MW00650332

De León

A TEJANO
FAMILY HISTORY

De León

A TEJANO FAMILY HISTORY

ANA CAROLINA CASTILLO CRIMM

UNIVERSITY OF TEXAS PRESS, AUSTIN

To my mother
Dr. Martha Lou Castillo
And to my mentor
The late Dr. Nettie Lee Benson

Copyright © 2003 by the University of Texas Press
All rights reserved
Printed in the United States of America
First edition, 2003

Requests for permission to reproduce material from this
work should be sent to Permissions, University of Texas
Press, P.O. Box 7819, Austin, TX 78713-7819.

⊛ The paper used in this book meets the minimum
requirements of ANSI/NISO Z39.48-1992 (R1997)
(Permanence of Paper).

Library of Congress Cataloging-in-Publication Data

Crimm, A. Carolina Castillo, 1946–
De León, a Tejano family history / Ana Carolina Castillo
Crimm.— 1st ed.
    p.   cm.
Includes bibliographical references and index.

 ISBN 978-0-292-70220-2

1. León, Martín de, 1765–1833.   2. León family.
3. Mexican Americans—Texas—Victoria—Biography.
4. Pioneers—Texas—Victoria—Biography   5. Victoria
(Tex.)—Biography.   6. Frontier and pioneer life—Texas—
Victoria.   7. Victoria (Tex.)—History.   8. Victoria (Tex.)—
Ethnic relations.   9. Escandón, José de, 1700–1770.
10. Frontier and pioneer life—Mexico, North.
I. Title.
F394. V6 C75   2003
976.4'125'004687200922—dc22

                                        2003013921

Contents

List of Maps

Notes on Terminology

There has been much controversy over the correct terms to use for those of Mexican heritage in Texas. I have chosen to use the term *Tejano* (pronounced *teh-hah'-no*) for those who lived in Texas during the years prior to Anglo colonization. These are the families whom the later Anglo arrivals called the "old Spanish families." I have continued to use *Tejano* throughout the book to differentiate these early settlers and their descendants from *Spanish,* those born in Spain or who lived under Spanish rule, and from the later arrivals from Mexico, for whom I have used the term *Mexican.* Finally, by 1845, it was appropriate to use the term *Mexican American* for immigrants from Mexico who accepted American citizenship. The "old Spanish families" remained the original Tejano settlers. I have used the term *Hispanic* for residents of Texas today who are in any way related to or descended from anyone of Spanish or Mexican ancestry. To avoid further confusion, I have not used terms such as *Latino, Ladino,* or *Chicano.*

For those from the United States, I have used the term *Anglo* or *Anglo American.* Mexicans object to the United States usurping the term *American,* since Mexico, too, is part of the American continent. There is also a problem with the term *Anglo,* which commonly refers to those of Protestant British ancestry. The Catholic Irish prefer not to be included with the British, and the term *Celt* or *Anglo Celt* has been used by some scholars. I have chosen to simply use the term *Irish.* For those of other European descent, I have used their nationalities.

Preface

This study follows the lives of three generations of the de León family as they founded ranches along the rivers of South Texas and settled the town of Victoria in present-day Victoria County, Texas. The last years of the eighteenth century and most of the nineteenth century were a time of radical change. The government under which the settlers lived shifted from Spanish rulers to a newly independent Mexican government in 1821 to the Republic of Texas in 1836 and finally to statehood in the United States. The society changed from autocratic to democratic, the economy from mercantile control to capitalistic investments. The story traces the de Leóns' success in founding Victoria and their exile from Texas during the Texas Revolution. Rather than end the history with the family's expulsion from Texas in 1836, I felt it was important to follow their return to Texas and to discover what happened to the family and to their land and culture. Their adjustments to the new society in which they chose to live, as do most human endeavors, brought opportunities as well as difficulties.

I first discussed this topic with Dr. Nettie Lee Benson at the University of Texas at Austin in 1987. A renowned scholar of Mexican history, Dr. Benson already had turned her insatiable interest toward Mexican Texas, as her article in the *Southwestern Historical Quarterly* of that year attests. Her queries and guidance led me to develop a study of the struggles of Martín de León, the first Mexican empresario. The result became my dissertation. Regrettably, though she worked vigorously until the end, Dr. Benson passed away at the age of eighty-eight, before I had completed the project. Her inspiration, however, continued.

Nuestra Señora de Guadalupe Victoria, the town founded by Martín de León and his family in 1834, was, with Stephen F. Austin's colony, the only completely successful colonization effort in Texas. De León's colony on the Guadalupe River followed Stephen F. Austin's colonization at San Felipe on the Brazos River by only two years. Each of them faced the challenges of equitably distributing land to settlers, of protecting the settlements, of maintaining peaceful relations with the Indians, and of smoothing over quarrels among the often-cantankerous colonists. It was inevitable that the two empresarios, one Anglo and the other Hispanic, should have had problems. That they were able to succeed despite periodic altercations is a testament to their dedication to their respective colonists and colonies.

This study crosses the time periods most frequently used by scholars and neither begins nor ends at any date convenient to historians of either Mexico or the United States. This book starts in the 1780s and ends one hundred years later. The chapter divisions are those which relate to the family, not those which many historians often use. The lives of the de León family members do not fit into the convenient time frames hedged around them by historians.

Nor do they provide neat solutions to scholarly theories. Their lives provide few grand, sweeping generalizations, and their actions offer scant support for broad theories or paradigms. Cliometricians struggle to find a large enough pool of individuals in Mexican Texas to make a study statistically significant, ignoring any renegade who may not conform to the pattern. But human beings are renegades and, more often than not, refuse to fit the mold. The reality which historians seek may be in the actions of individuals such as Martín de León rather than in the trends of a large number of generalized subjects.

Martín de León and his family lived through some of the most dramatic times in the intertwining histories of Mexico, Texas, and the United States. They had no idea their lives would span such changes, and their interest was to survive as best they could. De León began life in the Escandón settlements of northeastern Mexico, said to have been the site of the greatest land rush of all time. He spent the formative first ten years of his life in the exciting boomtown atmosphere of the mining village of Cruillas. He did not join Bernardo de Gálvez in the attack on British Florida, but early on, he chose a life of danger both as a muleteer and as a militia captain. His reason for settling Victoria will never be fully known, but if it was to protect his family, all of his children did receive land, in his eyes the ultimate source of wealth. He also left the conflict of the Texas Revolution to his sons and sons-in-law, who remained divided in their views, a split which is sometimes hard to comprehend for students of the Texas Republic. The family, led by Doña Patricia, his wife of forty years, faced the problems of exile and the difficulties of returning to an increasingly antagonistic society in Texas.

Don Martín's marriage partner, Patricia de la Garza of Soto la Marina, provides a clear image of the kind of women it took to settle the northern frontier. She offered her dowry to fund their first ranch and had the courage to leave their home in the civilized Escandón settlements to move to the wilds of Texas. For their ten children she demanded an education and did her best to bring them up as cultured members of society. Fearing that they might be labeled uncivilized barbarians, she asked that they not use guns, a request which was almost impossible to fulfill on the Texas frontier. She kept her family together after the death of her husband in 1834. She moved the family to New Orleans during the upheavals of the Republic of Texas and returned with them to Soto la Marina, her first home. It was Doña Patricia who insisted on returning to Texas in 1845 when it was safe to do so. Although some of her family chose to remain in Mexico, she encouraged her sons and daughters, and their sons and daughters, to make Texas their home, as she did in the last years of her life.

These early Tejanos who settled in Texas endured economic, political, and social upheaval in a time of dynamic shifts in ideas and outlook. Economically, in the years prior to 1800, Martín de León became an integral part of the new capitalist expansion of the Bourbon reforms taking place in the burgeoning Escandón settlements. He carried these ideas on into the settlement of his ranches and colony in Texas. Politically, from 1800 to 1880, as Mexico and then Texas struggled for independence, the de León family had to question their beliefs and adjust their loyalties from an autocratic Spanish empire to the concepts of a strange new form of republican government. Socially, by 1824, when de León founded his settlement in Texas, he ruled as the unquestioned autocratic empresario. The new concepts of social equality and democracy introduced by the Anglo-American arrivals were ideas that oftentimes made little sense, but he learned to live with them and with the multinational settlers in his colony. His sons and daughters adjusted to the beliefs of the new Texas to which they returned in 1845, but they retained much of their Hispanic culture.

As with all families who move to a frontier, there were times of hardship and suffering, but there were also times of joy in their successes. Above all else, there was a love of each other, a dedication to family, and an appreciation of community which has transcended their time and reaches down to the present day. The result has been thousands of Tejano descendants who reside in the communities of Victoria, Refugio, and Goliad, in the megalopolis of Houston, in Brownsville, McAllen, and Laredo, and in tiny towns scattered in so many South Texas counties on the American side of the border, as well as throughout the states of northern Mexico.

The de León family, although of the landed class, left few records. Like those of so many frontier settlers, their lives must be pieced together by combining the few facts which are available with what is known of the society around them at the time. The result is a narrative history that can help us determine how these individuals made the best of the circumstances in which they found themselves, something all humans struggle to do. In this work, I have explained my suppositions in text and endnotes. Everything for which there is documentation is also noted from sources in Mexico and in the United States.

Those Tejanos whose ancestors lived in the borderlands for many generations have long wondered what happened to their lands and their families during the years after the Texas Revolution. The story of Martín and Patricia de León and their descendants may help to answer some of their questions and to explain the complex problems that took place during a difficult and tumultuous time in Tejano history. There are no simple answers to the land loss and the deaths, but perhaps this book will help modern Tejanos understand, in part, the dangers those early settlers faced and how they survived to create successful lives for themselves and their offspring in Texas.

Acknowledgments

My first debt of gratitude is to the late Dr. Nettie Lee Benson, who first set me on this path, and to my dissertation chair, Dr. Ron C. Tyler, director of the Texas State Historical Association, who has continued to maintain an interest in my work over the past fifteen years. I am also deeply indebted to Jesús "Frank" de la Teja, without whose help and support this would never have been written, or rewritten. In addition to reading through several drafts and providing insightful comments, he gamely listened to a reading of the final manuscript on what must have seemed an interminable trip to Monclova. He kindly accepted it as an audio book read by the author.

Thanks are also due to the many scholars of the borderlands who have supported and encouraged me over the years, in particular all of the members of the Borderlanders' Breakfasts in Austin. Arnoldo de León has been unfailing in his encouragement and wisely recommended serious revisions in the first manuscript. I especially appreciate the friendship and suggestions of Armando Alonso, Adán Benavides, Elizabeth John, Dora Guerra, Betje Klier, Jack Jackson, and Andrés Tijerina.

I would like to extend heartfelt thanks to my colleagues at Sam Houston State University. Our inspirational department chair, Dr. James S. Olson, read the final manuscript and spent many hours correcting and suggesting improvements on the work. If this book succeeds, it will be due to his unfailing support and his kind encouragement. I am grateful for the friendship and support from Tracy Steele, who helped put the dissertation together so many years ago, and to Charlann Morris, who has kept me going with her cheerfulness when things looked bleakest. My thanks to Joan Coffey, who has shown us all how to be courageous in the face of adversity. I am particularly thankful for the friendship and laughter which Susannah Bruce and Nancy Sears have brought into all our lives. My thanks to Robert Ty Cashion, and to our ex-colleague Greg Cantrell, gone to North Texas but not forgotten at Sam, who has been a beacon and an inspiration and whose Austin book I have used as a constant reference.

One of the pleasures of taking ten years to complete a book has been meeting new friends and renewing old acquaintances at the research institutions in Texas and Mexico. The Center for American History (once known as "the Barker") has been a home away from home thanks to the kindness of Ralph Elder and his staff. Galen Greaser of the Texas General Land Office has become a special friend and has rescued me from numerous errors and pitfalls over the years, for which I am deeply grateful. Kinga Pryzcinska has been a great help on my many visits to the Catholic Archives in Austin. The staff members of the Texas State Archives have always been exemplary in their courtesy and helpfulness. Licenciado Alfonso "Poncho" Vásquez Sotelo, a loyal and helpful friend, and his hardworking staff at the Archivo General del Estado de Coahuila in Saltillo have been invaluable in providing information and hundreds of copies from documents in their files. At the Archivo General de la Nación in Mexico City, special thanks to Licenciado Alberto Partida, who allowed a tearful *gringa güera* to dig through the unindexed Guerra y Marina archives.

In Victoria, my deepest and warmest appreciation go to Social Studies Department Chair Charles Spurlin and his understanding wife, Pat, who made the whole project possible by gladly providing friendship and support as well as a job at Victoria College, a place in their home, and all of the facilities in Victoria and the surrounding area. I hope this work meets with their approval. The members of the Social Studies Department at Victoria College, in particular secretary Sandy Schrameck, and the staff at the library led by my good friend Beth Goodman were always gracious in their support and assistance.

While in Victoria, I also became acquainted with the many loyal and dedicated members of VH-GhoST, the Victoria Hispanic Genealogical and Historical Society of Texas. Their friendship, their knowledge, their avid interest in this topic — and their constant questions of "When is the book coming out?" — have kept me going during the long years. Gloria Candelaria and Estella Zermeño of Goliad have been priceless in their suggestions, support, and friendship over the years. Both have read the manuscript and offered inspired suggestions. Since no one knows the field better than they do, I have gratefully made every change and correction they suggested.

Special thanks are also due to the kind and generous descendants of the original de León family who have offered encouragement and advice over the years. I have especially appreciated the help from Wence de León, I. B. Benavides, and Gregorio de los Santos, who introduced me to the de la

Garza descendants. Ignacio Díaz also was kind enough to provide copies of important documents and information which has improved the book. My thanks to all the *primos* in South Texas, since we are all cousins after all.

Lastly, I would like to thank my family. To my mother, who has quietly worried about the length of time this has taken, my appreciation for helping with the final typing of the bibliography. My sister Sara and her husband, Dean, have kept me going with cards and calls and their faith in their "daughter" in college. Thanks to both of my brothers, Joe and Chuck, who have sent their support long-distance and prayed for me unceasingly. Finally, to my husband, Jack, my loving thanks for never nagging, for never asking when it would be done, and for taking care of me and the critters throughout all these years.

PROLOGUE

If Patricia de la Garza de León, wife of Martín de León, the founder of Victoria, Texas, were to return to her community one hundred fifty years after her passing, she would be amazed by the changes but pleased with how much remains the same. The buildings on the main plaza are different now, but she would be proud of the beautiful St. Mary's Church built on land she donated. She would be gratified to find that her husband is still revered by the citizens of the city, the descendants of their old friends among the early Tejanos as well as the Anglo Americans and the newer Mexican-American arrivals. Never a woman to flaunt her position, she would probably smile at seeing their names so prominently displayed on the plaques in the plaza. She could walk down the Street of the Ten Friends and remember those early settlers, her Irish friends, John Linn and his family, and that old reprobate Leonardo Manso. The rough bark of the now-giant oaks in the plaza would recall the memories of Martín laying out the dusty streets, of building their home on the town square, or of the little tortilla store on the corner, of Plácido Benavides' Round House, that Spanish *torreón* which provided refuge from the Indians. She would laugh at the memory of the city fathers struggling to build wooden fences around the plaza to keep the livestock out and protect the town well that Martín had built at such cost.

But the changes would not frighten her. Her family dared the wilds of Nuevo Santander and helped found Soto la Marina. Fear had not slowed Doña Patricia and her beloved husband Martín when they crossed the Río Bravo del Norte back in 1801 and settled next to the Apaches on the Nueces River with the first three children, nor when they dealt with Indians or Spanish or Anglo Americans. Nor when they moved, with all ten children, to the crossing on the Guadalupe to found Victoria in 1824. She had faced danger time and again, in 1814 from the dreaded General Arredondo during the wars for independence, in 1817 and 1821 from the Anglo filibusters and the Comanche and Norteño raids, in 1836 from the wild and uncontrollable Texian troops. No, fear had never stopped her.

Doña Patricia would ask, of course, after her family and the families of her friends. How did the marriage between her eldest son, Fernando, and Luz Escalera work out? Did they do well? She had always worried about Fernando. Had the inheritance she left young Francisco Santiago, her orphaned grandson, helped him? And what about her daughters Maria Jesús and Francisca? Had they lived comfortably from the mortgages? And had all of Felix's children kept the Mission Valley Ranch? Felix had been so distraught over his son Silvestre's drinking. Had Silvestre continued to drink? And dear Matiana, what a pair she and Luz had been, such business-women! Are their descendants still here?

"Yes, Doña Patricia, they are still here, the descendants of so many of the first families, the de León, Benavides, de la Garza, Carbajal, Barrera, García, Leal, Moya, and so many new ones added every generation. They are all here."

"What happened to the land?" she would ask.

"It is gone, Doña Patricia. Some was stolen, some was sold, and the rest was divided among the children and the grandchildren and the great-grandchildren until there was nothing left. There are still a few who keep the land. You remember the Pérez family that moved here from San Antonio in 1832? They still have land over around Bloomington, and they will only sell to *mexicanos*. And old Carlos de la Garza, down on the San Antonio? He tried so hard to keep the land together, but it is almost gone now."

She would shake her head sadly, perhaps, but it would not surprise her. She and Don Martín had given up the two ranches on the Nueces and the Aransas when they moved to Victoria. She, too, had sold ranch lands to survive when they fled into exile in Louisiana in 1836. But when they returned, and they always returned, she did not let her family give up without a fight. She had encouraged Fernando and Candelaria and the family to fight the court battles to regain their land, and they had won, in many of the cases. And when the land was divided among the grandchildren, better that all should have their *tierra*, their land, an *herencia*, an inheritance, no matter how small, than that some should be left with nothing. Yes, her family had suffered, but they had survived. Some had succeeded and prospered, others had failed and died in poverty. But, on the whole, as she looked around her community, Patricia de la Garza de León would be pleased.

CHAPTER I

SETTLING NEW SPAIN'S NORTHERN FRONTIER, 1750–1800

Genealogical Chart

BERNARDO DE LEÓN + MARÍA GALVÁN

    Martín de León (b. 1765, m. 1795)
    + Patricia de la Garza (b. ca. 1775)
        1. Fernando (b. 1798)
        2. María Candelaria (b. 1800)

    Santiago

    Juan

    José

Martín de León, gangly with the new growth of his fourteen years, raced up the dusty streets of the thriving town of Cruillas in northeastern New Spain. His heart pounded and his breath came fast. He had slipped away from his Franciscan tutor to carry exhilarating news to his father. In 1780, with war raging in Europe and now spreading to the New World, King Charles III, the great Bourbon king of Spain, had issued a call for more soldiers. He had ordered prayers for victory to be said in all of his dominions for the success of Commandant General and Louisiana Governor, Don Bernardo de Gálvez, the twenty-nine-year-old commander who planned in the early fall to attack the British in Florida. Don Bernardo had already done much to aid the rebellious North American colonists against the British, Spain's eternal enemy. He had been in communication with Patrick Henry, Thomas Jefferson, and Charles Henry Lee, had met with their emissaries, and had secured the port of New Orleans to help prevent the British from moving up the Mississippi. Victory for Spain and for the colonists was assured. The British would have to fight their war on two fronts, against the colonial English rebels in the north and against the growing power of Spain in the Gulf of Mexico.[1] Martín had thrilled with pride and excitement at the military exploits of Don Bernardo de Gálvez. The boy, hurrying up the narrow cobbled streets between the brightly painted, thick-walled adobe houses, assured himself that as a grown man of fourteen, he could certainly join Don Bernardo's military expedition against British West Florida and its capital at Pensacola. Little else was discussed in the plazas and homes of northern New Spain. The courageous commandant had launched brilliant attacks up the Mississippi and swept the British from their forts at Natchez, Baton Rouge, and Manchac.

Only a few months earlier, in January 1780, Don Bernardo had attacked and captured Mobile. The attack on Pensacola was scheduled for the fall. In the colony of Texas across the Río Bravo del Norte, the soldiers at the presidios and the mission fathers on the San Antonio River were gathering cattle to supply Don Bernardo's troops. Young Martín had been thrilled to hear that Cruillas would be included in the great effort. The mine owners in northern Mexico were pushing their workers to increase output, even hoping to reopen played-out mines. Surely his father could see that absolutely everyone was sailing to Cuba to join the war.

Martín crossed the main plaza, weaving his way around the Indian vendors squatting beside their brightly colored goods, the yellow piles of corn spilling over into the bright green mounds of chile peppers, the red tomatoes neatly stacked in small pyramids beside the bulging bags of brown

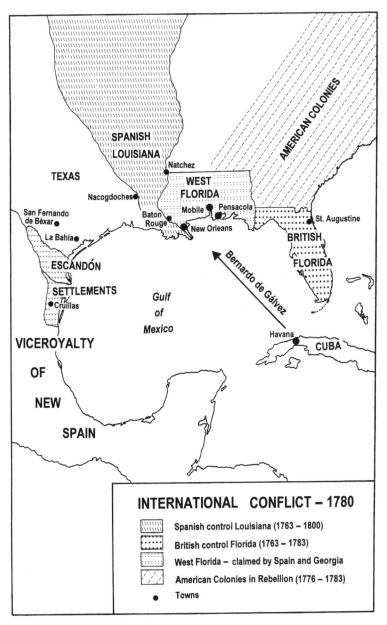

INTERNATIONAL CONFLICT – 1780

////	Spanish control Louisiana (1763 – 1800)
::::	British control Florida (1763 – 1783)
::::	West Florida – claimed by Spain and Georgia
////	American Colonies in Rebellion (1776 – 1783)
●	Towns

Map 1.1

beans. The usual gossips were standing at the stone water fountain in the middle of the plaza discussing the war. Three blocks from the main square, he turned down a street and reached the thick, iron-bound, wooden doors which opened into the stone-floored patio of his own home.

Martín's family, proud of their light skin and Spanish heritage, disdained the dark, single-room adobe homes of the Indians. In his own eyes he felt his family was as good as anyone born in Spain. To the newly arrived Spaniards, however, Martín and his family were second-class citizens, untrustworthy *criollos*, perhaps of Spanish blood but unfortunately born in the New World. As a *criollo*, his father had purchased their home a short distance from the square. Only the king's newly arrived Spanish officials could inhabit the homes immediately around the central plaza. Martín was pleased with their new home. It had been a side effect of the many economic changes wrought by Carlos III. New buildings in the neo-Classical style, all with elegant columns and arches around a Moorish patio, had been built throughout New Spain during the 1770s and 1780s as the economy of New Spain had grown. The de León house, however, consisted of large stone rooms, each ten meters on a side, with thick wooden beams, or *vigas*, across the high ceilings. The middle beam in the *sala*, or living room, was carved with their own name and the date and name of the builder. In the rooms behind the main house, mixed-blood mestizos and Indians worked in the kitchen fixing the meals on the tiled stove and in the adobe ovens. At the back of the house were the stables for the horses and rooms for the servants. The de León home was not as ornate as the stone houses of the rich Spanish government officials on the main plaza, but it was a fine, elegant home.

Young Martín entered the *sala* and greeted his father. Don Bernardo de León listened as Martín poured out the reasons he should be allowed to go to war with the great Conde de Gálvez. Don Bernardo nodded and agreed that it would be a great opportunity if his son were a little older. For the time being, however, Martín's father insisted that he remain at his studies. The decision, although devastating to the disappointed young man, proved to be a wise choice. That fall, a hurricane destroyed several ships in the Spanish military fleet, drowning hundreds of soldiers and forcing Bernardo de Gálvez to postpone the attack on Pensacola.[2]

By the summer of 1781, young Martín and all of Spain and her colonies celebrated the great victory over the British forces at Pensacola. Gálvez had led his ships into the harbor when his own naval commander had refused to brave the narrow channel. If he had gone, young Martín could

Remnants of eighteenth-century homes, such as the one in which Martín de León might have lived, still dot the small town of Cruillas in northern Mexico. Ana Carolina Castillo Crimm.

have shared in the glory of restoring Spain's power in the Gulf. Don Bernardo de Gálvez had been honored with the title of count and, for his courage in entering the port, King Carlos III had allowed him to place the motto "I ALONE" on his coat of arms. Someday, Martín was certain that, he too, would brave the dangers of the unknown.[3]

Martín's parents had taught him that education was, after all, the best way for young men to advance in the king's service. Royal officials needed a literate bureaucracy to handle the mountains of correspondence, the streams of orders, the monthly and yearly censuses, and the triplicate copies of land titles, reports, and letters. Since the advent of King Carlos III's inspectors in the New World, many higher-level positions were handed out only to trustworthy Spaniards brought from Spain, but there was still a need for local government officials and for a clerical staff in all of the Spanish governmental offices. Martín's father assured him that if he wanted to become one of the scribes or notaries so necessary to the king's bureaucracy, he needed to learn his letters. The rangy lad preferred the excitement of soldiering or muleteering, but he was obedient to his parents' wishes and returned to the small adobe home of the Franciscan friar his father had hired to teach Martín and his brothers — Santiago, Juan, and José.

The boys' father had spent much of his hard-earned money to pay for their education. Although the government often passed laws requiring the founding of schools, there were no governmental schools in Cruillas. The great Jesuit colleges throughout the Spanish empire had been closed since the expulsion of the Jesuit fathers in 1767. Those seeking an education had to pay for it themselves since the government spent its scarce funds on more critical needs, such as defending the colonies against the Indians.

Martín de León's love of excitement had been learned from birth, an integral part of his growing up in José de Escandón's colony of Nuevo Santander. The young boy was a product of one of the greatest land settlements of the Spanish empire. His father had often told him the stories of the founding of their colony on the northern frontier. Nuevo Santander had become critically important one hundred years earlier, in 1685, when the French began to encroach on Spanish territory. The boy's father recounted the story of the dedicated commander Alonso de León, who had spent years searching out and destroying the French settlement made by René Cavelier Sieur de La Salle in Texas. De León had helped found missions among the Caddo of East Texas to keep out the French. Although the Spanish attempts at converting the Caddo had failed, at least the French had been removed as a threat in the New World. No sooner were the French gone from Texas, however, than Spain itself fell under the control of France. The last of the Spanish Hapsburg kings had died in 1700 without heirs, and the great King Louis XIV of France had placed his grandson on the Spanish throne as King Felipe V, the first of the Bourbon line. With a French king on the Spanish throne, the Spanish colonists in New Spain would have to accept the French, who had returned to settle in Louisiana in 1702, as neighbors, like it or not.[4]

Years later, when King Felipe had passed away in 1746, everyone wondered if there would be a change in policy by his son, the new King Ferdinand VI, a man determined to keep Spain out of wars with either the French or the British. Ferdinand, now more Spanish than French, ordered the settlement of the northern territories in order to firmly establish a dividing line between the Spanish lands and the rapid expansion of the French at New Orleans. Certainly settling the frontier was dangerous. Menacing tribes lived hidden in the valleys and ravines and lashed out against settlers and Spanish slave raiders seeking workers for the silver mines. But colonists continued to come, always hoping to discover precious metals in the northern mountains. Monterrey had grown into an imposing city, and small settlements and ranches fanned out in the mountain valleys, always threatened by the local tribes. The king, however, wanted a more concerted and controlled effort to settle the northern frontier.[5]

The viceroy, the king's representative in Mexico City, began to explore the possibilities and called for proposals from any who wished to settle the northern frontier. It had taken seven long years for local officials to sift through the complex suggestions offered by the various proponents. Although the colonizer would be called on to use his own money to begin the settlement, there was also the potential to profit from the sale of goods to the new settlers. Their choice fell on José de Escandón, an ambitious and determined young officer from Soto la Marina in Spain. He had served throughout northern New Spain and knew the region well.[6]

Escandón was an optimistic and powerful salesman. The Spanish military officer sold his plan not only to the government but to thousands of settlers, both rich and poor in the provinces of México, Zacatecas, Guanajuato, and San Luis Potosí. Escandón offered them adventure and danger but inspired them with hope for their own lands, successful futures, and the protection of the Bourbon monarchs.[7]

Bernardo de León, young Martín's father, and his family were among those who had been swayed by Escandón's vision. With 2,500 other colonists, de León's family left Querétaro in December 1748 to settle in the new colony of Nuevo Santander. The colony stretched from the port of Tampico, north across the Río Bravo del Norte to the Nueces River, and inland to the foothills of the Sierra Madre. Escandón tried and failed to settle along the Nueces River with the Villa de Vedoya, which would have marked the northernmost settlement of Nuevo Santander. He settled the last of his colonists at the new port of Soto la Marina. In all, Escandón placed his settlers in twenty-four *villas* and fifteen missions. Bernardo de León's family had chosen to settle in Burgos, which Escandón established in early 1749. It was there, some years later, that Bernardo would marry María Galván. Burgos, the westernmost of the settlements in the foothills of the Sierra Madres, had been established to protect Nuevo Santander from the attacks of the small hunter-gatherer tribes hidden in the mountain recesses.[8]

By 1759 Carlos III, the dynamic, energetic Enlightenment monarch, ascended the throne of Spain. He fully supported the efforts of José de Escandón and encouraged him to enlist the local ranchers in his commercial enterprise. Ranchers had long been settled in the arid northern plains, in the neighboring provinces of Coahuila and Nuevo León, and along the Río Bravo del Norte. Unlike the absentee landlords in Mexico City, Saltillo, or Monterrey who visited only at roundup time, many of the northern hacienda owners lived on their lands and supervised their ranching operations. José Vázquez Borrego, at his hacienda of San Juan del Alamo in the state of Coahuila, for example, employed more than two hundred individuals to work on his farms, handle his cattle, run his mule train (the largest in the area), and serve in his personal militia unit, which was made up of a dozen armed men led by a sergeant.[9]

The town settlements and land grants which Escandón offered these investors were not for the mere aggrandizement of noble families. Escandón's poorer colonists provided a ready labor source for these hacienda owners, who could profit not only from the cattle and sheep herds, the hides and tallow, the wool and cotton cloth, but also from the *tiendas de raya*, or company stores which sold goods, sometimes at inflated prices, to the new ranch employees.[10]

Escandón had also offered the incentive of smaller ranches to his settlers who had hoped for the opportunity to start herds of their own. Bernardo de León and his family had not been among those wealthy settlers who owned the giant haciendas, encompassing thousands or even millions of acres. As a self-made man, he had wanted only a small *rancho* of a few hundred acres, his *tierra*, to pass on to his children.[11]

It had been hard for the wealthy to accept this new order in which the poor might advance to land ownership. Manuel de Escandón, son of the founder, had commented, "The majority of the *pobladores* (settlers) . . . maintain themselves in want and misery, barely succeeding in acquiring in one year, the salary of a working *peón*. But," he continued, "since they are brought up in that lifestyle, they remain content in the care of their small herds."[12] What the younger Escandón did not see was the hope that his father had held out to the thousands who chose to come north, staking their lives and their futures on homes in the river valleys and the mountains of the northeastern frontier. The ranch for Bernardo de León and his family meant individual freedom, some economic liberty, and a modicum of social equality. It did not take French philosophers or American revolutionaries to teach the new concepts to Escandón's settlers. They lived those ideas by moving north.[13]

For Escandón's colonists, in addition to their own land or jobs on the haciendas, there were other avenues of advancement. As his father constantly reminded Martín, an education assured a young man entry into the world of governmental bureaucracy, but the boy preferred the idea of a

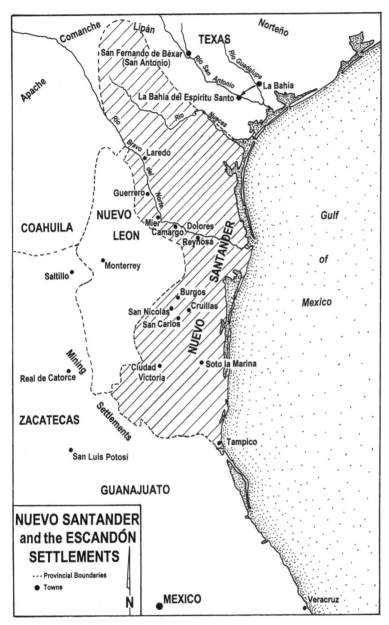

Comanche

Lipán

Norteño

TEXAS

San Fernando de Béxar
(San Antonio)

Río San Antonio

Río Guadalupe

La Bahía

Apache

La Bahía del Espíritu Santo

Río

Río

Nueces

Río Bravo del Norte

Laredo

Guerrero

NUEVO
LEON

Mier
Camargo

Dolores

Reynosa

COAHUILA

Gulf

NUEVO SANTANDER

Monterrey

of

Saltillo

Burgos

Mexico

San Nicolás
San Carlos

Cruillas

NUEVO

Mining

Ciudad
Victoria

Soto la Marina

Real de Catorce

ZACATECAS

Settlements

San Luis Potosí

Tampico

GUANAJUATO

NUEVO SANTANDER
and the ESCANDÓN
SETLEMENTS

- - - Provincial Boundaries
● Towns

N

● MEXICO

Veracruz

Map 1.2

military career. The military provided opportunities for men with brains and ambition if they were willing to risk their lives in campaigns against bands of native tribes. Young Martín could aspire to the rank of captain based on his own skills and abilities, although higher ranks were reserved for the elite. He would never be rich, since soldiers were most often paid in supplies rather than gold, but the eventual rewards might be grants of land and perhaps even royal favor.[14]

Business offered another avenue of promotion for Martín. Mule trains carried the majority of trade goods on the far northern frontier, where roads were rarely more than narrow tracks through steep mountain passes. The muleteers who supervised the mule trains needed both courage and intelligence, but if they succeeded in the dangerous field, they, too, could improve their positions in society.

Not everyone shared Escandón's optimistic reports of the new settlers. According to some of the Franciscan brothers who had come north to bring Christianity to the native tribes, many of the Spanish settlers were fleeing their native provinces to "evade their debts or crimes and the only thing they desired was to become owners of lands, water and grasses that should have belonged to the Indians."[15] The priests, however, had learned that the settlers were often brave, hardworking people who were determined to "reap the benefit . . . of prosperity by means of agriculture."[16]

Part of Escandón's planned colony extended beyond the immediate area of Nuevo Santander to include the new province of Texas, which had already excited young Martín's curiosity. The adjacent colony, with its missions to the Tejas Indians, had been successfully established in 1716 as a border with the French. Escandón wanted to use the fort, Presidio Nuestra Señora de Loreto, with its mission, Nuestra Señora de la Bahía del Espíritu Santo de Zúñiga, as part of his defensive network.[17] The colonial leader planned to link this combined settlement, better known as La Bahía, to his colonies in Nuevo Santander. As part of his scheme, he asked the viceroy to move La Bahía farther south, a day's ride closer to his towns. The viceroy agreed, and in October 1749, with the king's permission, the mission and presidio complex was relocated from the Guadalupe River to the San Antonio River.[18]

The new commander of the presidio, Captain Manuel Ramirez de la Piscina, who controlled the presidio for nearly two decades, from 1749 to 1767, encouraged his soldiers to establish ranches along the San Antonio River. He led the way by building his own large cattle ranch, the Rancho de San Joseph, better known to the local settlers as Rancho del Capitán, or El Capitán, some ten leagues from the presidio along the east bank of the San Antonio River. He had a reputation for paying his men fairly and did not overcharge for the food, clothing, and equipment which he sold to his troops. He had encouraged artisans, vendors and laborers to come to La Bahía from the Escandón settlements. Everyone was granted farm lands and town lots near the presidio, and the soldiers were permitted to request ranch lands on the east side of the river.

The west side of the river was reserved for the mission. There the friars trained their Indian neophytes in the techniques of roping and branding the herds of cattle which thrived on the rich grasses of the coastal prairies. Indians assigned to protect the herds in the outlying pastures brought in beef on the hoof in weekly or monthly consignments to feed those at the mission. Christianized Indians learned to plant crops and built the sturdy, stone chapel and the long outbuildings, where some of the tribespeople lived. Not all natives accepted the rigorous lifestyle of the missions, ruled by tolling bells and strange-sounding prayers. It was a difficult decision for them. Accepting the security of the mission, with the reliable food and warm clothing, meant giving up freedom and yearly treks to the coast to gather oysters and meet with other tribes, exchanging goods and perhaps acquiring new marriage partners. Not all tribes joined the missions, and of those who did, not all stayed.[19]

In 1755 Captain Piscina had tried to establish peaceful relations with the Indians by helping to found a mission for the aggressive Karankawa. The captain supplied his own funds and encouraged private benefactors to contribute to the establishment of the new mission of Nuestra Señora del Rosario de los Cujanes, upriver from the presidio. Although the Karankawa were never truly Christianized, the Rosario mission provided another protective bulwark for the growing civilian town. The community which Captain Piscina left upon his death in 1767 was small but solid and successful. So successful was the settlement, in fact, that La Bahía del Espíritu Santo became the eastern terminus chosen by the king's military inspector to anchor the line of defensive presidios and missions which stretched across the continent to California.[20]

Escandón's northern colonies at Nuevo Santander had not been as successful as those in the south. During the first two years, the settlers in the northern towns had laboriously planted their small patches of corn and vegetables and then watched their crops slowly wither and die in the heat of the northern dry lands. Martín's father had described the terrible hardships they had suffered. Many had to sell off some or all of their small herds to purchase the precious corn and the agricultural products they needed to survive. The government officials, who might have built irrigation canals to water the fields, were quickly dissuaded by annual devastating floods which raced down out of the Sierra Madre mountains to rip away and destroy the small settlements in their path. The floods had leveled the small *jacales*, or homes, which the settlers had constructed from the local cane, plaited together and plastered with mud. They had lost their few possessions, but they rebuilt, always hoping that it would be better next year. In addition, Indian raids were increasing, and there was never enough protection from government troops and militia units, who were, often, the poverty-stricken settlers themselves.[21]

By 1750 Escandón's optimistic reports and his hoped-for success had not fully materialized. Two years later, with the demise of the colony imminent and the prayers of his colonists ringing in his ears, Escandón had hurried to Mexico City. He requested more funds, and the king, desirous of insuring the prosperity of the towns, agreed to the cost overruns. The count saved his colonies at Nuevo Santander, swearing that he would maintain them even at the cost of his own blood or at whatever cost to the king's coffers.[22]

Escandón knew that he could not continue to ask for funds to support his colony. The northern towns needed something which they could trade for the abundant corn, beans, sugarcane, chile, vegetables, and fruit produced by settlers farther south. The northerners at last found their salvation in the many salt flats along the coasts. At Burgos, willing laborers could cut and rake out the salt and carry it to market on the same mule they used to plow and plant their crops in the spring. They could also hire on with the big *hacendados* such as Domingo de Unzaga, the captain of the *villa* or town of Hoyos, who needed muleteers to operate his fifty-mule team to carry the salt to the Saltillo Fair in the fall to exchange for foodstuffs and other goods from the interior. Mule trains hauled the salt over the steep, rocky passes in the Sierra Madres and across vast, dry, barren plains between the mountains to the mining establishments at Guadalcazar, San Luís Potosí, Mazapíl, and Sombrerete, where salt was needed for smelting ores in the mines. The salt also could be taken east to Soto la Marina, where it could be exchanged for the desperately needed corn and beans. Salt, as prized a commodity as corn, saved Escandón's settlers from destitution and his northern colonies from economic ruin.[23]

The port of Soto la Marina, named by Escandón for the town of his birth in Spain, was to be the jewel in his string of settlements. Already known for a hundred years as Río de las Palmas, the port had long been considered an excellent area for potential development. The merchants in Veracruz and Mexico City, however, had adamantly opposed the opening of a port which might drain off some of their trade. Escandón's argument that opening a port at Soto la Marina would prevent a shortage of supplies to the new colony and avoid speculation and the abuses of high prices at last won the support of the government, although the merchants continued to oppose him.[24]

With royal permission and governmental funds, Escandón built his port and completed it in 1752. Soto la Marina was connected by a network of roads to all of the towns in the settlement of Nuevo Santander as well as to the commercial centers at Monterrey and Saltillo. Hides and tallow, wool, cotton, and salt were loaded aboard Escandón's sailboat, the *Conquistadora*, for the twenty-four hour run to Veracruz. Everyone in Nuevo Santander reveled in the arrival of cheaper goods from Veracruz, unencumbered by the high costs imposed by the merchants and the battery of taxes paid on shipments carried north along the *caminos reales*, the king's roads, of the interior.[25]

The wealthy Mexico City merchants, accustomed to controlling the activities of New Spain through their hold on trade and the purse strings, were furious over losing the income from the northern trade. The merchants accused Escandón of running contraband through his new port and urged the viceroy to call for an inspection of the colony. The viceroy, under pressure, agreed, and sent José Tienda de Cuervo in 1756. For eleven months, Tienda de Cuervo went everywhere and questioned everyone. He had investigated the many claims and counterclaims against Escandón, including the allegations of contraband. His report exonerated Escandón, but he advised that the port of Soto la Marina be closed. The Mexico City merchants had also used their leverage with the viceroy by contributing 100,000 pesos in 1763 to the king's defense of Havana against the British. Although the Spanish crown lost that war, the merchants had won the closing of the port.[26]

The viceroy ordered Soto la Marina closed, but with far less haste than the merchants desired. The port remained open for several more years, and Escandón's colonists continued to benefit from the arrival of cheap trade goods. When the port was at last shut down in the 1770s, Nuevo Santander was combined with the adjoining states to create the Comandancia General de las Provincias Internas. The new governmental structure, aimed at drawing Nuevo Santander into the colonial trade network, did little but irritate the northern settlers. They complained bitterly over an *alcabala* (tax) of 8 percent and higher taxes on tobacco and pulque, a favorite alcoholic brew. The merchants, back in control of the northern markets, paid little for the settlers' raw materials, while they charged exorbitant prices for manufactured goods. It was little wonder, during the following decades, that the northern colonists like Bernardo de León grew increasingly bitter toward the king and his empire.[27]

Tienda de Cuervo had also emphasized the need to share political power with the colonists. Escandón had refused to follow the Spanish tradition of allowing the people to choose their own town governments, the locally elected *ayuntamientos*, or the *cabildos*, the municipal councils. He had presided over an autocratic military government. Passports or permits were required of all travelers. Government officials collected tithes and *alcabalas* and controlled the sale or purchase of goods, in particular tobacco, playing cards, and paper for legal documents. To keep people in the colony, the count had not permitted his colonists to move from one town to another without a governmental permit or to leave the province without permission. The restrictions, however, did not retard growth. By 1757 approximately 8,869 individuals from more than 1,500 families had settled in Nuevo Santander.[28]

The king continued to be concerned about his colony. Another royal inspector arrived in 1765. José de Gálvez, the king's visitor-general of New Spain, endured six years of hardships and often harsh weather conditions while traveling the rough *caminos reales* across New Spain. By 1771, when José de Gálvez returned to Spain, he was named to the post of Minister of the Indies, a position from which he could put a new economic system into place. Gálvez called for a mercantilist opening of trade within the Spanish empire, a halt to the monopolies held by wealthy merchants, an increase in the production of silver from the mines, the distribution of land to the Indians to make them part of the market structure, and the introduction of *intendencies*, a new French form of government already in use in Spain. The reforms dovetailed with Escandón's views.[29]

By the 1760s silver mining already had made a dramatic recovery in the northern settlements of Nuevo Santander. Encouraged by lower taxes, revised customs duties, the increased availability of mercury, and improved technology, the merchant *aviadores*, or investors, and mining experts had begun explorations in Nuevo Santander, where they found several potentially lucrative sites. In 1766 Escandón requested 6,685 pesos from the viceroy to establish mining centers in the colony. With the funds, Escandón established the *reales de minas* (royal mining towns) of San Carlos and Cruillas and the *villas* of Croix and Tetillas.[30] When Escandón's investors discovered veins of silver, copper, gold, zinc, and lead in the mountains around the towns, settlers from all over the region requested and received permission to move to the new mining communities.

Within a year, the population at San Carlos and Cruillas jumped to 15,000. Among those requesting permission to move to Cruillas was Bernardo de León, with his wife, María Galván, and one-year-old Martín, born in 1765. Bernardo's ambition, which he would instill in all his children, had been to acquire some wealth from the many opportunities in the boomtown. He had succeeded in doing so. Just because they had not been among the elite class did not mean that the avenues for opportunity were closed to them, especially not on the northern frontier of New Spain.[31]

In spite of the success of the new mines, the aging Escandón was called to Mexico City to answer allegations against him. His eighteen years of effort in founding and maintaining Nuevo Santander were forgotten. He had no defenders at the viceregal court. His many enemies—the bureaucrats who accused him of maladministration, the merchants who claimed he had robbed them, the missionaries who felt he had taken their lands, and those who envied his success—joined against him. The trial dragged on, slowly wearing down the old man's waning strength and optimistic spirit. On September 10, 1770, three years into the trial, José de Escandón died in Mexico City. It took three more years for his son, Manuel Ignacio de Escandón y Llera, to at last clear his father's name.[32]

In Nuevo Santander, with the founder gone, the viceroy ordered the reorganization of the government and granted land to the settlers. Each town was ordered to elect its own *ayuntamiento*. The original settlers received two *sitios*, or approximately 8,856 acres, for sheep and goats plus twelve *caballerías*, or approximately 1,272 acres, for planting.[33] *Agregados*, or those who had arrived later and had been in Nuevo Santander for less than six years, received two *sitios* for their sheep and goats and six *caballerías* of land. New settlers, such as the recently arrived miners, were granted two *sitios*. The military captains of the province received four *sitios*, or 17,712 acres, which could be used for summer pasture plus twenty-four *caballerías de tierra para siembra*, or 2,544 acres, of farmland. The settlers were required to take possession in two months and build a house in two years, and they could not sell the land for ten years. Bernardo de León, as one of the first settlers, received a ranch of over 10,000 acres on which he settled his family. They also maintained a house in town.[34]

Young Martín de León spent his first ten years in the exciting boomtown atmosphere of the new mining settlement of Cruillas. During those
critical, formative years, Martín reveled in the life of the busy town and enjoyed frequent visits to their family ranch. The plaza was always crowded
with traders and merchants, the salt and mercury coming in on the mule
trains, and heavily loaded mules carrying packs of ore going south over
the mountains to San Luís Potosí and faraway Mexico City. The mining
boom at Cruillas lasted until 1777. When the mines played out, many of
the settlers moved to the new mine at Las Minas de Catorce near San Luís
Potosí, but Bernardo de León remained at Cruillas with his family, where
Martín continued his education and learned ranching from his father.[35]

By the time Martín was eighteen in 1783, he turned down the opportunity which his father offered him for further education in Monterrey.
The adventurous young man had determined to pursue a career as a muleteer. Not many people chose this profession. Buying up an entire string
of mules was costly, and Martín may have used the money his father had
saved for his education to invest in the mule trade. In addition, the job was
dangerous and required responsibility, a good head for figures, excellent
business acumen, an ability to resolve problems, and the trust of the people
with whom the muleteer worked. For young Martín, it was an exciting
and potentially lucrative opportunity.[36]

Goods could not have found their way to the far north without the mule
trains. In agricultural areas, farmers might use their two or three plow
mules during the off season to supplement their income as small-scale salt
miners to carry the produce from their little farms to market in the nearby
towns or in far-off Saltillo. Most hacienda owners and mission fathers
had their own twenty- to fifty-mule trains to carry the produce from their
ranches to market, and it may have been in this trade that Martín began.
Mine owners often kept large numbers of muleteers and their mule trains
busy carrying the ore over the Sierra Madre to the smelters or bringing
back goods for the miners and laborers. The government also employed
muleteers to carry the restricted tobacco to the various *estancos*, or authorized stores, around the country. Only a few muleteers opted for the
carrera larga and became long-distance haulers with pack trains of more
than eighty mules to carry goods to the distant northern frontier. Of the
27,325 kilometers of roads in Mexico at the time, 28 percent of the roads
were usable by wagons or carts, while the remaining 72 percent were used
exclusively by mule trains.[37]

The entrepreneurial head muleteer, or *mayordomo*, such as Martín de

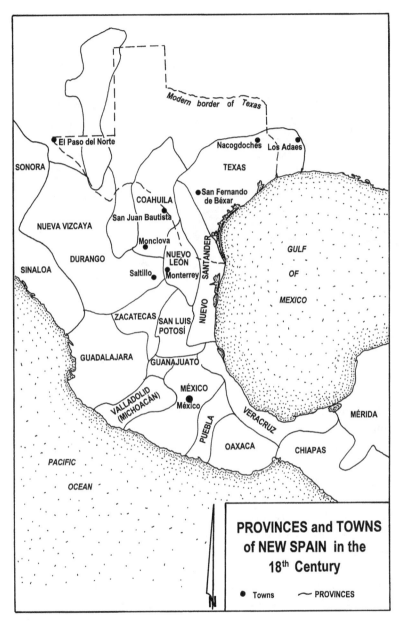

Map 1.3

Arrieros (Muleteers) by Carl Nebel, a nineteenth-century German artist who traveled in Mexico from 1829 to 1834 and painted the people of the newly independent country for his European audience. Courtesy of the Benson Latin American Collection, University of Texas at Austin.

León, was the key to the successful operation of the mule trains, especially in the mountainous north. In a description given by the Jesuits, a *mayordomo* had to be "faithful and loyal with his muleteers, intelligent in his art, trustworthy in the handling of the mules, and the goods they must carry."[38] A *mayordomo*, if he did not own his own team, had to have the complete confidence of the owner of the mule train. He was contracted to make sure the goods reached their destination, to handle all the bureaucratic customs permits and clearance certificates, pay all the taxes and duties, hire assistants and staff, pay for feed for the animals or the right to pasturage when they spent the night near a town, and ensure the safety of the cargo. The muleteer also might act as an itinerant tradesman, exchanging inexpensive local goods for the higher-priced merchandise he brought from Soto la Marina or Saltillo. In essence, the muleteer became a merchant, a moneylender, and a pawnbroker as well as a town crier and newsman.[39]

Martín would have had no trouble buying mules for his pack train. According to the report of Tienda de Cuervo in 1757, Burgos had 229 mules, and the town of Dolores, just down the Río Bravo del Norte from Laredo, had 1,600 mules. Hoyos and the mining town of Borbón had 732 mules, while Soto la Marina, because of its wetlands and the lack of pasturage, had only 142 mules. Mules were preferred over horses as beasts of burden due to their constitution. In addition to superior strength and endurance, mules were less costly to feed than horses, could eat whatever weeds or pasturage was available, and, unlike horses, never foundered themselves by overeating. Mules adapted better to climatic changes and were less excitable than horses. The surefooted mules, whose natural pace was to place one hoof directly in front of the other, could pick their way along the narrow, winding footpaths through the steep ravines and along the narrow ledges overlooking the deep, rocky valleys of the Sierra Madre. In addition, the fact that mules do not reproduce meant significantly more work time.[40]

Ideally, all the mules in Martín's train were of nearly identical height, weight, and color. Since the length of the mule's stride corresponded to its height, mules of the same size would walk at the same pace, without one mule overtaking the ones in front or delaying the ones behind. Mules could carry a pack which weighed half their own weight, or a load of between 400 and 700 pounds. When all the mules were the same weight, the loads could be divided evenly among them. Matching coat colors served, in addition to enhancing the elegance and beauty of the team, to distinguish one mule train from another, especially at the major entrepôts such as Saltillo or Mexico City, where hundreds of mule trains gathered. A lead mule carried a bell around its neck and led the train, usually without a pack, and outfitted with an elegant headstall and the *reata*, or rope, which was connected to each of the mules down the length of the entire train. The lead mule established the pace and set the time and distance for each day's trip, while the sound of the bell kept the train together, starting or stopping the mules along the road. In addition, if Martín had sufficient money, he could outfit his mules with elaborate matching saddle blankets carrying the de León family brand, intricately worked headstalls, and leatherwork and packsaddles decorated with silver. Most muleteers prided themselves on the elegance of their mule trains.[41]

Martín de León, as a *mayordomo*, hired his own staff of assistants, consisting of between three and ten or more men. The *hatajador*, or drover, led the train, riding ahead of or beside the lead mule, and was responsible for guiding the mule train over the mountain passes and along the network of narrow trails. The *sabanero* was responsible for the care and feeding of the mules and carried the hay or grain for feeding the animals when there was no pasturage at a night's stop. He might also help the *mayordomo* make arrangements for renting the transhumance pastures from the local towns through which they passed. He kept the mules from scattering during the night and gathered them in the morning for loading. A *cargador* or *aviador* was charged with loading and unloading the mules, caring for the cargo, and preventing it from getting wet or damaged. There might be several *cargadores*, depending on the size of the mule train.[42]

Each mule was loaded in the same order with the same pack each day. The *cargador* had to know his mules well enough to make sure that the mules, once loaded, would not buck or roll with the packs. Mules might also inflate their bellies as the packsaddles were cinched up, so the *cargador* had to check his wily animals and retighten the cinches to make sure the packs did not became loose or slip once on the road. The drover assigned the cargo according to the characteristics of each mule, varying in weight or the irregularities of the pack. The *cargadores*, who rode mules or horses within the train itself, kept a close eye on their mules and kept them moving together during the trip.[43]

Unlike the many mule trains in the center of the country, muleteering in the mountainous north was particularly dangerous. Aggressive native tribes, hidden in the mountain valleys, considered the passing animals prime sources for delectable mule meat. Even more attractive was the variety of Spanish goods which the mules carried. For the Indians, the trains were, in essence, their own personal marketplace on hooves. The majority of the cargo consisted of corn from the southern towns, salt from the coastal towns, and cotton, wool, hides, and lard from the haciendas. The muleteers also carried temptingly large sacks of gold coins which they had received as pay for their goods, and down-and-out Spanish settlers were lured by the potential for wealth and often tried robbing the muleteers and their heavily laden mule trains. Martín and his men expected attacks and rode well armed and ready for a fight. They staunchly defended their cargo and their money from any renegades and thieves whether Indian or Spanish.

Once a year, mule trains converged on Saltillo for the fall fair. There the produce of the north was exchanged for bolts of cloth, metal goods, knives, or merchandise from places as far away as Veracruz, Mexico City, Spain, or even China and the Philippines when the Manila galleons arrived safely in Acapulco. As long as the port of Soto la Marina was open, many mule trains carried goods to and from the local towns to the port on the growing network of roads in and around Escandón's towns.[44]

Martín de León had joined a tough group of men. They took considerable pride in their hard-earned reputations, and they were easily recognized by their attire, which indicated their social status. A contemporary described them as follows:

> They used a felt or straw hat with a wide brim and low crown, decorated with silver ornaments in various shapes (stars, heads of eagles, of bulls, etc.), and banded with a thick cord of felt or silver, or a band of flashing embroidery beads. Their jacket was short and made of wool or suede, with the cuffs and pockets embroidered in silk or brilliantly colored yarn; from the shoulders hung silk fringe or silver braid. They never omitted a thick woven scarf. They wore manly felt or suede trousers which buttoned up the sides, and their boots, which reached above the calf, were of the style called belled: these were made of two thick deer skins, embossed with different designs; each one of the skins was folded in half and again lengthwise, and then, thus folded, they are wrapped around the calf and tied with a rope; there are some which are richly embroidered. Truly typical was the famous snakeskin, always full of gold and silver, which was used as a belt . . . the trousers and jacket were buttoned with pieces of pure silver carved with whimsical designs.[45]

During his five years in the profession, from 1785 to 1790, Martín de León concentrated on the lucrative mining trade out of the town of Real de San Nicolás. He and his men supplied grain, tobacco, hides, wool, and cotton for the use of the miners. According to his biographers, he also supplied goods to San Fernando de Béxar in the province of Texas and Monterrey in the Nuevo Reino de León. It may have been during this period that de León, while transporting goods to La Bahía del Espíritu Santo or perhaps buying mules at Dolores, became familiar with the lands north of the Río Bravo del Norte, land which he would eventually request for settlement.[46]

During 1786, while Martín de León worked as a muleteer, Don Bernardo de Gálvez, having defeated the British and served effectively as governor of Louisiana, was named the king's viceroy for all of New Spain. Experienced and knowledgeable of the needs of the northern frontier, the famed general called for a vigorous war against those Indians not at peace with Spain. For the tribes who surrendered, he ordered that the small groups be settled near the presidios, where they could be bribed to remain peaceful with presents, poor-quality firearms, and enough liquor to keep them passive. For those who did not, Viceroy Gálvez called on the militia units, which had been improved and modified by the Royal Regulations of 1772. These regulations had been written up after the careful and detailed inspection by the Marqués de Rubí some five years earlier.

The rules prescribed that commanders train the men in handling fire-arms, including target practice, mounted drills, and military discipline. In addition, the men were to be paid 290 pesos annually, from which each soldier purchased his horses, uniform, armament, and equipment and received two *reales* (one quarter of a *peso*) daily for his own subsistence and that of his family. In addition the soldiers might receive "a *fanega* (approximately 1.6 bushels) of corn, a side of beef, two *reales* worth of soap and two of sugar loaves."[47] The actual success of each unit, however, depended on the honesty and integrity of the paymaster, the commander, and the local merchants, all of whom might conspire to defraud the soldiers of their funds.[48]

The benefits of the military life often outweighed the dangers and potential problems. For Martín de León, by now a mature twenty-five and seasoned by years as a muleteer, life in the military offered security. Although he was not wealthy and could not aspire to the posts of colonel or lieutenant colonel, positions held by the elite hacienda or ranch owners, he could still gain social distinction, some political influence, and an extensive *fuero*, or military legal right. The *fuero*, which protected the officers from local courts and allowed them trial by their own peers, was perhaps the greatest incentive for joining the militia.[49]

Martín had already learned to face danger and lead his own muleteers, so the discipline and danger of military life did not frighten him. For a ten-year enlistment, Martín could be assured of a pension and a land grant. In 1790 the young muleteer gave up his business and returned home to join the Fieles de Burgos. This defensive militia unit had been one of the many contingents established by the viceroy to protect the Escandón settlements from Indian attacks. After five years of muleteering, in which he had fought off Indian raiders with only his own small group of drovers and mule drivers, de León proved particularly adept at leading the soldiers of the regiment and finding the Indian encampments hidden in the mountain valleys.[50]

The Indians of the Sierra Madre, known collectively as Coahuiltecans, consisted of hundreds of small, independent family bands. They had defended themselves successfully for more than a century. Since the first arrival of the Spanish in 1519, many of the Indians, unlike the settled tribes of the interior of Mexico, had refused offers of Christianity and, because of their refusal, had been subjected to slave raids. By 1527 Nuño de Guzmán, the appointed governor of the Pánuco area, which included the lands that would become Nuevo Santander, had mounted a concentrated effort to capture, enslave, and relocate the native tribes to the Antilles, where their labor was needed to replace the dying Caribs and Arawaks. In response to the slave raids, the native tribes had maintained concerted and sometimes unified attacks on the Spanish residents in the area. The missionaries offered the only other option when they arrived hoping to convert the small hunter-gatherer tribespeople into settled farmers. Many of the tribes had refused this life also and had not accepted the strict regimen of a missionary *congregación*, or religious mission settlement. The advantages of accepting the new faith meant the natives were given food, clothing, and instruction in the new religion. The disadvantages meant having to work as farm laborers at the missions or working for Escandón's large hacienda owners.[51]

Nuevo Santander maintained the largest military force in the country due to the Indian threat to Escandón's settlers. The province had three *compañías volantes*, or mounted, fast-response cavalry units, each of which had a complement of seventy-five men and officers. They were assisted by twenty-six independent militia units, such as Martín de León's Fieles de Burgos, which were made up of the local settlers who armed and mounted themselves and were called up as needed. In Nuevo Santander this militia consisted of 2,358 men.[52]

The dilemma facing the king was the conflict between his desire to pacify and Christianize his Indian subjects and at the same time to protect his Spanish citizens. The greatest difficulty, according to Spanish military commanders, was that the Indians knew they were the king's "favored children" and soon learned they could get away with thievery so long as they came in periodically, acted repentant, and begged forgiveness. They received gifts, obvious bribes, from the mission fathers or the presidial commanders. The Regulation of 1772, implemented by José de Gálvez and the Marquis de Rubí, called for peace and protection of the king's native subjects. Captives were not to be abused but were to be sent to the interior, where they could be rehabilitated. The Indians were not as pleased with the later Instrucción of 1786, proposed by the knowledgeable Viceroy Bernardo de Gálvez, which provided more latitude for the local administrators and called for pacification through a combination of strong-arm tactics and negotiation. To the dismay of the northern Spanish settlers, de Gálvez died in 1786 after less than a year in office. Within three years, the new viceroy had suggested that although peace was preferable, warfare against the Indians was absolutely necessary in order to force them to return to peaceful ways.[53]

Those living on the frontier, especially groups such as de León's militia unit in Escandón's settlements, responded with all-out war. The settlers and their military commanders believed that the pacification of the hundreds of small nomadic tribes who operated from hidden encampments and settlements in the mountains—attacking the mule trains, the sheep and cattle herds, the silver mines and the settlers—could only be achieved through outright removal. The Indians responded in kind. Tribal chiefs such as Cabrito, who had united ten tribes against the Spanish, advised his people to steal all the Spaniards' horses, which would leave them "like chickens for the plucking."[54] Spanish horse and sheep herds disappeared. The Indians tortured, killed, and sometimes ate the Spanish men, at times keeping a few to ransom, but took the women and children hostage and put them to use as slaves. They stole Spanish mules and horses and traded with eastern tribes who had access to guns and ammunition from Louisiana traders. At one great Indian trade fair on the Guadalupe River in November and December 1782, the Apaches brought 3,000 horses, all carrying Spanish brands, to trade for 270 guns. Due in part to the great war going on between the Spanish and their American allies against the English (the American Revolution), the Apaches were angered by the lack of sufficient guns and had to take 2,000 horses back with them. Frustrated but not stopped by their failure to acquire the weapons, the tribes feasted on 4,000 head of stolen Spanish cattle.[55]

Although the small mountain tribes were an irritant, Martín de León's cavalry company most feared the dreaded mounted tribes such as the Apache, the Lipan, the Norteño, and the Comanche on the plains to the north. These tribes were far more aggressive. The governors and the vice-regal government alternated between trying to exterminate the aggressive raiders and attempting peace treaties which offered trade goods and annual presents to keep the Indians peaceful. The Indians took advantage of any periods of weakness or inattention on the part of the Spanish soldiers. In 1780 and 1781, thousands of cattle along with funds and soldiers had been diverted to Louisiana to feed Spanish troops. The Plains tribes stepped up their raids, hitting Spanish ranches as far south as Nuevo Santander and Coahuila.

Once the American Revolution was over, Governor Domingo Cabello of Texas struggled to reestablish a peaceful, if not always amicable, agreement with the various Indian groups. He spent years trying to balance the lack of funds with the promises of trade goods and annual gifts to bribe the Indian tribes into acquiescence.[56]

South of the Río Bravo del Norte in Nuevo Santander, Martín de León and his soldiers were constantly busy. For almost the entire ten years during which de León belonged to the Fieles de Burgos, his unit defended the colonies against both the local Indian tribes and the periodic raids of the well-mounted and heavily armed Texas Indians. The Fieles and their compatriots also went on the offensive against the smaller tribes in their mountain hideaways. Epidemics which raged throughout the Indian communities periodically during the last years of the eighteenth century and the first decades of the nineteenth devastated many tribes, leaving them too weak to defend themselves from either the Spanish or their own Indian enemies. By 1798, as Martín de León neared the end of his ten years of service, the Indian population of the eastern Sierra Madre stood at only 1,700 people, down from 25,000 just fifty years earlier. The militia units of Nuevo Santander had done the work which they had been established to do.[57]

During his years of service, Martín de León had been promoted through the ranks. After only five years, he was appointed captain of the regiment. The thirty-year-old captain had caught the eye of his commander's daughter, Patricia de la Garza. On the frontier, the number of appropriate suitors was slim for someone of the landed aristocracy such as the de la Garza family. The family may have hoped to find a Spanish official to marry Patricia, which would have ensured her success in the colonial society and perhaps even provided her with an entrée into Spanish society in Madrid. But such was not to be. Martín, although of Spanish blood, had been born in the New World and was, therefore, a *criollo*. He was not wealthy, but he was hardworking, and with the potential for a successful military career, he was still a promising prospect for the twenty-year-old Patricia. With the family's approval, the self-confident and dynamic captain courted and won her hand.[58]

In 1795, with the blessings of both families, Patricia de la Garza of Soto la Marina married Martín de León, captain of the regiment of the Fieles de Burgos. Although nothing is known of Patricia's early life, her dowry tells a great deal about her family. By the end of the eighteenth century, dowries were not essential and certainly not expected on the distant pioneering frontier of Nuevo Santander, but they were still considered proper among those who felt they belonged to the upper classes, whether Spanish or *criollo*. A dowry was property which a woman brought to the wedding to provide the new family with an income in the early stages of the marriage. Although Martín could administer the dowry and invest it for profit, the money belonged to Patricia and remained legally hers. The funds would serve to provide for Patricia in her widowhood. In urban areas such as Mexico City or even Monterrey, the most common dowries consisted of clothes, linen, jewels, furniture, and silverware. On the frontier, however, the dowry often consisted of animals to start a ranch.[59]

Such was the case with Patricia de la Garza's dowry. From her father, Patricia received twelve mares, four two-year-old colts, five tame horses, five unbroken colts, two proof jacks, sixteen breeding cows, one yoke of oxen, one donkey for plowing, one she ass, and one cow. The animals would give the young couple a good head start toward a successful future, but the truly substantial part of her dowry came from her godfather, Don Angel Pérez of Soto la Marina. From him she received 9,800 pesos in cash. In a study of Puebla, Guadalajara, and Monterrey, large dowries of more than 5,000 pesos made up only 14 percent of the dowries. For Monterrey, as a "frontier community with few wealthy individuals, there were almost no dowries over 5,000 pesos."[60] When Patricia received such a sizable sum, it is evidence that the de la Garza family, although perhaps not wealthy in their own right, were under the protection of the very well-to-do Pérez family.[61]

For the next five years, as the century ended, the couple remained in Burgos while Martín continued his service to the Spanish crown. The frontier was once more caught up in the problems of Europe. Carlos III died in 1788 and left Spain in the hands of the inept Charles IV, who surrendered the government to his wife's lover, Manuel de Godoy, while France erupted in revolution. The impact on Martín and his new family came when Godoy, more fearful of the growing expansion of the new United States, offered Louisiana to the French Directorate in 1795 in hopes of creating a buffer between the Spanish silver mines and the aggressive Anglo Americans just across the Mississippi. French spies and infiltrators appeared more frequently on the frontier, seeking to spread their revolutionary ideas. When Napoleon succeeded in acquiring Louisiana late in 1799, part of the secret treaty required that the land never be sold to anyone else. Three years later, when the treaty became public, Napoleon peddled the land to the United States, over Spain's objections. Martín and Patricia and the people of Nuevo Santander faced the very real threat of Anglo-American traders and settlers moving to the Mississippi River, just across from their colonies.

With the encouragement of the Spanish government, Martín and Patricia de León decided to use his captain's grant of land and her dowry to move to the increasingly important province of Texas. The cash was not enough to make a grand settlement, or *entrada*, like those of the early colonizers of northern Mexico such as José de Escandón. The young couple could not bring large groups of inhabitants and thousands of head of cattle, horses, and sheep or to create towns and receive large grants of land in exchange. But the dowry money and Martín's captain's grant was enough to bring their own family plus ranch hands and servants with their attendant families. It was also enough to pay for supplies to fill the squeaking, high-wheeled *carretas*, or carts, to load long lines of mules with household goods and to provide all of their people with homes, food, and protection. Martín felt confident that he and his men could protect the ranch from the Lipan, Apache, or Comanche. What protection they could not provide themselves would come from the government soldiers at the presidio of La Bahía del Espíritu Santo, two days' ride to the northeast, or from San Fernando de Béxar, two days ride to the northwest. The young couple, looking hopefully across the river and into the new century, were part of the slow but steady, ongoing Spanish expansion northward, filling in the spaces and protecting the frontier, no longer from the French but now from the intrusive Anglo Americans.[62]

CHAPTER 2

THE DE LEÓN RANCHES IN TEXAS, 1800–1813

Genealogical Chart

ARTÍN DE LEÓN (M. 1795) + PATRICIA DE LA GARZA

   1. Fernando (b. 1798)

   2. María Candelaria (b. 1800)

   3. José Silvestre (b. 1802)

   4. María Guadalupe "Lupita" (b. 1804)

   5. José Félix (b. 1806)

   6. Agápito (b. 1808)

   7. María de Jesús "Chucha" (b. 1810)

   8. Refugia (b. 1812)

On January 1, 1801, Martín de León and his wife of five years, Patricia de la Garza de León, stood before the notary public at Presas del Rey in the Eastern Interior Provinces of Northern New Spain. Patricia, then about twenty-six years of age and the mother of two children, signed over her dowry of almost 10,000 pesos in cash, goods, and livestock to her husband. The couple was investing everything they had to establish a ranch on the Nueces River in Texas, one of the four Spanish Eastern Interior Provinces.[1]

At the beginning of the new century, the threat from the acquisitive United States had boiled over again. What New Spain needed was another dynamic Charles III and a second José de Escandón to help settle Texas. What they had was the weak-willed Charles IV, who seemed to have little interest in the colonies of the New World except for what they could supply in silver bullion. The Spanish government no longer had the funds to encourage young men like Martín de León to make extensive settlements. Money was being siphoned off to defend Spain from Napoleon's armies. The French were sending spies and their propaganda into Texas, and the aggressive, land-hungry United States was surreptitiously encouraging illegal Anglo traders. In 1795 Brigadier Pedro de Nava, commandant general of the Eastern Interior Provinces, informed the Texas governor:

> A royal order, sent through secret channels, has arrived ordering the utmost care to prevent the passage to this kingdom of persons from the United States of America. The king has been informed on good authority that the United States has ordered emissaries to move here and work to subvert the population. Baron Carondelet, governor of Louisiana, has been ordered to work diligently against these greedy persons from the western states and says there has been some movement by them into the interior of this province.[2]

The immediate threat which sent Martín de León on his trek northward came from an Irish-American adventurer and horse trader named Philip Nolan. As early as 1794, Nolan had requested passes to enter Texas to collect horses as remounts for the Spanish governor of Louisiana while the area still belonged to Spain. Commandant General Nava signed the permits for the expeditions of 1794–1995. But within two years the Spanish Governor at Natchez had learned of Nolan's involvement with General James Wilkinson, who, it was rumored, planned to conquer the Spanish Southwest. Under orders to keep out all foreigners, especially Americans, Nava ordered Nolan not to enter Texas again. That fall, when Nolan ignored the order and crossed the Louisiana border into Texas with twenty to thirty men, the Spanish government in Mexico City leaped to the assumption that it was an invasionary force. Captain Martín de León and his Fieles de Burgos had been called up to defend the border and joined the militias from Nuevo Santander and Nuevo León as well as the garrisons along the Río Bravo at Laredo, Revilla, Mier, Camargo, and Reynosa and inland at Refugio. The units patrolled the roads from Nacogdoches to San Antonio and La Bahía looking for Nolan and his army. At last, in March 1801, Spanish troops from Nacogdoches located Nolan in the Waco Indian territory. Ordered to surrender, Nolan refused, and the Spanish forces killed him and captured his men. With considerable relief, the government ordered Captain de León and his Fieles de Burgos, along with the other militias, back to their home bases.[3]

Martín de León, perhaps already familiar with the region he and his men had been patrolling, determined to settle a ranch in the new lands. In 1801, with Patricia's support and her substantial dowry, Martín moved his family to La Bahía del Espíritu Santo on the San Antonio River. The hamlet was an active if not particularly large settlement. Since there were few large trees on the flat, expansive plains, most of the homes were *jacales* built of the local scrub wood and gathered close to the walls of the presidio. The officers and the slightly better-off ranchers (for no one was truly wealthy on the frontier) had built adobe or stone homes of one or two rooms along the road from the interior or scattered upriver toward San Fernando de Béxar. The population of almost 2,000 people consisted of soldiers or retired soldiers and their families and a growing number of civilians such as Martín and Patricia de León.[4]

During the mornings a constant bustle surrounded the presidio. Wood smoke from the breakfast fires mixed with dust from the corrals as soldiers brought in the horse herd from the pastures farther upriver to exchange for the mounts in the corrals. The half-wild horses, trapped on the vast Mustang Plains, provided rebellious but usable transportation. While the commandant and his scribe prepared the daily mail to go to San Fernando de Béxar and then on to Saltillo, Mexico City, and even Spain, the men saddled and bridled the squealing, bucking horses. Two of the soldiers prepared the saddlebags of outgoing mail, mounted, and rode off upriver on their two-day trip to San Fernando de Béxar. Across the river the Franciscan friars tolled the bells to call the Indians to prayers at the mission church. The bells also called the faithful together at the presidio chapel, where, although there was no resident priest, the women of the town gathered to recite morning prayers in the quiet of the candlelit sanctuary with its smell of incense and the ornate statues of the saints. Itinerant tradesmen or a mule train of goods for the mission might have arrived overnight from the Escandón settlements along the river. Although there was little hard cash, everyone in town would turn out to see their wares and perhaps offer to trade hides or lard or corn for a lace scarf, a length of cloth, or a copper pot. Gossip was always exciting, and the arrival of Martín and Patricia and their two children would have occasioned considerable comment.

There was very little unclaimed ranch land available on the San Antonio River for the young couple. Admittedly, the ranches were neither large nor elegant. Father Morfí, one of the mission fathers who arrived from Central Mexico several years earlier, had described the ranches as pathetic. Those who lived along the river, however, did not find them so. The lands up and down the San Antonio River had been carved up among dozens of owners. Upriver, the five San Antonio missions each held thousands of acres. Nearby, the mission of La Bahía del Espíritu Santo controlled the west side of the San Antonio River. Civilians from both San Antonio and La Bahía, the retired soldiers from the villa of San Fernando de Béxar, and soldiers and their families from the presidial garrison at La Bahía owned ranches along the northeast side. The only option for Martín and Patricia was to settle on the adjacent Aransas River or the more distant Nueces River.[5]

The young couple chose to settle on the Nueces. Martín and Patricia made a claim for his captain's land at the Paso de Santa Margarita.[6] It was an important low-water crossing on the road from Escandón's border towns to the presidio and mission at La Bahía. The crossing was also potentially dangerous. The ranch site lay adjacent to an Apache *ranchería*, a small farming community of relatively passive and semi-Christianized Indians. It was not the peaceful Apaches who threatened the small settlement at the crossing but the fearsome Comanches who hated the Apaches as much as or more than they hated the Spanish. The ranch site was many miles from the safety of the presidio at La Bahía or San Antonio, but Martín self-confidently believed he could defend himself from any potential Indian attacks. In 1802, while Patricia was pregnant with their third child, Martín took his ranch hands down to the river crossing and began the construction of the buildings which would house them all.

With Patricia's wealth, it had not taken long for the young couple to become an accepted part of the elite of the small community at La Bahía.

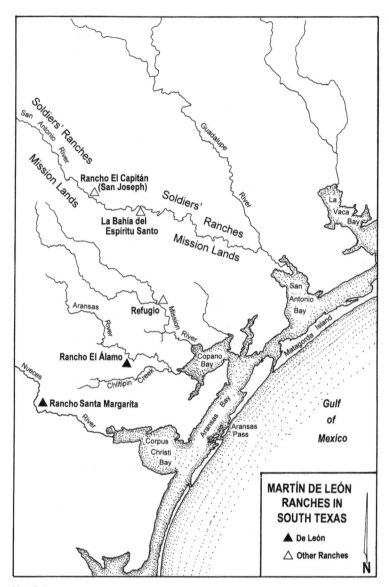

Soldiers' Ranches

San Antonio River

Mission Lands

Rancho El Capitán
(San Joseph)

Soldiers'
Ranches

La Bahía del
Espíritu Santo

Mission Lands

Guadalupe River

La
Vaca
Bay

San
Antonio
Bay

Aransas

River

Refugio

Mission River

Matagorda Island

Rancho El Álamo

Copano
Bay

Nueces

Chiltipin Creek

Rancho Santa Margarita

River

Corpus
Christi
Bay

Aransas Bay

Aransas
Pass

Gulf
of
Mexico

MARTÍN DE LEÓN
RANCHES IN
SOUTH TEXAS

▲ De León
△ Other Ranches

N

Map 2.1

Among their newfound friends were some of the local ranchers, in particular the Aldrete and Manchola families. Patricia knew it was never too early to begin planning two-year-old Candelaria's future. The Aldretes, a good ranching family, had three-year-old José Miguel Aldrete, who might provide an excellent match. Patricia gave birth to José Silvestre in 1802 and two years later to another daughter, María Guadalupe, known by the nickname Lupita. The family remained at La Bahía for another year, still waiting on their land. Their fifth child, Félix, was born in 1806, just before the completion of the ranch headquarters and the family's move to the ranch.[7]

De León's request for land—always a lengthy, expensive, and tedious process—had run afoul of changing land laws. Several years earlier, in 1800, the viceroy and the king's council had become concerned over the number of absentee landlords acquiring huge tracts for practically nothing on the northern frontier. Many of the landowners were acquiring land "not to increase their incomes, but to *señorear* . . . that is to be lord of the manor."[8] Forty to fifty *sitios*, almost a quarter of a million acres, could be purchased for 100 pesos. Unlike the profit-oriented ranchers whom Escandón had encouraged in Nuevo Santander, many of the owners of acreages in excess of 400 *sitios* had left the land unused.[9]

When Martín de León and his neighbors appealed for land in the province of Texas, they were forced to wait for more than three years. Among his neighbors were Miguel Delgado of the Rancho Delgado, Antonio Montreal of the Rancho San Pedro, and Manuel Vasquez of the Rancho El Carrizo. The king had appointed a special treasury council at San Luís Potosí to determine what should be done about the land issue. In 1805, following the advice of his committee, the king changed the regulation of the sale of lands on the frontier. The rich were permitted to purchase no more than thirty *sitios*, while the poor could acquire eight or ten *sitios*, an amount deemed sufficient to produce a respectable profit. For Texas, the council set the cost for dry lands at ten pesos per *sitio*, while irrigated lands or lands with wells or springs would cost thirty pesos per *sitio*, and lands directly on the river went for fifty to sixty pesos per *sitio*. Most property was situated on the river so that the families could use the water to irrigate their fields. Both wealthy and poor were required to settle the lands within two years, establish homes and productive ranches, and provide protection for travelers from marauding Indians. Once the government had made its decisions, Martín de León and his neighbors secured possession of their lands along the Nueces River. They still faced several years of time-consuming paperwork in actually securing a title, but in the meantime, the family could move in. As part of acquiring the land, Martín carried out the formal act of possession. Accompanied by the government official granting the land, Martín was taken by the hand and "pulled weeds and herbs from the earth in the name of his majesty the king and knelt in prayer giving thanks to God and the king."[10]

The Rancho de Santa Margarita, the name which Martín and Patricia gave their ranch, was ideally located to provide travelers with protection and a place to stay while crossing the Nueces River. When the couple arrived at the Nueces River, the ranch was described as arid and

> bounded on the South by the said [Nueces] River; on the North by the village of the Apaches and from this point toward the West, they are bounded by the creek *Nombre de Dios* and toward the East they extend as far as the lands owned by the Mission del Rosario.[11]

All ranchers, if they could, built their ranch headquarters on high ground and near water. The problem lay in being close enough to provide water for the ranch while still avoiding the yearly spring floods. On the flat plains of South Texas, the rambling, slow-moving rivers could easily rise thirty feet or more in a matter of a few hours, their deceptively smooth surfaces belying the powerful swirling undercurrents which could destroy a home, drown horses and cows, and wash a man away in an instant. Martín and Patricia, aware of the danger, chose the high ground overlooking the Nueces River. The ranch buildings at the crossing were built at the site of the modern town of San Patricio. The family remained at the crossing for several years, but like many other ranchers in the area, no government-appointed land commissioner ever placed them in possession of the land. They might be driven off by Comanche raids, and, since there was plenty of land along the Nueces for all, no one contested their right to the ranch.[12]

Unlike the Anglo-American settlers to come, no Spaniard went out into the wilderness alone. Martín de León and his neighbors settled their ranches in large family groups with numerous servants. The less well-to-do might have fewer servants, but they always settled in family units to provide help and support for one another. Directly assisting the ranch owner, or *patrón*, were his *vaqueros* (the name derived from *vaca*, or cow), the cowboys who handled the livestock and horses. The *peones*, or farm-workers, planted and harvested the corn, beans, squash, chiles, and tomatoes, the main staples of the ranches. The wives of the vaqueros and *peones* usually worked with the *patrona*, or wife of the owner, to prepare food,

Jacal con enramada (Hut with arbor) by Theodore Gentilz, a French artist and
surveyor who came to Texas with Henri Castro to help promote the Castro
colony during the 1840s. Courtesy of Mr. and Mrs. Larry Sheerin, San
Antonio, Texas.

clean house, wash clothes, and the myriad other chores necessary for survival on the frontier.[13]

When Martín at last brought Patricia and the five children to the ranch,
the *vaqueros* and *peones* had already completed some of the buildings. The
first structures were the simple, primitive *jacales,* easily assembled and comfortably cool in the hot, dry heat. De León had his *vaqueros* cut four- or
five-foot lengths from the plentiful shrubs and brushy trees, the more
crooked and covered with branching forks the better. The rough poles or
branches were laid horizontally between pairs of posts set into the ground
around the perimeter of the building, which could be as much as fifteen or
twenty feet square. Although some ranchers may have used the palisade or
picket form of *jacal* found in East Texas, with all the branches set vertically
and interlocking into a tightly knit fence or wall, South Texans preferred
the thicker, horizontal-branch walls for defense against the Indians. After
the branches were in place, the ranch hands mixed mud with straw and
plastered the thick mixture on the inner and outer surfaces, filling in the

crevices and providing a smooth finish which could be whitewashed to reflect the heat from the outside and to lighten the rooms inside. They constructed the roof of limbs or branches laid across a ridgepole extending from wall to wall, then attached a grass cover of thatch or *tule* which was tied to the cross members. The women pounded the floor flat and smoothed it with adobe or mud so that the surface, called a *tipichil*, was almost as hard as concrete and could be swept daily with a wet broom to keep it clean and smooth. Since there was little rain, the *jacales* were sturdy, lasted well in the heat, and could be easily defended in case of attack.[14]

As soon as work on the ranch permitted, de León began construction of the *casa grande*. Since there were few sources of wealth in Texas, no gold or silver mines, the great majority of the ranchers on the Nueces were men of moderate means, and none of the ranches was ever as grand or as fine as the huge haciendas of the Marqueses de Aguayo or the Sánchez Navarro families south of the Río Bravo. Still, each rancher aspired to have a *casa grande*, if for nothing else but to protect his family from the Indians. The "big house" was based on Moorish designs and consisted of as little as two rooms set side by side or as many as a dozen built around a courtyard with a well in the center. Each room was built as a large cube with walls and ceilings measuring between fifteen and twenty feet on a side. The rooms, with no windows but gun slits, *troneras*, in the outer walls, were built of brown sandstone or *caliche* (limestone), if there was any available, or of large blocks of adobe which were stacked and mortared into walls two to three feet thick.[15] The interiors of the rooms were smoothed with plaster or adobe and whitewashed. On the outside, the walls extended several feet above the flat roof as a parapet, which served as a defensive barricade against Indians.[16]

Much like in the home Martín remembered from his youth, the roof was supported by heavy cypress or mesquite beams, called *vigas*, which were built into the walls. The workers often carved a central *viga* with the date of the construction, the name or coat of arms of the family, and perhaps a family motto or religious saying. These hand-hewn rectangular beams were laid into the wall every two feet and were then overlaid by split or sawn boards called *tablas*. A further layer of roofing material of mud, grass, or gravel was spread over the *tablas*, followed by a top layer of lime, sand, and gravel smoothed and slanted to one edge. The flat roof was drained by *canales*, or channels, which extended through the parapet and might be made of carved wood or sandstone, sometimes formed into intricate gargoyle shapes. For safety, the gates into the patio were barred by thick, heavy paneled doors which could be closed with a Spanish self-locking hasp and a massive wooden bar.[17]

The rooms in the homes were based on centuries of tradition. A large *sala*, or hall, was built in the front of the house where the family gathered, met guests, or held parties. A built-in adobe or stone bench might ring the whitewashed room, covered and padded with brightly colored Saltillo *sarapes*. Cloth was tacked along the walls to keep the guests from brushing against the whitewash. There might have been tables, chairs, or chests in the center of the room, although such furnishings were uncommon. The larger ranches included a small chapel in one corner of the patio where itinerant priests could say mass, perform a baptism or communion, or where a marriage ceremony could be held. For the smaller ranchers, a niche built into the wall had to suffice with a statue of a saint or of the Virgin of Guadalupe.[18]

Ranchers often had little elegance in their lives. The bedrooms, each with its own large fireplace and hearth of stone, were outfitted with a rough bedstead made of mesquite or cedar and covered with a corn-shuck mattress and a handmade comforter filled with feathers. Clothes were hung from pegs in the wall or packed in large iron-bound wooden chests. A dining room contained a long table and usually benches or stools for seating. Only the very wealthiest had the elaborate Spanish red-velvet-cushioned oak chairs with high, straight backs and armrests. The most important room in the house was the kitchen, which had cooking utensils of clay, or if the owner had accumulated some wealth, like Patricia and Martín, graduated copper pots and cast-iron skillets and cooking vessels hung above the open hearth fireplace. In the *trasteros*, or cupboards, standing along the walls of the kitchen, with their locked double doors, the family silver plate was kept for special occasions.[19]

Skilled artisans were particularly prized. Carpenters or blacksmiths could make the many pieces of furniture used on the ranch, but there were few artisans on the northern frontier, and their work was highly valued. A skilled carpenter could use the mesquite or cedar to make carved and decorated chairs, tables, cupboards, wooden chests, benches, and stools. Even more prized was a carpenter who could make the heavy, iron-studded chests for storing clothing. Best of all was one who could create the Castilian *vargueño*, a Spanish-style chest or desk used to store the ranch documents and the business papers of the owners. The *vargueño* opened with a fold-down front to reveal dozens of small drawers and compartments. It might also contain a secret compartment for the family jewels or bags of silver and gold coins. It was placed on high legs so the rancher could use it as a desk to write letters or handle accounts. In the case of Martín and Patricia, their wealth may have enabled them to have a *vargueño* inlaid with ivory, mother-of-pearl, or precious metals.[20]

Equally valuable was a talented blacksmith who could manufacture anything needed on the ranch in iron, silver, or copper. He could create hinges and fasteners for the doors and windows, decorative details and closures for chests, bridle bits and hardware for the saddles, wagons, plows, and carriages. The blacksmith also made the branding irons with the family brand, which was stamped on furnishings as well as livestock. He also manufactured nails and forged or repaired the axes, adzes, hammers, and other tools needed to build the main house, corrals, sheds, and barns. The most prized smithies could make guns, and some few worked in silver and precious metals to create intricate designs for saddles, bridles, jewelry, or clothing fasteners.[21]

An important part of family life on the ranch was the occasional gathering of friends and family. For Martín and Patricia, the birth of their children was a cause for celebration and a chance to create a new set of familial networks through godparenthood. When Silvestre, Guadalupe, and Félix were born at La Bahía, Martín and Patricia, if possible, would have chosen their relatives in Burgos or Soto la Marina to serve as godparents at the baptism, but that was a long and dangerous trip. Godparents for the three youngsters came from the other settlers at La Bahía. It was a good way to begin to develop the important network which would help the family in the future.[22]

Upon the births of Agápito in 1808 and, two years later, María de Jesús, nicknamed Chucha, the parents turned to their new friends along the Nueces to act as *padrinos* and *madrinas*, or godparents. In so doing, the parents and the godparents became *compadres* and *comadres*, or co-parents, a relationship which was as close as and often closer than that of a blood relative. For the Spanish ranch families, whether along the Nueces or in Nuevo Santander, the concept of godparenthood had been expanded to become *compadrazgo*, the creation of an extended family. The Aldretes, as neighbors, united with the de León family as co-parents at the baptisms of the new babies. These godparents promised to help the parents protect the infants throughout their lives and bring the children up in the Catholic faith. Close friends were made into a powerful network of kin who could be depended on in time of need. Their help might include money, as it had in the case of Patricia de la Garza, or cattle, land, a job, a place to stay, and

even a home should the godchild or his or her family need it. Godparenthood created a defensive, protective system of intense and emotional relationships which lasted a lifetime and served the frontier community well.
It also protected them into the next century.[23]

By 1805 visitors began arriving at the Santa Margarita crossing on the
Nueces River. Soldiers, settlers, civilians, and government officials were
hastening from the interior of Mexico to La Bahía, San Fernando, and
the distant Louisiana border. After Napoleon sold the Louisiana territory to the Americans, abrogating his agreement made with the Spanish
king, it took two years for the secret to emerge, and when the news came
out, the Spanish government was furious. There was intense disagreement between Spain and the United States over the location of the boundary between Texas and Louisiana. The French had suggested to Thomas
Jefferson, although there were no maps or written documentation, that the
Louisiana Purchase included Texas. The Spanish vehemently disagreed
and continued to maintain that Texas was not part of Louisiana and that
the boundary was the Sabine River.[24]

Meanwhile, with the government changing around them, the Spanish
settlers in Louisiana had little choice but to accept the domination of the
United States or move to Spanish Texas. Many wanted to move to Texas,
but the commandant general in Chihuahua feared opening the borders to
potentially dangerous spies and infiltrators. The king, however, more concerned with his Louisiana citizens, approved the admission of his loyal,
hardworking farmers to help settle Texas, as long as they settled far from
the border with Louisiana, where contraband and the tempting trade with
New Orleans had become a major problem.[25]

The Spanish government ordered the creation of towns for the incoming settlers on the Trinity and the Brazos Rivers. Since funds for new
presidios were nonexistent, Governor Don Manuel Antonio Cordero y
Bustamante of Texas ordered soldiers from La Bahía and San Antonio to
move to the new sites on the Trinity and the Brazos to prepare the way and
protect the new colonists. Cordero sent his captain of militia to found Santísima Trinidad de Salcedo on the Trinity River. The settlers arriving there
from the dense cypress swamps of Louisiana were comfortably familiar
with the thick pine and oak forests of the East Texas river bottoms. For
the settlers from South Texas, however, the dense foliage was oppressive
after the open prairies they had known on the Río Bravo. Instead of vast
expanses of grasslands, the settlers had to clear dense underbrush and cut
down tall pines and oaks in order to provide fields for their cattle. For those

The purchase

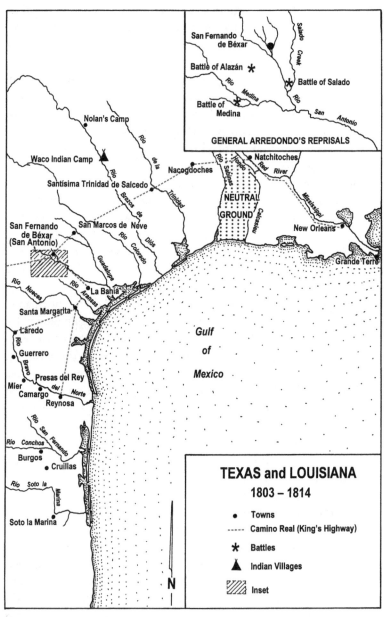

GENERAL ARREDONDO'S REPRISALS

San Fernando de Béxar

Battle of Alazán ✱

✱ Battle of Salado

Saltado Creek

Río Medina

Battle of Medina ✱

San Antonio

Nolan's Camp

Waco Indian Camp

Santísima Trinidad de Salcedo

Río de la Trinidad

Río Brazos de Dios

Natchitoches

Nacogdoches

Red River

Río Sabinas

Mississippi

NEUTRAL GROUND

Calcasieu

New Orleans

Grande Terre

San Fernando de Béxar (San Antonio)

San Marcos de Neve

Río Colorado

Guadalupe

Río Aransas

La Bahía

Río Nueces

Santa Margarita

Laredo

Guerrero

Río Bravo del Norte

Presas del Rey

Mier

Camargo

Reynosa

Río San Fernando

Río Conchos

Burgos

Cruillas

Río Soto la Marina

Soto la Marina

Gulf
of
Mexico

TEXAS and LOUISIANA
1803 – 1814

- •   Towns
- -----   Camino Real (King's Highway)
- ✱   Battles
- ▲   Indian Villages
- /////   Inset

N

Map 2.2

Louisiana refugees who did not care to remain on the Trinity, many moved on to La Bahía, then down the *camino real* to the Santa Margarita crossing, moving south to establish new homes in Nuevo Santander, Monterrey, or Saltillo.[26]

Martín de León, perhaps already interested in starting his own colony, listened to the travelers around the nightly campfires who described the founding of the town of Trinidad de Salcedo. When mule trains or soldiers passed through, he inquired after the success of the settlement. The lists of settlers requesting land at Trinidad de Salcedo included twelve residents of San Fernando de Béxar, a half-dozen soldiers from La Bahía, some French and Spanish Louisiana settlers, and two American traders from Nacogdoches, Guillermo Barr and Samuel Davenport. De León was particularly concerned over the increasing number of Anglo Americans who were already coveting the expanses of free land in Texas. Among those who came was Daniel Boone, a nephew of the Kentucky pioneer of the same name, "who swore that the United States did not 'suit' him,"[27] and moved on to San Antonio de Béxar as a gunsmith, where he was later killed by Indians.

The travelers sitting around the campfires at the Santa Margarita shook their heads in amazement over the audacity of Miguel Quinn, a settler at Trinidad de Salcedo. He had written "to a friend in the United States to inquire how far the Americans would go when they invaded Texas, so that he might buy cheap land in what was to be United States territory." Quinn, reported the campfire gossips, in addition to establishing a house in town on a *solar* (town lot) and *suerte* (the right to irrigation water), claimed a *sitio* for a ranch four and a half leagues downriver and requested permission to buy three more *sitios* at the crossing called El Paso Alto.[28]

Quinn did not get his wish to be annexed by the United States in 1803. During the next ten years, Martín noted that the small settlement held its own against Indian raiders and the new breed of illegal traders who sold guns to the Comanches. The muleteers reported that the members of the small community of Trinidad de Salcedo had gathered into a militia unit and defended the road from Nacogdoches to San Antonio, providing some protection and defense for the frontier. The second settlement at San Telésforo de los Brazos on the Brazos River, due to insufficient funds and a lack of settlers, was never implemented.[29]

By 1806, the Rancho de Santa Margarita was no isolated frontier settlement and had become a busy way station. The reason for the traffic was, once again, fear of war with the United States. American government officials had taken over at New Orleans, and while Martín de León and his family were settling in at the Santa Margarita, President Jefferson was sending American explorers into the new Louisiana Purchase. Commandant General Salcedo, after the problems over Nolan, trusted no one, and until the king had time to establish a boundary commission, all Anglo Americans were suspect. Salcedo ordered Simón Herrera, governor of Nuevo León, to move the militias of Nuevo León and Nuevo Santander into Texas. Martín de León, not long retired from the military, may well have recognized some of his old comrades-in-arms as they stopped for the night at his Rancho de Santa Margarita. Martín and Patricia de León and the ranch hands provided accommodations, food, and remounts for military units passing through from Nuevo Santander on their way to Nacogdoches, San Fernando de Béxar, or La Bahía del Espíritu Santo.

Others came through as well. Mule trains brought in supplies for the soldiers stationed around Texas. Government emissaries from Mexico City carried orders for their commanders at Nacogdoches. Louisiana émigrés, fearful of the upcoming war, packed their goods on mules and horses and moved back to Mexico from Louisiana or from the settlement on the Trinity. The mail carriers with military escorts came and went, each carrying his distinctive presidial pouches with individual seals and stamps. By 1806 Texas held more troops than at any other time in its history.[30]

Martín de León was not the only settler establishing himself in Texas. The Texas governors found another willing colonizer in Felipe Roque de la Portilla, whose wife, María Ignacia de la Garza Montemayor, was Patricia's cousin. Under orders from Governor Cordero, Roque de la Portilla, much like José de Escandón, founded the town of San Marcos de Neve on the San Marcos River, some twenty leagues northeast of San Fernando de Béxar, with settlers from Nuevo Santander. The colonizer left Nuevo Santander in the spring of 1807 with fifty-two colonists and all of their supplies, servants, and livestock. At the Rancho de Santa Margarita, Roque de la Portilla turned his settlers over to Governor Cordero's military unit and returned to Nuevo Santander for another group of colonists. In January of the following year Roque de la Portilla again stopped at the Santa Margarita with a group of settlers. Accompanying him were his wife and the first five of their eight children, including two of their daughters, Dolores and Tomasa. Roque de la Portilla made sure that among the settlers was Don Estéban, a teacher who could educate his children and the children of his colonists.[31]

Travelers relayed the gossip of the frontier as they sat around the sup-

Hacendados (Hacienda owners) by Carl Nebel. Ranchers on the northern frontier did their best to keep up appearances even if they might not be quite as elegant as these wealthy Mexican hacienda owners. Courtesy of Benson Latin American Collection, University of Texas at Austin.

per fires at the Rancho de Santa Margarita throughout 1806 and 1807. War appeared imminent. General James Wilkinson, head of the United States Army, with the support of Thomas Jefferson, was threatening to invade Spanish Texas, claiming the land as part of the Louisiana Purchase. In addition, it was rumored that Aaron Burr, the former vice president of the United States, was in Ohio scheming to separate the western United States and join it to Texas to create his own empire. The soldiers who stopped at the Santa Margarita said that Governor Cordero, concerned over the machinations of these madmen, had moved his troops into Nacogdoches, and Governor Herrera had taken his militia units to Los Adaes, the original capital of Texas, and far beyond the Sabine River into Louisiana.

General Wilkinson stalled until September 1806. Some said he was debating whether to join Burr in an invasion of Texas. When Wilkinson at last marched for New Orleans, Governor Cordero desperately wrote to Commandant General Salcedo in Chihuahua for orders. Governor Herrera, avoiding even the appearance of an attack, ordered the Spanish forces to pull back to the Sabine and then back farther still to Nacogdoches. The reason for the retreat, according to Bishop Marín de Porras, a visitor who had been through the area the previous year but had returned to Monterrey, was that

"[Governor Herrera's] only interest was the contraband trade. The uniforms for the troops were bought from the Americans, and even the hats, at a conspicuous profit for him, since he has distributed all among the troops at whatever price he has wished. And not content with this, he has flooded these provinces with contraband . . . by means of his acquaintances, who have gone to the most miserable ranches to expend the contraband goods."[32]

Whether the accusations of illicit activities were true or not, war had once again been avoided. Governor Cordero of Texas, Governor Herrera of Nuevo León, and General Wilkinson, in what has been called "the most hasty, ill-advised and unauthorized peace treaty in modern history,"[33] jointly agreed, without consulting either of their respective governments, that the Spanish troops would remain west of the Sabine, while the American troops, on the east, would not cross the Río Hondo, a tributary of the Red River. The "Neutral Ground" which was thus created formed a section of land which neither the Spanish nor the Anglo Americans controlled or supervised. It was true that some honest citizens established farms and ranches in the area, but the majority of the residents were bandits who attacked the increasing numbers of mule trains crossing between Mexican and American territory. Within five years the Neutral Ground would become a staging ground for a far more serious attack on Texas, but for the moment this arrangement was accepted by both governments as a semi-satisfactory solution to the boundary problem. The situation remained a thorn in everyone's side until the signing of the Adams-Onís Treaty in 1819. In Texas and on the Nueces, the threat of war was over, and the militia units were ordered to stand down and return to their homes. The accusations of the bishop were ignored, and both governors retained their posts. By 1809 Texas had gained a new governor in Manuel Salcedo, nephew of the commandant general in Chihuahua, who arrived in San Fernando de Béxar after a lengthy trip from Spain through the United States.[34]

Contraband had become a particularly tempting source of income for the ranchers in Texas. After 1803, having the horse-hungry Anglo Americans next door compounded the problem. Goods coming from Mexico City to La Bahía or San Fernando by way of the annual fair at Saltillo were both outrageously priced and heavily taxed. Goods in Louisiana, although illegal, were more accessible and far less expensive. Texas governors and presidial commanders at San Fernando, La Bahía, and Nacogdoches found it increasingly difficult to keep the local ranchers in and the American traders out. Most government officials finally reached the point that even if they did not actively participate, they often winked at the rapidly escalating contraband trade. Of the 1,187 horses and mules legally sent to Louisiana in 1802, as many as ten times that number may have been traded illegally. The increase in smuggling cases brought before the courts and in the ranch population on the Nueces and the San Antonio indicated that the ranchers were creating their own markets, with or without the permission of the government.[35]

The contraband cases involved prominent citizens as well as the lesser known. Presidial Captain Francisco Xavier de Uranga, who had been posted to La Bahía in 1799, was accused and convicted in 1803 of permitting horse trading with Louisiana. José Antonio de León of Camargo was caught and convicted of selling stolen horses in Louisiana. In 1809 José María Rioxas, a La Bahía resident, was convicted of stealing horses and mules to sell in Louisiana. In the following year, five more La Bahía residents were accused of taking horse herds to Louisiana. Whether Martín de León engaged in the contraband trade is unknown. If he did, he was never caught.[36]

Much of the reason for turning to contraband was the lack of profitable markets for goods produced on the frontier. Martín de León made part of his living from the hides and tallow of the feral cattle which roamed the plains. Horses, however, proved to be a more profitable commodity, especially with the growing demand from soldiers and settlers passing through the ranch. Each soldier needed more than a dozen horses in his *remuda*, or string of horses, in order to carry out military campaigns. Even the ranchers and settlers needed eight or ten horses each for cattle round-ups. Anything less and the horses became too worn out to carry a rider out of danger, which often meant the death of both horse and rider. The Mustang Fund report for 1807 at La Bahía showed that Martín de León paid 32 pesos (the 2 *real* head tax per horse) for 128 mustangs rounded up during that year. With this group of animals, de León had the beginnings of a horse herd from which he could produce a herd of marketable, tame *caballos de silla* or saddle horses. And if a few dozen wild horses joined the herd periodically, who was to know? With the good brood mares and the donkeys his wife had received as her dowry, combined with his experience as a muleteer, he could also breed mules for the many mule trains coming and going in Texas.[37]

Martín de León's horses, collected from the herds on the Llanos Mesteños, or Mustang Plains, were descendants of the first horses brought by the early Spanish settlers at the beginning of the eighteenth century. These wild mustangs showed their Arab and Barbary breeding. They were lighter, smaller, and swifter than northern European horses and had slender, arched necks, small delicate heads, large, wide-set eyes, and flaring nostrils. They stood about fourteen hands high and had developed great endurance on the scrub grass of South Texas. The herds of wild horses numbered well into the tens of thousands. The only way for Don Martín and his neighbors to capture the elusive mustangs was by driving a herd into traps with widespread fences that funneled the horses into large, round pens. Since many horses were trampled to death with this method, the ranchers used it only when their own herds had been depleted by Indian raids. The best of the wild herd were chosen from the pen and partially tamed by being tied beside mules or brood mares and herded back to the ranch.[38]

The horses that were to be used to herd cattle were called *caballos de campo*, and Don Martín allowed his ranch hands to choose these for their own *remudas* from the wild herd. The *vaqueros* tied the horses up, saddled them, and then rode them around the pen until they stopped bucking. The half-wild horses never completely lost their fear of the man-creature on their backs and frequently bucked when saddled. The *vaqueros* expected it. Part of the daily routine for the *vaqueros* was to stay on the bucking horses until they calmed down, a talent which translated into later competitive bucking horse events. Noah Smithwick, several years later, was among the first Anglo Americans to comment on the option of riding a mustang:

> Senor De León was the very essence of hospitality, as, indeed, I found the Mexicans everywhere to be. He had his *caballada* driven in for us to choose from. The *vaqueros* rode in among them, *carajoing* [cursing] and swinging their lariats, the horses reared and snorted, and we concluded walking would be a pleasant pastime compared to riding such steeds, so we continued our journey on foot.[39]

The best horses were reserved for Don Martín and his family and were called *caballos de camino*. These were saddle horses for travel or pleasure riding with a smooth gait, arched neck, high head, and good looks. The de León saddle horses were gentled as two- or three-year-old colts and fillies over a period of two years in order to preserve their spirit while developing full command over the animals. Don Martín might train his own stallion and expect his sons to train their own horses with the aid of the *caballerango*, or horse trainer. He often left it to his *mayordomo*, or ranch foreman, to train the rest of the horses, especially the riding horses for Doña Patricia and their daughters. Since the only other way for women to get around was by lurching coach or lumbering *carreta*, girls were taught to ride as early as their brothers. The girls, as they grew into capable, strong women, maintained their gentility and proper breeding by riding sidesaddle, spreading their wide, white, ruffled skirts so that only their boots showed in the stirrups. This style, called *escaramuza*, is still used by Mexican women in modern *charreadas*, or rodeos. The trusted and accomplished horse trainer would also be assigned to help the young sons, such as Silvestre, Félix, and Agápito, to train their own horses. A risk lay in losing the beautifully trained animals to Indian raiders, who appreciated the mannerly, obedient horses every bit as much as did the rancher and his family.[40]

For Martín de León and his Spanish rancher neighbors, the horse was an indication of gentlemanly status. The term *caballero* meant *horseman*, and in New Spain during the sixteenth and seventeenth centuries only Spaniards and *criollos* were permitted to ride horses. As the cattle industry developed in the north during the eighteenth century, however, few Spaniards stayed at the missions, other than the padres themselves, so Indians and mestizos were taught to ride and herd the thousands of cattle at the mission ranches along the San Antonio River and at La Bahía del Espíritu Santo. The result was the development of two different groups of riders. The first was the wealthy, elite Spanish or *criollo* ranch owner, a person of prestige, from whom the modern *charro* is descended. The second were his mestizo, or mixed-blood, ranch hands, the *vaqueros*. In the center of Mexico, "a great social and economic gulf" had already developed between the two groups of men,[41] who distanced themselves from each other by both the clothes they wore and the horses they rode. The Spanish gentleman was attired in

> linen shirts with short, usually brown, jackets of velvet or suede trimmed with embossed leather. Pants were split up the sides to reveal fine linen pantaloons and were held together with gold or silver buttons. An hacendado often wore a red silk or satin sash . . . His costume was completed by a *manga*, a mantle of rich cloth.[42]

For the northern ranchers such as Martín de León, the *manga* was frequently a beautifully woven *sarape* from Saltillo. The *vaqueros*, on the other hand, wore rough, homespun cloth shirts handmade by the women on the ranch. For protection, the working *vaqueros* wore leather jackets, and their legs were protected by leather leggings called *chaparreras*, which evolved into the modern chaps. The *vaquero's* only decor was hand-stamped leather designs which the *vaquero* himself might create. Their attire earned them the nickname *cuerudos* (from *cuero* for leather). On the northern frontier, where owners like Martín de León and his ranch hands lived and worked together, the differences between the ranch owner and the ranch hand were less pronounced.[43]

Although much of the profit came from horses and mules, Martín de León and his *vaqueros* still focused some of their interest on cattle that roamed the river valleys. The San Antonio River ranchers complained that few cattle were left after years of wanton and improvident slaughter. Thirty years earlier, in 1778, Commandant General Teodoro Croix had mandated that all unbranded cattle belonged to the king. His intent was to stop the cattle killing, to halt the quarreling over cattle ownership between mission fathers and San Antonio ranchers, and to bring in revenue for the crown. Anyone killing or capturing an unbranded cow had to pay a half-peso tax to the government. The constant Indian depredations were an obvious problem for the ranchers, especially those on the Nueces. How could it be fair to have to pay taxes again to replace cattle which the Indians had stolen? For Martín de León and his neighbors, the long arm of the law had a hard time reaching all the way to the Nueces River, and, although they did hold semiannual roundups, the men often felt little compunction about killing stray cattle in order to provide the day-to-day necessities for themselves and their ranch hands.[44]

By 1807 Martín de León and his neighbors were interested in the opportunity to expand their holdings. When Commandant General Salcedo ordered the removal of the Rosario Indians to Refugio and the closing of the mission, de León applied for a land grant between the Aransas and Chiltipín Creek for a second ranch. After several requests, he established a ranch on the Aransas River above present-day San Patricio. The ranch, known as El Alamo, was on the left bank of the Aransas River "where the river makes an elbow on the east side of the road now leading to the Mission of Refugio."[45] His new ranch was next to the four-*sitio* ranch belonging to the Aldrete family. Candelaria and her sisters enjoyed rides along the river with her brothers and the neighbors, including young José Miguel Aldrete.

The daily routine of the ranch centered around farming and ranching. Once the crops of corn, beans, squash, and chiles had been planted early in the year, in hopes that there would be sufficient rain to bring the crop in by fall, the remainder of the year was spent on the horses, mules, cattle, and sheep. During the mornings the *vaqueros* were assigned to the daily jobs around the ranch by the *mayordomo*. They might saddle up the horses to ride out and check the herds, bring in the *remuda*, train the new wild horses, or breed horses and donkeys to produce the sterile mules. They also periodically caught and slaughtered the feral cattle to produce such necessities as leather hides and beef jerky, or dried meat. The *vaqueros* tanned the cattle hides and softened them into leather, which was then used for everything from clothing, cots, and chair seats to mule packs, saddles, bridles, and harnesses. They also built fences for corrals with the limited lumber available and repaired or rebuilt the *jacales* and adobe buildings.[46]

Patricia supervised the women in preparing the meals and food for the house. The women ground the corn into a soft *masa*, or dough, on *metates*—flat, slightly concave stones—and then patted out the round tortillas for the lunch and evening meal. The women might make chocolate by grinding the expensive cocoa beans and stick cinnamon brought from San Fernando de Béxar and mixed with local pecans and cane sugar and dried into small square cakes. In the mornings, the chocolate was cooked in hot milk and beaten to a froth with wooden stirrers twirled between the hands. The family drank it with the *pan dulce* or sweet bread cooked in the adobe ovens. In the evenings they ate tortillas with meat from the cattle or goats, spiced with tomatoes and chiles and mixed with squash and beans. If the crops did not survive the heat of the summer, there were always stores of dried corn and beans which kept the families alive until food could be bought from San Antonio or La Bahía. The curds from the goat milk were formed into large blocks of cheese. The only sugar for the family came from sugarcane. The men fed the cane into giant rollers, crushed the juice out of the sugarcane, and boiled down the liquid until it crystallized into a granular molasses that was then pressed into conical holes carved into a log, forming *piloncillo*. The cheese and sweet sugar cones were used for family desserts.[47]

Patricia's daughters were taught to sew. They embroidered bedspreads, altar cloths, and upholstery, using the thread and dyes that they traded for in San Antonio, reds and blues from cochineal, indigo, and brazilwood. White, brown, and black wool from their own sheep was woven into blankets or rugs for the house or for saddle blankets, often with the family brand in the outside corners. The girls made sweet-smelling toilet soap from tallow, mixing it with melon seeds, rosemary, wild rose leaves, and bran starch, then patting it into round cakes and drying it in the sun. Patricia taught her daughters to make pomade to smooth their hair and make it shine by mixing strained beef marrow with rose leaves and rosemary, and she showed them how to hold their curls in place with lemon juice or sugar water.[48]

After lunch, during the heat of the day, everyone lay down for a two- or three-hour siesta. In the afternoon, they bathed in the river, enjoying the refreshing swim and washing off the sticky sweat of the day. Patricia and Martín also insisted that the children learn to read and write. During the day or in the evening, the children, boys and girls alike, sat down with the ranch teacher to learn their lessons. Martín and Patricia were adamant that all of their children should be educated. Patricia wanted them to be able to read their catechism so that they would be good Catholics, and Martín insisted that they be able to keep their own accounts, not having to depend on others.

Once a week the women washed the family clothes and the white skirts and petticoats, dousing the clothing in large copper pots full of boiling water and sudsing yucca root. They rubbed and pounded the wet clothes with flat paddles, rinsing them in the river and spreading them out to dry on the bushes. In the cool of the evening, the family gathered to sit in the main *sala* or outside on the adobe benches, the women with embroidery, the men talking, singing, playing cards, or gambling.[49]

Twice a year, the quiet routine of the ranch was broken for cattle round-ups. It would have been easier to just gather wild cattle as they needed them, but the king had decreed that they must brand their cattle, so round-ups were the only means of sorting out the various herds which had wandered and mixed along the river. The roundups in the spring and fall brought together ranchers and *vaqueros* and their families for miles around. Representatives from all of the ranches spent weeks riding into the thick brush and gullies along the river, flushing the cattle out, collecting the herds, and driving them to the nearest ranch headquarters. At the ranch, cattle were branded, castrated, and treated for illnesses. The cattle which were to go to market or be slaughtered for their hides and tallow were culled from the immense herds. In addition to sorting out the cattle belonging to the different ranchers, at least those which had not been taken by the Indians, and making sure the calves were branded with the cows' brand, the roundups provided all the local families a chance to socialize and share the traditional hospitality.[50]

At the conclusion of the roundup, the *hacendado* provided a feast for all the participants and their families. If the roundup was at the Santa Margarita, Don Martín had whole steers, goats, and pigs slaughtered and cooked overnight as *barbacoa* — a term later anglicized as "barbecue." The house servants placed the meat in rock-lined pits, each four or five feet deep, which had been heated for several days by fires in the bottom of the hole. Once the rocks inside the pits were hot, the ashes of the fire were removed and the meat placed in the pit, wrapped in banana leaves or burlap, covered with more heated stones, and sealed with dirt. After twelve to twenty-four hours, the pit was opened, and the tender, juicy meat was lifted out, the rich smells drifting across the ranch to tempt the hungry crowd. Doña Patricia, as the *patrona* of the ranch, with her daughters and servants had spent days preparing the tortillas, tamales, rice, beans, chiles, salsas, breads, cakes, and candies. The rich and plentiful foods were served outside on long boards supported on trestles. In the evening, for the dances, the ranch owners and their families had occasion to bring out their finery. The gathering gave the young people an opportunity to dance and flirt and laugh and find prospective marriage partners. The roundups also created the friendships among parents that would eventually result in the close-knit bonds of godparenthood connections.[51]

Part of the festivities always included good-natured competition among the ranches. Martín de León and his growing sons, especially Fernando and Silvestre, and their ranch hands competed for the pride of the Rancho de Santa Margarita. Match races were the most popular, in which two horses and riders from competing ranches were pitted against each other over a 200- to 400-meter straight track. The gambling and excitement were intense, and the victorious *vaquero* and his horse might be remembered in *corridos* or narrative ballads for generations afterward. The skills of the roundup were also displayed in competitions among the ranchers and their cowhands: roping, both on and off the horse, riding bucking horses or bulls, and *coleando*, or catching a bull or a steer by the tail and flipping him onto his back, a skill needed for branding. Although there were no prizes and no money involved, other than gambling among the men, for Martín de León and his family the pride of the ranch was paramount. Though barely more than toddlers, Félix and Agápito began learning the ranching trade and developing a pride in their roping and riding skills. Doña Patricia, meanwhile, made contacts among the ranch families.[52]

The annual visits to San Antonio, usually for the December festivities, after the fall harvest and cattle roundups and before the spring planting, were a place to find marriage partners for the children. It was also an opportunity to trade the ranch horses and mules for the luxuries offered in the mercantile stores. For several exciting days, the children and Patricia packed clothes into trunks, food into baskets, blankets and rugs into wicker hampers, and the soaps and candles which could be sold or traded for store goods. The trade goods, the tallow and hides, and the trunks and packages were packed onto mules. Several of the family retainers were sent on ahead to set up camp for the family. The *vaqueros* corralled the horse and mule herds for sale and saddled the family's *caballos de camino* with the best silver-covered saddles and bridles. Pride required that the family arrive in San Antonio on their finest horses.[53]

In December 1810, as the de León family rode into town, San Fernando de Béxar, now better known as San Antonio, was abuzz with news from the interior of Mexico. Not only was it Christmas, but word had come of a revolt in Guanajuato. Just four months earlier, in September, a parish priest named Father Miguel Hidalgo y Costilla from the small town of Dolores in Central Mexico had led a revolt of Indians and mestizos against the Spanish crown. Throughout the festivities, parties, and celebrations, everyone in town avidly, and at times angrily, discussed the varying views. While Doña Patricia, a dedicated and devout Catholic, attended mass in the beautiful stone San Fernando Cathedral, Don Martín discussed the news from the interior with his friends and fellow ranchers. The problems had begun two years earlier, in 1808, when Napoleon had forced the abdication of both the Spanish king and his son and placed his own brother, Joseph Bonaparte, on the Spanish throne. Confusion had ruled in Mexico City, as it did on the far northern frontier.[54]

While Martín de León built his ranch, opposition in Spain to Joseph Bonaparte had coalesced in the Central Junta of Seville. Throughout Latin America, the governments fell into disarray. Spanish-born *peninsulares* assumed responsibility for ruling the countries in the name of Ferdinand VII. The American-born *criollos*, on the other hand, maintained that they should rule the country through *juntas*, or elected councils, also in the name of Ferdinand VII. The conservative *peninsulares*, or pure-blood Spaniards, in Mexico City had chosen as viceroy the eighty-year-old Pedro Garibay, who ruled ineffectually for two years. During that time, in San Antonio, the commandants and governors had held two councils, begging for more troops, for more immigrants to be settled in the areas between San Antonio and the Sabine, and for the opening of La Bahía as a port. All of their requests were turned down, and Texas was left exposed to the incursions of infiltrators, spies, and propagandists, both French and Anglo American. In Spain, meanwhile, the Spanish Regency, ruling in the name of Ferdinand VII, had provided a new viceroy for Mexico. Lieutenant General Francisco Javier Venegas arrived in August 1810. Within a month of his arrival, Viceroy Venegas faced the Hidalgo uprising, the first of a series of crises.[55]

The gossip in San Antonio in December 1810 focused on revolution. The country was dividing between the loyalists who supported the viceroy, ruling in the name of the imprisoned Ferdinand VII, and Hidalgo's republican revolutionaries, who pushed for total separation from Spain. De León learned that Hidalgo's army, after destroying Guanajuato and killing hundreds of *criollos* and *peninsulares,* had moved toward Mexico City. There, on the outskirts of the city at the Battle of Las Cruces, Hidalgo's forces had been halted. Instead of taking Mexico City, his army had turned northward. Supporters of Hidalgo's cause were hoping for help from the United States. For the Spanish forces, Texas had become the last barrier to keep Hidalgo and his rebels from getting outside support.[56]

All of the political problems would have to wait, decreed Doña Patricia. The de León family joined the citizens of San Antonio to celebrate the feast of the Immaculate Conception and the day of Our Lady of Guadalupe on December 12. Patricia was busy with family decisions. It was time to choose godparents for the latest child—in 1810 it was María de Jesús, Chucha, who would be baptized in San Antonio. The older ones were also preparing to be confirmed in the church, and Patricia reviewed the catechism that they had learned from the tutor on the ranch.

While Martín debated the political dilemmas, the children thrilled at the fairyland of excitement at San Antonio. In spite of the fear of revolution from the interior, Governor Manuel Salcedo insisted that the festivities continue, although he did curtail nighttime activities. Zebulon Pike, the American who passed through San Antonio the year before, was not impressed with the mud-covered *jacales* of La Villita, the poorer side of town, but the children found them comfortably familiar. And the number of dwellings was, to their eyes, amazing. The children were impressed, as Pike had been, with the Casas Reales, the long, low, stone buildings which housed the governor's offices, and with the homes of the wealthy and the magnificence of the cathedral.

During the monthlong festivities of December 1810 the children wandered through the streets, around the military and market plazas, watching the religious processions, awed by the brightly lit booths offering entertainment, food, and games. The smells surrounded them. Roasted corn in the husk was peeled open and sprinkled with chile pepper. Rich meats, dripping with juices, were piled high on tortillas. Candied figs and orange peels, crunchy with sugar, were displayed in teetering pyramids. The dances and bullfights for the grownups were paid for by the wealthy of the town and brought together friends and family who might not have seen each other since the previous year, or new friends whom Martín and Patricia visited. Among them were the revolutionary Leal family, who would one day become in-laws, and the Pérez family, relatives of Patricia's godfather, Don Angel Pérez in Soto la Marina. Through it all, the debates continued to rage over the revolutionary ideas.[57]

Choosing sides in what was to become a civil war was difficult for many of the citizens of Mexico, especially self-made men such as Martín de León on the northern frontier. Governor Salcedo had appealed to their loyalty, enumerating the many benefits of Spanish rule. But the leaflets arriving from Louisiana and from the rebels in northern Mexico proposed new ideas of liberty, equality, and freedom.

Martín had been brought up in a tradition which respected authority. He had served as a military officer for ten years, and the concept of obedience was ingrained. He supported the Spanish ideals of monarch, religion, and order. The crown and its government could be arbitrary at times, but just as the king obeyed God the Father and the viceroy obeyed the king, so his subjects were expected to obey their governmental officials. If there were no obedience, how could Martín de León, as the *patrón*, demand obedience, respect, and reverence from his own family and his employees? Without obedience and authority, how could society exist? In exchange for obedience, Martín felt he took care of his people, just as the king protected his citizens.

If what the governor said was true, the revolutionaries under Hidalgo had caused terrible destruction and mass killings in Guanajuato. The revolution in France twenty years earlier, with the massacre of thousands at the guillotine, was an even worse vision of what revolutions might cause. These revolutionary ideas of individual freedom could not be right. In addition to causing death and destruction, this individualism had made the Anglos selfish and greedy for the lands of New Spain. The *egalité*, the equality which the French claimed, was ridiculous. For Martín it was ludicrous to think that a wild Apache Indian could be the same as a Spaniard, a soldier the equal of a captain, a *peon* on the same level as an *hacendado*, or his *vaqueros* equal to himself.[58]

And yet, Martín questioned the ideas of arbitrary rule. As a self-made man, did he not have the right, on his own merits, to be a lieutenant colonel or a colonel? By what right did the *peninsulares*, just because they were born in Spain, claim the highest positions? And why should a ruler, half a world away, and one who was not even of their own people, demand that those in the New World pay for his wars? By what right had the greedy *gachupín* merchants of Mexico City controlled and taxed and overpriced the trade which he had carried as a muleteer? And why should the wealthy receive forty *sitios* of land when he could only get two?

Their San Antonio friends, the Leal family, pushed him toward republicanism and revolution. They supported the new French and Anglo-American ideas. Patricia was already considering their daughter, Salomé, as a potential bride for young Félix. Should de León, horrified by the bloody excesses of the mestizo and Indian revolution, remain true to the royalists and the status quo? Or would he support the radical new republicans? It was a dilemma, and a dangerous one, if the death of the *criollos* and *peninsulares* in Guanajuato was any indication.[59]

Martín de León's answer to the dilemma was to return as usual to the ranch at the Santa Margarita at the close of the Christmas celebrations. The safety and security of his family outweighed all political considerations. Once again war was in the air, and while the number of soldiers increased, the civilians coming and going at the Santa Margarita crossing had dwindled to a trickle as Governor Salcedo ordered a halt to all unnecessary traffic in the province. Back at the ranch by the end of January, the de León family heard that the governor had ordered the soldiers of the Béxar garrison to prepare to march to the Río Bravo to repel the forces of Father Hidalgo.

Like de León, the main interest of the soldiers was the safety and security of their families, and they objected, especially when it was rumored that Governor Salcedo had sent his family to safety in East Texas. The news from family and friends in Nuevo Santander was equally upsetting. Many of Escandón's towns, settled by self-made men of the bourgeoisie with the vision of bettering themselves, had chosen to side with Hidalgo and the republican revolutionaries.[60]

By the end of January 1811, Martín and Patricia, safe at the Santa Margarita ranch, learned shocking news. Juan Bautista de las Casas, a retired militia captain from Nuevo Santander, had moved into San Antonio and overthrown Texas Governor Manuel Salcedo and was jailing all Spanish royal sympathizers and confiscating their goods. Within days, agents had come through the Santa Margarita ranch on their way to revolutionize La Bahía, Nacogdoches, and the settlements in between. Resistance was futile. Whether Martín de León agreed with the revolutionaries or not, in the interest of the safety of his family, it was best that he quietly accept whoever was in control.

By late February 1811, de las Casas and his cohorts controlled Texas. In order to protect his republican rule, de las Casas sent the royalist leaders, including ex-governor Manuel Salcedo and Nuevo León Governor Simón de Herrera, to Coahuila in chains. Removing the conservative pro-royalist leaders, however, saved neither de las Casas nor his revolution. Within six weeks, Martín heard that de las Casas had been overthrown by the royalists, who were back in power. As the loyal supporters of Spain regained control, they, in their turn, began to confiscate the possessions of the San Antonio revolutionaries. De León stayed out of the way on the Santa Margarita, more worried about the immediate concerns of fighting off the Indians. The many different tribes, encouraged by the internal battles among the Spanish, had increased their raids on the outlying ranches and settlements, stealing horses, cattle, and mules and capturing prisoners at will.[61]

March 1811 was a bad time for the revolutionaries. The short-lived de las Casas revolution was over, but the repercussions were not. With the defeat of de las Casas at San Antonio, the royalists in Texas had once again closed off supplies for the revolutionaries from the United States. That same month, Father Miguel Hidalgo, his leaders, and eight hundred of his troops, on their way to Texas, had been ambushed and captured at the Wells of Baján in northern Coahuila. Hidalgo was returned for trial and, after being defrocked, was convicted and executed. His head was placed on a pike outside the government offices at the scene of his revolt and left to rot. Governor Salcedo was on his way back to Texas, and in Nuevo Santander, General José Joaquín Arredondo had arrived to round up the remnants of the revolutionaries.

Although the northern provinces had fallen to the royal troops, José María Morelos continued the revolution in the center of Mexico. A revolutionary from Revilla in Nuevo Santander, José Bernardo Gutiérrez de Lara, with a dozen men, money, and supplies, had crossed the Nueces at the Santa Margarita ranch and headed for the United States. Gutiérrez de Lara carried a commission from the revolutionaries and a determination to gain the support of the United States for those in Mexico who still struggled for freedom from Spain.[62]

It took Gutiérrez de Lara almost a year and a half to return from the United States. When he came, he carried nothing but vague promises from the United States government. Those promises, however, and his

stories of meetings with government officials could be interpreted to sig-
nify deep American interest at the highest levels. In the meantime, from
the revolutionary hotbed of New Orleans, both Anglo-American and
French supporters continued to send leaflets and propaganda to the settlements throughout Texas and especially into Nuevo Santander. Martín de
León, at the crossing on the Nueces River, was the recipient of much of
the literature. To avoid any accusations of partisanship, he either burned
the material or turned the damaging tracts over to the government in
San Antonio. At the capital, one revolutionary emissary caught carrying
revolutionary propaganda, José Francisco Venegas, had been hanged for
sedition. It seemed best to keep one's opinions to oneself.[63]

Martín de León also learned of the return of Gutiérrez de Lara to New
Orleans. There, with the tacit support of the United States, Gutiérrez de
Lara had begun to form the nucleus of an army to invade Texas. Lieutenant Augustus W. Magee, having resigned from the United States Army,
joined Gutiérrez de Lara and was promoted to colonel and named military commander of the expedition. By promising each volunteer $40 a
month and a league of land in Texas, Gutiérrez de Lara and Magee had no
difficulty recruiting adventurers. The army gathered in the uncontrolled
Neutral Ground. Samuel Davenport, the one-time ally and friend to the
Spanish, outfitted the army with guns, ammunition, and supplies. In August 1812 Gutiérrez de Lara and Magee rode into Texas at the head of
the self-styled Republican Army of the North, a rabble of six hundred
to seven hundred Anglo-American freebooters, Mexican revolutionaries,
and renegade Indians.[64]

By mid-September 1812, for Martín de León on the Nueces River, war
was no longer imminent. It was on his doorstep. Gutiérrez de Lara and
Magee had taken Nacogdoches with ease when the soldiers refused to
fight and "remained to seek the safety of themselves and their families."[65] It
was not Gutiérrez de Lara's message of independence and freedom which
had won. It was self-preservation. The United States government, perhaps concerned over an escalating war with Great Britain in 1812 and
wanting to prevent Mexico from joining the British, decided it would be
best to deny any connection with or culpability for Gutiérrez de Lara's
army. As Magee's invading forces reached Trinidad de Salcedo in October, an American emissary, Dr. John Hamilton Robinson, arrived from
the United States on his way to see the commandant general in Chihuahua. He had been sent to express the American president's "regret and
anxiety" over the invasion and to assure Mexico of the "good faith" of the

United States. Magee and Gutiérrez de Lara, concerned and confused that the United States should deny its support, grudgingly let Robinson pass. Governor Salcedo, who met with Robinson in San Antonio and had him escorted to Chihuahua, gladly used Robinson's claims to prove that the United States was not in favor of New Spain's independence. He whipped up the resistance of the citizens of Texas against the illegal invading army of outlaws.[66]

Instead of moving toward San Antonio, where Texas Governor Salcedo and Nuevo León Governor Herrera defended the roads, the ragtag army turned toward La Bahía. Much to the consternation of Magee and Gutiérrez de Lara, the soldiers at La Bahía, like those at Nacogdoches, refused to join the Republican Army and simply abandoned the presidio to protect their families. On the Nueces, Martín and Patricia worried about their own family and waited anxiously to see which way the rebel forces would turn. Travel was not an option. Patricia had just given birth to Refugia, their eighth child.[67]

In 1812 Magee and Gutiérrez de Lara set up their defenses inside the strong stone walls of the presidio at La Bahía. Within six days of the rebels' arrival, Governor Salcedo and Colonel Herrera passed through the de León ranch and reached La Bahía, where they laid siege to the fort. In late 1812 the war was moving closer to the ranch. As November dragged on into December and January, neither side could gain an advantage. The invaders had begun to slip out of the fort and were raiding the cattle and harassing Martín and Patricia and their neighbors on the Nueces. It was time for the de León family to move to safety. Martín might have been willing to fight the Indians, but with eight children to protect, ranging from fourteen-year-old Fernando down to newborn Refugia, Martín and Patricia were unwilling to have the family endangered any longer.[68]

Soto la Marina, Doña Patricia's home, offered the best safe haven despite the rumors of revolutionary ideas bubbling up there as well. Doña Patricia hurriedly supervised the packing of the clothing, the kitchenware, the religious statues, the heirlooms, and the family silver, while Don Martín organized the loading of the mules and horses. They took everything they could, knowing full well that the ranch would be raided by both Indians and revolutionary forces. But there was much they could not take. Don Martín placed the herds of horses and cattle in the care of his *mayordomo* and a handful of faithful *vaqueros* who would supervise the spring planting and protect what they could of the ranch equipment and buildings. Doña Patricia's *casa grande*, which had grown large and comfortable over ten years as rooms were added to accommodate the new children, would have to be abandoned. For the children, their neighboring friends, favorite animals, and well-known haunts would be left behind. The family waved their goodbyes to those who remained and mounted their horses for the ride south. The *vaqueros* were sent on with tents and food to set up the rest camps along the road. Unlike the happy visits to San Antonio, this trip was carried out in haste, and the children could feel the fear. With the exuberance of youth, however, the de León children were soon enjoying the excitement of the trip and looking forward to meeting the many family members in Burgos and Soto la Marina.

CHAPTER 3

NUESTRA SEÑORA DE GUADALUPE VICTORIA, 1813–1828

Genealogical Chart

M ARTÍN DE LEÓN (M. 1795) + PATRICIA DE LA GARZA

  1. Fernando (m. 1823) + María Antonia Galván (d. 1825)

  2. María Candelaria (m. 1818) + José Miguel Aldrete
     2-1. José María (b. 1820)
     2-2. José de Jesús María (b. 1822)
     2-3. Trinidad (b. 1824)
     2-4. Rafael (b. 1826)

  3. Silvestre (m. 1828) + Rosalía de la Garza
     3-1. Francisco Grande (b. 1825)

  4. "Lupita" (m. 1824) + Desiderio García

  5. Félix (m. 1828) + Salomé Leal

  6. Agápito (m. 1824) + María Antonia C. de la Garza
     6-1. León de León (b. 1824)

  7. "Chucha" (m. 1824) + Rafael Manchola
     7-1. Francisca "Panchita" (b. 1826)

  8. Refugia (b. 1812)

  9. Agustina (b. 1814)

  10. Francisca (b. 1818)

In the spring of 1813 Martín de León led his weary family and their *vaqueros* and servants, and the long line of dusty pack mules into the small village of Soto la Marina. Riding with him were his four sons, Fernando (just turned fifteen), José Silvestre (eleven), José Félix (seven), and Agápito (five). Behind them rode the rest of the family. Patricia de la Garza, nearing forty, led her daughters, thirteen-year-old Candelaria and nine-year-old Lupita. Behind them, the servants carried three-year-old Chucha, restless and irritable at being confined for long hours on the horse, and the infant Refugia, snoozing in her basket. Because of the children, they had hurried to leave before the terrible heat of the summer. They made the long trip from the Nueces in easy stages, stopping to rest often. They had crossed at Laredo, sending the *vaqueros* on ahead each day to set up the next day's camp, then followed the river southeast through Revilla, Mier, Camargo, and Reynosa. Leaving the river, they dropped south and skirted the foothills of the Sierra Madre to Burgos and Cruillas, where they stopped to see the de León family. From there they rode down to Soto la Marina, still some thirty miles from the coast, but a port city nevertheless.

Soto la Marina was no longer the active place it had been in its heyday under Escandón, but it was home. Patricia de la Garza settled in among friends and family, while Martín discussed the scandalous affairs in Texas with his in-laws. He soon found that it was dangerous to discuss politics openly. Ever since Father Hidalgo was beheaded in 1811, Hidalgo's supporters under José María Morelos y Pavón had struggled to continue the rebellion. Nuevo Santander had long been a source of incipient rebels. The government had assigned General Joaquín Arredondo to seek out and exterminate revolutionaries throughout San Luís Potosí and Nuevo Santander. Because of the general's success, by the time Martín and Patricia arrived in Soto la Marina in 1813 Arredondo had been given control over all of the Eastern Interior Provinces, which included Nuevo Santander, Nuevo León, Coahuila, and Texas. After clearing Nuevo Santander of revolutionaries, his assignment was to stop Gutiérrez de Lara and the rebels in San Antonio.[1]

Just as Martín and Patricia arrived in Soto la Marina, General Arredondo gathered an army from settlements along the Río Bravo (later called the Rio Grande) and marched northward to put down the invasion. Martín avoided the call to arms by Arredondo. The government couriers and the ever-present muleteer network reported rumors coming from Béxar of victories for the forces under Gutiérrez de Lara. His invasionary army had defeated the royalist forces under Governor Salcedo at Salado

Creek and had marched triumphantly into San Fernando de Béxar on April 1, 1813. With disgust, the muleteers reported that on the night of April 3 Antonio Delgado, one of the rebel captains, took Governor Salcedo, Colonel Herrera, and their aides out of town and, after tormenting them, slit their throats and left the bodies in the field. The *bexareños*, although some may have agreed with the revolutionary ideals in principle, were appalled at the carnage. They feared throwing their support to Gutiérrez de Lara, an outsider who might or might not succeed. Like the soldiers at Nacogdoches and La Bahía, the residents of Béxar were more interested in protecting their families than joining a revolt. Worse yet, Colonel Magee had died, and it appeared that Gutiérrez de Lara was losing support from his Anglo-American backers.[2]

Gutiérrez de Lara was not the puppet the United States had hoped for. He had refused to separate Texas from Mexico, and his constitution, the first for Texas, followed the Spanish customs and traditions, including protection of the Roman Catholic Church, an idea that further alienated the United States government. Hearing of the independent actions of Gutiérrez de Lara, the U.S. government representatives in New Orleans hastily recruited José Alvarez de Toledo, a more amenable Cuban revolutionary. He was given more American volunteer troops and sent to Béxar. Gutiérrez de Lara was still winning battles, but it did him little good without the support of the United States. In June he won a victory against General Arredondo's subordinate at Alazán Creek, but the following month Toledo arrived in San Antonio. Toledo, with the new contingent of Anglo-American troops, forced Gutiérrez de Lara from power and assumed command. The United States government, however, had bet on the wrong man. On August 18, 1814, Arredondo met Toledo's troops at the Medina River and decisively defeated the rebels.[3]

Martín and Patricia feared for their friends in San Fernando de Béxar. Reports arrived in Soto la Marina that any who had supported the revolutionaries were in deadly peril. Rumor was soon replaced by fact. By September, Arredondo had executed 327 insurgents in Béxar and imprisoned their wives and daughters for fifty-four days, forcing them to cook and feed his army of several thousand men. Arredondo sent his subordinates on to the settlements on the Trinity and Brazos, where they captured and executed an additional one hundred rebels. Only later did Martín and Patricia learn that the Leal family had escaped the slaughter. With a handful of others, the Leal family had returned to Béxar and begged for pardons from Arredondo.[4]

With royalist control reestablished throughout the Eastern Interior Provinces and peace at hand, Martín and Patricia decided to move back to Texas. Patricia was pregnant once again, but there were other motives for returning. Candelaria was fourteen, and it was time to begin making serious wedding plans. Those plans had to be made in Texas, where José Miguel Aldrete had grown into a very acceptable suitor. The family packed up their possessions, regretfully said goodbye to Patricia's family, and started northward once again.

International affairs had little effect on their movements. Word had spread that the British had defeated the mighty Napoleon and were settling their war with a new and still weak United States. In Spain, with Napoleon out of the way, Ferdinand VII was restored to the Spanish throne. Glad to regain his throne, the monarch accepted the new constitutional monarchy and the representatives from throughout the empire, whose obeisance he fully expected. When they did not oblige, the honeymoon period following his return did not last. The autocratic monarch soon nullified the representative Spanish Cortes and sent home the elected delegates from New Spain. Debates once again raged over the right of the king to deny his people representation.[5]

On the Nueces River, Martín and Patricia de León found that their Santa Margarita ranch had been badly damaged in their absence. Rather than rebuild so far from La Bahía, the family gave up their claim to the land and settled at the Aransas River ranch on Chiltipín Creek, halfway between the Nueces River and the presidio at La Bahía del Espíritu Santo. Part of the reason for choosing the site may have been the suggestion of the Aldrete family, who had also moved to the Aransas River. This time Martín had the help of his sons in building the small *jacales* for the ranch hands and the new *casa grande* for the family. By the time Patricia gave birth to Agustina in late 1814, the family was settled on the Aransas River ranch. Of major importance for Doña Patricia was the romance which was blossoming between seventeen-year-old José Miguel Aldrete and fourteen-year-old Candelaria. The following year, Candelaria would turn fifteen, and it was time to begin planning her *quinceañera* or "coming out." If they announced the engagement at the end of the year, there would be time to begin gathering the dowry and planning the wedding for the following summer.[6]

Don Martín, meanwhile, continued to profit from the sale of horses and mules both in Saltillo and, perhaps, in the burgeoning town of New Orleans. Contraband and smuggling had always been part of life in Spanish Texas, and New Orleans had provided a ready market and source for illegal goods. When the United States acquired the Louisiana Territory from the French in 1803, a small settlement of independent pirates, free-booters, and smugglers was firmly established on Grande Terre Island. The pirates squatted in a town of shanties, huts, and warehouses on a sandy, pine-covered island six miles long by three miles wide facing the Gulf of Mexico at the mouth of Barataria Bay. The island, south and east of the town of New Orleans, was ideally located to control traffic in and out of the mouth of the Mississippi River.

The freebooters on the island had little organization or strength until the arrival in 1804 of the French Lafitte brothers, Pierre and Jean, from Española. Within two years, Jean Lafitte and his elder brother, although blacksmiths by trade, had taken over the operation on Grande Terre. Jean Lafitte organized the freebooters, held shares in many privateers, created an efficient method of capturing shipping coming into New Orleans, set up a capable, businesslike sales force to carry the stolen goods into New Orleans for sale, and acted as a banker and commercial agent. With a ready market developing in Texas and Nuevo Santander, Lafitte and his freebooters were quick to profit from selling contraband at Soto la Marina and in the protected bays and inlets along the coast of Texas. The presidial companies at La Bahía and Nacogdoches had no access to boats and could do little to stop the ships entering and leaving the hidden harbors.[7]

Martín de León may have met the Lafitte brothers in New Orleans sometime during 1813 or 1814. By making arrangements to trade with Lafitte at the coast, de León could ship goods with little danger and could trade for any of the luxury items his daughter might require for her dowry and trousseau. Louisiana Governor William C. C. Claiborne had tried unsuccessfully to stop the Lafitte trade. When he arrested the pair, Jean Lafitte had hired the best lawyers in the territory, Edward Livingston and John R. Grymes, for $20,000 each. Grymes had resigned as district attorney to defend Lafitte, and when the new prosecuting attorney accused Grymes of having been "bribed from the path of honor,"[8] Grymes challenged the attorney to a duel and shot him through the hip, crippling him for life. The Lafitte brothers were acquitted and continued their trade with Martín de León and the rest of their loyal clientele.[9]

In January 1815, Lafitte and his Baratarian pirates proved their bravery at the Battle of New Orleans and helped the new United States Army under General Andrew Jackson win a decisive victory over the British. Their reward was a pardon from the United States government, but the brothers realized that the opportunities for illegal commerce at Grande Terre Island had come to an end. Undaunted, they moved to Spanish Texas and opened new headquarters on Galveston Island in Louis Michel Aury's Green Flag Republic. From there they could still trade in Spanish Texas and Nuevo Santander and continue their profitable contacts.

According to Martín de León's biographers, a pirate named Ramon Le Fou had offered to ship de León's goods in exchange for a pardon from the Spanish officials. De León agreed to contact the government officials in Nuevo Santander, among them relatives of Doña Patricia. Le Fou and his men had offered transportation, and when de León came aboard with his son, Félix, they had ensured de León's success by holding Félix as insurance. De León acquired the trading papers for the buccaneers, and Félix was released. The pirates continued to play a part in the contraband and smuggling for de León and in the periodic invasions of Texas during the next eight lucrative years.[10]

At the de León ranch on the Aransas throughout 1815, Candelaria, as a grown lady of fifteen, was allowed for the first time to be courted by the young men from La Bahía and San Fernando de Béxar. Any excuse was a reason for a party. Saints' days and religious holidays throughout the year brought families together either at the de León ranch or at neighboring ranches. The Christmas season at Béxar took on special meaning for Candelaria. Her sisters watched in envy and excitement as Candelaria was introduced by her proud parents to Béxar society. By the following year, Candelaria would be expected to choose a husband and begin plans for a wedding. The choice of bridegroom was no surprise. Seventeen-year-old José Miguel Aldrete had grown up with Candelaria, and the two had known each other for most of their lives. By marrying, the young couple would join two of the major ranches of the La Bahía area, something which would benefit both families.[11]

The marriage of María Candelaria and José Miguel Aldrete, the first for a daughter of the de León family, had to be a lavish affair. The latest fashions could be acquired from New Orleans, with the help of the buccaneer traders, along with laces, fans, gloves, and the most beautiful jewels. Many of the clothes, in particular the delicate undergarments, had to be hand-sewn by Doña Patricia and her daughters from the silks and satins and laces purchased by Don Martín. It would take more than a year to make all the preparations and plan the wedding. The ceremony was set for the spring of 1817, but affairs far from La Bahía once again interfered.

Nuevo Santander, despite the best efforts of General Arredondo, had continued to be a source of revolutionary republicans. With New Orleans as a haven for the plotters, Galveston Island as a base of operations, and the Neutral Ground as a source of mercenaries, new rebellions were inevitable. Early in 1817 Francisco Xavier Mina, a would-be liberator of New Spain, assembled a force of Spanish, Anglo-American, and French buccaneers at Galveston Island in the pirate Green Flag Republic. Mina's army sailed down the coast of Nuevo Santander and, hoping for support from local rebels, took Soto la Marina on April 18, 1817. Henry Perry, a member of Mina's expedition, left Soto la Marina and marched north to capture La Bahía.[12]

With Mina's revolutionaries in Soto la Marina, Don Martín could not safely take the family back to Doña Patricia's hometown. There was little choice but to remain on the ranches. With the invading army on the way, the de León family, along with many of the other ranch families, barricaded themselves and prepared to fight the latest invaders. Henry Perry, however, bypassed the ranches and attacked the stone presidio. Without major artillery, he failed to take the presidio or defeat the royalist forces at La Bahía. Within two months, Spanish government troops destroyed his command, and Perry was executed. Meanwhile, Mina and his liberal troops at Soto la Marina were defeated by the harried Commandant General Arredondo. Mina fled south to join other rebels but was captured and executed on October 27, 1817. The ranch families around La Bahía were once again at peace, and plans for the wedding could proceed.[13]

A wedding was no simple matter, even on the frontier. During the spring of 1818, Candelaria and José Miguel were each expected to provide between two and five character witnesses who could attest that they were free to marry each other. The parish priest from San Antonio interviewed the couple and their witnesses to determine that the couple was not related by consanguinity and that neither of them was engaged or married to someone else. Once the depositions were taken, the priest required a three-week period during which the marriage banns were announced in the church during each of the Sunday masses. Anyone who knew of any reason the couple should not marry was required to speak up. When there were no objections, Candelaria and José Miguel were free to marry.[14]

Although there is no record of the ceremony in 1818, other descriptions of weddings from the same period indicate that the wedding was an occasion of festivity for the entire town. The chapel at the presidio of La Bahía was gaily decorated and ranch families from far and wide rode in for the

El convite para el baile (Invitation to the dance) by Theodore Gentilz depicts young men arriving to invite a young lady to a dance, often a prelude to later marriage. Courtesy of Daughters of the Republic of Texas, San Antonio.

ceremony. All were dressed in their most elegant attire, jewels, silks, and satins from as far away as Mexico City, New Orleans, or even Europe. The wedding mass for Candelaria and José Miguel was celebrated in the candlelit chapel with family and friends in attendance. Afterward, the entire town was treated to a feast which Doña Patricia and her family had worked for months to arrange, followed by festivities, music, and dancing that lasted for three days. It was a wedding which people spoke of for years afterward.[15]

After the celebration, the young couple settled down on the Aldrete ranch and began to build their own home and family. Both fathers supplied *vaqueros* and servants to help with the construction of the small *jacales* and the beginnings of the large ranch house, which would fill with children. Patricia, sometime during the same year, had given birth to their last daughter, Francisca, destined from birth to remain single and care for her parents in their old age. For Martín de León, the nagging problem of providing land and ranches for all of his children had become a growing concern.[16]

The settlement in 1819 of the boundary question between the United States and Spain should have brought peace and security for the de León family in Texas, but it did not. The Adams-Onís Treaty formalized the boundaries between the United States and New Spain at the Sabine River, leaving Texas on the Spanish side; but it would be two more years before the United States ratified the treaty. Spain still attempted fruitlessly to stop the illegal trade between Texas and the United States, but at least the Neutral Ground with its bandits and marauders was no longer a threat. Many among the Anglo-American community in New Orleans and Louisiana felt that the Neutral Ground as well as Texas had been part of the original Louisiana Purchase. The Adams-Onís Treaty, in their view, had illegally given up land which should have belonged to the United States. A group of citizens in Natchez, led by Dr. James Long, a New Orleans doctor, angry over what they perceived to be flagrant land theft, determined to take Texas for the United States. In March 1820, after a brief sojourn on Galveston Island, where Dr. Long and his wife, Jane, dined with Jean Lafitte, the couple settled on Bolivar Peninsula just across the pass from Galveston Island to make preparations for the invasion of Texas.[17]

National affairs in the center of Mexico had once again occasioned great debate in Texas. At La Bahía as well as on the Aransas River ranch, Martín de León and his neighbors discussed the incredible changes taking place in Mexico City. Spanish control in the New World was rapidly waning. In 1820 Spanish rebels in Madrid had forced Ferdinand VII to accept a liberal constitution. In an attempt to keep the American colonies part of a new Spanish commonwealth, the Spanish government ordered that representatives should once again be elected and sent to Spain to sit in the Spanish *cortes*.

On the local level, provincial deputations were reestablished throughout the Spanish world. The debates raged on the ranches, at La Bahía, and at Béxar about whether representatives should be sent. In Texas, Commandant General Arredondo, who had spent the previous ten years fighting against all revolutionary ideas, refused to call for elections or to reinstitute the Spanish constitutional government. Finally, by November 1820, seven months after the rest of the country had adopted the Spanish constitution, Arredondo allowed elections in Texas.[18]

The delegates sent to Madrid from the Spanish colonies in the New

World were vitally interested in the question of colonization. During the first few months of 1821, the liberal Spanish Congress in Madrid, in particular the Mexican deputy from Saltillo, José Miguel Ramos Arizpe, a cousin of Patricia de León, revived the concept of civilian settlers. In March 1821 the Spanish minister for overseas affairs in Madrid reported to the Spanish Congress that the "distribution of land in [Spanish] America was of the greatest importance . . . and that the King expected the most marvelous results in both aspects."[19] He did, however, warn of the dangers and suggested that it "required the most urgent circumspection as well as the greatest prudence in the matter of . . . that immense territory."[20] By June 1821 the Committee on Overseas Affairs, meeting in Madrid and chaired by Ramos Arizpe, proposed an extensive Project for the Colonization of the Americas. Included in the thirty-one proposals were suggestions to use European settlers and grant them land but to protect the lands of those already living or owning land in the area, such as Martín de León, the Aldretes, and the many settlers around La Bahía.[21]

Moses Austin, a one-time resident of Spanish Louisiana in the Kaskasia area of Illinois, was one of those who requested a right to colonize in the last year of Spanish Texas. Like the Louisiana settlers who had come to Trinidad de Salcedo in 1803, Austin had the right to apply for settlement as a citizen of Spain's Louisiana colony. In 1821 Governor Antonio Martínez turned down Austin's request. By chance, Austin had become acquainted in New Orleans with the baron de Bastrop, one of the original settlers of Trinidad de Salcedo. The baron had since moved to San Antonio, where he found Moses Austin, dejected over the governor's refusal to grant him a colony. The baron, ever interested in colonization, spoke to the governor on Austin's behalf. The governor agreed to send the paperwork for the colonization contract on to the higher authorities. The contract was approved by a reluctant Commandant General Arredondo. Before Austin could put the project into action, however, Spanish control of Mexico ended.[22]

The king's citizens in his Spanish colonies, including Mexico, had splintered into two groups—conservatives who favored centralized autocratic monarchical rule with protection of the privileged elite against liberals who believed in republican, popular elections with local power. Neither group was happy with the Spanish government. During 1821 the conservatives united under Colonel Agustín Iturbide to declare independence from Spain in the Plan de Iguala. The liberals, who also demanded independence, agreed to support Iturbide as long as there was a constitution, which they presumed would be republican and liberal. In August 1821 an elderly but respected liberal, Viceroy Juan O'Donojú, arrived from Spain to try to maintain Spanish control and keep Mexico part of the Spanish empire. With little support from either the liberals or the conservatives, O'Donojú had no recourse but to sign the Treaty of Córdoba on August 24, 1821, granting Mexico its independence from Spain.[23]

For Martín de León and the other ranchers in Texas, the independence of Mexico from Spain had less impact than a far more present danger. Dr. James Long, still angered over the American loss of Texas, determined to take advantage of the recent upheaval in the center of the country. Leaving his wife at Bolivar in September 1821, Long gathered troops from the Neutral Ground, marched on La Bahía, captured the garrison, and seized the town. This time, Martín and Patricia worried not only about their own ranch but about the Aldrete ranch, where their new grandson, José María, had been born to Candelaria and José Miguel Aldrete. Long did not have the manpower to threaten the ranches, and within weeks the invader was quickly defeated and captured. As an illegal alien, Long was sent to Mexico City to await trial. There, perhaps accidentally, Long was shot and killed. His wife remained, alone and uninformed of her husband's fate, on the peninsula at Bolivar.[24]

James Long was not the only threat. The Anglo Americans were coming, no longer in military assaults, but they were arriving, nevertheless, some legally and some illegally. Moses Austin had died during his return to the United States, and his son, Stephen F. Austin, had taken up his father's idea of colonization and was on his way to Texas. Others were slipping across the Sabine, settling on Bolivar or in Galveston, moving into Nacogdoches, and building illegally along the rivers farther south. In Mexico City, liberal politicians had hoped for help from the United States in their bid for independence as a sister republic. Martín de León and the other ranchers of La Bahía could have told them that the Anglos were more interested in helping themselves to Mexican land at the expense of their Spanish-speaking neighbors.

Martín de León grew increasingly concerned when he heard that the new Mexican leaders, both liberals and conservatives, had taken up the torch of colonization. Tadéo Ortíz, a liberal, offered to bring ten thousand Catholic settlers from Ireland and the Canary Islands to settle six thousand leagues of land in Texas. The plans fell through, but Martín de León was worried that the best lands in Texas might soon be gone, leaving none for himself and his sons. The newly established Mexican Congress, in its first year of existence under Emperor Iturbide, hesitated to grant land. The dilemma centered on questions of who owned the lands—the individual states or the central government—and who was to be admitted as settlers. Deputy Juan Bautista Valdés of the Eastern Interior Provinces, which included Texas,

> urged the greatest circumspection in the admission of all classes of foreigners because ... [of] the risk of dismemberment of that part of America in which Texas was located. Texas had always excited the envy of the United States and colonization would afford the United States the easiest and most advantageous method to obtain it.[25]

All colonization petitions were tabled until a colonization law could be enacted by the Mexican Congress. On December 29, 1821, the Commission on Foreign Relations determined that Texas should be settled by colonists from Mexico, from New Orleans, and from Europe, in particular Catholic Irish and Germans. Anglo Americans, as settlers, were not included. The Commission warned:

> If we do not take the present opportunity to people Texas, day by day, the strength of the United States will grow until it will annex Texas, Coahuila, Saltillo, and Nuevo León like the Goths, Visigoths and other tribes assailed the Roman Empire.[26]

Before a law governing colonization could be enacted, Ortíz had lost interest in the Texas project and Stephen F. Austin had arrived in Mexico City and requested a contract to bring Anglo-American settlers to Texas.[27]

Emperor Agustín de Iturbide, meanwhile, had taken a personal interest in Texas. In 1821 the Mexican Congress, in gratitude to Iturbide for bringing about Mexican independence, granted him a portion of land in Texas measuring twenty leagues on a side, or almost two million acres of land. In May of the following year, when La Bahía's *alcalde*, José Antonio Gutiérrez de Lara, requested an easing of the restrictions on trade in Texas, Iturbide offered to open the state and "made an attempt to better the conditions of the people in the distant province of Texas."[28] What that meant, exactly, Martín de León and his neighbors were not sure, but they did know that Stephen F. Austin, with his empresario contract, had arrived in Texas. In September 1821 Manuel Becerra was ordered to escort Austin to the Colorado River to inspect the lands which he had been granted for his colony. On the way, Becerra reported:

We went as far as the Guadalupe River where we stopped, and the said Austin wanted to be taken to examine the site of the old mission, Nuestra Señora del Refugio, and its presidio; although I answered that I was ordered by the government to go straight to the margins of the Colorado River, the said Commissioner told me that it was also necessary for him to examine those places, and I could do no less than to grant his requests . . .

We proceeded east, reconnoitering the environs of the old presidio, and having noticed that they were mapping all those places, it seemed that it was not proper to give them information about those lands . . .

Lastly, I thought it important to mention that during the time of this trip in company of the eleven foreigners, no religious act was observed. I report this observance according to the order issued on this matter.[29]

Becerra's report evidently did not reach Iturbide. Stephen F. Austin had traveled to Mexico City to plead his case with the new government for the continuation of his father's colonization contract. Much to Austin's relief, and to the growing distress of Martín de León and the ranchers in Texas, Iturbide signed the Imperial Colonization Law into effect on January 4, 1823, and granted Austin permission to carry out his settlement. All of Iturbide's good intentions, however, came to naught and any hope for the improvement of conditions in Texas faded when Iturbide abdicated the throne on March 19, 1823. He also lost his grant of Texas land.[30]

With the fall of Iturbide, a liberal constituent congress began work on creating a federalist government. The congress gave power back to each of the states as part of a new Acta Constitutiva which created the federated republic. The Eastern Interior Provinces were divided into four separate states—Nuevo Santander, Nuevo León, Texas, and Coahuila. Erasmo Seguín of San Fernando de Béxar represented Texas, and Ramos Arizpe, the influential Saltillo politician, spoke for Nuevo León. Seguín and Arizpe debated whether Texas, with its minuscule population, should remain a territory or be joined to one of its sister states. Ramos Arizpe pushed for Texas to be joined to Coahuila until it could acquire a larger population. Meanwhile, as the politicians wrangled in Mexico City, *bexareño* residents elected their own provincial deputation in April 1823 to control the activities in the state of Texas. Included among their duties was the granting of colonization contracts.[31]

Martín de León, by 1823, could see that Stephen F. Austin was rapidly filling the Colorado and Brazos River valleys with Anglo Americans, although perhaps not as rapidly as Austin would have liked. If de León was to secure lands for his own sons and daughters, the only alternative was to

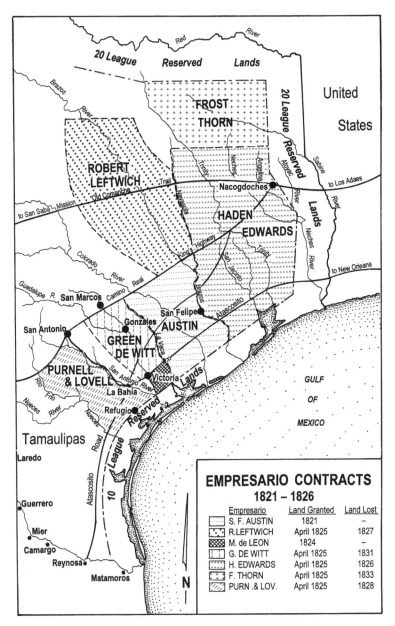

Red River

20 League Reserved Lands

Brazos River

FROST THORN

United States

20 League Reserved Lands

ROBERT LEFTWICH

Old Comanche Trail

Trinity

Navasota

Neches

Angelina

Atoyac

Sabine

to Los Adaes

Nacogdoches

to San Saba Mission

King's Highway

HADEN EDWARDS

Neches River

to New Orleans

Colorado River

Real

Brazos

San Jacinto

Guadalupe R.

San Marcos

Camino

San Felipe

AUSTIN

Gonzales

Atascosito

San Antonio

GREEN DE WITT

La Vaca

San Antonio River

PURNELL & LOVELL

Victoria

Reserved Lands

GULF

OF

MEXICO

La Bahia

Refugio

Reserved

Rio Frio

Nueces River

Nueces

Tamaulipas

Laredo

Atascosito Road

10 League

Guerrero

Mier

Camargo

Reynosa

Matamoros

N

EMPRESARIO CONTRACTS
1821 – 1826

Empresario	Land Granted	Land Lost
S. F. AUSTIN	1821	–
R.LEFTWICH	April 1825	1827
M. de LEON	1824	–
G. DE WITT	April 1825	1831
H. EDWARDS	April 1825	1826
F. THORN	April 1825	1833
PURN .& LOV.	April 1825	1828

Map 3.1

request an empresario contract of his own. As Martín de León well knew, establishing an empresario colony was not something entered into lightly.

An empresario was not, like Escandón, the pre-eminent noble of the past and master of all he surveyed. He was, however, much more than a real estate agent in charge only of granting land. The duties of an empresario were onerous and expensive. In addition to bringing the settlers, the empresario acted as military, judicial, and political leader. For his troubles, for every one hundred families he brought in, an empresario received approximately 23,000 acres (five leagues and five labors) for his own ranch. What tempted Martín de León, however, was the right to grant land to his own family and to become the patriarch of his own colony.[32]

While Erasmo Seguín and Ramos Arizpe debated the future of Texas in Mexico City, Martín de León gave up the ranch on the Aransas and moved the family back to Nuevo Santander. It was time to make plans to establish his own colony and protect his family. Part of the decision had been based on the marriage of twenty-five-year-old Fernando to María Antonia Galván. If Fernando and María Antonia were to have a sizable ranch of their own, Don Martín needed to have the power to grant lands. The empresario settlement was the best method to achieve his goal of providing ranches for all of his children. Each family would be authorized to receive one league (4,428 acres) as a ranch and one labor (177 acres) for a farm, usually irrigable land along a river. Single men such as Silvestre, Félix, and Agápito were given proportionately less, although they could apply for the larger amount once they married. Settlers could also request a town lot. De León had already determined that the best lots around the main square, with the exception of the east side, which was dedicated to the church and the west side for the governmental offices, would be reserved for his family.

During the summer and fall of 1823, de León traveled throughout Nuevo Santander recruiting settlers. Unlike Escandón's *entrada* one hundred years earlier, de León had a hard time finding families willing to move to Texas. There was still sufficient land available in Nuevo Santander, and the economy supported the local population with room for expansion. There was little incentive to come to Texas where *indios bárbaros* (wild Indians) constantly raided ranches and where military invasions still threatened settlers. By the end of 1823 he had only found little more than thirty interested prospective colonists. By including his own family, he could list forty-one potential settlers. Leaving the family in Nuevo Santander, he returned to Texas.[33]

On April 8, 1824, de León appeared before the Honorable Provincial Deputation of the city of San Fernando de Béxar. He stated that he was a *vecino*, or resident, of the town of Cruillas, Mexico, and respectfully petitioned for permission to found a colony on the Guadalupe River in Texas ten leagues beyond La Bahía del Espíritu Santo. De León promised, as empresario, to bring forty-one families from Nuevo Santander at his own expense to establish the town of Villa de Nuestra Señora de Guadalupe de Jesús with a plaza and streets as the law required. He also requested that his colonists be relieved of taxes for ten years as had been done for the recently appointed empresario Stephen F. Austin.[34]

The list of proposed settlers (m-married, s-single, wid-widower) included:

Fernando de León (m)	Victoriano Olivares (m)	Antonio Ortiz (m)
Silvestre de León (m)*	3 sons of Olivares (s)	1 son, 1 daughter
Félix de León (s)	Gabriel de Olivares (m)	Antonio Cisneros (m)
Agápito de León (s)*	4 sons of G. de Olivares (s)	Nepomuceno Cisneros (m)
José M. de las Casas (m)	José M. Cantu (m)	Antonio Treviño (wid.)
1 Son of de las Casas	2 sons, 4 daughters	2 sons

* Silvestre may have been engaged at the time, but he was not married yet, and Agápito was about to be married.

Juan Treviño (s)	Gregorio Ortiz (s)	José Manuel Garcilaso (m)
Trinidad Gonzales (m)	Juan de Dios Gonzales (s)	Antonio Mayorga (m)
Rafael Quintanilla (m)	Juan Pablo Garza (s)	1 son, 4 daughters
2 daughters	Simon Gonzales (m)	Ramon Molina (s)
Bernardo Saldivar (m)	2 grown sons	Julián Garcia (s)
4 sons, 2 daughters (s)	Feliciano (m)	Pedro Gonzales (s)
José Miguel Treviño (m)	2 sons, 1 daughter	Victoriano del Castillo (m)
3 sons	Juan Franco Vela (m)	3 sons
Ignacio Quintanilla (m)	3 sons, 1 daughter	Juan Garcia (wid)
Polinario Gonzalez (s)	Seferino Leal (m)	2 daughters
Cecilio Olivares (s)	1 son, 1 daughter	Dionisio Sorido (m)
		3 sons, 2 daughters
		Luis Arrizola (m)

Very few of the settlers on the list became colonists, but the names satisfied the provincial deputation and fulfilled the letter of the law. Martín's

Ismael Aldrete was said to have looked very much like his grandfather, Don Martín de León. Courtesy of Institute of Texan Cultures, San Antonio.

main purpose—providing lands for his sons and daughters—would be accomplished.[35]

During discussions between de León and the provincial deputation, the government made several changes to de León's petition. The officials added the word *Victoria* and changed the name of the colony to Villa de Nuestra Señora de Guadalupe de Jesús Victoria. They may have been ingratiating themselves with Guadalupe Victoria, a hero of the war for independence who had changed his name from Manuel Félix Fernández and was a member of the temporary triumvirate which ruled Mexico throughout 1823. Although no one knew it at the time, Guadalupe Victoria would go on to become president of the new republic seven months later.[36] Since the new Texas Provincial Deputation sitting in Béxar had complete jurisdiction over land grants, de León's petition, unlike Austin's, did not have to be sent to Mexico City for approval.

The provincial deputation approved de León's colonization project on April 13, 1824, only seven days after he requested the grant and barely a month before the power to grant land was taken from them. The provincial deputation of San Fernando de Béxar was terminated on May 7, 1824, when the constituent congress in Mexico City, under pressure from Ramos Arizpe, combined Texas with Coahuila. The government in Saltillo, which became the capital of the combined states, received most of the political power.

Martín de León at last held the power of an empresario, the right to grant lands to his sons or to whomever he wished, as well as the prestige of being the patriarch and leader of an entire settlement. De León had chosen his land on the Guadalupe River. The boundaries of his contract included the land between the lower Guadalupe and La Vaca Rivers, extending from the Atascosito Road on the northwest to the El Sabinal crossing at a line measured ten leagues from the coast. This area of ten littoral leagues was to remain unsettled in order to prevent anyone from acquiring contraband goods from ships passing along the coast.[37]

From 1824 until 1828 Mexico struggled to establish a new republican government under Guadalupe Victoria, the first president. The economy was in a shambles, and there was no money to pay the standing army. Debts left over from Iturbide's monarchy went unpaid. Taxes were avoided, smuggling and contraband were rampant, and the Spanish who had controlled the purse strings for so many years were quietly removing their funds from the country. In Spain, Ferdinand VII had bitterly refused to accept the loss of his colonial empire and threatened to invade and retake all of New Spain.

Agustín de Iturbide, the one-time emperor of independent Mexico, exiled first in Italy and then in England, heard rumors of the intended assault by Ferdinand VII. Iturbide, ever loyal to the land of his birth, notified the Mexican republican government that he was willing to help fight off the invasionary forces. He and his family embarked for Mexico without waiting to hear that Guadalupe Victoria's government had passed legislation that he should be shot for treason if he landed. He arrived in Soto la Marina, and it was not long before Patricia de la Garza's relatives and others in the small town realized who had appeared in their midst. The legislature of the state of Nuevo Santander, now Tamaulipas, fearful of repercussions for harboring a traitor, ordered the execution of the one-time leader. Iturbide, standing before the firing squad on July 19, 1824, gave one last emotional speech: "Mexicans! Even in this act of my death I recommend to you love of our fatherland and observance of our holy religion . . . I die for having come to assist you, and I die happy because I die among you. I die with honor, not as a traitor."[38]

The liberal government of Guadalupe Victoria had returned power to the states and local governments, something which had pleased Martín de León. The problem was that Texas and Coahuila were now controlled from Saltillo, high in the cool peaks of the Sierra Madre, where the federalist politicians favored granting colonization contracts to anyone and everyone. The new state government placed such importance on the issue of settlement that the first law passed for the combined state was the Colonization Law of March 24, 1825, even before the completion of the state constitution.[39]

The Saltillo government, like the bureaucratic Spanish government which it replaced, closely regulated the granting of land. Each piece of property, even on the remote frontiers of Texas, had to be surveyed, titled, and registered with the state before the government would send a land commissioner to place the owners in possession of the land. At San Felipe, the capital of Austin's settlement, and Victoria, the capital of de León's colony, the two empresarios were required to survey each lot or ranch and request that a title be issued to the owner. As had been the case with Martín de León's ranches on the Nueces and Aransas, the settlers could move onto the land and build homes, but the land was not technically theirs until a land commissioner, appointed by the governor, placed the owners in possession of their land, issued titles and deeds, and provided, with the help of the surveyor, maps showing the metes and bounds and a map or plot plan which was registered with the Mexican government. Each owner would eventually receive an original title. One copy would be retained by the empresario, one copy went to the state files in Saltillo, and one to land offices in Mexico City. There were still problems, however, with overlapping deeds, since maps were often inaccurate and the government did on occasion accidentally grant the same land to two or more empresarios. It was a problem which Martín de León would face on several occasions.[40]

As an empresario, Martín de León would now more widely assume the title of *don*. The term was frequently used as a mark of respect for the elders of large families. Less often it was a title given to leaders who supported and protected the members of their community, including their

own family and those over whom they had extended godparenthood protection. Almost like nobility, de León would become "Don Martín" and
his wife would be "Doña Patricia" to the entire community and not just
to their ranch hands and servants. They would be admired and esteemed
for their support and protection of those around them.[41]

In the spring of 1825, Don Martín de León returned to Nuevo Santander and gathered his family and some of those who had chosen to throw in
their lot with him. Among those who came was Julián de la Garza and his
wife, María García, accompanied by their children, including their daughter María Antonia Concepción de la Garza. Evidently, while the de León
family was in Camargo, sixteen-year-old María Antonia had fallen in love
with her cousin, Agápito, Martín's youngest son, also a precocious sixteen years old. The two fathers, Julián de la Garza and Martín de León,
had no time for discussion or extensive plans. Hurriedly, they gave their
permission for the young couple to marry in 1826. Agápito and his young
bride joined the colony with the rest of the family. The long mule trains
once again moved north, this time with everything necessary to settle an
entire colony—seed, tools, and supplies. Long dust plumes rose from the
plodding herds of cows, sheep, goats, pigs, and donkeys. The first twelve
families who arrived on the Guadalupe River consisted of Don Martín's
family, his wife's relatives, and the retainers from the Aransas and Nueces
River area.[42]

The small settlement on the Guadalupe was busy with activity. The site
chosen by Don Martín was a small bluff overlooking a curve on the northeast side of the Guadalupe River at a low-water crossing. Cypress, pecans,
elms, live oaks, and huisache grew along the banks of the river, and a vast,
flat prairie with grass five to six feet high spread away as far as the eye could
see. Don Martín, now sixty years old, depended on his sons to help him
establish the colony. With the help of Fernando and Silvestre, Don Martín
supervised the laying out of the town itself. Félix and Agápito wrote up
titles, laboriously hand-copied the detailed documents, and carried on the
correspondence and reports which the government required. Without advanced surveying equipment but rather the chains and stakes the Spanish had used throughout the New World for hundreds of years, the men
marked the streets and leveled the ground for the town lots. Fernando rode
out with the settlers, exploring the riverbanks and pastures so that each
could choose the location of his own ranch along the rivers. His brother
Félix chose the long-abandoned site of the old mission of La Bahía, far
upriver and tucked among an outcropping of hills and rocks for protec-

tion. Across the Guadalupe River was Silvestre's ranch on the flatlands that spread out from the river. Fernando and Agápito chose their ranches nearer the coast. Don Martín, concerned over completing the contract and placing his colonists in possession of their lands, waited to claim his five leagues and labors.[43]

Setting up a town was far more complex than establishing a mere ranch headquarters. The excitement of building the new settlement was contagious. While the men discussed plans for the town, the excited children were free to run and play, shouting and splashing in the river or chasing each other on their horses through the tall grass and out across the vast prairies. Patricia and the women cheerfully compared the benefits of town lots, each choosing the site for her family's town home. They tended the campfires, ground corn for tortillas, and prepared the simple meals of beans, chiles, and meat to feed the hungry crews of men. Don Martín and his colonists, armed with axes and machetes, cleared the smaller mesquite and huisache shrubs from the riverbank, then cut the sturdy live oaks, elms, and cypress to build the first government buildings.[44]

Don Martín located the town center an eighth of a mile from the Guadalupe, safe from floods but close enough to the river to allow for bathing, washing, and supplying water for the town's residents. He planned two town squares, one for the church and government and the other for the market. He laid out the town streets in the approved Spanish grid pattern. His own home he placed on the south side of the government square. The rest of the town lots around the government square were assigned to his family members. Everyone shared in the construction of the first government building.[45]

Politically, the town of Guadalupe Victoria would remain under the control of La Bahía. Don Martín, as empresario, would continue to resolve judicial and legal problems for the small colony. In October 1825 Don Martín applied for a *licencia de capilla*, a permit to construct the first church in town. He also requested a priest, but there were no clergymen available. Doña Patricia donated $500 in gold and the furnishings to help found the Church of Nuestra Señora de Guadalupe. Even if there was no priest, small statues of the Virgin of Guadalupe and the saints could be installed with pomp and ceremony, and everyone gathered to pray and ask for blessings on the new settlement. Don Martín's settlers chose their own lots and began to build their small *jacales*, corrals, and barns. Once the home sites were selected, the women, with the help of the children, laid out their gardens and built brush fences to protect the first corn, bean, squash, chile, and tomato crops.[46]

Doña Patricia, while settling into their new home, was vitally interested in the education of her growing family. She established a school in the new town for the children of all the settlers. She paid for the teacher and made certain that all of the children attended the classes. She was also busy planning weddings and baptisms. Perhaps it was the potential for large grants of land which made her sons and daughters attractive marriage prospects.

The parties and weddings were almost continuous as Doña Patricia married off six of her ten children and welcomed new grandchildren into the family. Fourteen-year-old Chucha, perhaps with the selective assistance of her parents, was betrothed to twenty-four-year-old Rafael Manchola, the militia captain of La Bahía. It was an excellent match for Chucha, but it was even better for promoting Don Martín's political connections, since the Manchola family were influential at La Bahía. Chucha and Rafael Manchola were married in the presidial chapel in 1824 and settled down in La Bahía, where Chucha was close to her sister, Candelaria Aldrete. Candelaria, now twenty-three, had just given birth to her second son, José de Jesús María, and the two girls had much to discuss while they played with Candelaria's two babies. Their husbands, meanwhile, became closely involved in La Bahía town government, supporting and defending their father-in-law's small colony at Victoria whenever necessary.[47]

The same year, to Doña Patricia's intense relief, Lupita, practically a spinster at twenty-one, married twenty-year-old Desiderio Garcia, the son of one of Don Martín's newly arrived colonists. Silvestre, who would become the *alcalde* (a combination judge, mayor, and sheriff) for Victoria, made another good connection by marrying Rosalía de la Garza, the daughter of Julián de la Garza, who had become an important and well-to-do rancher at Refugio. Four years later, in 1828, while the family was visiting in Cruillas, Tamaulipas, eighteen-year-old brother Félix married sixteen-year-old Salomé Leal, daughter of their San Antonio friends. The remaining children—Refugia, twelve, Agustina, ten, and Francisca, eight—remained with Don Martín and Doña Patricia in their town home. Sadly, in 1825 the family faced its first tragedy. Fernando's wife of only two years, María Antonia Galván, passed away, the first death in the new colony.[48]

As the Victoria colony prospered, new settlers arrived from Tamaulipas, Monterrey, and San Antonio. A number of the settlers on the original list had not appeared, and if Don Martín was to complete his forty-one families, he needed additional colonists. Among those who were welcomed to the town were Diego and Valentín García, Manuel Zepeda, Fulgencio Bueno, the Escalera family, and José María Hernández. Among the later arrivals were the Carbajal family and the four Benavides brothers. De León also found sixteen Anglo-American families who had already moved into the area illegally, including John Linn, John D. Wright, and Joseph Ware. These settlers, even though they were Anglos and not on the list of settlers de León had submitted, were accepted as members of the Victoria colony. Jean Louis Berlandier, visiting in 1828 with the Mexican Boundary Commission, indicated that there were individuals in the Victoria colony from Canada, the United States, Ireland, France, and Germany. Unlike Austin's settlements on the Colorado, Martín de León's colony was, by necessity, multicultural from its inception.[49]

Not everyone approved of the mixture of colonists. At La Bahía, the town council was irate over the settlers at Victoria. In spite of the defense of Don Martín by Manchola and Aldrete, the remaining members of the government did not approve of the varied ethnic flavor of the Victoria colony. In a letter dated March 26, 1825, Juan José Hernández, *alcalde* at La Bahía, complained to Governor Antonio Martínez in San Antonio about Martín de León's failure to follow protocol. According to Hernández, who held legal jurisdiction over the new colony of Victoria, de León had not reported who was settling in the Victoria colony and had allowed foreigners to settle without the authorization or permission of the government.[50]

During the next three months, numerous letters were exchanged among officials of La Bahía, San Antonio, and Saltillo. The various government officials carefully reviewed de León's contract. San Antonio Political Chief José Antonio Saucedo informed the governor that de León had only brought in a dozen settlers, mostly his own family members. He had not only failed to bring in the promised number of colonists from Nuevo Santander, now Tamaulipas, but Saucedo agreed with La Bahía *alcalde* Hernández that de León was encouraging the settlement of foreigners. When questioned by Saucedo, de León assured the government that the remaining twenty-five families had been held up by drought along the Río Bravo. De León's assurances satisfied the Saltillo government. By October 5, the Saltillo governor's office notified the political chief in San Antonio that de León's foreign colonists were to be accepted and that a land commissioner would be named to put them in possession of their lands. The

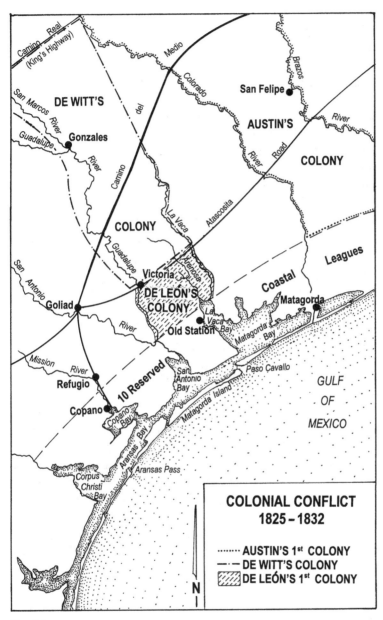

Camino Real (King's Highway)

San Marcos River

Guadalupe

DE WITT'S

Gonzales

del

Camino

Medio

Colorado

San Felipe

Brazos

AUSTIN'S

River

River

Road

COLONY

COLONY

Guadalupe

River

La Vaca

Atascosita

Victoria

Arenosa

Leagues

Coastal

San Antonio River

Goliad

DE LEÓN'S COLONY

Old Station

La Vaca Bay

Matagorda

Matagorda Bay

Mission River

Refugio

10 Reserved

San Antonio Bay

Paso Cavallo

GULF
OF
MEXICO

Copano

Copano Bay

Aransas Bay

Matagorda Island

Corpus Christi Bay

Aransas Pass

**COLONIAL CONFLICT
1825 – 1832**

········· AUSTIN'S 1st COLONY
—·— DE WITT'S COLONY
▨ DE LEÓN'S 1st COLONY

N

Map 3.2

Saltillo government eventually named Fernando de León as the colony's land commissioner.[51]

De León's policy of open acceptance of anyone interested in settling at Victoria enabled him to complete his contract within two years of the initial settlement. By March 24, 1826, he had made good on his promise to colonize Victoria. He had not only completed his first contract for forty-one families but had introduced a total of more than one hundred families, many from Tamaulipas and a few from the United States. In payment, he requested and received the five league and five labor Rancho El Sacramento on Garcitas Creek, extending south toward Matagorda Bay and west with the Arroyos del Zorrillo and Palo Alto.[52]

Martín de León had been right to worry about the imminent arrival of hordes of Anglo-American settlers. In the United States many farmers had been left destitute or deeply in debt by the Panic of 1819. Austin himself was fleeing a debt of more than $10,000, and, as one citizen of Louisiana complained, "many persons having left this place who are in debt to me and having gone to your section of the c'try . . . all of whom are slave holders."[53] In addition, land in the United States was selling for $1.25 an acre. Land speculators were buying up the large tracts and offering smaller portions of ten or twelve acres to farmers for as much as $800 or $1,000 with no credit available to help ease the financial burden.

When Austin advertised in newspapers in New Orleans, Kentucky, and Tennessee, his Texas land grants of more than 4,600 acres at a cost of $12 to $100, farmers in the United States found the bargain almost inconceivable. American Senator Henry Clay could not believe that the Mexican government was making such contracts and commented, "The Mexicans must have little interest in holding Texas, they are giving it away."[54] Thousands of Anglo Americans were willing to move to Texas, claim adherence to a religion they did not believe in, and swear allegiance to a country which some of them despised, in order to get the land. The newspapers in the Western states downplayed the huge grants, fearful of losing their own settlers to Austin's Texas colony. Unless one had slaves, they noted, no single farmer could ever hope to clear and plant that much land. The would-be emigrants, on the other hand, already envisioned a tidy profit from the sale of the excess land to later arrivals.[55]

Austin and de León were not the only two interested in becoming empresarios. The Saltillo legislature was besieged by requests from Anglo Americans in 1825 when the Mexican national government transferred control of land sales to the states. The Texas Association, a group of merchants, doctors, and lawyers in Tennessee, had sent Robert Leftwich to apply for land contracts first to Mexico City and then to Saltillo. Other Anglos such as Haden Edwards, Andrew Erwin, Frost Thorn, and Green De Witt, had waited in vain in Mexico City throughout 1822, 1823, and 1824. During 1825 and early 1826, the Saltillo government granted contracts to these men who promised to bring in some 2,400 families. Some of those who received contracts, such as the Texas Association, were interested in speculation, not settlement. A very few, such as Green de Witt and Haden Edwards, were personally interested in settling in Texas.[56]

Martín de León was soon embroiled in problems with his new neighbors. Green de Witt, following closely in Austin's footsteps, had contracted with the Saltillo government on April 15, 1825, to bring four hundred families to Texas within six years. The government was unaware of the fact that the contract for Green de Witt partially overlapped de León's colony. Unlike Austin, Green De Witt had not inspected the lands of his contract prior to his request and had left it up to his surveyor, James Kerr, to locate and mark out the boundaries of the colony. Kerr chose the confluence of the San Marcos and Guadalupe Rivers for the capital of the new colony, which was named Gonzales, after Rafael Gonzales, the governor of Coahuila and Texas.

The capital of the De Witt colony was well beyond the boundaries of de León's colony, but Kerr had also chosen a landing place for the settlers at the new port on Matagorda Bay at La Vaca, whose name Kerr modified to Lavaca. This port lay within the jurisdiction of de León's colony. By mid-1825 Kerr had conducted the first boatload of settlers to Gonzales. Empresario De Witt, meanwhile, was in the United States recruiting more colonists.[57]

In the fall of 1825 Martín de León and his settlers were startled to see strangers passing through the Victoria colony on their way up the Guadalupe River. De León did not stop them but informed the Saltillo government of what he had seen. Juan Antonio Padilla, the interim secretary, responded on October 6, 1825. He ordered that De Witt be reminded that he was not to bother any of the citizens of the Villa of Guadalupe Victoria nor to hinder any of them in the continuation of their labors. The Anglo farmers in the small colony at Gonzales, intent on clearing land and planting their first crop, had no intention of causing difficulties. For six months they made a small but successful settlement at Gonzales. An Indian raid in July 1826, however, drove many of the frightened Anglos out of their new homes and back toward the coast. James Kerr, realizing that he did not have the manpower, militia, or presidial soldiers to protect the settlers, moved as many of the Anglo colonists as possible back to Port Lavaca, by this time called Old Station.[58]

In August, Kerr also petitioned the Béxar government to allow the by-now suffering settlers the right to remain at Old Station and to grant to De Witt the entire valley of the La Vaca River including the ten coastal border leagues. He explained that the coast was more protected from the Indians, that more of the settlers came by water from New Orleans, and, finally, that if the ten littoral leagues were measured from the outer islands, Old Station was legal, or almost. While waiting for a response (which took more than a year), Kerr settled the colonists at Old Station, divided the land among them, and built homes and a warehouse for supplies arriving from New Orleans.[59]

Green De Witt, meanwhile, had returned from the United States with more colonists. Kerr and De Witt traveled to Gonzales to check on the few settlers who had remained. While passing through de León's colony De Witt "noted that a portion of his [De Witt's] grant had already been occupied by settlers."[60] According to de León, De Witt did more than just note. De Witt, said de León, "alarmed my settlers and caused many . . . to suspend their operations and thus became [so] discouraged . . . that they were about to abandon their possessions."[61] De León complained to Saucedo at Béxar and to the governor in Saltillo, claiming right to the land by prior contract and by the fact that Mexicans, according to the new state colonization law, were to be given preference.[62] Much to De Witt's annoyance, the government ruled in de León's favor. The difficulties between the two men, already off to a bad start, escalated in the years ahead.

Some of the problems between de León and De Witt lay in the misunderstandings by Anglo Americans of the Spanish and Mexican legal systems. The network of rules and regulations which had grown up over three hundred years was entirely different from what they had left in the United States. The Spanish used a conciliatory method which was "communally based and had few of the accouterments of formal law."[63] Jurisdiction was vested in the *alcaldes* as judges. The judge had the right to question the parties, carry out his own investigations, and control the proceedings. The purpose was to attempt to "resolve conflict in a way that preserves, rather than destroys, a relationship."[64]

For cases involving less than $200, each party named an arbitrator to assist the local *alcalde* in reaching a decision. Anything above $200 was handled by the judge of the colony, usually the empresario himself. Juries were unheard of in the class-oriented Spanish culture where no self-respecting upper-class Spaniard would have accepted a judgment from a member of the poorer classes. For larger or more complex cases, it often took so long to receive a resolution from San Antonio or Saltillo that Anglo-American *alcaldes* learned to improvise, much as the early Mexican settlers had, although their improvisations were usually "along the lines familiar in the United States."[65] The system which had developed on the frontier had evolved not from the "languid procedures of a pre-industrial, pastoral people,"[66] but from necessity. Settling a crisis required local judges to find some method of immediate conciliation between the parties. Only in this way could the frontier communities continue to operate successfully.[67]

Under the British common law system used by the incoming Anglo Americans, judges acted as umpires and juries made the decisions. The judges and juries, who had no right to investigate a case, remained uninformed of the facts beyond what was presented in court and made a determination based solely on the presentations of the opponents. For the "free Yankee population who consider they are competent to judge for themselves,"[68] the conciliatory courts of Mexican Texas implied that judges were "a superior class over them," which for the Mexicans was indeed the case in terms of education and social standing, as judges were chosen from the "better sorts" of society.[69]

Law and order and the effective functioning of the government were important to Martín de León. De León, as the chief and the only official of his colony, was supplied by the La Bahía government with the standard legal documents and the current laws and decrees of which he was to inform his settlers. At La Bahía, the government consisted of an *alcalde* and a *cabildo*, or town council. Those who sat on the town council exerted "considerable influence on community affairs,"[70] and it was here that José Miguel Aldrete and Rafael Manchola, Don Martín's sons-in-law, provided their backing. Don Martín could rest assured that the problems of Victoria would be protected. While Austin struggled to combine Mexican and American laws for his colonists, de León continued the semi-autocratic control which was expected of an empresario.[71]

Even an autocrat, however, had to respect the laws. Several years later, Silvestre de León, Don Martín's second son, as judge for Victoria, was called on to rule on a case involving his own father. Don Martín was accused of shooting a hog belonging to a Mexican resident of Victoria. In court, Judge Silvestre asked his father if the allegations were true. Don

Martín admitted to killing the hog but maintained that it was because the hog had destroyed his garden. Silvestre asked his father if he had a "lawful fence" to keep the hog out. Don Martín replied that it was not of the best, but he asked if Silvestre would rule against his own father. John Linn, who was in the court, recounted the result:

> Don Silvestre replied that in his capacity of a public officer the ties that bound him as an individual were inoperative. On the bench he would perform his duty with strict impartiality, but off the bench he became again the dutiful son. With this prelude the alcalde announced that he would assess the damages sustained by the plaintiff in the loss of his hog at twenty dollars. Don Martín promptly paid the amount, with the remark that he was proud of such a son, to the disappointment of a crowd that had collected to see some fun.[72]

Another source of friction between Martín de León and the incoming Anglo Americans was tobacco. The Mexican government, following the lead of the Spanish, held a monopoly on the sale of tobacco. Government cigarettes were sold in *estancos*, or tobacco shops, controlled by local governments. Anglo-American settlers in Austin's colony, for whom *estancos* had not yet been established, were expected to buy their cigarettes at San Antonio, La Bahía, or Nacogdoches. The Mexican government had hoped to receive more than two million *reales* in income from the sale of tobacco during the heady years after independence, but the government had been able to collect less than one-tenth of that amount across the entire country. Frustrated over the drop in income, the Mexican government cracked down on the tobacco being brought in from the United States.[73]

Austin and De Witt advised their colonists that they could not bring tobacco into Texas. During 1825, while many of the incoming settlers professed ignorance of the law, José Antonio Saucedo, the political chief at San Antonio, allowed them to sell their illegal tobacco to the government at a price of eleven *reales* rather than having it taken from them. By the following year, however, Saucedo warned the settlers that they could be arrested and imprisoned and their goods confiscated if they were caught trafficking in tobacco.[74]

On August 23, 1826, just as the boundary problem between de León and De Witt was escalating, a De Witt settler named Thomas Powell arrived at Old Station on the schooner *Escambia* from New Orleans. Powell had almost twenty mule-loads of goods including a large quantity of tobacco. Martín de León, the nearest government official, was notified that the schooner was carrying contraband. When de León arrived with a contingent of the La Bahía militia, he found Thomas Powell and Dr. Oldivar, a French officer, planning to sell their cargo to local settlers. De León notified Saucedo of the problem and requested back-up. He then arrested Powell and Oldivar, confiscated the goods, and took the men and contraband to Victoria.[75]

At Victoria, empresario de León could have resolved the situation by conciliation. The Anglo Americans at Gonzales, however, fearing that they would lose a court case, appealed to Political Chief Saucedo at Béxar and to Austin at San Felipe. On October 25, Saucedo notified Green De Witt, who was by this time at La Bahía, that de León had been ordered to release Powell and all confiscated goods except the tobacco. Four days later, to prevent any violence, Saucedo ordered the La Bahía garrison under Rafael Manchola, de León's son-in-law, to march for Victoria immediately with "all the armed force at their disposal" and to seize the cargo of the schooner *Escambia* so that it could be checked. Grudgingly admitting that it had been his responsibility to prevent the arrival of the tobacco, De Witt sent a letter of apology to Saucedo, and de León released Powell from the Victoria jail. He turned Powell over to De Witt, and the two Anglos returned to Gonzales. Powell and De Witt took the goods from the *Escambia* with them, including, it appears, some of the tobacco.[76]

De León and Manchola, now at Victoria, learned of the illegal action. The empresario and Manchola set out toward Gonzales to resolve the problem and collect the tobacco. The settlers at Gonzales, hearing from an old colonist named Francis Smith that the two government officials were on their way, immediately assumed the worst. Panic spread among the colonists, who armed themselves, assured by Smith that de León planned to kill De Witt. Smith claimed that de León had sworn to take De Witt's head back to Victoria tied to his saddle. The sixty-two-year-old empresario Martín de León and Manchola arrived at Gonzales, totally unaware of the furor and certainly without any bloody plans to take De Witt's head anywhere. Kerr was able to keep the frightened colonists from attacking the two government officials. After negotiations were conducted between Kerr and de León, the matter ended without any bloodshed. De León apprehended Smith for inciting the riot and returned to Victoria with what little they could find of the contraband.[77]

De León kept Powell's and Oldivar's guns, six barrels of flour, two sacks of coffee beans, a barrel of sugar, and a white wool cape belonging to one Francisco Wuytel. Kerr again complained to Saucedo, who ordered de León to return the goods, including the guns, as long as the Americans promised not to use the weapons against the Mexicans but only against the Indians. The colonists continued to claim that they did not get all their guns back, while Manchola and the Mexican officials maintained that they never found all the tobacco.[78]

Rafael Manchola was soured by the episode. He no longer trusted the Anglo settlers. As he commented in his report to Mateo Ahumada, the commandant of Texas, in October 1826,

> no faith can be placed in the *norte americano* colonists because they are continually demonstrating that they absolutely refuse to be subordinate, unless they find it convenient to what they want anyway, all of which I believe will be very detrimental to us for them to be our neighbors if we do not in time, clip the wings of their audacity by stationing a strong detachment in each new settlement which will enforce the laws and jurisdiction of a Mexican Alcalde which should be placed in each of them, since under their own colonists as judges, they do nothing more than practice their own laws which they have practiced since they were born, forgetting the ones they have sworn to obey, these being the laws of our Supreme Government.[79]

Manchola, who went on to represent Goliad at the state congress in Saltillo, was influential four years later in writing the restrictive provisions of the Law of April 6, 1830, which halted Anglo colonization in Texas. His suggestions also led to the erection of forts around the state to control contraband as part of the same law.[80]

De León complained continually throughout 1825 and 1826 about the "evil and malicious" men who were passing through Victoria.[81] Horses, already broken and trained by the Mexicans and which usually grazed at large, were the easiest items to steal and the most readily marketable to the Indians. In March 1825 de León reported two Americans for selling branded Spanish horses to the Indians. In September of the following year he made a claim for one of his citizens of a horse stolen by a group of Anglo Americans from the Brazos River who were passing through Victoria with a herd of horses.[82] Nothing came of the claim, and the accused were never apprehended.

In late 1826 another revolution in distant Nacogdoches disturbed Martín de León at Victoria. Haden Edwards, an empresario in the Nacogdoches area, had received his contract on April 15, 1825. Within the year, Mexican settlers in Edwards' colony around Nacogdoches accused him of ignoring the claims of longtime colonists and rigging elections to place his handpicked people in office, including Edwards' own son-in-law. Even the new colonists he was bringing in from the United States complained that he arbitrarily overcharged for land. Saucedo, from San Antonio, and Austin, at San Felipe, warned, cajoled, and finally threatened Edwards to no avail. Saucedo demanded the reinstatement of the duly elected sheriff whom Edwards had removed. On November 22 and again on December 16, 1826, José Antonio Saucedo sent letters of reprimand to the Nacogdoches colony, threatening the loss of the contract. Five days later, while Haden Edwards was in New Orleans recruiting more settlers, Haden's brother, Benjamin, angered by the reprimands from the Mexican government and fearful of losing the colony, gathered eighty Anglo settlers and declared the Republic of Fredonia. Benjamin Edwards received no support from Austin or the Anglo settlers. The La Bahía and San Antonio militias were ordered to subdue the rebels at Nacogdoches. Austin, fearful of the repercussions to his own colonists who might lose their lands, and Kerr, likewise concerned about the fate of De Witt's colony, joined the government's forces. Except for one small skirmish on January 4, 1827, the Fredonia rebels were captured without a fight. Haden Edwards was stripped of his empresario contract, and he and his brother were expelled from Texas.[83]

Problems also occurred with Stephen F. Austin. In December 1826 the La Bahía town government was called on to settle a dispute between Martín de León and Thomas Grey, one of Austin's settlers. Grey had bought and paid for a donkey which he had purchased from de León. Grey had left the donkey to graze with de León's herds, and when he sent for it several months later, de León demanded a payment of twenty-five dollars or a cow and calf for grazing the animal. Grey refused to pay, and de León refused to release the donkey. Some months later, de León sent his son Fernando with a wagonload of corn to sell to Austin's Colorado River colonists. An altercation ensued between Grey and Fernando. Grey detained Fernando at gunpoint and locked up the corn, cart, and yoke of oxen. Fernando, infuriated and insulted at the affront, threatened Grey's life. Austin jailed the furious Fernando but allowed him to send word to his father. Martín de León appealed to the La Bahía militia for help in securing his son's release and demanded an apology from Austin's colonist Grey. After threats and counterthreats, Fernando and the cartload of corn were released. Grey, however, had disappeared and no apology was ever forthcoming.[84]

By August 1827 Martín de León faced additional problems with his immediate neighbor Green De Witt and the settlement at Old Station. This time, however, the results worked in de León's favor. De Witt still had not moved the colonists back to Gonzales, and contraband was increasing rapidly. Commandant General Anastacio Bustamante, writing from Mexico City, complained of the "secret introduction of prohibited goods which is being carried on at the Lavaca and the disturbances of public tranquillity."[85] He ordered Saucedo to remove the De Witt colonists. On August 29 Saucedo notified De Witt that the colonists had one month to leave Old Station and return to De Witt's designated empresario area around Gonzales. James Kerr, without whom the inept and increasingly drunken De Witt could not have survived, carried a petition to Béxar requesting an extension of time. On September 28 Saucedo allowed the colonists to remain at Old Station until December 1, 1827. Green De Witt had proved to be incompetent, but Kerr saved the day. Kerr clearly understood the Spanish concept of *Obedezco pero no cumplo*, or "I obey but do not comply," in which citizens could petition for redress and postpone unwanted rules and regulations. He continued the petition process to Governor Viesca in Saltillo. The governor, as Kerr had hoped, extended the removal of the colonists to June 1828. By that date, the De Witt colonists had moved back to Gonzales, built a fort, and begun to clear land for their farms, and de León had accepted their presence.[86]

Don Martín de León's colony on the Guadalupe River was successfully established by 1828. Don Martín no longer received complaints from the La Bahía government where he and Patricia visited frequently to see the new grandchildren. The aging couple had to make plans for the baptisms and choose the godparents for the rapidly arriving grandchildren from among the members of the community at La Bahía. José Miguel Aldrete and Candelaria had their third son, Trinidad, in 1824, and their fourth son, Rafael, was born in 1826. Also at La Bahía in 1826, Candelaria's younger sister, Chucha, wife of Rafael Manchola, had given birth to Francisca, who would be known as Panchita to distinguish her from her Aunt Francisca, who still cared for Don Martín and Doña Patricia. Back in Victoria, Doña Patricia also needed to find godparents for León de León, the first and only child of Agápito and his wife, María Antonia.

In comparison to the growing problems with the Anglo colonists, Don Martín's colony — with its loyal, Catholic settlers from Tamaulipas and from the Escandón towns on the Río Bravo — had become an example of what the government had hoped for in setting up the empresario system. Even Austin, who was as honest and conscientious an empresario as there was among the Anglos, was having his own difficulties keeping troublemakers from the United States out of his colony. When Martín de León had problems with the influx of Anglo Americans without government permission or passports, he turned to Austin to resolve the problems. Austin himself complained that "the North Americans are the most obstinate and difficult people to manage that live on earth."[87] Saucedo required that Austin keep a close track of the strangers in the area and submit a census to San Antonio listing their names and locations on a regular basis. Austin struggled unsuccessfully to do so. As Don Martín had foreseen, there was no stopping the Anglo Americans, but at least his family was settled on their own ranches and had built their town homes. His sons and daughters had received their lands and, in his waning years, he and Patricia could face the future with tranquility, happily visiting their growing family on the ranches around Victoria or at La Bahía and San Antonio. Don Martín knew he could do little about the trouble which he was certain was brewing in the Anglo colonies on the Brazos and the Colorado rivers.[88]

CHAPTER 4

PROBLEMS, 1828–1834

Genealogical Chart

M ARTÍN DE LEÓN (D. 1834) + PATRICIA DE LA GARZA

1. Fernando (wid. 1825)

2. María Candelaria (m. 1818) + José Miguel Aldrete
    2-1. José María (b. 1820)
    2-2. José de Jesús María (b. 1822)
    2-3. Trinidad (b. 1824)
    2-4. Rafael (b. 1826)

3. Silvestre (m. 1824) + Rosalía de la Garza
    3-1. Francisco Grande (b. 1825)
    3-2. Martín (b. 1830)

4. "Lupita" (m. 1825) + Desiderio García
    No children

5. Félix (m. 1828) + Salomé Leal
    5-1. Santiago (b. 1829)
    5-2. Patricio (b. 1830)
    5-3. Silvestre (b. 1834)

6. Agápito (d. 1833) + María Antonia C. de la Garza
    6-1. León de León (b. 1824)

7. "Chucha" (m. 1824) + Rafael Manchola (d. 1833)
    7-1. "Panchita" (b. 1826)

8. Refugia (m. 1832) + José María Jesús Carbajal
    8-1. Antonio (b. 1833)
    8-2. José María (b. 1834)

9. Agustina (m. 1831) + Plácido Benavides
    9-1. Pilar (b. 1834)

10. Francisca (b. 1818)

In June 1828 José Miguel Aldrete, Rafael Manchola, and the ranchers of La Bahía stormed out of the governmental offices on the plaza at the town of La Bahía. The *ayuntamiento* had just received word from Saltillo that confirmed the rumors. After years of promises, the vast pastures of La Bahía del Espíritu Santo had at last been secularized, but none of the local ranchers would have a chance at the land. To their shock and dismay, on June 11, 1828, the state government at Saltillo had granted all of the La Bahía mission property to two Irish Catholics—James Hewetson, a Monclova doctor, and James Power, a Monterrey lawyer.

With the group of ranchers was twenty-seven-year-old Carlos de la Garza. He had grown up at La Bahía, a descendant of three generations of presidial soldiers. All his life he had heard that the mission lands were about to be turned over to the local ranchers. As a soldier's son, Carlos had hoped for his own ranch. The grant to Power and Hewetson, however, meant the new colonists would get it all. For twenty years, his family had fought rebels and filibuster armies, and Carlos had learned to dislike and distrust the foreigners who brought revolt and revolution. His upbringing made him conservative, and his experiences placed him bitterly against the incoming settlers.[1]

At La Bahía, Carlos and his ranch neighbors hoped for redress of their land claims, but hope was dwindling. The old stability of the Spanish empire had given way to frustrating and irreconcilable internal conflict in Mexico. The liberal states-rights advocates, better known as the federalists, and the centralists who demanded more autocratic control by the government in Mexico City had reached an impasse over colonization. The federalists in Mexico City and in Saltillo encouraged bringing in Anglo Americans to settle Texas, while the wealthy, elite centralists frowned on Anglo ideas of democratic individualism. Carlos de la Garza, although neither wealthy nor elite, staunchly supported the centralists.

The government in Mexico held its second general election in 1828. With little input in the Saltillo legislature, the Tejanos, or Mexican Texans, remained on the edges of the escalating political upheaval, listening with growing concern and dismay over the widening rift in Mexico City between the liberals and conservatives. Manuel Gómez Pedraza, the centralist conservative candidate for president and an experienced politician, was elected by the state legislatures, but liberals refused to accept the verdict, claiming that the military had rigged the votes. Within three months the liberals, and in particular their champion, Santa Anna, had forced the con-

servatives from power and placed their own federalist candidate, Vicente
Guerrero, in the presidency. Guerrero, as a liberal, should have supported
the Anglo immigration to Texas, but he opposed slavery and abolished it
in 1829, an act which threatened Austin's colonists.

Of more concern to the settlers at La Bahía and to Don Martín and
Patricia at Victoria was the last attempt by Ferdinand VII of Spain to re-
capture his empire. While Manuel Becerra ran the Victoria colony, Don
Martín had been conducting business in New Orleans. By chance, his ship
docked at Havana, where Spanish troops reportedly were being readied
for an attack on the Mexican coast. Hastening home, Don Martín reported this distressing news. Within the month, King Ferdinand landed
Spanish troops at Tampico and at Patricia's hometown of Soto la Marina.
In Mexico City, President Guerrero called on Santa Anna to repel the invaders. By October 1829 Santa Anna succeeded in driving the Spanish out
of Mexico, and the threatened invasion failed. Spaniards were expelled
from Mexico and took their bullion and investments with them.[2]

During 1828 and 1829, Carlos de la Garza and the citizens of La Bahía
had a chance to express their views and concerns directly to one of Mexico's
most prestigious and brilliant government representatives, Manuel de
Mier y Terán, during his official inspection tour of Texas. Carlos de la
Garza and his neighbors, pleased at first to host the large entourage from
Mexico City, were soon disillusioned. The elite members of the Boundary
Commission, traveling through Texas sneered at La Bahía and labeled the
small Texas towns "miserable."[3] But if the Tejano settlers were pathetic,
Mier y Terán noted that the Anglo Americans were truly dangerous.

According to Mier y Terán, the growing ranks of illegal immigrants
were arrogant and had neither become Catholic nor sworn allegiance to
Mexico. Expecting Anglo-American immigrants to become honest, loyal,
hardworking Mexicans had been a pipe dream. In the eyes of the commissioners, who left the area as promptly as possible, the solution was to
encourage more European settlers, such as Irish Catholics, since Mexicans from the interior had no interest in moving to a land that had little
civilization and many Indian raids.[4]

Receiving no help from the commissioners, in 1828 more than one hundred La Bahía ranchers applied to Tadéo Ortíz de Ayala, director of colonization. Not only were the local Tejanos denied a chance to claim the
mission properties, they were in danger of losing their own lands to the
new arrivals as well. La Bahía, they complained, "had been ignored by

the Supreme Government in spite of the fact that the oldest settlers in this area counted themselves among the first who had taken the oath of allegiance to the independent Republic in 1821."[5]

By 1829 José Miguel Aldrete and the angry La Bahía ranchers learned that Power and Hewetson, for their first contract, promised to settle two hundred Irish Catholic families on the mission lands. On May 25, 1831, the two empresarios signed a second contract to settle an additional two hundred families at the abandoned mission of Refugio. As compensation for their efforts, the empresarios expected to receive twenty leagues and twenty labors, or more than 92,000 acres, of premium land. Aldrete, Carlos de la Garza, and the Mexican ranchers along the San Antonio River were thoroughly disgusted at the "flagrant neglect of the Republic which once promised so much."[6]

The members of the La Bahía *cabildo*, including Aldrete and Rafael Manchola, appealed once again for intervention from the state government. The local settlers' petitions were "not being taken up [by Power and Hewetson] for consideration or were being refused altogether."[7] The only concessions which the governor in Saltillo would make was that the new empresarios were to accept all Mexican families in the area as legal colonists. The La Bahía ranchers, also known as *badeños*, were to have their land respected up to a league and a labor, and the locals were to be given titles to their ranches. This did little to assuage the local feelings, since many Tejanos had no ranches of their own, while others such as Aldrete and Manchola had ranches covering far more than a league and a labor. Power and Hewetson, hopeful that they would be able to bring in their quota of Irish settlers, refused to offer the local La Bahía residents a chance at the premium lands.[8]

James Power brought the first group of colonists from Ireland via New York and New Orleans in 1829. The Irish immigrants arrived in a pathetic condition, sick from the long voyage, with little food and little hope. For want of shelter, the small group settled at the empty Refugio mission. Much to the astonishment of the frightened Irish families, Carlos de la Garza and the locals came to their aid. With traditional Mexican hospitality, the ranchers took in the starving Irish. Carlos de la Garza invited several of the Irish families to his father's ranch and provided food, clothing, and supplies for them. Among the families were Nicholas Fagan, John Dunn, George C. McKnight, Antonio Sideck, Edward McDonough, and Peter Hyne. In addition, some of the settlers from De Witt's failing colony, such as Peter Teal, came to join their fellow Irishmen. Carlos and his Tejano neighbors helped the Irish settlers carve out their small farms along the San Antonio River near the old mission. Notwithstanding his friendship with his new neighbors, Carlos continued to oppose the empresario settlements.[9]

For Carlos de la Garza, acquiring his own ranch had taken on added importance. He was getting married. In May 1829 Carlos de la Garza invited his new Irish neighbors to the wedding celebration at the small presidial stone church at La Bahía del Espíritu Santo. Twenty-eight-year-old Carlos de la Garza, third-generation descendant of La Bahía's presidial soldiers, was marrying Tomasita, newly arrived from the Río Bravo. According to Annie Fagan Teal, "The Spanish ladies were dressed in silks that would stand alone, costly laces, jewels rich and rare of beautiful Mexican workmanship."[10] With his new family to consider, Carlos appealed to the government officials and to Power and Hewetson for ranch lands. Once again his petition was ignored.[11]

Power and Hewetson had worked quickly to secure their lands. The government in Mexico City had received the report of Mier y Terán and the Boundary Commission and was planning to end Anglo-American colonization. Even the English-speaking Irish were suspect.

The first land commissioner appointed in 1830 for the Power and Hewetson grant was Juan Guajardo, whose sister would later marry empresario James Hewetson. When Guajardo did not respect the requests of the La Bahía settlers for mission lands in issuing titles, Carlos and the local Tejano ranchers complained to Saltillo again. The state government replaced Guajardo with Land Commissioner Manuel del Moral, who arrived in Goliad several months later. He too failed to give lands to the Tejanos, and within a year, del Moral resigned under pressure. The *ayuntamiento* of Goliad also objected to the third land commissioner, Santiago Vidaurri, but they had little choice. It was not until Power realized that he could not meet his contract of four hundred families with Catholic Irish settlers that he relented and accepted the petitions of the Tejanos.[12]

In 1833 and 1834 James Power finally asked Land Commissioner Vidaurri to grant titles to the local Mexicans on the mission lands east of the San Antonio River. Vidaurri provided deeds and titles to more than fifty local Mexican families. Among them were the Aldrete, Carbajal, Castillo, Galán, González, Serna, Menchaca, de los Santos, Valdéz, Moya, and Carlos and Julián de la Garza families. After their long wait, Carlos and Tomasita established Carlos Rancho nine miles south of La Bahía on the San Antonio River.[13]

CAMERON

WAVELL

Red River

FILISOLA

TEXAS ASSOCIATION
– NASHVILLE CO.
to
AUSTIN & WILLIAMS

Colorado

Llano River

ROBERTSON COLONY

Guadalupe

San Marcos

San Antonio

Gonzales

DE WITT
to
de LEÓN

McMULLEN

McGLOIN

San Antonio River

Nueces River

San Patricio

Refugio

POWER & HEWETSON

Goliad

Victoria

BURNET

Trinity

Navasota

Brazos

San Jacinto

Neches

Angelina

Sabine River

Nacogdoches

GALVESTON BAY &

ZAVALA

TEXAS LAND CO

VEHLEIN

Liberty

Bastrop

Colorado

AUSTIN'S

San Felipe

COLONIES

La Vaca

Brazos

GULF

OF

MEXICO

Río Grande (Río Bravo del Norte)

N

SECOND EMPRESARIO
CONTRACTS 1828 – 1835

Empresario	Land Grant	Land Lost
FILISOLA, CAMERON	1828	1830
D. BURNET	1829	
J. VEHLEIN	1829	to GB & TL Co.
L. ZAVALA	1829	
GALV.BAY & TX LAND CO	1830	1835
TEXAS ASSOCIATION	1826	to Austin & Wms.
ROBERTSON COLONY	1834	1835
POWER & HEWETSON	1829	1835
McMULLEN & McGLOIN	1832	1835
DE WITT	1832	to de León

Map 4.1

The Irish soon learned to appreciate the culture of their new Tejano neighbors. The Irish were amazed to learn of the Spanish laws regarding marriage and the rights of women and children under the Hispanic legal tradition. The prevailing Irish and Anglo-American customs they had left behind gave women few rights. After marriage, a woman's possessions belonged to her husband, and both her earnings and the proceeds from any lands to which she might have once held title also went into his pocket. Her only protection upon his death was to receive one-third of the lands while the remainder was divided among the children. Under Spanish law, on the other hand, a wife had the right to retain her dowry, to share equally in her husband's earnings, to keep property in her own name, set aside profit from the sale or produce from her own land or cattle, and, in the end, when her husband passed away, to reclaim her dowry before the land or goods were divided among the children. Within the home, the Tejana woman's word was law. The Irish settlers who lived so closely with the Spanish and *law* saw the benefits of the system were influential in later inserting these laws into the Anglo-American Texas legal codes.[14]

The Tejana women like Tomasita, Doña Patricia, Candelaria, and Chucha, made their own decisions and played an important role in family matters. Women may have remained subservient to their husbands, but they were never subservient to their sons or nephews or grandsons. Spanish and Mexican cultures gave their women the right to demand respect, obedience, and power within the family. The Tejana women did not see any benefit in what Anglo women called independence and freedom and saw no reason to envy the utter lack of rights which Anglo women suffered. While men faced the outside world, women's duties kept them at home. Their jobs included preparing food, healing illnesses and injuries, teaching religion, and educating the young.[15]

Food for the family, the retainers, the servants, the ranch hands, and any guests or visiting kin was the domain of the women, both daily and on feast days. Tomasita kept her larder stocked with sugar, cornmeal, flour, coffee, salt, beef jerky, raisins, cinnamon, and wine. As soon as she and Carlos had moved to the ranch, she planted fruit trees, tomatoes, squash, potatoes, and melons, in addition to the ever-present corn, beans, and chiles.

The importance of corn and beans in combination had long been noted by the earliest peoples. Without understanding why, the Aztecs and their descendants had found that corn tortillas when eaten with beans provided a healthy diet. Only recently, as scientists have unlocked the mystery of food chemistry, has the answer become evident. In order to support protein synthesis in the body, the body must have a source of complete proteins such as those from milk, eggs, meat, and other animal products which were often unavailable to the poor or to people on the frontier. Together, the beans and corn or rice dishes provided complete proteins for the frontier dwellers.[16]

To celebrate festivities, Tomasita and the women shared the creation of one of the most popular among the holiday foods: the tamale. Tamales were a family affair. More than just a food, the preparation of tamales united the women in the family. The ritual and cooperation of cooking tamales provided women with a powerful network of supporters who not only cooperated in the production of the food but also sustained each other in the face of family or marital problems.

The strength of a marriage was assured by the network of large numbers of female relatives who made it their business to see that the marriage succeeded. When meeting to cook tamales, the women shared their most intimate secrets. The possibility of abuse or excessive authority by the men would be quickly halted when the women, in particular the man's mother, to whom he owed complete obedience, united in support of his wife. Although Tomasita might have left her family behind in Mexico, Carlos' mother, sisters, aunts, and cousins would have brought her into their family circle as they made their tamales. Tejana women still gather during the holidays to continue the time-honored and time-consuming tradition of making the tasty dish.[17]

Recipes for tamales varied from family to family and were passed from mother to daughter. The women ground the corn into soft dough known as *masa* while they cooked a hog's head. They picked the meat off the bones and then mashed the meat up with chiles and spices. The women spread a thick layer of dough into a corn husk, laid the meat in the center of the dough, and wrapped the corn husk around the mixture, folding one end of the husk up to keep the tamale from unwrapping. To cook the dough, they steamed the tamales in a huge cauldron. Together, the women worked in the kitchen, gossiping and laughing, discussing the antics of the children, commiserating over marital problems, and sharing happiness and sorrows while the tamales cooked over the large fires.[18]

Tomasita, like Doña Patricia and most Tejana women, also treated medical problems. Since there were no hospitals, all illnesses had to be dealt with locally. Some women felt a calling to become healers, believing that they had received a *don de Diós*, or gift from God. They might become *parteras*, or midwives, *sobadoras*, or folk chiropractors (the term actually means someone who rubs), or *curanderas,* healers who used medicinal herbs and ritual cures to treat injuries or illnesses. Indefinable illnesses were often attributed to *mal agua,* bad water, or *mal aire,* an evil wind which could be treated with specific herbs and incantations. The "evil eye," or *mal de ojo,* was always a real and present danger which could cause someone to "wither away with unexplainable fever, or other biological or mental disorders which, if gone untreated, could result in death."[19] The women learned their trade by apprenticeship to older women healers and passed their traditions on to subsequent generations. The herbs and potions needed by these women are still available and the skills still present among the Tejano families of Victoria and Goliad.[20]

Religion was also an integral part of Tomasita's duties. Most ranches had chapels where the visiting mission priest could say mass during family celebrations. During the early days at Carlos Rancho, Tomasita made do with a small altar in the main *sala,* where a crucifix was prominently displayed with statues of saints and angels for whom the women sewed elegant vestments and beautiful satin and lace clothes for festivities. Within two years Carlos built a chapel which served not only his own ranch but the Irish Catholic community around him. Bishop Odin, the representative of the Catholic Church in Texas, included Carlos Rancho and its loyal Catholic residents on his visits through the area. By Catholic tradition, the children often received the name of a family patron saint as well as the Holy Family. Most boys, therefore, were named for Joseph, or José, while girls' parents included María, or Mary, in their names. Throughout the year, Tomasita and the other ranch women often taught the children to read and write by using the Catholic catechism. Father Timon, a French priest and the first of the representatives of the Catholic Church to revisit Texas after the Revolution, commented:

> The ... Mexicans were willing to die for their religion, yet they hardly knew what their religion was. How could they know? Their Faith seemed rather a divine instinct that grew from their Baptism than a faith of knowledge.[21]

What he failed to realize was the tremendous effort which women such as Doña Patricia and Tomasita and the *abuelitas,* the black-gowned grandmothers, had expended over the years to teach the catechism. The simple questions and answers were repeated endlessly by the children until the concepts became a part of their very being. Tomasita and the women on the distant ranches were often without benefit of priests for months at a time. Even though there was no one to say mass, hear confession, baptize or marry the faithful, or give final rites to the dying, the religion was never lost. The lessons which Doña Patricia had learned in Soto la Marina as a child or which women such as Tomasita brought with them from Mexico were profitably repeated, training anew generation after generation of Catholics.[22]

Education was also an important woman's duty. Although the *ayuntamiento* of San Antonio and the Coahuila y Texas state government passed laws early in the 1800s requiring the establishment of public schools at San Antonio and La Bahía, the ranches were far removed from town. While Doña Patricia had established a small school in Victoria, Tomasita and her neighbors, including the Aldretes, hired tutors and educated their children at home on the ranches. Sometimes the children of the ranch hands and the servants also attended. Few among the poor saw any need for an education when the *patrón*, or the ranch owner, was available to handle any reading or legal affairs that might come up. Tomasita and Carlos de la Garza felt so strongly about education that within ten years Carlos Rancho boasted a Catholic boys school for the de la Garza sons as well as for all the neighboring Irish Catholic boys.[23]

The Irish, led by their empresario James Power, gradually adopted elements of Tejano culture. In 1832 Power married Dolores Portilla, the daughter of Felipe Roque de la Portilla, the same explorer and settler who twenty years earlier had visited the de León ranch at the Nueces River on his way to colonize San Marcos de Neve. Power, accompanied by his new bride and her family retainers, chose to build their home, known as The Chimneys for its two massive stone chimneys, on Live Oak Point near the coast and just downriver from his settlement at Refugio. From Dolores he learned to eat Tejano foods, share Tejano traditions, and accept Tejano family customs, in particular after the birth of their two children. When Dolores died, he married her sister, Tomasita, and had five more children, all of them educated in Tejano ways. His Refugio colony became the center of a growing multinational community which included other mixed marriages, such as the merchant and military leader, Philip Dimitt and his Mexican wife, Maria Luisa Laso, whose children also were brought up in Tejano traditions.[24]

From 1828 onward, the population in Texas skyrocketed. A second group of Irish settlers, led by John McMullen and John McGloin, settled on the Nueces River on August 17, 1828. The site they chose for their capital of San Patricio was none other than the Santa Margarita crossing on the Nueces River—Martín de León's abandoned ranch. Like Power

and Hewetson, McMullen and McGloin were also having trouble finding enough residents. Indians raided the small, unprotected settlements,
scaring off prospective settlers. The Irish farmers, plagued by the dry conditions of South Texas, soon gave up farming and took up raising cattle
and horses, a trade which they learned from the Tejanos. McMullen and
McGloin, in an attempt to encourage other colonists from Matamoros to
come settle on the Nueces, held a giant fiesta on Agua Dulce Creek near
San Patricio. The Irish empresarios, unfamiliar with local customs, had to
hire local Tejano ranchers to help with planning and putting on the feast.
Never willing to miss an opportunity to party, many Mexicans arrived
from the ranches at Matamoros and along the Río Bravo for the fandango,
but few stayed beyond the four days of the party. Despite the failure of
McMullen and McGloin's recruiting efforts, the name Banquete (Feast)
is still used today for the site of the party on Agua Dulce Creek.[25]

Farther north on the Guadalupe River, Martín de León's small colony
had grown despite Indian raids, conflicts with neighbors, illegal colonists,
and sixty-three-year-old de León's attitude. Louis Berlandier, the scientist
with the Mier y Terán expedition, had accused de León of being

a capricious man . . . [who] sometimes intrigued unscrupulously to make a family
abandon lands which it had cleared and which that great man coveted, either for
himself or for others.[26]

Evidently not everyone felt that way about Don Martín. Juan N.
Almonte, a government official who visited the colony a few years later,
found the colony of Nuestra Señora de Guadalupe Victoria to be one of
the most prosperous establishments in the Department of Béxar.[27]

At Victoria, thirty-year-old Fernando had begun to learn English, while
Irish settlers John Linn and his brother Edward learned Spanish. Although all governmental affairs were carried on in Spanish, English was
becoming increasingly useful in Victoria. Fernando, widowed and alone,
was busy during the day with land affairs, but in the evenings, when he was
not expected at his parents' home on the square, he and the Linn brothers
had become close friends and relaxed over cards and drinks or attended
horse races during festivals. While the young men laughed and talked,
they learned each other's language. As more Anglo Americans appeared in
Victoria requesting land, Fernando's command of English improved and
became an important and useful tool.[28]

Martín de León's achievements at Victoria were closely tied to the success of the settlement at La Bahía del Espíritu Santo. In 1829 Rafael Man-

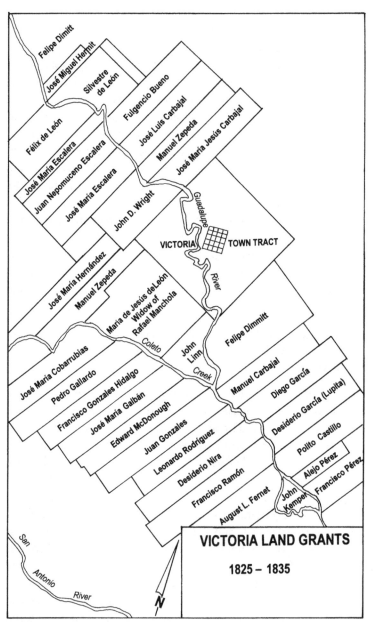

Map 4.2

chola, Don Martín's son-in-law, had petitioned to change the name of La Bahía to Goliad, an anagram to honor Father Miguel Hidalgo, the man who had inspired Mexican independence. Martín and Patricia were frequent visitors at the newly renamed town of Goliad. José Miguel Aldrete and Candelaria, now with four children, had become successful ranchers, as had Rafael Manchola and María de Jesús with their four-year-old daughter, Panchita, thanks to the land titles from Power and Hewetson. During this period, Martín de León had come to depend on his two *badeño* sons-in-law, who helped him handle all his legal affairs.[29]

In March 1829 Martín de León petitioned for the separation of his town from Goliad so that Victoria, too, could have its own town council. The state government at Saltillo rejected the petition since a land commissioner had not yet been sent from Saltillo to grant titles to all of the colonists at Victoria. De León was, however, permitted to have his representative sit on the Goliad *ayuntamiento*. Rafael Manchola sat on the town council of La Bahía as Martín de León's attorney. The Saltillo government had also appointed Fernando de León land commissioner for Victoria to grant titles to all the settlers of the Victoria colony.[30]

By 1830, while McMullen and McGloin were attempting to bring in enough Irish settlers to fulfill their contract, conditions in Mexico City had worsened. The new president, Vicente Guerrero, had been overthrown by his centralist vice president, Anastasio Bustamante. With the help of staunch conservatives, Bustamante and the centralist government worked to weaken the states and increase the power of the central government. When Bustamante received Manuel de Mier y Terán's final report on conditions in Texas, everyone's worst fears were confirmed. The Irish Catholics, although relatively loyal to Mexico, were too few in number. Austin's colonists, no longer among the majority of the Anglo Americans, remained loyal out of fear of losing their lands. It was the new Anglo-American immigrants who were causing problems by not settling in empresario grants or requesting land titles. At the recommendation of Mier y Terán, Bustamante's conservative government determined to halt the disloyal and often illegal immigrants. The Mexican congress passed the Law of April 6, 1830. Among its provisions the law called for colonization of Texas by German and Swiss immigrants, the prohibition of settlement in the area ten leagues from the coastline, the construction of forts and customs houses around the existing settlements, and the opening of coastal trade with Mexico, although not with the United States.

Of greatest importance to Carlos de la Garza and the other Tejanos, the new law prohibited any more slavery in Texas, closed the borders to all Anglo Americans, and canceled the contracts of any empresarios who had failed to bring in the number of colonists stated in their agreements. Only the contracts of Austin, de León, and Green De Witt remained in force. Even the Irish Catholics lost their contracts. McMullen and McGloin had brought only eighty families and even some of those settlers deserted the small colony on the Nueces for the relative security of Power and Hewetson's Refugio settlement. Although Power and Hewetson had brought in more than one hundred settlers, the Irishmen had failed to complete the promised four hundred families. The Law of April 6, 1830, destroyed all of their hopes.[31]

For Martín de León at Victoria, the new law had its benefits. The seven forts called for by the law would finally ease some of the problems Don Martín had been having with illegal immigrants. According to Mier y Terán, the forts were to encircle Texas. Two forts, at Port Lavaca and on the Nueces at Lipantitlán, would control trade from Mexico and along the coast. Another at Tenoxtitlán protected Austin's settlement on the Brazos from the Comanche and Norteño Indians. The remaining four were placed along the eastern rim of the colonies, one at Velasco on the mouth of the Brazos, one at Anahuac on Galveston Bay, one at Terán on the Neches River, and the last one at Nacogdoches. Both Mier y Terán and Don Martín hoped the forts would stop Anglo-American squatters while protecting the colonies from Comanche and Norteño raids. They would also serve to collect taxes and stop contraband, in particular tobacco. Don Martín was most grateful when the government also increased the contingents of soldiers at San Antonio, Goliad, and Nacogdoches.[32]

The forts, however, rather than serving their purpose in controlling immigrants, became sites of conflict between increasingly restive Anglo Americans and the overly officious Mexican government agents. Juan Davis Bradburn, a Kentuckian who had adopted Mexican citizenship, took charge of the fort at Anahuac. He had spent the previous twenty years fighting for Mexican liberalism and independence throughout Mexico and knew the Texas area intimately. He had been a part of the Gutiérrez-Magee expedition into Texas, had joined Mina in his attack at Soto la Marina, and aided Vicente Guerrero in his bid for the Mexican presidency. Bradburn was a liberal at heart, but like Mier y Terán, he was perfectly willing to shift his allegiances to the centralists then in power in order to secure a paid position. He accepted the post of commandant of the new fort at Anahuac and the onerous task of enforcing the Law of April 6, 1830. It was also his duty to help Mier y Terán bring law and order to the illegal, crazy-quilt settlements in the Atascosito district. The settlements lay to the east of Austin's colony and within the coastal reserve, those lands ten leagues from the coast where settlement was prohibited. These reserved leagues had been closed to settlement by the national government to prevent contraband and to protect the country from possible invasions, but the Anglo settlers neither knew nor cared about government policy. In October 1830 Bradburn arrived in Galveston Bay to establish the fort at Anahuac.[33]

The newly arrived commandant, appointed by the national government, immediately quarreled with the Coahuila y Texas state leaders over land titles for the colonists. Illegal settlers had continued to pour into the Atascosito district, although the borders had been closed to new immigrants in 1830 by the Law of April 6. Bradburn feared that a land commissioner might grant titles to many who had no right to the land. On the state level, the government officials of Coahuila and Texas wanted more settlers. The state had remained liberal and federalist under José María Viesca and his brother, Agustín Viesca, both of whom supported Anglo immigration. In 1830 the Viesca brothers had sent a land commissioner to Nacogdoches, but the commissioner had been jailed by Bradburn and no titles had been issued. In January 1831 the Viescas tried again. They appointed José Francisco Madero to provide titles to landholders who lived outside the boundaries of the empresario contracts, in particular those in the Atascosito district. Passing through San Antonio on his way to the Anglo settlements, Madero hired a young, English-speaking *bexareño*, José María Jesús Carbajal, as his surveyor.[34]

José María Jesús Carbajal was perfectly suited for the job. He had been born in San Antonio in 1809, one of eleven children descended from a line of San Antonio soldiers. In 1821 his widowed mother, perhaps suffering from a lack of funds, accepted the offer of Stephen F. Austin and Ben Milam to send her precocious eleven-year-old son to the United States for an education. José María accompanied Littleberry Hawkins to New Orleans and then up the Mississippi to Frankfort, Kentucky. While in Frankfort, young Carbajal became a member of the fundamentalist church of Alexander Campbell, whom he later followed to Lexington, Kentucky, and then to Bethany, Virginia. He picked up an education as best he could, between apprenticeships in a tannery and a saddle shop. By 1830 José María returned to San Antonio, where he received training as a surveyor and be-

Stick Stock by Theodore Gentilz depicts the difficulties of surveying lands in Texas during the nineteenth century. Courtesy of Mr. and Mrs. Larry Sheerin, San Antonio.

came involved in the local politics. Carbajal possessed a number of valuable qualifications for surveyor — he was well educated, understood surveying, and could speak English.[35]

José Francisco Madero and Carbajal arrived on the Trinity River in January 1831. For unknown reasons they did not pay the requisite courtesy call on Commandant Bradburn at Anahuac. Madero began at once to issue titles to the residents of the Atascosito district. Furious over Madero's flagrant disregard for protocol and angered that Madero had begun making out land grants, Bradburn ordered the arrest of the land commissioner and his surveyor. The men were jailed at the new fort at Anahuac. Both Bradburn, from the fort, and Madero, from his jail cell, appealed to their superiors. After a flurry of letters, Bradburn, much to his disappointment and chagrin, received orders to free his prisoners.[36]

As soon as they were released, Madero and Carbajal hurried to grant titles before further orders arrived. During March, April, and May 1831 they provided deeds for sixty tracts, all within the reserved leagues, as well as several other grants of land for Mexican land speculators. In addition, Madero established a popularly elected *ayuntamiento* for the residents of the Atascosito area. He formally named their community on the Trinity the Villa de la Santísima Trinidad de la Libertad (Town of the Sainted Trinity of Liberty), later shortened to Liberty by the residents. Bradburn considered this a flagrant violation of the law, but there was little he could do about the *fait accompli*.[37]

In Victoria, Martín de León benefited from the Law of April 6, 1830. De Witt's constant stream of problems at Gonzales had cost him colonists who feared Indian raids and a loss of land. By the end of De Witt's six-year contract in 1831, the often-inebriated empresario had failed to settle his agreed-upon four hundred families. The following year the Viesca government in Saltillo transferred De Witt's contract to Don Martín de León. The Mexican empresario took over control of the colony, its settlers, and the town of Gonzales. In addition, through his attorney and son-in-law Rafael Manchola, de León requested a strip of land to the north of the La Bahía–Nacogdoches road, extending from the La Vaca River to Coleto Creek, as well as the area from the Guadalupe River west to Coleto Creek, and finally the ten coastal border leagues between the Guadalupe and the La Vaca south to the coast. In spite of their previous problems, he hired the trustworthy James Kerr as surveyor for both colonies.[38]

Almost immediately the contract came under fire from de León's neighbors. The northern strip infringed on Green De Witt's settlers. When de León attempted to remove twenty-five settlers from the area of the new contract, they appealed to the Saltillo government, and de León was ordered to leave them in possession of their lands. To the southwest, the original lands of the La Bahía mission had extended to the Guadalupe River, including Coleto Creek. Power and Hewetson had received first right to the area from the Coleto to the Guadalupe River. After a bitter four-year court battle, the Irish empresarios won title to the land along the Coleto. The land to the southeast, toward the coast, however, remained in the hands of the aging but still active Martín de León.[39]

Among the new settlers in the de León colony during 1832 were two young men who were to have a tremendous impact on the de León family. The first, Plácido Benavides, had come to Texas a few years earlier with his three brothers. The four men had requested land grants from Don Martín de León and had become settlers in the colony. The second was

Early *vaqueros,* similar to those who would have worked on the de León ranches handling cattle on the open ranges of South Texas. Courtesy of Local History Collection, Victoria College.

the surveyor José María Jesús Carbajal. These two men, like Aldrete and Manchola, became indispensable to the elderly empresario.[40]

Plácido Benavides arrived in 1828 at the de León colony from Reynosa, Tamaulipas. He and his married brothers—Ysidro, Nicolás, and Eugenio—had requested and received their portions of land south of the town of Victoria toward the coast. Plácido, who was twenty-two and still single, remained in town. He began construction of what would later be called Plácido's Round House. The building was in fact a Spanish-style *torreón,* the circular, towerlike, defensive turret, with *troneras* or gun slits on the lower floors, a style which the Spanish had learned from the Moors and had used for decades on the frontier for defense against the Indians. His round house served the community as a bastion against Indian attacks on many occasions over the years. Plácido, a sagacious and intelligent tactician, led the colony's militia against the Coco and Karankawa tribes.

Since Plácido could read and write, Martín de León hired him to carry on the correspondence and handle the paperwork of the colony. Plácido also became the colony's teacher. As the youngsters trooped through his classroom, he caught the eye of fourteen-year-old Agustina de León, who may well have been one of his students. Doña Patricia was pleased with the possible match and encouraged the romance.[41]

José María Jesús Carbajal, meanwhile, had returned to San Antonio from Liberty in 1831. In the summer of 1832 a smallpox epidemic ravaged the city of San Antonio while leaving the neighboring towns untouched. Carbajal gathered several members of his family, including his mother, and joined other San Antonio residents as they fled to Victoria. Martín de León, always seeking colonists, was happy to accept the new arrivals. In particular, he was glad to have the services of the young English-speaking surveyor. After granting land to several members of the Carbajal family, the empresario hired Carbajal to join James Kerr as a surveyor. It was not long before Carbajal, then twenty-three, was introduced to Don Martín's twenty-year-old daughter, Refugia.[42]

The bright, energetic José María Jesús proposed within the year. The only problem was his religion. Doña Patricia, a staunch Catholic, disapproved of her daughter marrying a Protestant. Patricia was also concerned at his frequent absences from home. His work as a surveyor required trips throughout Texas, and as a politician, he was popular in the many Anglo-American communities, especially in Liberty, where he had been so instrumental in establishing their titles. But José María won over his future mother-in-law. The courtship was accepted by Don Martín and Doña Patricia and proceeded rapidly, interrupted only by José María's trips to and from Liberty, Nacogdoches, and San Felipe. Doña Patricia came to believe so strongly in him that she later invested thousands of dollars in his attempts to create a republic on the Río Bravo.[43]

The match between Plácido Benavides and Agustina was more to Doña Patricia's liking. Plácido was hardworking, determined to succeed, and, above all, Catholic. He had also become indispensable to Don Martín, for whom he served as *alcalde*. He worked with his brothers-in-law Fernando and José María Jesús Carbajal, and the three young men became a tight-knit group, sharing ideas and discussing the politics of the period. By 1832 the romance between Plácido and Agustina, now eighteen, had become serious. Doña Patricia, already involved in the wedding plans for Refugia and Carbajal, added Agustina to the arrangements. The women of the de León family spent the year sewing beautiful trousseaus for the two sisters. With their parents' blessings, in late 1832 Refugia married José María Jesús Carbajal and Agustina married Plácido Benavides. Only Francisca was left at home to care for her parents.[44]

Political problems in Austin's colonies spread to Victoria, and having Carbajal in the family created the beginnings of a rift among the de León brothers. Politics had become the dominant topic of conversation during 1832 and 1833. During feast days, the sixty-seven-year-old patriarch and his nine sons and sons-in-laws sat at the long wooden table in the *sala* of the family home on the Victoria town plaza. They debated national politics and the most recent problems at the new settlements. Carbajal had become closely involved with the Anglo-American community. In May 1831 he was elected to an Anglo-American caucus to petition the Mexican government for redress from Bradburn's excesses. By November he was appointed to the civil government of San Felipe, Austin's capital, and in 1832 he served on the Nacogdoches town council. He also worked with the settlers at Liberty to set up their town council. He continued as the only bilingual surveyor, making contacts with both Tejanos and Anglo Americans all over Texas.[45]

Following the problems at Anahuac with Bradburn, General Mier y Terán had appointed George Fisher, another Mexicanized American, as customs collector at Galveston and had ordered Fisher to require all captains before sailing to have their ships' papers approved by Commandant Bradburn at Anahuac. The requirements, which the Anglo Americans vehemently and violently opposed, had led to several shooting incidents. When word reached Victoria of the problems, Carbajal supported the views of the Anglo settlers. Only Plácido and Fernando joined him.[46]

By 1832 Doña Patricia's family at Soto la Marina reported that the disorder and civil war from the interior of Mexico had reached the northern coast. President Bustamante had failed to resolve the country's problems, and the opposition liberals had called on Santa Anna to intervene. At Matamoros battles between Bustamante's centralist forces, led by General Mier y Terán, and Santa Anna's liberal forces under Colonel José Antonio Mejía had erupted. Doña Patricia worried when she heard that General Mier y Terán had established his headquarters outside Soto la Marina. Mier y Terán battled valiantly to save the conservative government. Facing imminent defeat and believing that Texas would be lost to Mexico when the new liberal government opened the borders to the Anglo Americans, Mier y Terán wrote to his friends:

> How could we expect to hold Texas when we do not even agree among ourselves? It is a gloomy state of affairs. If we could work together, we would advance. As it is, we are lost ... Texas is lost ... What will become of Texas? Whatever God wills.[47]

Mier y Terán, certain of defeat, abandoned the field of battle. Depressed at the thought of losing Texas and overcome by the failure of the Mexican government to establish a workable solution to the political conflict, the general gave up all hope. The following morning, he walked to the same spot just outside Soto la Marina where Agustín de Iturbide, Mexico's first leader, had been shot. Grim and determined to die with honor as Iturbide had, General Manuel de Mier y Terán took his dress sword, braced its handle against the stone wall and drove it through his heart.[48]

Mier y Terán's death and the eroding support for Bustamante and the centralists in Mexico City was good news for Carbajal. The successes of Santa Anna and the federalists in the field had also helped resolve the problems between the Anglo Americans and Bradburn. With Carbajal's help, the Turtle Bayou Resolutions had been recast to reflect support for Santa Anna and the federalists. Bradburn was removed, and the resolutions were presented to the new federalist commander, Colonel José Antonio Mejía, who had arrived to retake Texas from potential rebels. Carbajal continued his support of the federalist cause and of his friends at Liberty.[49]

Two months later, in August 1832, Don Martín was shocked to receive an invitation to a convention from Austin's colonists who planned to "define their position and redress their grievances."[50] Rafael Manchola at Goliad had also received word of the meeting. When the family gathered in Victoria there was considerable disagreement over whether the two communities should send representatives to San Felipe de Austin. Don Martín basically agreed with the complaints expressed in the invitation, but he disapproved of the Anglo method of town meetings. Like the Turtle Bayou assembly, the convention was illegal. By Spanish and now Mexican law and tradition, grievances were to be brought by individuals before a duly elected and legally constituted local government, which would then forward the complaints through the proper chain of command to San Antonio, Saltillo, and at last to Mexico City.[51]

Don Martín, without doubt fulminating at the scandalous actions of the Anglos, found that his family members had divided in their views. During the heated debates in the grand *sala* of the de León town house, Fernando and Silvestre sided with the pro-Anglo Carbajal, while Félix and Agápito vehemently opposed getting involved in the Anglo actions. Plácido Benavides was a strong supporter of Carbajal, while José Miguel Aldrete and Desiderio García appear to have done so with considerable hesitation. Rafael Manchola still opposed the activities of the Anglos, but when Don Martín at last agreed that Victoria and Goliad should send representatives, two of his sons-in-law agreed to attend. José María Jesús Carbajal, representing Victoria, and Rafael Manchola, attorney for Goliad, set out for San Felipe several days late to join the other fifty-six delegates. Austin was pleased with the arrival of the two Tejanos, for he felt safer with the Tejano communities supporting the reform movement.[52]

By the time Carbajal and Manchola arrived at San Felipe, the complaints of the settlers had been laid out. Among the reforms which the convention respectfully requested were "liberal tariff privileges, repeal of the ban on immigration from the United States, and most important, separate statehood."[53] Manchola, with Carbajal's help, wrote an even stronger set of demands than those already made by the convention. The Anglos voted to send William H. Wharton to Mexico City with the resolution, bypassing both San Antonio and Saltillo. Manchola and Carbajal, aware of the impropriety of such an action, brought their version back to Victoria and Goliad, where the two towns subsequently approved the Manchola resolution, and sent them on to San Antonio for endorsement. Carlos de la Garza, on his ranch down the San Antonio River, judiciously remained out of the politics, although he vehemently disagreed with the Manchola resolution.[54]

Ramón Músquiz at San Antonio, like Don Martín, agreed with the complaints of the delegates to the San Felipe convention, but he could not countenance their actions. Músquiz annulled the convention and ordered Wharton to abandon his trip. By November 1832, however, the San Antonio *ayuntamiento* had written up its own list of grievances, based in part on Manchola's resolution and the ideas of the Anglo colonists. These included demands for help in solving the problems of

> renewed hostilities by Comanches; inadequate support for government troops and militia; colonization laws that failed to take local needs into account; deleterious effects of article eleven of the notorious law of April 6, 1830; . . . an inadequate judicial system, and the lack of trained judges; poor schools and teachers; and military intervention in civilian affairs.[55]

Ramón Músquiz apologized to the governor for such effrontery, then sent the requests on to Saltillo in December 1832. Four days later, in Mexico City, Bustamante and the centralists gave up control of the government, and Santa Anna and his federalist liberals entered the national capital. At Victoria, Carbajal assured his family that as soon as Santa Anna was elected, the problems of the Tejanos would be resolved.[56]

Carbajal was only partially right. By March 1833 all nineteen state legislatures had voted unanimously to elect Santa Anna to the presidency. The problems of Texas, however, were tabled as Santa Anna turned over the day-to-day operations of government to his liberal vice president, Valentín Gómez Farías, who focused his attacks on the conservative and centralist clergy and military in Mexico City. For six months, Gómez Farías attempted to restrict the military and strip the clergy of its wealth. The centralists, in particular the clergy, feared losing church lands and their power and prestige. They turned to the one man whom everyone believed could be their savior, Santa Anna, who had gone into seclusion at his magnificent estate at Manga de Clavo near Veracruz. From April until December 1833, the centralists pressured Santa Anna to turn against the liberals and come to their aid.[57]

By April 1833 Carbajal's Anglo friends in Texas were once again stirring up problems. Despite the warnings from Ramón Músquiz against holding any more extralegal meetings, Austin's increasingly radicalized settlers called for another convention in April 1833. This time Martín de León refused to let either Victoria or Goliad participate. Both Carbajal and Manchola agreed that their demands had been expressed to the proper authorities and that Músquiz had forwarded their complaints to Saltillo and Mexico City. There was no need for another convention and even less for the proposed constitution which the delegates planned to write. The Mexican national government, in its own good time, would eventually repeal the Law of April 6, 1830. Only the application for Texas statehood and its separation from Coahuila had merit, and that request had already been made. Carbajal and Manchola did not attend. Austin, meanwhile, had been bypassed by his own people when they chose William H. Wharton to lead the two-week convention. Without the support of Tejanos Carbajal and Manchola, Austin was desperate to regain the good will of his settlers. Austin agreed to take the resolution, the new constitution, and the application for statehood to Santa Anna in Mexico City.[58]

Stephen F. Austin, arriving in Mexico City from Texas in July 1833, appealed to Gómez Farías for the repeal of the Law of April 6, 1830, and the separation of Texas from Coahuila. His best hope for redress lay with Gómez Farías and the federalists who supported most of the demands of the resolutions from Texas, in particular renewed Anglo immigration. Austin spent the summer lobbying for the changes, and by October 1833, the federalist Congress had repealed the Law of April 6 and sent it to Gómez Farías for his signature.

Days later, Santa Anna returned from Manga de Clavo to reassume the presidency, this time as a centralist. He immediately began to dismantle his own vice president's federalist attacks on the clergy. Austin met with Santa Anna and received a positive answer to the majority of his requests, but he was still unable to convince His Excellency that Texas and Coahuila should be separated. The Coahuila representatives refused to surrender control over the sale of Texas lands.

During this time, Austin made a dangerous political error. He sent a letter to the *ayuntamiento* of San Antonio suggesting that Texas would have to be detached from Coahuila by force, "even though the general government withholds its consent."[59] Austin's seditious comments, although he did not realize it as he started for Texas in December 1833, would lead to his arrest.[60]

While Don Martín and his sons and sons-in-law debated politics, Doña Patricia and the women discussed family matters. The women agreed it was a shame that Fernando seemed to be growing more attached to José María Jesús Carbajal and his Protestant leanings. What he needed, Patricia was certain, was a good Catholic wife who could bring him back to the fold. As Patricia and her daughters reviewed thirty-four-year-old Fernando's marriage prospects in Victoria and surrounding towns, there did not seem to be any likely candidates with whom Fernando felt compatible. The women shook their heads. Otherwise the family was growing and prospering, though, and Doña Patricia could not have been more pleased.

Candelaria Aldrete, the eldest daughter, had succeeded beyond anyone's expectations. Her husband, José Miguel, had acquired thousands of acres in payment for his duties as a government official at Goliad. The couple had more than enough money to hire a tutor out on the ranch for their four boys — José María, José de Jesús, Trinidad, and Rafael — who ranged in age from twelve to six. At the ranches upriver on the Guadalupe, Doña Patricia, as a proud grandmother, was concerned with finding godparents for new grandchildren. Rosalía de la Garza, Silvestre's wife of four years and mother of two-year-old Francisco, had just given birth to their second child, Martín. Salomé Leal, Félix's young wife, with two boys, three-year-old Santiago and two-year-old Patricio, was pregnant again, and newly-wed Refugia Carbajal awaited her first child. The godparents chosen for all the grandchildren would be critical to building networks in the rapidly growing community. The family remained concerned over María Guadalupe and Desiderio Garcia's failure to have any children despite all of Doña Patricia's prayers and the many candles she had lit for them. Agápito and María Antonio, young though they were, only had little León. Still and all, life was very good for Doña Patricia and her family as the women laughed and talked in the kitchen of the big house.[61]

During the summer of 1833 cholera swept through Texas from New Orleans. In June, Don Martín learned of the epidemic. He ordered Doña Patricia and as many of the family as possible to move out to the ranches. The disease had started in Europe the previous year and spread to the East Coast of the United States and then to the port of New Orleans. From there, James Power's Irish colonists contracted the disease. Seventy of his settlers died in New Orleans before leaving port, and the remainder sailed for Texas, carrying the infection with them to Brazoria, Refugio, and Matagorda. Dozens more died upon arrival in Texas. The Anglo-American colonies at San Felipe de Austin and Matagorda were especially hard hit, while some cases were reported at San Antonio, Victoria, and Goliad. As the horrifying disease spread, the remainder of Don Martín's settlers scattered to their outlying farms and ranches, hoping to avoid infection.[62]

At Victoria, Martín de León and his sanitation committee followed the lead of San Antonio and Goliad in cleaning up the stagnant water and the filth in the streets. Although no one at the time understood how the disease spread, they had intuitively chosen the best path to avoid contamination. The bacteria, which was carried in fecal matter and propagated in water supplies, had spread quickly. Don Martín and his family could not avoid the horrible illness. At Victoria in July 1833, twenty-five-year-old Agápito and thirty-three-year-old Rafael Manchola succumbed to cholera. The de León family was devastated. As the epidemic slowly passed, Doña Patricia brought her family back together. At Doña Patricia's insistence, Agápito's widow, María Antonia de la Garza, with seven-year-old León de León to raise, moved into the house in Victoria. Chucha or María de Jesús Manchola, now the widow Manchola, also moved in with Doña Patricia, bringing her seven-year-old daughter, Panchita. Doña Patricia particularly enjoyed the company of the two women who had been added to the household, and the two young cousins, Panchita and León, had lightened the mood of the house on the plaza.[63]

The following year, in June 1834, cholera reappeared, striking first at Goliad, perhaps again introduced by the incoming Irish settlers. Don Martín had stayed in town to supervise the sanitation committees, but cleanliness was not enough. Twenty-three people died in Goliad during the first week of June, and the San Antonio councilmen quarantined Goliad to prevent the spread of the disease. The San Antonio political chief warned the town councils of Gonzales, Liberty, San Felipe, Mata-gorda, and Nacogdoches about the dangers and authorized them to use government funds to hire doctors, clean up their towns, and care for the indigent. At Goliad, three of the four members of the town council died, and the San Antonio political chief authorized the appointment of coun-cil members from previous years. Ninety-one of Goliad's less than one thousand residents died. Even on the ranches, no one was safe. Carlos de la Garza's young son died along with a half-dozen residents and ranch hands. At Victoria, Don Martín, dedicated to the care of his people and perhaps already weakened by his efforts in their behalf, was stricken with the cholera in July 1834.[64]

Doña Patricia, hurriedly called back to town from the ranch, arrived to find seventy-year-old Don Martín near death. Severe cholera-induced diarrhea had dehydrated him. Through it all, Don Martín could still speak, murmuring in pain from his sick bed. Patricia and her *curanderas* struggled to help him drink *manzanilla* (chamomile) tea and other potions. Their efforts were fruitless. The constant vomiting continued to deplete his fluids. Don Martín's frail body cramped and twisted painfully. Patricia was helpless to stop the progress of the disease or ease his pain. There was not even a priest to provide the comforts of a confession or the blessings of the last rites. Patricia, Francisca, and the few remaining servants knelt around the bed to pray in the darkened room. On July 18, 1834, Don Martín de León — founder, empresario, and father — was gone. His colony of Victo-ria passed to a new generation.[65]

CHAPTER 5

TEJANOS AND THE TEXAS REVOLUTION, 1834–1835

Genealogical Chart

MARTÍN DE LEÓN (D. 1834) + PATRICIA DE LA GARZA

1. Fernando (wid. 1825)

2. María Candelaria (m. 1818) + José Miguel Aldrete
   - 2-1. José María (b. 1820)
   - 2-2. José de Jesús María (b. 1822)
   - 2-3. Trinidad (b. 1824)
   - 2-4. Rafael (b. 1826)

3. Silvestre (m. 1824) + Rosalía de la Garza
   - 3-1. Francisco Grande (b. 1825)
   - 3-2. Martín (b. 1830)

4. "Lupita" (m. 1825) + Desiderio Garcia
   - No children

5. Félix (m. 1828) + Salomé Leal
   - 5-1. Santiago (b. 1829)
   - 5-2. Patricio (b. 1830)
   - 5-3. Silvestre (b. 1834)

6. Agápito (d. 1833) + María Antonia C. de la Garza
   - 6-1. León de León (b. 1824)

7. "Chucha" (m. 1824) + Rafael Manchola (d. 1833)
   - 7-1. "Panchita" (b. 1826)

8. Refugia (m. 1832) + José María Jesús Carbajal
   - 8-1. Antonio (b. 1833)
   - 8-2. José María (b. 1834)

9. Agustina (m. 1831) + Plácido Benavides
  9-1. Pilar (b. 1834)
  9-2. Librada (b. 1835)

10. Francisca (b. 1818)

By August 1834 the cholera epidemic had subsided, and life in Victoria had returned to normal. Residents had gradually drifted back to town. The strict cleanup demanded by the late empresario Don Martín de León and the city fathers had relaxed, and pigs and chickens had returned to rooting through the fruit rinds and vegetable peels collecting in the streets between the adobe houses and the wooden *jacales*. Doña Patricia de la Garza de León, dressed in somber black, had begun the painful process of living without her husband of thirty-nine years. She had returned from the ranch to their home on the main square of Victoria. Patricia had ordered the servants to scrub down the giant wooden four-poster bed with the family brand carved into the headboard. The big bedroom had been freshly whitewashed, the dirt floor swept, the carpets beaten, and her clothes aired out and hung back on the pegs in the wooden armoire. Don Martín's clothes had been locked away in trunks and stored in the back rooms.

The days after Don Martín's death had been a blur. His body had been quickly buried along with dozens of others. Because of the cholera, there had been no great funeral, no chance for the people of the town to pay their last respects. As they returned to town, however, Tejanos, Irish, Anglo, French, and Germans had lit candles in the small wooden chapel on the square for their empresario and for the others who had died during the summer. All of Don Martín's abruptness—his anger at the escalating problems with the Anglos, what some had called his tyranny—was forgotten. They spoke only of his concern for the colony, of his goodness to them. When Father Refugio de la Garza had arrived from San Antonio, the family and the colonists had been able to at last join in a requiem mass for Don Martín.

The emptiness of losing Don Martín would remain with the family, but the colony and the busy household demanded attention. Widowhood with its black garb was one of the sad but accepted burdens of old age, but Doña Patricia was determined that her daughter Chucha Manchola and daughter-in-law María Antonia were too young to remain widows. Eighteen-year-old Francisca could not marry while she cared for her mother, but Doña Patricia set out to find appropriate husbands for the other two women. Agápito's widow, Antonia, had chosen to keep her son, León, with Doña Patricia under the protection of the de León family, although she could have returned to her de la Garza kin in Tamaulipas. Chucha, the widow Manchola, was only twenty-two and, even with a seven-year-old daughter, could still find an appropriate match. The two young

Martín de León's four-poster bed, where he is said to have passed away from cholera in 1834. The bed is currently preserved by the O'Connor family in Victoria, Texas. Courtesy of Louise O'Connor, Victoria.

cousins León and Panchita added laughter to the household, and the two young widows lightened the load for both Doña Patricia and Francisca.[1]

For all the deaths, there had been births as well. Refugia and José María Jesús Carbajal's new baby, José María Chico (Junior), joined his brother, one-year-old Antonio. Refugia and the babies often stayed with Doña Patricia while José María made his trips to the Anglo-American colonies. In town, Silvestre had taken over the post of *alcalde*. He and Rosalía had five-year-old Francisco and two-year-old Martín. Out on the Mission Valley Ranch, Félix and Salomé now had four boys, six-year-old Santiago, five-year-old Patricio, three-year-old Samuel, and two-year-old Silvestre.

Of all of Doña Patricia's remaining children, only her eldest, Fernando, had no children and no wife, a problem which Doña Patricia needed to alleviate. Gatherings at Doña Patricia's home on the town square brought together the large family, and the family jointly resolved the problems of the colony.[2]

With the death of Don Martín, the family had to be called together to decide who would carry on the various duties associated with running the family and the colony. Family gatherings meant a great deal of work for the women. Doña Patricia, Francisca, Chucha, Antonia, and perhaps Refugia often began the day with a cup of whipped chocolate and a small sweet bread which they had baked the day before. There was much to do for a big family dinner—fresh produce to buy, food to cook, the house to prepare, new black dresses to complete—but first there were always their religious obligations. After breakfast, Doña Patricia and her daughters and daughters-in-law, dressed in black, stopped at the small chapel across the plaza, dimly lit by dozens of flickering candles for the victims of the epidemic. There they knelt quietly in prayer, murmuring the familiar words, their rosaries slipping smoothly through their fingers as they prayed for the dead and for the living as well.

After their morning devotionals, they walked two blocks to the market square, where other women from town were busily picking through the produce in the booths and stalls. During the summer, with the cholera, it had been impossible to maintain the small garden behind the house in town. It was easier to buy from the mission Indians. Although no longer living at the mission, the Indians made a living from the sale of their produce, grown on the small bits of land they had been granted for farms when the missions were secularized and the reverend fathers left them to fend for themselves in the Spanish world. The women could browse through the bright colors and fragrant aromas of fresh fruits and vegetables spread out in front of the itinerant Indian vendors around the edges of the market square. At the far end of the square, the strong, rich smell of fresh-cut beef and plucked chicken attracted the women. One of the new recipes which Doña Patricia could use was chicken with some of the *mole* sauce which had originated in Puebla, in the interior of Mexico. The unusual recipe called for Indian chocolate mixed with chile peppers and chicken broth to produce a thick, rich, pungent brown sauce in which pieces of chicken were cooked. Accompanying the chicken she could choose rice, beans, and squash, as well as tortillas for the evening meal.[3]

Doña Patricia and her daughters and daughters-in-law would have been

Las Tortilleras (The tortilla makers) by Carl Nebel shows Indian women grinding corn into *masa* and patting the dough into tortillas cooked on the *comal* over a fire. Courtesy of Benson Latin American Collection, University of Texas at Austin.

greeted by everyone as they bartered with the peddlers and exchanged gossip. They were respected by the community. When anyone had problems, they knew they could turn to Doña Patricia, as the empresario's wife, the *patrona*, for help. Even with her husband gone, she still had responsibility for the townspeople and their problems. She often stopped here and there to ask after a sick child, to leave a coin or two, or to discuss family problems. On the way home the women stopped by the small mercantile store on the corner of the market square to see if any goods had been shipped in from New Orleans or if the mule trains had returned from Saltillo.

The latest addition to the town was a small store which sold tortillas. Inside, the women stood in line, smelling the hot, steamy, acrid odor of lime as it boiled and softened the corn in the giant vats. Some of the Indians and mestizas who had moved to town from the mission knelt in the back grinding the corn into the soft, yellow *masa*, on the heavy stone *metates*. Other Indian women behind the counter patted the dough into tortillas and flipped them onto the large, hot, metal *comal*, turning them quickly as they cooked. With their purchases, Doña Patricia and her daughters returned across the plaza.[4]

A few blocks away on Calle de Independencia, workers were busy erecting a new street sign. The main road into town from the coast was to be named The Street of the Ten Friends. With so many changes and so many deaths by 1834, it seemed only right to remember and honor the original founders of Nuestra Señora de Guadalupe de Jesús Victoria, men who had served as *alcaldes* and shared the responsibilities of governing the small community, as well as some of the more recent developers. Among the ten friends listed on the sign were: Don Martín de León; his two eldest sons, Fernando and Silvestre; three of his sons-in-law, Manchola, Carbajal, and Benavides; two of his children's fathers-in-law, Valentín García and Julián de la Garza; and two wealthy newly arrived land investors, Pedro Gallardo and Leonardo Manso. As soon as a priest returned from either San Antonio or San Felipe, there would be a large fiesta to name the street and to celebrate the September 16 *fiestas patrias*, the patriotic feasts of Mexico.[5]

The Independence Day festivities had grown over the years since 1821. At La Bahía the soldiers and wealthier citizens contributed to the parades and performances. Local citizens took the roles of Spaniards and Mexicans during the wars for liberation and fought mock battles. In honor of the Indian heritage of Mexico, twelve of the ladies from town, often Doña Patricia's daughters and daughters-in-law, dressed in their richest silks, laces, and pearls and accompanied a carriage in which an Indian girl sat dressed in an elegant costume of feathers, gold, and silver. The ladies each held the ends of white ribbons attached to the carriage and led the parade through town. The citizens, led by the de León family, ended the parade with great feasts, horse races, and bullfights.[6]

While the women prepared for the evening's festivities, Fernando de León, the eldest son and land commissioner, with Plácido Benavides, the newly appointed colonial administrator, worked in the long, low, government building on the main square. Three weeks earlier Fernando had sent word to San Antonio requesting the appointment of Plácido as the new head of the colony, and the request had just been approved. Fernando would have taken his father's position, but he was already the government land commissioner. In that job, Fernando's duties consisted of surveying, mapping, and granting titles. It would have been a conflict of interest for him to administer the colony as well, so the family had decided that Plácido, who had taken care of most of the paperwork during the previous four years, would serve as *alcalde*. Silvestre agreed to continue as a *regidor*, or judge.[7]

The de León family had much to decide during that fall of 1834. After the feast the family adjourned to the large *sala*. The women joined the men, for much of the discussion centered on their land and their futures as well. The ten grandchildren played outside in the patio, the older ones responsible for their younger siblings and cousins. José María Jesús Carbajal, wealthy in his own right from his surveying work in East Texas, administered the division of Don Martín's assets. Doña Patricia would keep the town house where Chucha, María Antonia, and the grandchildren could remain with her and Francisca. The ranch on the Garcitas was also hers as the replacement for the dowry money which she had given Martín in 1801. Part of the land lay within the boundary of the Department of the Brazos, which was controlled from San Felipe de Austin. It was important to have the state government of Coahuila y Texas transfer the jurisdiction of the ranch from the Department of the Brazos to the Department of Béxar, which remained under the control of San Antonio. If José María Jesús Carbajal was chosen as one of the deputies to the legislature in the spring of 1835, which seemed likely, he would see to the change.[8]

The family considered the possibilities. Doña Patricia had no real need for the big ranch with its large homestead and extensive outbuildings, although it was family land and there was sentimental value in keeping it. Her *vaqueros* lived on the ranch and cared for her cattle and horses, sending in meat and produce whenever it was needed. The de Leóns and their extended family, including the Benavides brothers, Valentín Garcia, and Leonardo Manso, effectively controlled the peninsula along La Vaca Bay and down toward Matagorda Island. They were in a position to ask whatever price they chose for the land. But there was little reason to sell the land and plenty of time to decide. The Anglos were willing to pay good money for land near the coast, and the potential for profits was enormous.[9]

Land had become a source of intense speculation in Texas. José María Jesús Carbajal had surveyed much of the land for the Anglo settlers. With the borders open, speculators from as far away as New York, London, and Paris were interested in acquiring land. During the spring of 1834, the Coahuila y Texas government under Agustín Viesca had moved from Saltillo to the northern town of Monclova at the foot of the mountains. There the legislature had passed laws which allowed the Anglos to purchase land on easy terms. With the approval of Santa Anna, the Viesca

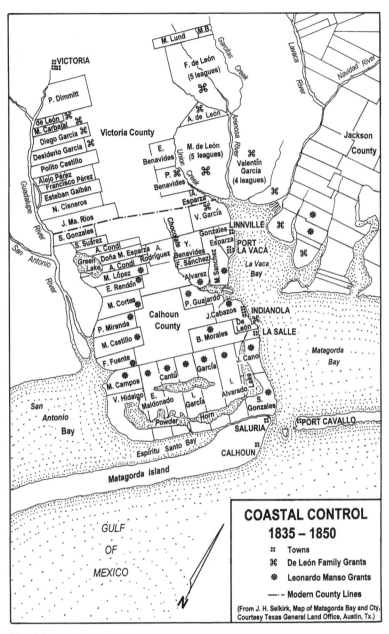

VICTORIA

P. Dimmitt

de León
M. Carbajal
Diego García
Desiderio García
Polito Castillo
Alejo Pérez
Francisco Pérez
Esteban Galbán
N. Cisneros
J. Ma. Ríos
S. Gonzales
S. Suárez
A. Condi
Doña M. Esparza
Green
Lake
A. Condi
M. López
E. Rendón
M. Cortes
P. Miranda
M. Castillo
F. Fuente
M. Campos
V. Hidalgo
E.
Maldonado
Powder

Victoria County

Guadalupe
River

San
Antonio
River

M. Lund   M.B.
F. de León
(5 leagues)

Garcitas Creek

Lavaca River

Navidad River

Jackson
County

A. de León

E.
Benavides
P.
Benavides

M. de León
(5 leagues)

Valentín
García
(4 leagues)

Union Creek

Arenosa River

I.A.
Esparza
V. García
Gonzales   LINNVILLE
Y.   Esparza
Benavides   PORT
F. Sánchez   LA VACA
Alvarez
La Vaca
Bay

A.
Rodríguez

Chocolate

M. Sánchez

P. Guajardo
Calhoun
County

J.Cabazos   INDIANOLA
De
León   LA SALLE
B. Morales

J. Cano

Matagorda
Bay

García

I.
García

L.
Horn

Alvarado Lake

I.
Alvarado
S.
Gonzales

SALURIA

PORT CAVALLO

San
Antonio
Bay

Cantú

Espíritu Santo Bay

CALHOUN

Matagorda Island

GULF

OF

MEXICO

N

COASTAL CONTROL
1835 – 1850

:: Towns
⌘ De León Family Grants
⚙ Leonardo Manso Grants
— · — Modern County Lines

(From J. H. Selkirk, Map of Matagorda Bay and Cty,
Courtesy Texas General Land Office, Austin, Tx.)

Map 5.1

brothers no longer limited the incoming Texans to the league-and-labor grants from the empresario settlements. They sold eleven-league grants, or 56,655 acres, in Texas with no empresario requirements attached. By the decree of April 19, 1834, the governor had been authorized to sell four hundred leagues of land to pay militiamen to suppress the Indian tribes. Carbajal reported that General John T. Mason had purchased three hundred leagues under this law for little more than pennies an acre.[10]

Fernando de León was well aware of the activities of the land speculators. As land commissioner for the Victoria colony, his duties to hand out titles for land continued. As his English improved he received newly arrived colonists, sometimes found places for them to stay in town, and rode with them to survey parcels of land in which they were interested. Nor was he averse to adding land to his own holdings. Although not an empresario like his father, Fernando had claimed his own ranch of five leagues and five labors, also on the La Vaca Bay peninsula. Government officials were often paid in land, and the ranch seemed fair compensation for his efforts as land commissioner, a job which had become increasingly difficult as the number of settlers seeking land had expanded.

Among those to whom he had granted lands was Leonardo Manso, a new arrival in the colony. With Fernando's help, Manso devised an ingenious means of acquiring more than the eleven-league grants without the cost of paying for the land in Saltillo. Manso proposed to bring in fifteen Mexicans from Tamaulipas or Monterrey who could claim to be colonists of the de León colony. Each one could request a league and a labor, land which Fernando granted to them for the cost of the paperwork. Manso could then buy the certificates from all fifteen men and transfer the deeds to his own name.

Within two years Leonardo Manso had carried out his plan. He paid each of the men between $250 or $300 for their land, or approximately five to six cents per acre, then sent them back to Mexico with their profits, and he kept the land. In this way, Manso gained more than fifteen leagues at a cost of a little over $5,000, a considerable investment for the times, but far less than the $21,000 cost of eleven leagues in Monclova. Within four months Manso had acquired more than 66,400 acres in his own name.[11]

As the de León family well knew, one could also profit from an empresario contract which became, in essence, free land for those who held the contract. José María Jesús Carbajal had reported on the efforts of the Galveston Bay and Texas Land Company in East Texas around Nacogdoches. Their contract, as with all empresario grants, defined fixed boundaries, included many rules and restrictions, and required the expense of bringing settlers to Texas. It appeared, from what José María had seen, that the new empresarios were not overly concerned with bringing settlers or fulfilling the niceties of the law. They had illegally sold out to New York investors who created the Galveston Bay and Texas Land Company and began selling scrip to gullible prospective settlers. During the years from 1830 to 1834, while the borders were closed, the company's promises of title were worthless, but sales of scrip continued throughout 1832 and 1833.[12]

By March 1834 the company's Mexico City contact, General José Antonio Mexía, who had accumulated 243,540 acres in his own name, reported that the law banning Anglo-American immigrants had at last been rescinded. The floodgates were opened. General John T. Mason, the Texas representative for the Galveston Bay and Texas Land Company, actually outfitted one thousand families to come to Texas. It was not an empresario colony such as Austin's or Martín de León's. Not all the families received titles to their land, nor did the company establish a town for them or carry out the myriad duties required of an empresario. The Galveston Bay and Texas Land Company did, however, net a considerable profit. After an outlay of a little over $141,200, the company was able to report an income to its stockholders of somewhere between $300,000 and $880,000 on the land sales, depending on the honesty of the person giving the report.[13]

Fernando, Plácido, José María Jesús, and the Victoria colony had felt the impact of the new arrivals. The immigrants were arriving at the rate of almost one thousand a month at Brazoria and Galveston. They had come expecting the promised league and labor, almost five thousand acres of land. The problem for the new arrivals was finding an empresario colony that was granting land. Those who wanted to settle in Austin's colony had found that the best lands were already taken, and they were disgruntled at the high prices which Austin's longtime residents were asking for the smaller pieces. At Victoria, Fernando and Plácido were still welcoming colonists. There were many good pieces of land available north of La Vaca Bay and along the coast. Fernando stayed busy taking settlers down to Matagorda Bay to pick out property. Since José María Jesús Carbajal was surveying in the Anglo colonies, James Kerr was often hired to survey for the Victoria settlers, spending a month or two at a time surveying the leagues and labors at a cost of between $60 and $80.[14]

Surveying in Texas by 1834 had become a highly lucrative profession. For Carbajal, Kerr, and others willing to brave the dangers of attacks by Indians or wild animals, surveying could provide a good living. Many of the settlers had little money and often paid in kind with land, cattle, horses, oxen, or corn. Kerr, Carbajal, and the dozens of other surveyors often had to pay their own crews in kind and use the little cash available to buy the expensive equipment needed to carry out accurate surveys.

Alexander von Humboldt, the German explorer who had come through Mexico in 1803, left a list of his valuable surveying equipment. The items included a time keeper, a demi-chronometer, a telescope, a sextant, a theodolite (with azimuth circle), an artificial horizon, a quadrant radius of one foot, a dipping needle, and a variation compass, in addition to the transit and chain. For the Texas surveyors, without access to Humboldt's funds, the compass, transit, and chain were usually sufficient. The chain itself was made of a series of six-inch-long flat strips of brass, each linked together to form a chain approximately twenty *varas* long. A *vara*, a measurement which originated in Spain, was approximately 33⅓ inches long and had been used to survey lands in Texas since 1731. By the time the Anglos arrived in the 1820s the Anglo-American surveyors converted the approximately one-yard-long *varas* to the English measurements of feet and yards.[15]

Surveying was not easy. Carbajal's surveying crew consisted of approximately a half-dozen men. Two chainmen used the twenty-yard-long brass chain to measure the length of the line. They were aided by several brush clearers who used machetes to cut the thick brambles and underbrush away from the line. Since the chain measured only twenty *varas* at a time, the chainmen could take several days to lay out the length of one side of a league of five thousand *varas*. The labor grant for farming consisted of 177 acres, which measured one thousand square *varas* on a side. The total for a standard league was 25 million square *varas* and extended far inland from the river or the coast. Because of the vast extent of the land, few owners worried about where their land ended, and the newly arrived surveyors, unlike the precise and careful Carbajal, often simply "dropped the line" when they got inland, leaving the survey incomplete and approximating the sides on the hand-drawn title maps.[16]

Carbajal, as the surveyor and leader of the team, was the linchpin of the system. The lead surveyor had to be able to read and write and cipher in order to determine the sizes of the land. He usually owned the compass and transit or telescope which he used to determine the direction of the line. The sides of the survey had to be accurate not only to the degree but down to minutes and seconds as well. Even a small error of a second or two on the compass might mean the line could be off by two hundred yards or more at the far end of the measured line. By looking through the transit and sighting along the compass, Carbajal motioned for his chainmen to move either left or right as they laid out the chain and moved down the line. He kept a notebook in which he recorded the physical features at each of the corners in addition to the distance and direction of each of the lines. Upon his return from a surveying trip, Carbajal used the measured distances, today called metes and bounds, to prepare a legal title, write out the description of the property, and draw out the map of the land with the length and direction of each line. Carbajal, unlike the Anglos who had a difficult time writing out the titles in dictionary Spanish, often included notes on the kind of terrain, suggested crops, and made detailed descriptions of the flora and fauna from his notebooks.[17]

A critical component of Carbajal's surveying crew was the guards. Their duty was to kill game to feed the crews and to protect the surveying team from the Comanches, Tawakonis, Waco, and Taovayas, in whose territory much of the surveying was being carried out. The native tribes were often frightened by the noisy surveying parties, who yelled back and forth, hacked, and chopped their way through the underbrush, fired at game — sometimes killing it — and marked the trees with strange symbols. It did not take the native tribes long to learn that the arrival of the surveyors meant that settlers were not far behind. The Comanche labeled the compass "the Thing that Steals the Land" and did not hesitate to attack, kill, and scalp any surveying party they encountered.[18]

It often required considerable diplomacy to convince the Indians not to attack. Fernando de León, surveying with James Kerr down near the coast, had been attacked by a small group of Karankawa. Turning their cooking pots on their sides to simulate cannons, Fernando convinced the tribe that his men were ready to do battle if they were attacked. After a considerable debate and a combination of threats and bribery, Fernando convinced the Karankawa, with the help of tobacco and food, to move across the bay onto Matagorda Island and leave the surveying team in peace. The Karankawa agreed, and Fernando and James Kerr continued with their survey.[19]

Unlike Carbajal and Kerr, who did their best to get along with the Indian tribes, the Anglos often brought on the attacks themselves. In one case, two peaceful Caddo chiefs — Canoma and Dorcha — had been hired by settlers on the Colorado to find stray horses. As the two chiefs were returning with the horses, a band of whites traveling through the area captured them and assumed they were horse thieves. Although the Caddo explained their mission and showed the gifts they had been given, the whites refused to go to the settlement to verify their story. The two chiefs were tied to a tree and riddled with bullets. Canoma's wife, a witness, reported the murder to the Caddo people, who took their revenge on the settlers along the Colorado and on the surveying parties in particular.[20]

All surveyors marked their surveys to indicate the corners of the property. Carbajal's mark was two horizontal lines above an X and two more horizontal lines below the X. At each corner and on any large trees along the line, one of the brush clearers would hack out the distinctive imprint, leaving it as an indication to other surveyors. Some of the newly arrived Anglos learned from what they saw and adapted to the requirements of the Mexican laws.

By 1834 Carbajal was not only carrying out surveys but also accepting and checking surveys for the 103 Anglo surveyors, many of whom made do with just the chain and a compass and carried out one or two surveys for family or friends. In a list of fourteen surveyors for the Robertson Colony from March to July 1835, eleven had surveyed one league or less. Only three surveyed larger amounts. The pay for a survey, normally $3 per mile, ranged from as low as $12.50 for a 436-acre survey to $28 for 1,903 acres and could go as high as $2,000 for the eleven-league grant. For Carbajal, who frequently made the surveys for the large grants, the profits could be enormous when, and if, he could collect his payment.[21]

As the de León family gathered that fall of 1834, José María Jesús Carbajal had much to report from the Anglo colonies. He had worked closely with Samuel May Williams, the secretary for the Austin colony, and had been involved with the problems between Williams and Sterling C. Robertson, one of the would-be empresarios who claimed land northwest of Austin's colonies. Much of the difficulty, according to Carbajal, stemmed from the absence of Stephen F. Austin, who had left for Mexico City with the requests of the Anglo colonists.

Austin had at first been successful upon his arrival in Mexico City in 1834 with the requests for changes proposed by the consultations among the Anglo colonists in Texas. The state legislature at Saltillo, and Santa Anna on the national level, had approved most of the requests made by Austin as well as those of Manchola and Musquiz, who had sent their petition the previous year. Texas had been divided into three administrative areas — Béxar, Brazos, and Nacogdoches — and Texas had been granted an additional representative in the state parliament of Coahuila y Texas. English was accepted as an official language, and Anglo settlers were permitted to use juries for their trials, something which Fernando found particularly foolish, since most of the incoming Anglo settlers were illiterate farmers with no knowledge of the laws.

The one request which had not been granted, however, was the separation of Coahuila y Texas into two states. Austin, because of his letter suggesting the forceful division, had spent much of 1834 in jail in Mexico City, although he had been removed from the jail and placed under house arrest after the first six months. He might have still been hopeful that Texas would achieve statehood, but Carbajal and his brothers-in-law were not as sanguine about their chances.[22]

Carbajal reported that Austin's enemies were at work. Robertson, in particular, and those who wanted to profit from land speculation which Austin had long opposed, were at work destroying the character and efforts of the beleaguered empresario while he languished in jail in Mexico City. Everywhere he went, Carbajal had heard Austin vilified and slandered. From Juan Almonte, the Mexican inspector who was touring Texas during 1834, Carbajal had learned that Anthony Butler, the United States consul in Mexico City, was one of the most avid in his attacks on Austin. Butler, it seemed, had even been writing letters to the colonists encouraging revolt. Almonte had suggested that Butler's meddling was the result of the machinations of American President Andrew Jackson, who seemed to be determined to gain Texas for the United States.[23]

Of most concern, according to Carbajal, were the changing political views of the Anglo Americans. Although belligerent individualism prevented the settlers from uniting with any one group for long, a new radical faction known as the War Party had formed. Those who tried to unify the different parties soon threw up their hands in disgust, concluding that "the people ... are damned stupid and easily ruled by Demagogues and factions."[24] The militants, however, were staunchly opposed to the Mexican government and advocated force in separating Texas either from Coahuila or from Mexico itself. The members consisted of newly arrived young men, most of them single, who were either slaveholders or Southerners who supported slavery. Unlike Austin's longtime residents, these newcomers felt they had received no benefit from the Mexican government and included, according to Carbajal, one newly arrived resident named Sam Houston, who was said to be in close contact with President Andrew Jackson.

Austin's settlers, in opposition to the outsiders, however, had formed a Peace Party which opposed revolt. It was made up of the older, married colonists who had lived in Texas almost since the inception of the colony.

Most had emigrated from the northern United States, as had Austin, and did not own slaves. Like Austin, they preferred Mexican benign neglect, even with the recent taxes. Carbajal was unsure which of the two groups would prevail, since the Anglo Americans had not been able to agree among themselves.[25]

The de León family was also divided over whether Texas should separate from Coahuila. Carbajal supported the incoming Anglos, since the new arrivals came with cash and an intense interest in buying land which would have to be surveyed. For Fernando, the advantage of being separate from Coahuila meant that San Antonio and, by extension, his Victoria colony would control their own land sales and the attendant profits. The disadvantage, however, would be that the four thousand Tejanos would be quickly outnumbered by the Anglo settlers, who now numbered in the tens of thousands.

National politics were also increasingly disturbing. Juan Almonte quietly discussed the situation of Texas with Carbajal and suggested the possibility that Santa Anna might consider coming to Texas to resolve the problems, much as Arredondo had years before. José María Jesús Carbajal remembered all too well the terrors of 1814. Only five years old at the time, Carbajal had watched in horror as General Arredondo and his Lieutenant Santa Anna had devastated San Antonio. José María still shuddered when he recalled the coarse shouts of the soldiers, the screams of his mother and the other women as they were herded into the dark, cramped barracks where Arredondo decreed that they would feed his men until the rebels had been found and executed. Since the soldiers had appropriated the homes of the citizens, he and the other children had been abandoned in the town to fend for themselves. They had eaten what scraps they could find, slept huddled in corners, and fought to survive. At first they had cried when they heard the shots of an execution, but as the bloodshed continued day after day, the children had grown numb to the horrors. They could hear their mothers crying as the women ground the corn hour after hour in the prison darkness. The women had known, with every shot, that someone's father or brother or son was dying. Now, twenty years later, Carbajal still feared the arrival of troops in Texas and especially of Santa Anna.[26]

As the situation in the center of Mexico worsened in late 1834, Carbajal and Refugia and their children left Victoria for San Antonio. Carbajal was determined to do what he could to stop Santa Anna, and his best chance was in Monclova, where the federalist Viesca brothers still op-

D. ANTONIO LOPEZ DE SANTA ANNA,

General de División,

varias veces Presidente de la República Mejicana

General Antonio López de Santa Anna, styled the Napoleon of the West, had learned about Texas from his expeditions with General Arredondo. Courtesy of Benson Latin American Collection, University of Texas at Austin.

posed Santa Anna's centralists. Carbajal's many skills were appreciated in San Antonio, and he promptly went to work as the interim secretary to the Bexar *ayuntamiento*. In February 1835 he was elected representative for the Béxar District to the Coahuila y Texas State Congress in Monclova, which would convene in March.

Word had reached Texas, meanwhile, that the congress had ousted Gomez Farías, Santa Anna's liberal vice president. In short order, Santa Anna changed sides and joined the conservatives who abrogated the federalist constitution of 1824, after its ten short years in existence, and placed all power in the hands of the central government. Militias were ordered reduced throughout the country to prevent problems, but the state of Zacatecas, with the largest militia and confident from the wealth of its silver mines, had risen in revolt. Santa Anna, the self-styled Napoleon of the West, marched his troops against the large militia force. The poorly led weekend warriors were no match for his trained soldiers. Within days, news of the blood and death he left in his wake reached the northern frontier.[27]

Carbajal hastened to get his affairs in order. Concerned over the repercussions in Zacatecas, he collected monies owed him where he could, sold off land, settled debts, and made sure that Refugia and the children would be taken care of by friends of his mother's family in San Antonio. What money he could gather he sent to his bankers in New Orleans. He recommended to Fernando that he and Plácido should complete the remainder of the land grants and titles as soon as possible and make certain their own affairs were in order. Carbajal held out little hope that the situation in the interior of the country would improve.[28]

By March 1835 José María Jesús Carbajal arrived at the state congress in Monclova to join the other ten delegates from Parras, Leona Vicario (Saltillo), Béxar, Brazos, and Nacogdoches. The national government's order to reduce the local militias would have left Texas with no protection against Indian raids and was resisted by everyone. Santa Anna's new government had also begun to force the state governments into subservience to the central powers. In Monclova the eleven representatives at the Coahuila y Texas State Congress disagreed over the actions of Santa Anna and his centralist congress in Mexico City. The centralist faction, consisting of the three representatives from Saltillo, supported Santa Anna, while the federalist faction made up of the remaining eight men backed the Viesca brothers.

During the previous month a centralist governor, Juan Bautista Elquézabal, had been elected for Coahuila y Texas with Santa Anna's approval. On March 4 the Viesca brothers convinced eight of the congressional delegates, a majority, to disallow Elquézabal's election and order his resignation. Elquézabal refused either to resign or to publish the announcement of his resignation and fired off a letter to the Monclova congress demanding a retraction of its order. The Viescas ignored the order. In a fury over the high-handed acts of the federalists, the three centralist deputies representing Leona Vicario (Saltillo) presented their written protest and stormed out, leaving the congress without a quorum. They reported the federalist disloyalty to Santa Anna in Mexico City. Undaunted by their lack of a quorum, the remaining eight members of the congress in Monclova re-examined the election returns and named Agustín Viesca governor. With this evidence of brazen illegality, Santa Anna ordered General Martín Perfecto de Cos, his brother-in-law, to march north and close down the rebellious Coahuila y Texas state government.[29]

By March 12, 1835, the Monclova congress, knowing it had precious little time, got down to business. Carbajal, along with James Grant, the deputy from Parras, and John Durst, the deputy from Nacogdoches, were appointed to the Committee on Civic Militia and Colonization. In spite of orders from Mexico City to the contrary, Carbajal's first act was to authorize a militia of the residents of the Béxar Department to campaign against the Tahuacanos, Huacos (Wacos), and Tahuayas (Taovayas) in order to protect the settlers in the area. Since there would be no pay, the militia was permitted to divide the spoils of their raids. The committee then moved to organize a militia for the defense of Texas against the imminent arrival of General Cos. For this, however, the government needed money.

Carbajal met with his old friend Samuel May Williams, Austin's secretary and right-hand man. Williams suggested a new law which would allow Agustín Viesca to sell not just the eleven-league tracts, but four hundred leagues, or approximately 1.2 million acres of Texas land. The land sales would ostensibly provide the funds needed to hire a defensive force. Within two days of the passage of the land bill, the entire four hundred leagues was purchased by Samuel May Williams, James Durst, and James Grant. The money would be forthcoming soon, the men promised. A month later, with Cos expected any day, Governor Viesca sold an additional four hundred leagues to Williams and two other investors in exchange for a promise to outfit five hundred soldiers to defend the state from General Cos. That, too, would be done "soon." The congress also granted Agustín Viesca and Ramón Músquiz eleven-league grants.[30]

With the help of his friend Carbajal, Samuel May Williams intended to expand his interests in Texas. Williams first requested that the legislature return to himself and Austin the lands which had been granted the previous year to Sterling Robertson and the Leftwich colony. Williams suggested that Robertson had only received the land by using bribery and that Robertson had done nothing to bring settlers to the area. The congress agreed with Williams and ordered William H. Steele, the Robertson colony land commissioner, not to grant any more land. Samuel May Williams also received a charter to establish a bank in Texas and offered Carbajal a chance to purchase some of the stock. Within days, Williams had sold more than $85,000 of stock in the new bank to his fellow legisla-tors. Both the land sales and the bank stock were paid for in promissory notes, so neither provided hard cash for Williams or for the Viescas.[31]

When word reached Texas of the massive land sales, Williams and his partners were condemned as speculators for planning to profit from control of the remaining public lands in Texas. Although Williams and his partners maintained their innocence, the "Mammoth Speculation at Monclova" destroyed their reputations. Austin, who disapproved of the speculation, had been in jail when the transactions were taking place, but because Williams was his secretary, Austin was blamed as well. He spent the remainder of his days denying any involvement and disassociating him-self from his one-time friend. Samuel May Williams, perhaps the most hated man in Texas, never did gain all the land he had been promised nor make good on any of the promissory notes.[32]

Just as Carbajal had feared, Cos arrived in Saltillo in June 1835 and ordered the arrest of all of the members of the congress. Cos ordered his soldiers to capture every member of the illegal government and prom-ised a firing squad. Carbajal packed what he could on his horse and raced north for his life, along with the other members of the Monclova congress. General Cos quickly captured Governor Viesca, but Carbajal had reached Texas, where he warned his Anglo friends of the imminent arrival of Mexi-can troops. Most dismissed his counsel as exaggeration. He slipped into San Antonio to gather Refugia and the children and rode on to Victoria.

On June 21, just as Carbajal left town, Colonel Ugartechea received word from General Cos that Carbajal was guilty of voting for the sale of the lands and was to be arrested and tried for treason. Ugartechea sent his soldiers in hot pursuit.[33] Arriving exhausted in Victoria, Carbajal sought aid from his de León kin. Doña Patricia and Fernando moved Carbajal, Refugia, and the children to safety on the outlying family ranches. Mean-while, Plácido Benavides, as *alcalde*, called a town meeting of the citizens of Victoria. Thirty men convened and agreed to protect their most eminent citizen.

When Ugartechea's soldiers arrived on the far side of the Guadalupe River, the ferryman sent word to warn the town as he slowly ferried the men across. The soldiers thundered into the town plaza, and their com-mander called for *alcalde* Plácido Benavides. At a leisurely pace Plácido came in from his cornfields along the river, making the soldiers wait in the plaza. The thirty Victorians, meanwhile, drifted into the town square, leaning casually on their rifles as they encircled the soldiers. The soldiers, who had unsaddled their horses, suddenly found themselves surrounded by silent and determined armed men.

> Presently the alcalde, Señor Don Placido Benavides, arrived and inquired of the officer what was wanted. The officer replied by handing him an order from Colonel Ugartechea demanding the body of Carbajal. Placido Benavides returned the order and said to the officer that he could inform Colonel Ugartechea that neither the body of Carbajal nor the body of any other citizen of Victoria would be delivered into the hands of the military, as he was a constitutional officer, and not at all amenable to the military.[34]

The officer, fearful of precipitating a crisis, ordered his soldiers to saddle up, and they returned to San Antonio empty-handed to face the fury of General Cos.[35]

Problems were also occurring among the Anglos around Anahuac. Led by the fiery William B. Travis, the radicals were whipping up opposition to the Mexican government, in particular Captain Tenorio, in command at the fort at Anahuac. The captain had been ordered by the Mexican government to collect taxes and inspect boats entering and leaving Galveston Bay. To his surprise, Tenorio found support from the citizens of nearby Liberty, who feared the Anglo extremists who planned to attack the small fort. At the end of June 1835 Travis and a force of fifty men with two cannons attacked and captured the fort at Anahuac. Captain Tenorio and his men were forced to abandon their post and return to the interior of Mexico. While Travis and his radicals crowed over their small victory, Carbajal's friends at Liberty protested their innocence, fearful of Santa Anna's wrath.[36]

At Victoria, July and August of 1835 passed quietly. Doña Patricia could only hope that the threat of war would not materialize. Carbajal and Refugia remained in hiding. Carbajal passed the time translating all of the Mexican laws into English for the use of the Anglo colonists. The de León family determined to maintain a semblance of peaceful innocence.

Austin had been freed as part of Santa Anna's amnesty program and was on his way back to Texas. Carbajal knew that a vocal majority of the Anglo-American colonists, many of them Austin's original settlers, opposed insurrection and the radicalism at Anahuac and San Felipe. Throughout August a consensus developed among the Anglo colonists to call a general meeting to discuss the problems of the state. Even the radical War Party, hoping to gain converts, supported the meeting.

From Saltillo, General Cos and the Mexican government flooded the state with assurances that law-abiding settlers had nothing to fear. General Ugartechea at San Antonio continued to search for the troublemakers. Among those the government sought were the land speculator Samuel May Williams, the rebels at Anahuac led by Travis, the federalist instigator Lorenzo de Zavala, who was still selling land scrip around Nacogdoches, and, of course, the delegates to the Coahuila legislature including Carbajal, for whom there was no amnesty.[37]

September 1835 marked the turning point for Texas and for the de León family. Word reached Victoria that Austin had returned to the acclaim of his settlers, but he had shifted his support to the War Party. He joined in support of the illegal consultation which had been called for October. The most frightening news, however, was that General Cos had been ordered to march to Texas to capture the rebels. The de León family, along with the settlers throughout Texas, had to choose sides. Would they support the legally constituted government, even if it was a centralist regime? Or would they fight for federalist views and the Constitution of 1824? Few Tejanos considered standing with the Anglo War Party, whose demands for total independence from Mexico were too radical.[38]

The de León family could not agree. Fernando and Plácido Benavides threw their support wholeheartedly to Carbajal, who feared for his life now that General Cos was headed for Texas. Silvestre hesitated. He opposed the Anglo extremists, but he also objected to the centralist regime. Danger for his family lay in either direction, but he grudgingly agreed to support his brothers-in-law. Félix refused to take part in any armed insurrection. He would remain out of the way of the problems on his ranch in Mission Valley. At Goliad, the Aldrete men also sided with Carbajal and the federalists, but, like Félix, they stayed on their ranches. Doña Patricia had always opposed violence. For years, even when the colony was threatened by hostile natives and bandits, Patricia de León had refused to allow her children to use guns against anyone. She had declared that she did not want them to be known as bandits, and she vehemently opposed the actions of her sons-in-law. Like Carbajal, her memory of Arredondo's treatment of rebels was clear. Bandits were shot.[39]

Anglo settlers could not agree, either. Knowing full well that Texas had limited means and a disunited citizenry, Austin hesitated to condone outright war. His own colonists opposed him, while Travis and the War Party felt that Austin had vindicated their position and called for armed insurrection and immediate independence. Lorenzo de Zavala arrived from Nacogdoches and joined Austin. The two began planning the creation of a new government while struggling to bring unity to the colonists.[40]

On September 20 General Cos and two ships loaded with troops landed at Copano Bay. His first stop was Refugio, where he demanded that "all local dignitaries from Goliad and Victoria come to pay their respects."[41] The citizens of Goliad, San Patricio, and Victoria split into opposing camps. Brother was pitted against brother, neighbor against neighbor, and friend against friend. Victoria, controlled by the de León family, sent no representatives to meet with Cos. Arriving from Goliad, however, was Carlos de la Garza, the thirty-five-year-old rancher, accompanied by Juan and Agustín Moya and a detail of soldiers from Presidio La Bahía led by Captain Manuel Sabariego. His neighbors may have been surprised to see de la Garza taking sides. He had never played a part in the government of the town of Goliad and had remained on his ranch, building up his cattle herds, and aiding his Catholic Irish neighbors. With the arrival of the Mexican forces, however, he chose to support General Cos and offered to form a loyal cavalry troop made up of his fellow Tejano ranchers and a group of Karankawa Indians.[42]

As they marched toward Goliad, Cos ordered Colonel Ugartechea at San Antonio to collect the cannons at Gonzales and Victoria which had been given to the colonists for protection against the Indians. At Victoria, Plácido Benavides peaceably turned over the small three-pound cannon which was mounted on truck wheels and was of little use. On October 2 soldiers from San Antonio arrived in Gonzales and demanded the cannon. The citizens had bedecked the cannon with a sheet on which they had painted "Come and Take It." When the citizens refused to surrender the cannon, a few shots were exchanged, but the Mexican officer, who had been ordered not to attempt to take the cannon by force, returned to San Antonio without the cannon.[43]

While Carlos de la Garza and the centralists formed their reconnaissance troop on the San Antonio River to support Cos, Plácido Benavides, on the Guadalupe River, had created his own mounted force of thirty men to oppose the Mexican general. With Plácido rode Silvestre de León and Mariano Carbajal, José María's younger brother. Plácido and his small band joined George M. Collinsworth and his twenty men, who were marching from Matagorda to take the fort at Goliad. Many of the federalist Tejanos opposed General Cos, but they were equally opposed to an outright break with their native country. Perhaps at the instigation of Silvestre and the Tejanos, Collinsworth and his volunteers agreed to draw up a covenant in which they pledged their support to Mexico and the Constitution of 1824. Talk of independence was in the air, but it was not an idea which most of the Tejanos could condone.[44]

Collinsworth's small contingent, now numbering more than 125 men with the addition of Plácido's volunteers, had planned to take Goliad and capture General Cos and his war chest, but Cos was already in San Antonio. Even without Cos, Plácido and Collinsworth agreed that Goliad was a prize worth taking. Control of the stone fort on the river meant that they could cut off General Cos from Copano Bay and his supply lines to the coast. From the Aldretes Plácido learned that Cos, having received the support of Carlos de la Garza, had not expected any attack and had left the fort defended by a small force of fifty men. Plácido informed Collinsworth, and the combined force marched on Goliad, where they demanded the surrender of the town. The Goliad town council, without Aldrete, was in the hands of the local centralist supporters, who refused to hand over the town. The following day Collinsworth and Plácido, with help from Aldrete and his federalist friends, broke down the doors and captured the fort. They found a stash of supplies, lance heads, and bayonets, but the major victory was control of the valley ranches which could be tapped for "contributions" to the cause of the Texians, or Anglo-American Texans. Captain Philip Dimitt and Colonel James W. Fannin arrived to take charge of the fort. The two men would be overseen by an evenly balanced supervisory body made up of Colonel James Power from Refugio, Major James Kerr, José María Jesús Carbajal, Plácido Benavides, and several other Victoria federalists.[45]

By October 15 word reached Carbajal and Benavides at Goliad that Stephen F. Austin, at the head of the self-styled Army of Gonzales, was on his way to expel Cos from San Antonio. Plácido and his Tejanos, along with many of Collinsworth's company, joined the expedition. As the small army encamped around San Antonio, volunteers continued to arrive, both Anglo and Tejano, swelling Austin's force to four hundred men. Dissension in the ranks, however, increased. Austin's officers, many of whom were delegates to the consultation which was to take place on November 1, felt that Austin should withdraw and avoid a confrontation with Cos, whose force numbered more than six thousand men and was strongly entrenched behind the adobe walls of San Antonio.[46]

Austin continued to insist on the need to take San Antonio. Time after time he planned assaults, only to have his men refuse to attack. While Plácido and his Tejanos scoured the countryside for cattle to feed the hungry men and maintained a close watch on the Mexican troops in San Antonio, the Anglo contingent quarreled. Insubordination and desertions increased. Even those who were willing to fight disobeyed Austin's orders.

James Bowie and James Fannin, deployed to reconnoiter the Mexican forces, were instructed to send for Austin and the remainder of the army as soon as they made contact with the Mexicans. Disdainfully, Bowie and Fannin, with their force of one hundred men, did not notify Austin but rushed to attack a superior force of four hundred Mexican cavalry near Concepción mission. The Anglo victory was due more to the efficacy of their long rifles and their hidden positions along the river bottom than to any attempt at strategy. An irritated Austin arrived just in time to see the Mexican army retreating toward San Antonio. He pushed for an immediate attack on the town while it was in disarray, but his officers once again refused.[47]

The only bright spots in Austin's command were the 135 Tejano volunteers led by Plácido Benavides from Victoria and Juan Seguín from San Antonio. They did not question his authority, debate his orders, or vote on his commands. They remained loyal, trustworthy, and obedient, and they provided Austin with provisions for his hungry army and supplied information on the activities of General Cos and his men. The Tejanos could also be cold and cruel when the need arose. Plácido Benavides, while searching for horses with James Bowie south of San Antonio, learned from a Tejano farmer that a local herder had hidden some horses. Benavides and James Bowie tied the man's hands behind his back and hung him from a tree until he was almost dead. It took three tries, but the man at last revealed the location of the horses.[48]

While Austin struggled to control the army at San Antonio and Fernando de León moved the women of the de León family out to the ranches, Philip Dimitt at Goliad was also having problems which could only be solved by the Tejanos. On October 30 Captain Dimitt, in order to extend control over the land south of the old presidio, ordered a detachment of men under Ira Westover to march on Fort Lipantitlán on the Nueces River. Dimitt had been unable to gather enough horses or supplies to outfit his men. Carbajal and Silvestre de León, through their local connections with their Aldrete in-laws, supplied twenty mounts for the expedition and thirty head of cattle from the Victoria and Goliad ranches to feed the men.[49]

The raid on Lipantitlán, better known as the Battle of Nueces Crossing, again proved the importance of the Texian long rifles and Tejano support. Eager for a chance to join the fight, the advisory board from Goliad — including James Kerr, John Power, and John Linn from Victoria — along with a reluctant Silvestre de León, joined Westover. They had all been elected delegates to the consultation, but they postponed their political duties to ride to Lipantitlán. Francisco de la Portilla, son of Don Martín's old friend Felipe Roque de la Portilla, safely guided the small contingent around the Mexican dragoons and toward San Patricio, the site of Don Martín's first ranch. Although Silvestre had spent some of his youth on the ranch, he remembered little of the area.

The detachment arrived to find that the fort on the far side of the Nueces was nothing more than a few wooden rails and an embankment of earth. Linn maintained it might have served as a "second-rate hog pen." As the combined contingent of Anglos and Tejanos came south, the Mexican forces at Lipantitlán had been ordered north to attack Goliad. Westover and the men arrived to find that the fort was guarded by a skeleton force that quickly surrendered. Westover's troops tore down what they could of the embankment, took the two cannons and some horses, and prepared to return to Goliad.[50]

Many of the Irish at San Patricio opposed Westover and the rebel federalists. One of them had ridden hastily to recall the Mexican forces. Before Westover and his Tejanos could escape, the Mexican military returned. Joined by their local Irish allies, the Mexicans launched an assault on the Texian forces. Westover and his men had taken cover in the woods along the Nueces River, which rendered the Mexican cavalry ineffective. Having to dismount and fight on foot, the Mexican military was decimated by the Texian long rifles. Unwilling to face the Texian rifles a second time, the Mexican force gave up the fort and fell back to Matamoros, leaving their loyal San Patricio Irish supporters to face the wrath of the Texians alone. Westover, without sufficient men and supplies to hold the fort, pitched the cannons into the river, abandoned Lipantitlán, and returned to Goliad. Upon their return, Dimitt complained bitterly to Austin of Westover's disobedience and failure to hold Lipantitlán. Equally at fault, from Dimitt's perspective, were Carbajal, Silvestre de León, and John Linn, who — angered by Dimitt's insulting remarks — left Goliad in disgust.[51]

By the time de León, Kerr, and Power returned from Lipantitlán on November 12, the consultation was nearly over. The council of delegates at San Felipe de Austin had achieved a quorum on November 3. Had Silvestre arrived in time, it is doubtful that he would have been impressed with his first glimpse of democracy at work. Like the military, the nearly sixty Texian men could agree on almost nothing. The critical vote for independence failed. The Peace Party, joined by the moderates, successfully defeated the War Party's bid for independence and pledged to create a provisional federalist state government within the Mexican republic. Much to the disappointment of the rabble-rousers, they also voted to maintain the Constitution of 1824. For the following two weeks the disparate groups quarreled and bickered. They did agree on sending Austin, who was still at San Antonio fuming over the ineptitude of the Texian troops, to the United States to gather funds. The War Party placed the ambitious Sam Houston in charge of a nonexistent army and established a government consisting of a governor and general council made up of one representative from each district. Their choice of Henry Smith as provisional governor proved to be a disaster. Within weeks of the end of the consultation, Smith had fought bitterly with the council members who tried to oust him, while he in turn tried to remove the council. If this was Anglo government, Silvestre wanted no part of it.[52]

Austin, who had received word of his appointment as emissary to the United States, made one last frustrating attempt at the end of November to convince his men to attack General Cos. When his officers again refused, Austin paraded the troops and gave a farewell address in which he had a hard time not expressing his recriminations. The next morning he packed his bags for New Orleans and turned over the army to Edward Burleson. Burleson found that the seven-week siege had destroyed morale and was causing mounting dissension among the Texians.

The Tejano mounted patrols led by Seguín and Benavides continued to provide information and supplies. Following their example, the Texians mounted up to patrol the roads, intercept couriers, and keep reinforcements from reaching General Cos. The mounted troops had some small successes. William Travis captured a *caballada*, or horse herd, of three hundred horses, which was sent up to Juan Seguín's ranch to recuperate and resupply the Texian cavalry. Jim Bowie, bent on a fight, rode out to attack a mule train which was rumored to contain silver to pay the men in San Antonio. The entire Texian camp emptied, racing after Bowie in hopes of a fortune. Shots were exchanged, and the Mexican military abandoned the mules, which turned out to be loaded with nothing more than cut grass. Others, urged on by James Grant, determined to march on Matamoros. The mood in the camp was not improving. At the beginning of December the few remaining officers called for a retreat to Goliad, and the camp degenerated into chaos. The Texians realized that their own disorganization could cost them the war. Juan Seguín and Plácido Benavides watched in dismay.[53]

Ben Milam, a one-time supporter of the Mexican federalists and member of the James Long expedition, returning from a scouting expedition on December 4, was equally appalled to learn that the siege would be abandoned. After a bitter debate with Burleson, Milam called for volunteers to storm the town. Three hundred men responded, and with the small group Milam ordered the assault for the next day. With him were Juan Seguín, Plácido Benavides, and sixty-seven Tejanos. At dawn, the Texians and their Tejano allies attacked the entrenched forces of General Cos.

The battle raged for four days. By the fourth day the Mexican troops, running low on supplies, food, and water, had become desperate. The bloody fighting degenerated into a house-to-house, and hand-to-hand melee in which the Mexican forces grudgingly gave way inch by inch. Convict reinforcements brought in by Ugartechea proved to be a liability rather than an advantage. The sullen prisoners would not fight and devoured the limited food supplies in the Mexican camp. Although some contingents of the Mexican troops refused to give up or destroy their honor, on December 9 a disillusioned and bitter General Cos surrendered. According to the terms of his surrender, he agreed not to fight the Texians again, and he retreated with his men south of the Rio Grande. At the request of the local *bexareños,* he took the convict reinforcements with him. The Texians, certain that their victory had ended Santa Anna's interference in Texas, joyfully returned to their homes. Juan Seguín and the *bexareños* began patching up their war-ravaged homes. Plácido Benavides and his men, exhausted but exhilarated, set out for Victoria.[54]

Doña Patricia welcomed her family home with great relief. Joined by Fernando and the women, she looked forward to a peaceful Christmas season. First among the festivities in the small chapel on the plaza was the baptism of Plácido and Agustina's newborn baby daughter. He and Agustina named her Librada in honor of the liberty for which he had fought. Silvestre, with back-slapping congratulations from his brothers, returned to learn that Rosalía was three months pregnant. José Miguel Aldrete and Candelaria arrived from Goliad with their four boys, now seventeen, thirteen, twelve, and ten. The boys had wanted desperately to join the Tejano patrols, but Doña Patricia was thankful that their father had not allowed it. The conversation had become stiff and stilted when Félix and Salomé arrived with Desiderio García and Lupita. Their opposition to the war and to the Anglo Texians had put them at odds with the rest of the family, and only their obedience to Doña Patricia's request that they come had brought them in from their ranches for the family gathering. She hoped that with the war over, the political discord among her family would dissipate. The threat of Santa Anna, however, was impossible to ignore.

José María Jesús Carbajal knew better than to think Santa Anna would be so easily stopped. He warned the family that Santa Anna would exact his revenge on Texas. Bitterly, Félix and Desiderio blamed the Anglos for the warfare. Any repercussions from Mexico would be their fault. Plácido Benavides and Carbajal defended the actions of the Texians. Cos and the centralists in Mexico had to be shown that Texas would not bow down to a military state.

Fernando and the men discussed the possibility of the Anglos pushing for complete independence. On this the family could agree. Mexico was still their country, and having seen the ridiculous squabbling of the Anglos, they wanted no part of an independent Texas where Anglos would be in control. If the new consultation planned for March called for independence, Plácido and Silvestre agreed that they could no longer support the Texian cause. Carbajal felt that independence was the least of their worries. Their greatest danger came from Santa Anna. If the Napoleon of the West should launch an attack, Carbajal, a federalist politician with a price on his head, and now Fernando, Silvestre, Plácido, and the Aldretes as well, had no recourse but to fight for their lives or flee to safety. The family looked into a gloomy future. Texas, torn by dissension and disunity, had no money, no arms, and no army with which to defeat the angry general. And Carbajal knew that Santa Anna was coming.[55]

CHAPTER 6

REVOLUTION AND EXILE, 1835–1845

Genealogical Chart

ARTÍN DE LEÓN (D. 1834) + PATRICIA DE LA GARZA

    1. Fernando (wid. 1825)

    2. María Candelaria (m. 1818) + José Miguel Aldrete
        2-1. José María (b. 1820)
        2-2. José de Jesús María (b. 1822)
        2-3. Trinidad (b. 1824)
        2-4. Rafael (b. 1826)

    3. Silvestre (d. 1843) + Rosalía de la Garza (d. 1838)
        3-1. Francisco (b. 1830)
        3-2. Martín (b. 1832)
        3-3. Francisco Santiago (b. 1836)

    4. "Lupita" (m. 1825) + Desiderio Garcia (d. 1842)
        No children

    5. Félix (m. 1828) + Salomé Leal
        5-1. Santiago (b. 1829)
        5-2. Patricio (b. 1830)
        5-3. Silvestre (b. 1834)
        5-4. Olivia (b. 1837)
        5-5. María de Jesús "Chucha" (b. 1840)

    6. Agápito (d. 1833) + María Antonia C. de la Garza +
       Manuel Carbajal (m. 1837)
        6-1. León de León (b. 1824)

7. "Chucha" (m. 1824) + Rafael Manchola (d. 1833)

    7-1. "Panchita" (b. 1826)

8. Refugia (m. 1832) + José María Jesús Carbajal

    8-1. Antonio (b. 1833)

    8-2. José María (b. 1834)

    8-3. Crecencia (b.-d. 1836)

9. Agustina (d. 1842) + Plácido Benavides (d. 1838)

    9-1. Pilar (b. 1834)

    9-2. Librada (b. 1835)

    9-3. Matiana (b. 1836)

10. Francisca (b. 1818)

José María Jesús Carbajal was right. Santa Anna would have his revenge. When word reached Mexico City of Cos' defeat, the *generalísimo* acted immediately. In less than a month, by the end of December 1835, he had extracted 400,000 pesos from a reluctant church and citizenry, gathered an army of more than six thousand men, and started for Texas. In Texas the provisional state government could do little but squabble. The government had split into two warring factions. Governor Smith headed one pseudo-government, while the council headed another. Houston had no army and no money. Austin, William H. Wharton, and Branch Archer had been sent to the United States on a fruitless search for funding. A few Anglos dismissed Santa Anna as harmless. Others, in particular Austin's old colonists who feared losing their land, remained loyal to Mexico. Still others itched for a fight and began gathering at Gonzales and San Felipe to join the emerging military companies.

Doña Patricia had tried in vain to keep her family out of the looming violence. Fernando and José María Jesús were intent on helping the armies that opposed Santa Anna. Accompanied by Peter Kerr, brother of the surveyor, the men had gathered a herd of horses from the nearby ranches and headed east to sell them in New Orleans. The men were well known in the Crescent City and their horses always in demand. They exchanged the horses for over $3,000 in arms, ammunition, food, and supplies and secured passage aboard the schooner *Hannah Elizabeth* bound for Matagorda. Santa Anna, however, had ordered warships to patrol the coast to prevent just such resupplies. At Paso Caballo the Mexican ship *Bravo* ran the small schooner aground. Resistance was futile, and Fernando and Carbajal hastened to throw overboard their cargo of "two boxes of muskets, rifles and other arms, and eighteen kegs of powder" to prevent the precious cargo from falling into the enemies' hands.[1] Even Carbajal's glib tongue could not help them when the captain and Mexican prize crew boarded the schooner. While Peter Kerr and fifteen other passengers were imprisoned on the *Hannah Elizabeth*, Fernando and José María Jesús were transferred to the *Bravo* in chains and taken to Matamoros, where they were jailed as traitors.[2]

The sight of a wreck on the coast set off bells in Matagorda. For the local citizens, a wreck meant profit for those who could help salvage the ship, and they scrambled to be the first to reach it. The laws of salvage which governed wrecks had originally existed to help rescue the passengers and crew of wrecked vessels. In exchange for saving the survivors, the rescuers had first claim to the cargo. The captain of a salvage ship could either claim the whole prize, if he had his own paid crew, or auction off the goods to those who had come with him. The goods would then be transported back to the harbor and sold on the docks for a considerable profit.

Salvage was technically legal. In a letter to the government, however, James Fannin had noted, "Our sea coast has for years presented nothing but a scene of fraud, corruption and piracies to the unfortunate, who, either by misfortune or design, have been driven on our shores." He was "well aware of the intrigue, management, and downright roguery which has been universally practised [sic] by the unprincipled speculators, and always to the great injury and frequently total ruin of the unfortunate."[3] In some instances the denizens of the beaches and waterfronts had been accused of intentionally moving lights and channel markers to ensure a profitable wreck, although such was not the case with the *Hannah Elizabeth*.[4]

On December 19 a small band of men hurriedly set sail for the pass. In the self-righteous words of the crew, "a number of our fellow citizens ... fell into the ranks and marched under orders ... [and] embarked on board the *William Robbins*, a small schooner, commanded by Captain W. A. Hurd, armed and equipped to repel the enemy, or afford such assistance as the case might require."[5]

The profiteers retook the *Elizabeth* from the Mexican prize crew and commandeered the cargo. Peter Kerr, who was still on board, tried to claim his goods. According to Johnson, "Mr. Kerr, who seemed more like a crazy than a sane man, begged Captain Hurd that his property might not be sold, but that in lieu thereof, pay as salvage, fifty percent on the invoice cost."[6] Captain Hurd agreed and allowed Kerr to remove one hundred barrels of flour, two hundred bales of tobacco, five casks of gin, five casks of brandy, and twenty-two barrels of whiskey at a cost of $1,270.50. One of the crew, William L. Cazneau, then auctioned off the remainder of the cargo. Since the salvagers had no cash with them, Captain Hurd agreed to take their notes. The total profit for Captain Hurd was $2,993.50 less Cazneau's commission of $149.67 as auctioneer. The goods were removed to the shore of Matagorda Island with, as Captain Hurd noted, "great difficulty, exposure and labor." Each man then had to get his goods off the island and back up the bay as best he could.[7]

Fannin and the provisional government tried to regain the goods, which they felt had been promised to the Texian army. Accusations flew, but it was too late, as the goods had already been sold to buyers in the waterfront taverns along Matagorda Bay. Hurd and the prize crew were highly offended by the implications that they had engaged in piracy. Peter Kerr never could find the money to pay for his liquor and flour and lost his entire investment to Hurd and his crew. Neither Carbajal nor Fernando de León ever received credit for their attempted contributions to the Texian cause.[8]

In Matamoros, meanwhile, Fernando de León and José María Jesús Carbajal, imprisoned at the stone fortress called Casamata, had gotten word to Victoria of their predicament. Plácido Benavides was stationed at Goliad and requested permission from Major Robert Morris to undertake a spying mission to Matamoros. As part of that mission with or without Morris' knowledge, he would do what he could to help his brothers-in-law. Morris agreed, and Benavides and his troops slipped into Matamoros early in February. They found the town filled with centralist troops preparing to march northward. Blending in with the crowds, Benavides and his men made their way to Casamata. Using de León family gold, Benavides arranged the escape of Fernando and Carbajal. As the small group attempted to slip back out of town, they were discovered, and in the wild flight, twenty-two of Benavides' scouts were captured. Plácido escaped with the remainder of his men and his brothers-in-law. By February 6 Plácido reported to Morris at Goliad that there were one thousand centralist troops at Matamoros and another one thousand troops marching toward Central Texas from the Rio Grande. Fernando and José María Jesús returned to Victoria with little to show for their efforts.[9]

As Benavides had warned, Santa Anna arrived at the Rio Grande in early February. The Texian government had almost no defenses. Governor Smith had appointed Houston to command the still scarce forces, while the council authorized Dr. James Grant, Philip Dimitt, and Frank Johnson to attack Matamoros. Callously, Grant stripped the miniscule garrison at San Antonio of food and clothing and headed downriver to Goliad. Under Governor Smith's orders, Houston arrived in Goliad to find that Grant had assumed command of the forces and would not countenance his interference. Houston, opposed to the expedition and still hoping to gain control of the men, competed loudly for the allegiance of the U.S. volunteers. James Bowie, a longtime resident of San Antonio and a supporter of Houston, obeyed the general's orders to go to the Tejano capital. Meanwhile, Houston abandoned hope of gaining Grant's volunteers for his own army and returned to Gonzales.[10]

While Sam Houston ordered troops to destroy San Antonio, the Tejanos around Victoria had other things to worry about. General Urrea was marching up the coast from Matamoros to capture the critical towns of

José María Jesús Carbajal, married to Martín and Patricia de León's daughter Refugia, was an English-speaking surveyor and supporter of the Anglo colonists around Liberty. Courtesy of Local History Collection, Victoria College.

San Patricio, Goliad, and Victoria. Plácido Benavides, this time without Silvestre, once again left his family in the care of Doña Patricia in Victoria and hurried south. He reached San Patricio and joined Grant and Johnson with their Matamoros expedition. Grant, in need of mounts, asked Benavides to help him and two dozen men collect a herd of horses on the vast plains along the Nueces. They were unaware that General Urrea had already arrived.

On February 27 Urrea and his men captured San Patricio and the fort at Lipantitlán and easily defeated Johnson's scattered troops. The Irish cen-

tralists from San Patricio informed Urrea of Grant's imminent return with
the horse herd and helped him set a trap along Agua Dulce Creek. Grant,
Benavides, and Ruben R. Brown were riding a half-mile ahead of the men
with the *caballada* when sixty mounted Mexican dragoons charged out of
the woods. Benavides and the Anglos never stood a chance. According
to Brown, Grant ordered Plácido to ride for Goliad and notify Fannin of
Urrea's advance. Plácido, better mounted and a better rider, avoided capture by the Mexican cavalry, but Grant and Brown, attempting to escape in
the confusion of the wild horse herd, were run down and captured. Grant,
well known to the Mexicans as a landowner in Coahuila, was impaled on
their lances for his treachery. Brown was roughly bound up and taken to
Matamoros for questioning.[11]

Plácido reached Goliad on March 1. Fannin, now in control of the fort,
was unsure what to do. He knew Travis needed help, but Houston was
ordering him to come to Gonzales or at least retreat to Victoria. Plácido
knew that Fannin had no support from the local Tejanos, whom Captain
Dimitt had alienated with his harsh demands for food and supplies. Dimitt
had taken their horse herds, appropriated their corn, and forced any he
could catch into cutting wood and carrying water. Carlos de la Garza on
the San Antonio River had reorganized his Guardia Victoriana from volunteers among his Tejano neighbors, including Manuel Sabariego and the
Moya brothers Juan and Agustín. With the local Tejanos controlling the
countryside, Plácido knew there was little he could do to help Fannin. Plácido rode on to Victoria to form his own Tejano cavalry to oppose the
oncoming Mexican forces.[12]

Carlos de la Garza and his Guardia Victoriana joined General Urrea at
San Patricio. They became indispensable. As scouts they notified Urrea of
Fannin's movements and prevented the Texians from learning of Urrea's
whereabouts. They also warned Urrea that Fannin had sent out Captain
Amon King to evacuate the settlers in Refugio. A few days later, they re-
ported that Fannin had ordered William Ward and his Georgia Battalion
to King's aid. Ward and King, instead of moving promptly and getting
the settlers to safety, used their two military units to attack and punish
the local centralist ranchers, including the de la Garza family at Carlos
Rancho. Carlos de la Garza, riding for Urrea, could not come to their aid.
Teresita and the women with the few remaining *vaqueros* fought off the
Anglo forces from behind the stout stockade fences which had protected
them from many Indian raids. On March 12 Urrea came to the rescue of the
Refugio ranchers. He trapped King and Ward at Mission Rosario. Once

again, the Texas long rifles kept Urrea's men at bay throughout the day. By evening, however, Ward and King were low on ammunition. Their only recourse was escape. Carlos de la Garza and his Guardia Victoriana took revenge for the attacks on the Refugio centralists. King and his men were easily overrun and captured. They were returned to Goliad, where Urrea ordered them held until orders were received from Santa Anna. Ward and his Georgia Battalion escaped downriver, and the few survivors struggled throughout the next month to reach Fannin or Victoria.[13]

General Urrea marched toward Goliad and Victoria. His scouts informed him of the strange antics of General Fannin. The anxious Anglo commander could not decide whether to start for San Antonio to reinforce the army at the Alamo, to march toward Victoria, or to join up with Houston at Gonzales. General Urrea's troops discovered Fannin and his men on the prairie outside of Goliad, too far from water at Coleto Creek, and burdened with heavy artillery which Fannin refused to abandon. Surrounded and outnumbered, Fannin at last surrendered. He and his men were marched to Goliad, where they were imprisoned with King's small force.[14]

Carlos de la Garza and his Guardia had combed the prairies looking for Ward's men. Failing to find them, Carlos returned to report to General Urrea at Goliad, where he learned that a number of his Irish neighbors had been a part of Fannin's Texian army and were imprisoned at the fort. A courier arrived from Santa Anna with orders for their execution. Carlos appealed to General Urrea for their release, but the general remained adamant.

That night Carlos de la Garza, disobeying orders and jeopardizing his own life, effected the escape of James W. Byrnes, John Fagan, Nicholas Fagan, Edward Perry, Anthony Sidick, and John B. Sidick. He hurried the men downriver through the night, and by morning they were safely hidden on Carlos Rancho. No one, however, came to save Mariano Carbajal, José María Jesús' younger brother. Plácido had learned too late of his capture, and there was nothing Carbajal or the de León family could do to save him. The next morning, March 27, Palm Sunday, Fannin and the remainder of his men, including Mariano Carbajal, were marched out of the little town and executed. De la Garza had saved his neighbors from the execution at Goliad. It was an action for which they gratefully repaid him with their support throughout the rest of their lives.[15]

In mid-March, while General Urrea was capturing Fannin, Plácido reached Victoria to find the town in an uproar. All the news was grim.

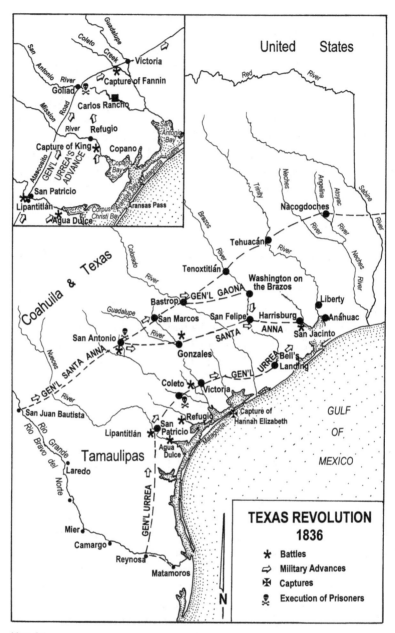

**TEXAS REVOLUTION
1836**

✳ Battles
⇨ Military Advances
✠ Captures
☠ Execution of Prisoners

Map 6.1

Santa Anna had annihilated the defenders of the Alamo, and General Urrea had massacred all of King and Fannin's men at Goliad. Fernando gathered the de León clan for a hasty meeting. Félix and Desiderio, angry over the outcome of the events, felt certain that there was little doubt they, too, would be killed. After expressing their bitter recriminations, they rode off up the Guadalupe to barricade their ranches and protect their families. Doña Patricia, remembering the many times she and Martín had avoided the military, advised moving out of town. Her sons agreed that the women would be far safer on the ranch. She had already begun packing, loading wagons, and moving her daughters, daughters-in-law, and grandchildren to safety at the family ranch on Garcitas Creek. Leaving Fernando in town, Doña Patricia led the creaking exodus of wagons and carriages winding its way along the Street of the Ten Friends out of Victoria. Others in town followed her example.

John Linn, fearing for his family's safety, had called on Fernando and asked him to protect his wife, his fifteen-day-old child, and the other women of the household while Linn marched northward to join Houston at Gonzales. Fernando provided two oxen and a cart to take his friend's family to safety at Linnville, where they hoped to find a ship to take them to New Orleans. The Linns arrived to find that there were no ships available on which to make their escape. The town had been ransacked, and the warehouses were empty. Their only sustenance was a barrel of flour.

The women had started back for Victoria when Fernando found the bedraggled family on the open prairies. Fernando insisted that their only choice was to join Doña Patricia on the de León ranch, where there was both food and shelter. When the frightened Linn family arrived, Patricia hurried them into hiding and, within minutes of their arrival, a Mexican officer showed up with five soldiers. He was seeking traitors, he said, but informed Doña Patricia that General Urrea did not intend to "molest the inhabitants of the country who remained at their homes and took no part in the war." He did, however, explain that Urrea expected the citizens to provide subsistence for the troops and that "the principals of the various ranches must present themselves at headquarters within three days." Doña Patricia refused the men entrance and sent them on their way. None of the de León family appeared at the general's headquarters.[16]

Only Fernando remained in town. The rest of the men of the de León family, divided in their loyalties, had separated and ridden off to protect their own homes. Carbajal, known for his federalist sympathies and his attendance at the Monclova congress, had remained in hiding with Doña Patricia. He was too well known in Victoria to be safe from Urrea. Plácido, already committed to the military, insisted on riding with his scout troop. He had earned the respect of the officers in the Texian army for his efforts at Concepción and against Cos in San Antonio. Despite the opposition from some of the newly arrived volunteers from the United States who wanted to segregate the Tejano forces, Plácido had been appointed first lieutenant of cavalry in the newly organized Texas militia along with Manuel Carbajal, another brother of José María Jesús. Riding as a guerrilla unit, he and his men continued to attack General Urrea and his forces as they moved up the coast.[17]

Fernando, who had not taken part in the military action, was convinced that he was in no danger. Needing support from the Tejanos, the Texians had given Fernando a commission with the Texian army, and he had bought supplies for them, but Fernando did not believe that Urrea would know of it. Fernando was wrong. When General Urrea arrived in Victoria on March 21, Fernando was called before the general. Some of the inhabitants of Victoria, eager to please Urrea, reported that de León was hiding supplies destined for the Texian army. Fernando denied having any supplies for the rebel forces and assured Urrea that he had not taken part in the uprising. Urrea, learning from Fernando's enemies that the de León family had sympathized with the federalist cause, imprisoned him. Chained to the wall in his own jail, beaten, and tortured, Fernando at last disclosed the location of the supplies. Not even his influential family could help him now. The newly revealed centralists "became extremely insulting to the few Americans who remained,"[18] butchering some of the hapless rebels.

Disregarding the danger to herself, Doña Patricia, with faithful Francisca at her side, hastened in from the ranch, leaving the remainder of the family in hiding. She did not arrive crying and pleading. With the self-confidence of a Spanish matriarch, expecting to be obeyed even by a general, she demanded that Urrea let her tend to her son. She could not secure his release, but she insisted on the right to care for him. To the surprise of those in town, the general agreed. She moved her things back into her Victoria home. Daily, she and Francisca carried meals to her eldest son and tended to his wounds. Fernando remained in the Victoria jail for the remaining two months of the war.[19]

In April, General Urrea left Victoria in the hands of his centralist supporters, protected by a small contingent of his troops, and continued his march up the coast, paralleling Santa Anna's movement and pursuing the fleeing Texian government. Plácido, having slipped into town to see Doña Patricia and gain news of Fernando, was hurrying to join his troops south of town. On the prairie south of Victoria he came across Isaac D. Hamilton, who, although bayoneted and shot, had escaped the Goliad massacre. For nineteen days Hamilton had been struggling to reach help. Having known Hamilton at Goliad, Plácido found a cart and loaded his friend into it. They had traveled only a short distance when a Mexican cavalry patrol stopped them. There was nothing that Plácido could do. He could not fight the patrol, and if he tried to outride them he would be caught or killed. If the patrol realized who he was and that he was helping a condemned rebel to escape, he would be shot on the spot. Instead, Plácido "called out that he had captured one of the rebels, coolly demanded a receipt for his prisoner, and handed Hamilton over to Urrea's lancers."[20] While Plácido rode off, Hamilton was tied onto a horse bareback, beaten by the soldiers, and hauled to Victoria for execution. He was saved by Francisca Alvarez, a woman he called "the Angel of Goliad." Hamilton never forgave Plácido and spent the rest of his life trying to find and kill him. Hamilton also destroyed Plácido's good reputation among the Texian troops.[21]

By early April 1836 both centralist and federalist Victorians wondered what had happened to Houston's small army. Hardly anyone put much faith in Houston's success against thousands of Mexican soldiers. Word reached Victoria that Houston had retreated from Gonzales, then San Felipe, and then the Brazos. Santa Anna had moved north and east out of Béxar, combing the countryside for the elusive Texian government and the "backwoods drunkard who presumed to call himself a general."[22] Texian citizens fled in the face of the approaching troops, taking what little they could carry through mud and rain and bitter cold, in what would later be called "the Runaway Scrape." Some of their own Texian soldiers burned the homes and possessions of the settlers to keep them out of Santa Anna's hands. Other Anglos cruelly rode up on the small groups, shouted that the enemy was coming, then, as the pathetic stragglers dropped their goods and fled, stole what little was left.[23]

Everyone in Victoria was certain that Houston's force was doomed. Santa Anna, unsure where Houston was, had divided his army into separate hunting parties. Santa Anna at last learned that Houston had moved down the Brazos River and reached Harrisburg on the coast. Certain Houston would retreat toward Nacogdoches, Santa Anna moved to capture Lynch's Ferry on the San Jacinto River. Houston beat him to it and slipped behind the Mexican army. Although surprised to find the enemy to his rear, Santa Anna was still confident that he could defeat the ragtag band.[24]

Santa Anna had every reason to be self-confident. Houston's men were quarreling with their commander once again. On April 20 a small mounted division launched its own unsuccessful attack on the Mexican dragoons. The following day, facing almost certain mutiny in the ranks if he did not attack, Houston at last launched the assault. He pitted his 910 untrained men, including Juan Seguín and his volunteer Tejanos, against Santa Anna's proven army of 1,200 troops. Within less than an hour, much to everyone's surprise and Santa Anna's chagrin, Houston's motley army had defeated the Mexicans on the battlefield at San Jacinto. The Texians, joined by Seguín's Tejanos, took revenge on the Mexican soldiers for the Alamo and Goliad. They slaughtered hundreds of the defeated Mexican forces even as they surrendered.[25]

Houston, wounded in the ankle, ordered his men to find Santa Anna. Without the general the victory would mean nothing since thousands of Mexican troops under Filisola and Urrea were closing in on the San Jacinto. Houston knew his men could not face another battle. The following day Houston's soldiers discovered Santa Anna. Houston refused to let his men hang the general, although they clamored for his head. To save his own life, Santa Anna accepted Houston's terms that he order the Mexican troops to leave Texas. General Filisola, Santa Anna's second in command, was encamped along the Brazos. Hampered by bad weather, lack of supplies, and dysentery among his troops, he was only too glad to retreat from the marshy forests of East Texas to the open prairies of South Texas. He continued across the Rio Grande and into Mexico.[26]

General Urrea, however, was still moving up the coast. He had won every battle and skirmish that he had fought and had taken supplies from the ranches along the way. His men were healthy and ready for action. In late April, Urrea received the orders from General Filisola to leave Texas. Urrea could not believe his ears. He objected vehemently and sent bitter letters to the Mexican secretary of army and navy pointing out the potential for success against Houston's army. But he complained to no avail. General Urrea was ordered to turn his soldiers south and he abandoned Carlos de la Garza and the faithful Guardia Victoriana.[27]

Victorians were stunned by news of Houston's victory. General Urrea and his gloomy soldiers marched back through town in mid-May. Fernando had been freed from prison when news of San Jacinto reached town. Suddenly the handful of centralists were scrambling to join the Mexican army on its march south. There was little doubt that the Texians would be vengeful.

Thomas Rusk, appointed the new general of the Texian Army, had followed Urrea down the coast to make sure that he returned to Mexico. Rusk had chosen Victoria as his headquarters, and the local government was now in the hands of Anglos. The Spanish laws and customs had disappeared. Everywhere Doña Patricia looked there were raucous Anglos, camped in the square, breaking into houses and barns, stealing horses and corn, killing cattle, brawling with each other, and weaving drunkenly down the streets. With Fernando, she and Francisca hastened to pack their things and move back to the ranch. Rude gangs assaulted any Mexican they found. Volunteers from the United States were still pouring in, frustrated that the war was over and looking for a fight. No Tejanos were safe.

Rusk struggled to keep the men under control. He begged for supplies to feed his unruly troops. The Texian government, mired in financial difficulties and now under the command of interim President David Burnett, had nothing to send. The men soon turned to scavenging through the homes in the town and on the outlying ranches. The volunteer troops were also angry over the rumor that Burnet was trying to reduce the size of the army, which now exceeded 2,500 men, most of them from the United States and all of whom wanted their land grants. Others eyed the vast open prairies and took land where they wanted. Doña Patricia was appalled, but worse was to come.[28]

Fernando de León, just released from jail for aiding the Texian cause, was accused of having disclosed the location of the supplies to the Mexican army. Rusk sent his soldiers to the ranch, and to the family's unbounded surprise and disgust, Fernando was taken back to Victoria in manacles. De León was again jailed for several days, this time as a traitor to the Texian cause. Rusk, aware of the position of his prisoner, kept a loose rein and allowed Fernando to take daily baths in the river. A group of volunteers under a man named Brantley, however, thought it fine sport to take pot shots at the unarmed Tejano bather. When Fernando was struck by a bullet, Rusk's soldiers quickly pulled him from the water to find that he was still alive. The drunken men had missed their aim, inflicting only a flesh wound. Rusk, embarrassed by the episode, freed Fernando and returned him to his mother's house for treatment. Doña Patricia and Francisca returned to town once again, and Doña Patricia demanded help from Rusk in driving the drifters and derelicts from her home. Like Urrea, the harried Rusk complied.[29]

Others among the Anglos, as Noah Smithwick remarked, "were not engaged in any of the battles, and acknowledged no authority, either military or civil."[30] Members of one of the brigand bands, with much laughter and guffawing, appropriated two mules from Doña Patricia's corral. Acceding to his mother's entreaties, Fernando, recuperating from his wounds, marched into Rusk's offices in the government building and demanded a return of the mules. Rusk accompanied Fernando to the leader of the band. The "captain of the thievish band . . . refused to surrender them, and Rusk was not in a position to force their release, inasmuch as the men were not regularly enlisted and a conflict with them was not advisable."[31] Even María Antonia, Agápito's widow and wife of Manuel Carbajal, was forced to give up sixty head of cattle, for which she requested a certificate of impressment. It took over a year and repeated demands before she finally received the document.[32]

By mid-June 1836, General Rusk was increasingly worried about the possibility of a return attack by General Urrea or the Mexican forces at Matamoros. He ordered the removal of all citizens, especially Goliad centralist sympathizers likely to help the Mexican army. For Carlos de la Garza and his neighbors on the San Antonio, leaving was not an option. They had opposed the Texians and their independence, but once the change was accomplished, they chose their land over political loyalties. Despite the danger of what might be perceived as treasonous actions, de la Garza and most of his Guardia chose to remain at Carlos Rancho. The heavily defended ranch headquarters, where Irish and Mexicans united for protection, became the center of county affairs. When Rusk's soldiers arrived at the ranch and ordered the families to move toward Louisiana, de la Garza ignored Rusk's orders, and "none durst molest him."[33] The attack by the Mexican forces never materialized, and the Tejano settlers of Goliad grimly remained on their ranches.[34]

Other Tejanos, terrorized by the attacks, preferred to leave Texas. Fernando offered to buy their lands as they left, or at least to take the property into his safekeeping. During late May and early June he took possession of thousands of acres abandoned by fleeing Tejanos. Whether he simply promised to keep them safe or actually paid for them is unknown, but by mid-June, Fernando held titles to more than 100,000 acres of land. There was no time to register the title transfers, but Fernando stored the documents in a trunk at his mother's house.[35]

Doña Patricia de León protested to Rusk the rude treatment which she had been accorded at the hands of his Texian soldiers. It did little good. When she and Fernando received Rusk's orders to move east, Doña Patricia had already decided "to make a summer sojourn in New Orleans."[36]

Doña Patricia did not just pack up the women and children. She insisted the whole family get out of Texas. The Aldretes, with their four boys loaded into mule-drawn wagons and carts, arrived from Goliad. Félix and Salomé came down from Mission Valley with their four boys, along with Desiderio and Lupita García; Silvestre and Rosalía arrived in a wagon with their two older sons and their newborn, Francisco Santiago. From the ranches to the south came Plácido, a pregnant Agustina, and their two girls. The two small Carbajal boys rode with their father, while Refugia, like her sister-in-law, was confined to a wagon with the baby Crecencia. Francisca, aided by the two widowed sisters-in-law, Antonia de León and Chucha Manchola, packed up the town house while the two cousins, León and Panchita, said their goodbyes to favorite haunts and longtime friends. With the family came indispensable *mozos* (manservants) to handle the baggage and family *nanas* (nursemaids) to care for the babies. In the bustle and confusion, the Anglos crowded around rudely to jeer, reaching out to snatch jewelry from the women. Rusk sent troops to quiet the commotion but took the opportunity to appropriate the family horses from the corral. Doña Patricia, refusing to leave her possessions, ordered Fernando to secure fifteen mules from Phillip Dimitt. She loaded them with everything she could. Finally, under the protection of Rusk's troops, Doña Patricia led the family to the small chapel for a last prayer. In the flickering candlelight, the Tejano family prayed for safety on the voyage ahead and for their future. In that emotional moment, the family did not know that most of them would be gone from their homes not for a summer, but for almost ten years.[37]

Much remained behind. According to a claim for restitution made by Fernando many years later,

> Previous to leaving, in compliance with the order of General Rusk, your petitioner and his family had been forcibly deprived of a large amount of property, consisting of clothing, furniture, plate and jewelry by men professing to be patriot volunteers ... who won their chief laurels by taking the ear rings and jewelry from the persons of helpless females belonging to your petitioner's family ... Your petitioner was hurried off on foot (his corral being full of horses at the time, but it was said, they were all needed for the army) to the Government vessel and landed with his family in New Orleans.[38]

Rusk, from his own accounts, "sent men with them to see that they went on board the vessels" at Matagorda Bay.[39] The de León family was joined at Linnville by other Tejanos, including Plácido Benavides' three brothers

La Mantilla by Carl Nebel shows elegantly dressed Spanish women in attire similar to that worn by Doña Patricia and her daughters during their stay in New Orleans. Courtesy of Benson Latin American Collection, University of Texas at Austin.

and their large families and the Escalera, Campos, Carbajal, Navarro, Sánchez, Hernández, Germán, and García families. At Linnville, Doña Patricia was thankful to find John Linn and his family. Although Rusk had assigned the de León family to the *Durango*, the group of seventy refugees boarded Linn's own barque, the *C. P. Williams*, for the trip to New Orleans.[40]

When the families disembarked on the bustling quays of the growing city, they found a town accustomed to refugees. There was not a country in South American or the Caribbean whose revolutions had not produced its own flood of survivors who found safety in the port city. Anyone who needed an army, or the money to raise one, came to New Orleans. Rebels and revolutionaries could buy arms and ammunition, as Fernando and José María Jesús had done only six months earlier. Revolutionary plans were mapped out in backrooms and bars. Anglo Americans had flocked to New Orleans, delighting in the liquor which flowed freely, losing their stakes in dimly lit gambling saloons and their virginity in the plush boudoirs of the creole prostitutes before embarking for Texas. Ships crowded the wharves.

Shops along the narrow cobblestone streets offered goods from around the world, everything from guns, swords, and Napoleonic uniforms to the latest bonnets and dress styles from Paris, satins and silks from the Far East, dainty Dutch lace, rich Russian pelts, and brightly colored English cotton ginghams. New Orleans had something for everyone.[41]

Unlike some refugees, the de León family had been in New Orleans before. Fernando and José María Jesús found lodgings for the many relatives in the hotels and rooming houses near the center of town. After settling in, there was little for the family to do but meet for tea or coffee in the small cafés, visit the shops, and explore the streets. Doña Patricia enjoyed the sonorous, early morning masses in the magnificent cathedral. After church she and the women visited dressmakers and boutiques, fanning themselves in the sticky summer heat, while the men played cards, watched cockfights, or gambled on horse races at the edge of town. After noon, everyone ate a light lunch and retired to their rooms to change into light chemises and loose shirts for the afternoon siesta. They frequented the bathhouses, thankful for the tubs of water, but they missed the refreshing afternoon dips in the rivers of Texas. In the cool of the evening they strolled down to the main square to admire the city's elite, dressed in the latest Parisian fashions, parading past on high-stepping horses or in their elegant carriages. For once, Doña Patricia and her family were not the center of attention. Doña Patricia was pleased when María Antonia, Agápito's widow, found a new husband in Manuel Carbajal. The two married quietly with little pomp or elegance. Agustina and Plácido provided the biggest excitement for the family when she gave birth to Matiana, the twentieth grandchild.

The children enjoyed the new town. Seventeen-year-old José María Aldrete tried to remain aloof from his twelve- and thirteen-year-old brothers, Trinidad and José de Jesús, and begged to be allowed to go with the men on their outings. Left to their own devices, the mischievous boys, joined by their ten-year-old brother, Rafael, and the inseparable cousins Panchita and León, learned their way around the narrow streets and alleys, often escaping their *mozos*, to roam the quays and wharves and to watch the sale of slaves at the French Market. The nine younger children, shepherded by their *nanas* with the two babies in strollers, played in the big, grassy park in front of the government house. The children watched the fireworks on the Fourth of July and listened to the unintelligible shouts of politicians vying for office in front of the government buildings during the election of 1836.

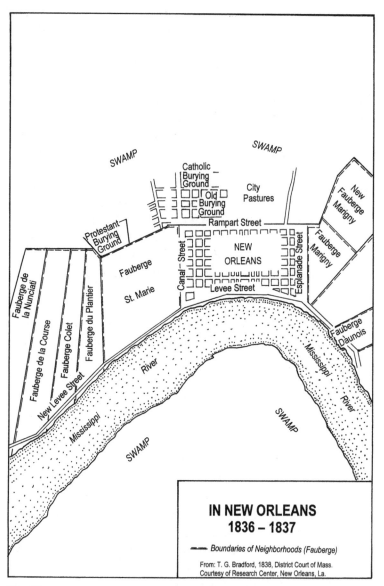

SWAMP

SWAMP

Catholic
Burying
Ground

Old
Burying
Ground

City
Pastures

New
Fauberge
Marigny

Protestant
Burying
Ground

Rampart Street

Fauberge
Marigny

Fauberge
St. Marie

NEW
ORLEANS

Canal Street

Esplanade Street

Fauberge de
la Nunciati

Fauberge de la Course

Fauberge Colet

Fauberge du Plantier

Levee Street

Fauberge
Daunois

New Levee Street

River

Mississippi
River

Mississippi

SWAMP

SWAMP

IN NEW ORLEANS
1836 – 1837

—••— *Boundaries of Neighborhoods (Fauberge)*

From: T. G. Bradford, 1838, District Court of Mass.
Courtesy of Research Center, New Orleans, La.

Map 6.2

It was an exciting world, but it was rapidly eating up the family's capital. The days drifted into months, but news from Texas was still bad. The Comanches, Tonkawas, Cocos, and Karankawas were attacking at will, and the government could do little to stop them. The new Republic of Texas had no money to pay for a military, and the militias were ineffective. President Houston, opposed at every turn by Vice President Mirabeau Buonaparte Lamar, struggled to find funds and solve the problems of the government. By fall, John and Edward Linn returned to Victoria. So did Ysidro, Nicolas, and Eugenio Benavides with their families. Doña Patricia was distressed to hear that José Miguel Aldrete would also leave for Texas. He packed up Candelaria and the children, and they bid their farewells.

Pressed for funds, Plácido recommended that the family move to Opelousas, where there were Benavides kin. Doña Patricia and Fernando agreed, and the large group packed once again and rented mules to transport their goods northwest to the small community in the pines. The narrow, marshy roads wound through dark forests of tangled cypress draped with soft, gray, Spanish moss. They arrived in Opelousas to the warm welcome of Plácido's relatives. The family found the wooden log homes pleasant with their wide porches and open central halls. For the natives of the open expanses of the South Texas prairies, however, it took a while to feel comfortable among the dense trees and thick underbrush. After the bustle of New Orleans, the family, especially Fernando and the men, felt depressed by the small community, the quiet broken only by an occasional mule or wagon train going or coming from Texas or by the mail carriers arriving from New Orleans. The men often returned to New Orleans on the pretext of business matters. For those left behind, there was always hunting and cooking and cleaning to be done. The irrepressible children adjusted quickly. Led by seventeen-year-old José María Aldrete, they explored the countryside, hunting for small game which they proudly brought home. Even the grownups soon acclimated, grateful for the Benavides hospitality.[42]

By the time the Linns and the Benavides had returned to Texas, taxes threatened all landowners. Ysidro Benavides wrote to Fernando immediately, warning him of the threat to the family ranches. Houston's government had first attempted to collect taxes in 1838 and 1839, setting a rate of between $1 and $1.25 per acre, an amount which almost no one could afford. The de Leóns were overwhelmed. The taxes were exorbitant, especially for Fernando, who now held titles to over 100,000 acres. If he failed to pay the taxes, the county sheriff had the right to sell the land.[43]

Fernando scrambled to find the funds. His reputation in New Orleans was impeccable, and he was rapidly adjusting to the Anglo society. It was also well known that he owned thousands of acres of land in Texas. Local moneylenders accepted his assurances that he would eventually repay them, whether in land, cattle, or horses, and they lent the requisite money. Fernando began sending letters of credit to Ysidro to settle his debts. He had to be selective, however, since try as he might, he could not pay for all of the land. He chose to keep the Escondido Ranch on the Garcitas and approximately 50,000 acres in smaller parcels around the rest of the country. The remainder he abandoned to the sheriffs' sales.[44]

Fernando had many enemies, and his land was as attractive as carrion to vultures. In 1839 Fernando de León lost 30,000 acres, or 6.75 leagues, to George Sutherland, who paid $124.50 at a sheriff's sale. The following year James Schenk paid $1,340.60 for a five-league tract (22,140 acres) belonging to Fernando. Not content to take his land through the slow process of sheriffs' sales, his enemies sued him for everything they could get, both legally and illegally. As his friend John J. Linn noted,

> Fernando de León was subsequently persecuted by the presentation of unjust claims against him, and, owing to the prejudice then existing against the Mexicans, many illegal and unfair judgments were rendered against him. Thus was a princely landed estate dissipated, and its owner died in comparative poverty.[45]

Beginning in 1838 a series of cases revolved around Fernando de León's giving supplies to the Mexican military during the revolution. George Sutherland, John Menifee, Thomas Menifee, and Andrew Neill all claimed that their goods had been lost to the Mexican army because of Fernando de León's treason. Suits were brought in the court of Judge James Robinson, who, ludicrously, appointed Andrew Neill, one of the claimants, as a lawyer for de León. With little fanfare, the judge promptly found against de León and issued a writ of attachment for the sale of his property. Sutherland acquired 5,029.75 acres for $2,514.88. Judge Robinson also ruled against Fernando in the amount of $2,200, resulting in the loss of 1,636 acres to Andrew Neill for $290.[46]

During the remainder of 1838 and 1839 de León's enemies continued to attack him in the Texas courts. Judge James Robinson proved to be his most determined enemy. In *Menifee v. De León* (1839), in *McGuffin v. De León* (1839), and in cases brought by Andrew Neill to recoup legal fees as de León's attorney, the judge ruled against de León and ordered pieces of his land sold to satisfy the claimants. One of the purchasers of the land was the judge himself. Working through Edward Linn, Fernando from New Orleans appealed the case to the district courts, which overturned Robinson's ruling. An overjoyed Linn wrote to Fernando that they had won the case. Menifee and Sutherland, however, were not through. They appealed the case to the Supreme Court of the Republic of Texas, and the case dragged on for two more years. Fernando's hopes sank. Frustrated and angry and trapped in Louisiana, he had lost a total of 58,805 acres.[47]

Félix, too, had become embroiled in legal battles. Before he left Texas he had been involved in an altercation during 1836 with Caleb Bennett, a newly arrived Anglo settler. Two years later, Thomas G. Western, executor of the estate of Caleb Bennett, accused Félix of murdering Bennett and stealing $3,500 of his property. Again working through Edward Linn, Félix proved that he had neither killed Bennett nor stolen any of his property. Judge James Robinson had no recourse but to rule in favor of Félix. Western's petition was disallowed, but that did not end Félix's legal problems.[48]

Félix de León's property on the Guadalupe River was a particularly lovely home, called Mission Ranch, situated in the hills outside of Victoria. It had long been famous as the second location of the mission of La Bahía from 1726 to 1749 and was well known in the community as the Mission League. The old dams and ditches of the church still existed (as they do today). On September 1, 1839, Edward Linn paid the taxes on Félix de León's league of land and registered his brand. Two years later, however, Sheriff Daniel McDonald issued an execution against Félix de León for the 1839 taxes of $133.32 and the cost of the suit, claiming that the taxes had not been paid. The successful bidder at the sale was the attorney A. S. McDonald, who bid $216.88 for the land around Mission Hill. Félix and his six children lost the family ranch.[49]

Silvestre, too, was concerned about losing his land. He trusted those with whom he had fought during the revolution, but he knew that newcomers had no interest in whether he had been on the side of the Texians. Silvestre, over Rosalía's objections, returned periodically to Texas to check on the ranch and his cattle.[50]

From Austin, Senator John Linn wrote to the de León family, worried about the problems facing the new country. President Lamar had plunged Texas even more deeply into debt. By 1841, when Houston returned to the presidency of the floundering republic, some of the large land grants had shifted into the hands of lawyers and wealthy merchants. Complaints from politically well-connected Texians had temporarily ended the land

John J. Linn, an early Irish settler in Victoria and later a senator from Victoria, like his brother Edward remained a friend of the de León family throughout his life. Courtesy of Institute of Texan Cultures, San Antonio.

taxes under Lamar. Houston reimposed the land taxes to prevent national bankruptcy. The 1844–1845 taxes were considerably lower than the earlier taxes. Tax on an entire league of land (4,428 acres) was only $12, and most taxes ranged from $1.50 to $6.00. Even with the lower amounts, there were fifty-two sheriffs' sales during this period. The Tejanos, now familiar with methods of paying the taxes, lost no land. Most of the sales came from land belonging to recently arrived German and Anglo-American immigrants who had settled on small tracts of one to twenty acres.[51]

Ysidro Benavides and John and Edward Linn reported that everyone, not just Fernando and Félix, was losing homes to crooks. Even judges, or perhaps especially the judges, such as Robinson and Thomas Jefferson Chambers, claimed land where it suited them, regardless of settlers already living there. The pioneers had to repurchase their cleared and settled lands or take up their certificates and settle elsewhere. Land titles, even if the colonists had them, could not be traced, since many of the original empresario records had been misplaced or lost. When settlers claimed to have original deeds, swindlers appeared with forged papers. In addition, boundaries often overlapped, especially since maps and often surveys were inaccurate. Like the early Spanish grants, the Texas government also granted land to two or more owners. The paper-trail difficulties created endless bickering in Austin, the new capital of the republic.[52]

The General Land Office itself had become the center for much of the problem. Noah Smithwick, one of the original settlers, complained:

> There was still another class of land sharks who victimized those who through ignorance of the law had not exactly complied with the requirements. These lynx-eyed land grabbers had their emissaries in the land office and whenever a flaw was discovered in a settler's title they had certificates ready to file on the land, thus compelling the settler to buy the land from them or lose his improvements. And often there was no flaw, but these unscrupulous villains would persuade the holder that there was, offering to make the settler a deed to the land if he would lift his certificate and transfer it to them. By this means they came into possession of many genuine certificates in exchange for land to which they had no title whatever.[53]

Land certificates given as pay to soldiers in the Texas army posed the greatest problem. Soon after the Battle of San Jacinto, special grants went to soldiers who had fought in the Army of the Republic. When they mustered out, their pay was in land scrip, or promissory certificates, to make claims on untitled land. Soldiers who had fought during the Texas Revolution were granted bounty certificates of 320 acres for every three months served and donation certificates of 640 acres for having fought at Goliad or San Jacinto.[54]

Land certificates were also used to entice new settlers. Newly arrived immigrants who desired lands for farms and ranches received land grants, known as headrights. The amount depended on the date of their arrival in Texas. Heads of families who had arrived in Texas prior to the Declaration of Independence on March 2, 1836, and who did not hold Mexican grants, received first-class headrights of a league and a labor (4,605.5 acres), which continued the Mexican government's generous policies. Single men arriving before independence received one-third of a league. Second-class headrights were granted to all those who had arrived between March 2, 1836, and October 1, 1837. Heads of families received 1,280 acres, and single men were granted 320 acres. Third- and fourth-class headrights of 640 and 320 acres were given, respectively, to families and single persons who came to Texas between October 1, 1837, and January 1, 1842. These headrights could be claimed anywhere there was vacant land. To the newly arriving immigrants who had been used to small farms with neat fences and gates in the United States, the wide-open land looked vacant.[55]

Senator John Linn reported that the new General Land Office was inundated by requests for the location of land claims and was struggling to keep up in the face of chaos. Established in 1837 by the Congress of the Republic, the Land Commission had attempted to collect records of titles from each of the empresarios. Many of the empresario records, like those in Fernando's trunk now in Opelousas, were no longer available. Until the Texas General Land Office could verify claims, local knowledge, usually in the form of a surveyor who knew the area, was the only way to be certain of available land. Few sales could take place without a clear title, and only those with the original written Mexican or Spanish titles could claim a legal right to land. But even those were rapidly becoming suspect.[56]

Anyone with a good title, if he or she acted quickly, could expect to find a market among the investors, bankers, and land speculators in the gambling town of New Orleans. But the economy of the United States was weak. In Washington, President Andrew Jackson had destroyed the Second Bank of the United States, and Carbajal, in New Orleans, had heard that a crisis of worldwide proportions was in the making. A few speculators and investors in New Orleans still dealt in specie, and Carbajal recommended to his in-laws that they sell their land quickly. Because of the problems with the titles in Texas and unsettled economic conditions in the United States, speculators offered less than the usual market value of $1 per acre for the land, but it was better to get something than nothing.[57]

Many Texas landholders were selling their land to buyers in New Orleans. The de León family in Opelousas received word that their old friend Leonardo Manso had arrived in New Orleans with the fifteen titles to the land on La Vaca Bay. He had invested $5,000 in purchasing the land from the Mexican titleholders, and he sold the 66,000 acres to Peter W. Grayson for $11,000. Grayson had also purchased titles from William Arrington, Valentine García, Diego García, Samuel May Williams, Joseph Coffin, and Thomas Jackson. He also acquired an eleven-league grant from Michael Muldoon, the frequently inebriated Irish Catholic priest. Grayson died before he could profit from his purchases, but his heirs sold the land to Levi Jones, another New Orleans speculator, who eventually lost his entire investment when he tried to establish a town and sell the lots.[58]

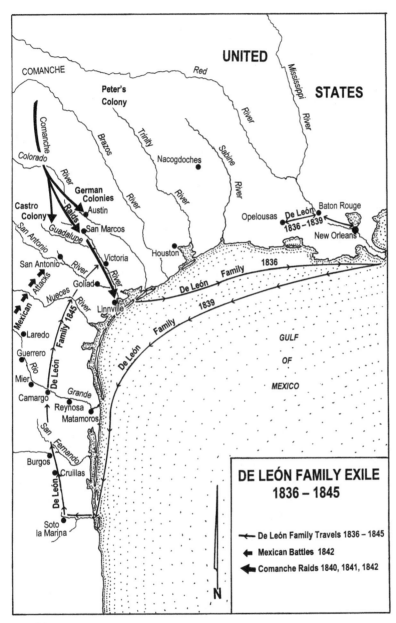

UNITED STATES

COMANCHE

Peter's Colony

Red

Mississippi River

Comanche

Colorado

River

Brazos

Trinity

Nacogdoches

Sabine River

River

German Colonies

Castro Colony

Raids

Austin

Guadalupe

San Marcos

Opelousas

De León
1836–1839

Baton Rouge

New Orleans

San Antonio

Victoria

Houston

1836

De León Family

San Antonio

Attacks

River

River

Goliad

Linnville

1839

De León Family

Mexican

Nueces

River

De León Family 1845

Laredo

GULF

Guerrero

Río

De León

OF

Mier

Grande

MEXICO

Camargo

Reynosa

Matamoros

San

Fernando

Burgos

Cruillas

De León

Soto
la Marina

N

DE LEÓN FAMILY EXILE
1836 – 1845

← De León Family Travels 1836 – 1845

← Mexican Battles 1842

← Comanche Raids 1840, 1841, 1842

Map 6.3

In Opelousas, Doña Patricia called a family council. Although Fernando, José María Jesús Carbajal, and the rest of the men could live on their letters of credit, the women could not. They needed funds, and Doña Patricia discussed the option of selling land. Ysidro, who had arrived from Texas, agreed that it was a good time to sell. The New Orleans speculators were interested in buying, and it was best to make a deal before the land was stolen by squatters, land thieves, or the courts. María de Jesús Manchola had the right to sell her land as Rafael Manchola's widow, but María Antonia, because of her marriage to Manuel Carbajal, needed the family's permission to sell her son León's land. The family agreed that she should. Doña Patricia had claimed the 20,000 acres of Martín de León's first ranch as her dowry right. José María Jesús and Fernando chose Pleasant B. Cocke, a New Orleans investor, as the purchaser. From her trunks Doña Patricia produced the title to the land, signed by Fernando as land commissioner, and unearthed the decades-old document in which she had given Martín the $10,000 in goods and cash from her dowry to start their long trek into Texas.[59]

On January 3, 1837, the family came before George King, the parish judge for St. Landry parish. José María Jesús Carbajal, since he spoke the best English, acted as lawyer for the family. Present at the gathering were Fernando and Félix de León, Plácido and Ysidro Benavides, Manuel Carbajal, and Francisco Nida, a family friend.

In the first order of business, Pleasant B. Cocke, having arrived from New Orleans, purchased from Doña Patricia de la Garza de León the title to a tract of land containing five leagues and five labors, or approximately 22,728 acres. Her late husband, Martín de León, had received the land for the completion of his first empresario contract in 1829, and the land had come into her possession upon his death. She claimed the land as her dowry right and produced the document dated 1801 as proof of her legal license to the land. Pleasant B. Cocke offered $10,000 for the land, which was accepted by Doña Patricia with the approval of the gathered family.[60]

The second order of business was the tutorship of León de León. Since his father Agápito de León had died and his mother remarried, the law required that his mother and his new stepfather, Manuel Carbajal, legally accept guardianship over him. José María Jesús announced that the appellant, María Antonia de la Garza, asked to be reinstated "in the natural tutorship of her said minor child, León de León, which was forfeited in consequence of her marriage with Manuel Carvajal [sic] after the death of

Agápito de León."[61] Jointly, the family decided that half of María Antonia's family ranch, a "League or Sitio superficial quantity Texian or Mexican measure,"[62] inherited from Agápito jointly by María Antonia and León, should be sold. P. B. Cocke agreed to buy the 2,200 acres of unimproved land on the Garcitas and Marcado Creeks for $1,000, half in cash and the remainder in equal installments in six and twelve months from the day of the sale. The family also agreed that Manuel Carbajal would be united with his wife, María Antonia, in the tutorship of León de León and that the boy should be placed under the protection of José María Jesús Carbajal, who was appointed the undertutor to young León.[63]

Pleasant B. Cocke also purchased land from María de Jesús "Chucha" Manchola, and with the documents signed and sealed by the judge, the family received their money from Cocke.[64] León de León and Panchita Manchola could look forward to comfortable futures and good educations, although the idea of being stuck in Catholic boarding schools for months at a time, even if they were in New Orleans, may not have appealed to the two cousins. Doña Patricia, who placed little faith in the banks in the United States, purchased mortgages on property in Opelousas and saved the remainder of her funds for those rainy days when her family might need her help. Meanwhile, Félix had rushed Salomé to New Orleans for the birth of their fifth child, Olivia.

By the time Ysidro returned to Texas, he wrote Fernando that the land problems had indeed gotten worse. "There were those who came to the state after its annexation and bought up or manufactured old Spanish grants, and, with witnesses made to order, robbed the old pioneers of their hard earned homes."[65] The government, unable to stop the larceny, had little choice but to stop sales and transfers of property altogether. After having opened it little more than a year earlier, the government closed the General Land Office. Those who did have title to land which they had gained before the revolution "held their land at such prices that those who came to the country under the hope of getting land for nothing or at least at very reduced sums, were neither able nor willing to pay."[66] New arrivals, therefore, were left to "rent or do nothing."[67] According to an interested observer in 1837, should the new government make the mistake of opening the land office,

a scene of strife and confusion must follow which will surpass even the worst conception the mind can form. Each tract of good land will be stained by the blood of opposing claimants; surveys will be fraudulent, and litigation endless ... The world must expect to see an agrarian struggle when the office opened, that would shake to its foundations, as by an earthquake, the strongest and best settled government of the earth.[68]

The Republic of Texas certainly could not claim a strong government. That such a gloomy prediction did not come to pass, according to John Linn, was due to the efforts of local surveyors such as his brother Edward. On the local level, the early settlers and the surveyors knew their boundaries although there were no fences, and neighbors knew who owned land upriver and downriver from their own claims. Some of the difficulty lay in the immense size of the Spanish and Mexican grants. Newcomers, trudging across the wide-open prairies, had settled in any pine grove or oak motte that looked appealing. Landowners often had no idea that claim jumpers had settled on their extensive properties until they were called into court to prove their boundaries.[69]

Edward Linn reported to the de León family that even the newspapers had begun to attack them. An article in the Houston *Morning Star* claimed that since the de León family had "[taken] up arms against Texas and joined the army of Santa Anna during the revolution, their property was considered as forfeited."[70] Edward defended the de León property when he ran surveys or when he came across squatters, but incoming settlers believed the newspaper account and felt free to take de León property. Those who had squatted on the lands or bought them from sheriffs' sales swore to "defend their land even if they had to use violence to remove the Mexicans who were trying to reclaim their land through law suits."[71] From Louisiana, there was little the de León family could do but trust Edward Linn and their Benavides kin.

Summer in Texas may have been hot, but Opelousas in 1838 was worse than anything the family had ever experienced. They suffered from the stuffiness of humidity and the constant attacks of mosquitoes. Even smoke and cheesecloth over the windows had no effect. That summer, yellow fever broke out among the small populace. Little Crecencia Carbajal, just months old, died in the oppressive heat. Many in the family succumbed to the fever, lying limp and motionless, their lips parched, skin parchment-yellow, begging for water. Those who hadn't fallen ill dragged buckets of water up from the dark, murky swamps. Plácido had worked hard to save the others, carrying water, cutting wood, and bringing back game from long hunting trips. Worn out by his exertions, Plácido came down with the dreaded disease. There was no medical help, and the family was devastated when he died that summer. The family buried him beside little Crecencia in the Benavides family plot. The following year, death struck again. Silvestre's wife, Rosalía, succumbed. She, too, was laid to rest in the cemetery at Opelousas, Louisiana, far from their Texas home.[72]

By 1839 Doña Patricia decided it was time to leave the mosquito-infested swamps of Louisiana. Texas was still dangerous, but at least Soto la Marina in northern Mexico was relatively safe. While José María Jesús Carbajal returned to New Orleans to book passage for the family to Matamoros, Fernando and Félix arranged for wagons to carry the women and children and for mules to haul the family's possessions. Doña Patricia and her daughters organized the packing of the trunks and boxes, and the long train of mules and wagons headed for New Orleans once again. It was a far less cheerful group that returned to the Crescent City, but at least, Doña Patricia felt, they were headed home.

Matamoros, Soto la Marina, and all of Mexico were abuzz with excitement when the de León family landed in the spring of 1839. The French and British were threatening Mexico for failing to repay its debts. Once again the political parties were feuding, and there was talk in Spain of invading and retaking Texas to keep it out of the hands of the British. While Carbajal and Refugia traveled up the Rio Grande to a new ranch which he had just purchased along the river, Doña Patricia hurried the rest of the family away to Soto la Marina and the haven of the de la Garza ranches. Silvestre rejoined them from Texas and reported continuing problems with the insolvent Republic of Texas. He and his *vaqueros* had maintained a constant watch on his lands, patrolling the ranch, running off squatters, and buying the goodwill of the Indians with gifts of tobacco and cattle.

The Comanches, coming in great waves with thousands of mounted riders, had attacked Victoria in 1840. The citizens in town had fled to Plácido's Round House, the defensive Spanish *torreón* with its gun slits and thick walls. The settlers had escaped the wrath of the Indians with their lives, but the town was destroyed. Ranging farther south, the Comanches had surprised the settlers at John Linn's small port town on La Vaca Bay. Without a *torreón* for protection, Linnville was burned to the ground, and the Comanches massacred and scalped the settlers. Only the best-fortified ranches had withstood the raids. Carlos de la Garza, on the San Antonio River, provided refuge for his neighbors and the people of Refugio. The local ranchers had formed a ranging company for the defense of the small community, based on ideas of the Mexican lancers and de la Garza's Guardia Victoriana. Everyone worried, however, when they learned in 1842 that the Mexican forces under General Woll planned to invade Texas. Not only would the Indians feel free to assault the outlying settlements, but the Texians would feel justified in attacking the Tejano ranches. By the fall of 1842 the invasions had failed, but the countryside was once again subjected to raids by Indian tribes and cattle thieves.[73]

Doña Patricia, concerned over her family, grew more worried when Agustina, weakened by her bout with the yellow fever, fell ill once again. Patricia sent for the doctors in Matamoros, but there was little they could do. Even the old *curandera* on the ranch, with all her potions and powders, was helpless. Only a year after Plácido, Agustina passed away, leaving her three little girls orphaned. Doña Patricia and the ever-faithful Francisca took over the care of Pilar, now eight, Librada, seven, and six-year-old Matianita. Back in Texas, Ysidro promised to care for their land and protect their *herencia* (inheritance) and notified the Texas courts that he would act as guardian for Plácido and Agustina's estate.[74]

Death seemed to be a too-frequent visitor at Doña Patricia's doorstep. During the sojourn in Soto la Marina, Desiderio Garcia too had fallen ill. He was only thirty-eight when he died, leaving Lupita, at thirty-nine, a widow with no children to console her. In 1840 Desiderio had sold some of their land in Victoria, which provided Lupita with a small income. Doña Patricia took in her widowed daughter, glad to have her take the empty spot left by María Antonia's marriage to Manuel Carbajal.[75]

Early in 1843 Silvestre returned to the ranch on the Guadalupe and joined his *vaqueros*. They rode out to begin the sweep of the ranch and to check on the stock. Topping a small rise, Silvestre and his men surprised Mabry (or Maberry) Gray, also known as "Mustang" Gray, and a gang of men running the brands on the de León cattle. They had started a small fire and were using a straight bar to mark over Silvestre's brand, changing its appearance. Buyers on the coast, giving the cattle a cursory inspection, would not have noticed the change. Only a suspicious cattle inspector checking the undersides of the hides of slaughtered cattle would have been able to tell who the original owner had been, and Gray did not plan to let that happen.

Silvestre tried to avoid a violent confrontation. He pointed out to Gray that he was on de León land and that the cattle were legally branded and belonged to the de León family. Gray did not hesitate. Before Silvestre and his men even had time to swing their rifles, Gray and his men had drawn their weapons and fired. Silvestre and his *vaqueros* fell in a hail of bullets. Assuring himself that all the men were dead, Gray stripped the bodies and rode off with the cattle. That evening, *vaqueros* from the ranch went out in search of Silvestre and the missing men. They found the mangled remains of their *patrón* and the evidence of the cattle theft. The loyal *vaqueros* carried the bodies back to the ranch and dug graves for the dead on the small hill overlooking the ranch house. Two of the *vaqueros* rode for Soto la Marina to carry the sad news, while the others rode to Victoria to report the killings.[76]

Gray continued to prey on other Mexican families, including other de León relatives. In 1842 "Mustang" Gray had joined a "company of organized bandits and cut-throats called 'the Cow-Boys' whose leader was one Wells."[77] This group had rampaged at will across the countryside and had killed a group of seven Mexicans who had come up from Mier to visit Ysidro Benavides, Plácido's brother. The Mexicans were encamped south of Goliad for the night when Gray approached the camp. They invited him to join them for supper but soon found themselves surrounded and imprisoned by the rest of the gang. The Mexicans were tied hand and foot, and the gang opened fire on them. Among the group who was gunned down was Cayetano Moreno, the brother of Ysidro's wife. One of the seven survived the executions and reported the deaths to the authorities. Nothing was done during the years of the Texas Republic to arrest Gray or stop his marauding.[78]

That fall Silvestre's land went on the block for failure to pay taxes. Judge Palmer, as probate judge, appointed Milton H. Hardy to handle the estate of the deceased. Creditors appeared in 1844 to make claims on the estate. Hardy sold all of Silvestre de León's 4,428 acres to satisfy their demands. The land was sold at a sheriff's sale for between thirteen and nineteen cents per acre to Thomas Ingram, Thomas Newcomb, W. S. Newman, William Gamble, and S. W. Van Norman, all claimants in the case. Like his brothers, Silvestre had been divested of his property.[79]

At Soto la Marina, Doña Patricia had three more grandchildren who had been left orphaned. Sorrowfully, she explained to fourteen-year-old Francisco, twelve-year-old Martín, and four-year-old Francisco Santiago that their father would never be coming home again. Their grandmother and the family gathered to determine what to do with the growing boys. The three Benavides granddaughters were already a handful for Doña Patricia. After the loss of Silvestre's land, there was no income to help pay the boys' way. Fernando, Félix, and Doña Patricia met with Rosalía de la Garza's parents at Soto la Marina. They agreed that the boys should move in with Rosalía's parents. Little four-year-old Francisco Santiago, Fernando's favorite among the nephews, begged to stay with his uncle. Fernando promised that one day they would be back together again. Little did he know how true that would be.

CHAPTER 7

FIGHTING FOR THE LAND, 1845–1853

Genealogical Chart

MARTÍN DE LEÓN (D. 1834)
+ PATRICIA DE LA GARZA (D. 1850)

1. Fernando (wid. 1828, m. 1848, d. 1853) + María de la Luz Escalera (m. 1848)
    1-1. Francisco Santiago "Frank," nephew (adopted 1848)

2. María Candelaria (m. 1818) + José Miguel Aldrete
    2-1. José María (b. 1820)
    2-2. José de Jesús María (b. 1822)
    2-3. Trinidad (b. 1824, m. 1846) + Andrea Ramírez
    2-4. Rafael (b. 1826)

3. Silvestre (d. 1843) + Rosalía de la Garza (d. 1838)
    3-1. Francisco (b. 1830)
    3-2. Martín (b. 1832)
    3-3. Francisco Santiago (b. 1836, adopted 1848 by uncle Fernando)

4. "Lupita" (wid. 1842, m. 1849) + Cesario de la Garza
    No children

5. Félix (d. 1850) + Salomé Leal (d. 1852)
    5-1. Santiago (b. 1829)
    5-2. Patricio (b. 1830)
    5-3. Silvestre (b. 1834)
    5-4. Olivia (b. 1837)
    5-5. "Chucha" (b. 1840)
    5-6. Samuel (b. 1846)
    5-7. Candelaria (b. 1847)

6. Agápito (d. 1833) + María Antonia C. de la Garza +
   Manuel Carbajal (m. 1837)
   6-1. León de León (b. 1824)

7. "Chucha" (m. 1824) + Rafael Manchola (d. 1833)
   7-1. "Panchita" (m. 1847) + Cristobal Morales

8. Refugia (m. 1832) + José María Jesús Carbajal
   8-1. Antonio (b. 1833)
   8-2. José María (b. 1834)
   8-3. Crecencia (b.-d. 1836)

9. Agustina (d. 1842) + Plácido Benavides (d. 1838)
   9-1. Pilar (b. 1834)
   9-2. Librada (b. 1835)
   9-3. Matiana (b. 1836)

10. Francisca (m. 1849, d. 1852) + Vicente Dosal
    10-1. Jesús (b. 1850)

In June 1845 John Linn wrote to Fernando from the new capital at Austin that the United States had finally accepted Texas as a state. All that remained was for the citizens of Texas to vote for or against annexation. Linn reported that the ex-president, Mirabeau B. Lamar, continued to oppose the union, still hoping that New Mexico and California would join Texas to form one great southwestern country. According to Linn, Sam Houston and most Texans were certain to vote for annexation since Texas had been unable to solve its economic problems or defend itself against Indian attacks. With the help of American money and U.S. troops, Texas would at last be safe. Linn also sent congratulations to Fernando. The Texas Supreme Court had ruled against Sutherland and had remanded Fernando's land case back to Victoria County for a new trial. Judge Robinson had been removed, and there was hope that Fernando could now win a fair ruling.

The de León family conclave met in Soto la Marina in 1845 to discuss the possibility of returning to Texas. Political revolutions were brewing in northern Mexico as centralists battled federalists. Texas was now the safer of the two places. The family also still held land there. Thanks to their Benavides kin and Edward Linn, the de León family owned their town homes, numerous lots, and acreage along the coast. Squatters had lived in the houses, and vandals had long since taken their possessions, but the property still belonged to them. There was hope, and there was reason to return. Doña Patricia had rebuilt before, and she would do it again.

As they gathered at Soto la Marina, many changes had transpired within the family. Doña Patricia was concerned for the orphans—Silvestre and Rosalía's three sons and Plácido and Agustina's three daughters. Lupita, widowed by the death of Desiderio Garcia, joined her widowed sister, Chucha Manchola, in Doña Patricia's household. Fernando, also widowed, was still alone at 47. There were new grandchildren, however, and the older ones were going off to school. The Aldretes had just returned from New Orleans, where they had placed Rafael and Trinidad in Charles Cuvellier's boarding school. They had offered one-third of a league in exchange for the schooling, passage, and room and board for both boys, who now could join their cousin León at the elite school. They had checked on Panchita, who missed her cousin León but did not often escape the watchful eyes of the nuns at the convent school.[1]

José Miguel and Candelaria Aldrete reported that the lawlessness and the Indian raids in Texas had diminished. The Indians had been pushed farther west, where Alsatian colonists under Henri de Castro had settled outside San Antonio. Led by Prince Carl von Solms Braunfels, the Germans were landing at Indianola and renting wagons to make the long trek northwest and settle in the rocky hill country between San Antonio and Gonzales. Braunfels was giving them small farms of ten or twenty acres. To the Aldretes the size of the land grants seemed ridiculously small, but the Germans seemed happy. They were farmers, after all, not cattlemen. The sensible Germans had even gone back to the old Spanish method of bribing the Indians with goods to keep them peaceful, and it seemed to be working. Victoria was busy and prosperous as the wagon trains of Germans came through. Some had stayed and bought land along the coast or from the large landowners around Victoria. The hardworking German farmers bothered no one. They stayed on their small farms and kept to their own communities. Even Victoria was beginning to attract "the better sort," the Aldretes reported.[2]

Not everyone chose to return. José María Jesús Carbajal and Refugia, with eleven-year-old Antonio and ten-year-old José María Jr., remained on the Rio Grande, settling on their ranch at Camargo. José María Jesús had high hopes that the northern states of Tamaulipas, Coahuila, and Nuevo León would form a new country dedicated to the federalist ideals. His brother Manuel and Antonia would be staying in Mexico, too, although they promised that León would come visit his grandmother often in Victoria. Silvestre and Rosalía's three boys, Francisco, Martín, and Francisco Santiago, were left in Mexico with the de la Garza family. Félix and Salomé, with their four boys and three girls, knew that if they wanted to leave their sons and daughters any inheritance, it would take fighting for their Texas land. Fernando, too, felt he had nothing to lose by returning and challenging his enemies in court.

It was a hard decision for Doña Patricia and the other women. They could stay in Soto la Marina, where they might be safe from the revolutionary uprisings, but Patricia placed her hopes in her homeland of thirty-five years. Francisca, now twenty-eight, knew that she would go with her mother. Chucha Manchola, alone since Panchita had started school in New Orleans, also determined to return with her mother in order to care for her three orphaned nieces, Pilar, eleven, Librada, ten, and Matianita, nine. Lupita García, so recently widowed, joined her sisters and her mother in the long trek back to Victoria.[3]

Although she returned to an Anglo Texas, Patricia's ties and those of her family to her Mexican homeland were never broken. Texas might become part of the United States and she might be called American, but her language and her customs would remain Spanish. Her home, wherever it was, became the heart and soul of the family. In time of need, the family could be called together to make important decisions or extend help to a relative in trouble. It was also the center for family gatherings for weddings, births, baptisms, deaths, and religious holidays. With the danger of Indian attacks declining, the families from Mexico regularly braved flooded rivers or trekked across the dry South Texas chaparral to make the yearly trip to Doña Patricia's home in Victoria. The road had been improved, and travelers in carriages and coaches could make the crossing in less than a month. Potential marriage partners, godparents, and kin made the long trip across the dry plains of South Texas with increasing frequency.[4]

Upon their return to Victoria, Doña Patricia and Fernando found that the Aldretes and the Linns were right about the changes in Victoria. The streets were still dusty and the pigs and chickens still rooted in the gutters, but the governing council was busy civilizing the town. Wooden sidewalks lined the main streets. A fence had been put up around the market square to keep out the animals. Strict rules governed the merchants and food vendors. Mission Indians, with their fruits and vegetables, no longer dominated the market square. Strange-speaking German farmers sold their goods from carts or small mercantile establishments. The street names had been changed, and Patricia did not recognize most of the new wooden buildings which had been erected a few years earlier. As they entered the main square, she almost did not know her old home.[5]

One thing was the same — John Linn's home. This time it was Fernando who was grateful for his friend's protection. John Linn was older, more serious, graying at the temples, a distinguished statesman, and the senator from Victoria, but Doña Patricia still found in him her friend Juan, who had brought her presents from New Orleans. This time she had small gifts for him, from Soto la Marina and Matamoros. Edward Linn came for dinner, and the friends laughed and talked of the old times long into the night.

The next morning Doña Patricia and her daughters accompanied the Linns to church. The small chapel that she and Martín had built had been replaced with a larger wooden structure. Doña Patricia met the new resident priest, Father Estany, a Spanish-speaking Vincentian priest who told her of the new bishop for Texas. The dynamic and dedicated Frenchman, Bishop John Mary Odin, had taken good care of the parishioners. He had chosen priests who spoke Spanish as well as English and often German and Polish for the community of mixed backgrounds.[6]

Upon their return from church, John Linn asked about their plans. He was certain that Doña Patricia could get her home back if she wanted it. Robert Carlisle and Bridget Quinn had been living in the house, long emptied of all of her furnishings. Rather than agonize over painful memories, Doña Patricia asked about the possibility of selling it to them and holding the mortgage. John Linn agreed, and within days Patricia had sold her home for $7,000, of which Carlisle and Quinn agreed to pay $700 a year. It would be more than enough to keep her family comfortably in a small house in town until the court cases were settled. Since Fernando had no wife, Doña Patricia insisted that he join the all-female household.[7]

With John Linn's help and advice, Fernando found a good lawyer. A. H. Phillips agreed to take his cases in exchange for a league of land. More than four thousand acres seemed a high price to pay, but to regain almost fifty thousand acres, Fernando felt it was worth it. Fernando sold one of his town lots to Dr. Felix H. Webb for $100, enough to give him working capital, and he and Phillips formed a partnership which lasted successfully for ten years. Fernando at first felt uncomfortable among the Anglo lawyers and landowners who stared at him as he entered the courthouse, but he was determined to be accepted in the new society. He had even brought a slave back with him from New Orleans who acted as his manservant. Fernando still spoke accented English, but it improved quickly as he and Phillips discussed their legal options. When the courthouse hangers-on found out that the de León family had the support of Senator Linn and his brother, surveyor Edward Linn, some changed their attitudes, greeting the de Leóns with care. Others, however, especially those afraid of losing land, treated them with undisguised disdain. Fernando learned to ignore their looks and snide comments.[8]

District court was the social event of the year for small towns like Victoria. While the court was in session, "litigants, witnesses, prospective jurors, friends of persons on trial, spectators, gamblers, and an occasional peddler crowded courtroom, grogshops, and streets . . . Indeed, court week furnished one enthralling substitute for formalized amusements."[9] In the evenings, after court, lawyers and spectators swapped stories, recounted humorous tales, and drank themselves into oblivion. Fernando and Phillips held boisterous suppers for their own supporters, where laughter and cigar smoke filled the rooms, and liquor flowed freely.

The first action Phillips recommended was to dislodge the squatters. During the spring term of 1847, to the fascination of the gossips on the courthouse steps, Fernando launched an all-out attack. He filed case after case. He sued Andrew Neill, S. A. White, M. I. Hardy, and Murphree and Van Bibber, all for ejectment. Witnesses, many still carrying the ten-year-old scars of the Texas Revolution, came forward to testify for Fernando; these included Edward Linn and the senator. They described his efforts to help Texas, the sale of horses to buy the supplies which had been lost aboard the *Hannah Elizabeth*, his military rank with the Texas Militia, his mistreatment at the hands of the Mexican troops, and the travesty of being dislodged by General Rusk and forced to leave his home and Texas. The Anglo landholders fought back with ugly rumors, detailing Fernando's complicity with General Urrea, his willingness to side with the Mexican forces, his abandonment of Victoria for the safety of New Orleans. The testimony piled up, session after session, year after year, and still the cases dragged on. Fernando refused to back down. The land had been stolen, and he would not accept defeat. At last, a shocked and stunned crowd heard the judge rule in favor of Fernando de León in the case against Andrew White. The precedent had been set. The judge's gavel came down again and again for Fernando—against S. A. White, M. I. Hardy, and Murphree and Van Bibber. When the trials ended, Fernando hugged Phillips in a giant Mexican *abrazo*. Fernando had regained not only his Rancho Escondido but more than twenty thousand acres of his original property as well.[10]

But Fernando and Phillips were not through. Fernando was determined to win back his land from the judge who had ruled against him so many times. It gave him particular satisfaction to initiate the case of *F. De León v. James Robinson*. Robinson, frail and white-haired, sitting across the courtroom from Fernando, suddenly looked far less intimidating than he had in his black robes behind the bench. Fernando's recent victories made Robinson and his lawyers nervous. The testimony slowly mounted against them as witness after witness spoke for Fernando. Judge Robinson, as some still called him, sat hunched and silent throughout the trial. In 1848, two years into the trial, worn down by the lengthy case and the hours of testimony, Robinson died. Fernando considered giving up the case, but Phillips assured him that his chances of winning were better than ever. After an administrator had been appointed and the estate had gone through probate, Fernando and Phillips reopened the case in 1851 against Robinson's estate. Without old Judge Robinson sitting there sullen but determined, the case ended quickly. Again Fernando won and regained his property. The courthouse hangers-on, the lawyers, and even some of the Anglo ranchers now greeted him by name, shaking his hand and congratulating him on his success. For the Anglos he was no longer a common Mexican—he was one of the "old Spanish families." He did, after all, own more land than almost all of the Anglo ranchers who complimented him. Fernando and his family celebrated their great victories.[11]

In 1846, while fighting his own cases, Fernando de León and Phillips appealed Silvestre's case in *De León v. Hardy.* Fernando de León and his lawyer seemed to be in the courthouse all the time, agreed the gaggle of rumormongers, alternately spitting and whittling as they sat on the benches in the shade of the trees around the government square. First one case and then another. What on earth was to happen to the settlers already living on the property in question? Getting them off the land would be a row, they agreed. But Fernando and Phillips were not concerned. It would be the sheriff's problem to execute the judge's orders.

Silvestre's case was more complex than Fernando's. Since it had been a probate case, the district court's ruling would have to be overturned, and that meant appealing the case to the Texas Supreme Court. Fernando and Phillips packed up the written testimony on mules and set out toward the state capital. Austin was still a new town, its unpaved streets muddy in the spring and dust-dry in the fall. The town itself consisted of a 640–acre tract "fronting on the Colorado and nestled between Waller Creek on the east and Shoal Creek on the west."[12]

A collection of temporary one and two-story clapboard wooden buildings—saloons, mercantile establishments, law offices, and rooming houses—lined Austin's main street, now called Congress, which extended from the river to Capital Square. The rest of the streets had been named for the rivers of Texas and were bisected by numbered streets which began at the river and wandered off into the hills east and west of town. The French consulate on the bluff east of town had been appropriated by Swedes who had renamed it Swedish Hill. Germans and Irish and Poles had settled down toward the Colorado River, where warehouses and docks leaned against each other and saloons alternated with houses of prostitution in which congressmen discreetly entertained themselves while away from their homes. The one-story wooden courthouse building was close to Capital Square and within easy walking distance of Senator John Linn's newly completed home, where Fernando and Phillips found rooms and a hearty welcome.[13]

The case for Silvestre's land was tried before Chief Justice John Hemphill, a vigorous and determined judge who dominated the Supreme Court from 1840 to 1857. Phillips explained the case. In essence, Silvestre had been divested of his lands by unscrupulous individuals who, he said, had falsely claimed that debts were owed to them from the estate. The witnesses who came forward to testify in Silvestre's behalf included Senator John Linn. Phillips introduced the piles of depositions and testimony which they had brought from Victoria. To the surprise of the court crowd, the judge promptly reversed the ruling of the lower court and remanded the decision to the Victoria courts. After celebrating with the Linns, Fernando and Phillips repacked the mules and returned to Victoria.[14]

Once back on home ground, Phillips was now certain they would win. He was right. In the next session, the district judge invalidated Thomas Hardy's sales of Silvestre de León's land, and the court returned the entire league of land to Silvestre's estate. The courthouse buzzed with the news. Many of the settlers would have to be removed, and there would be considerable opposition. Fear of the conflict was not something which worried Fernando.[15]

Overjoyed, Fernando wrote to Rosalía's family to let the boys know that they would each receive 1,476 acres, more than enough for a sizable ranch or sufficient to sell for an excellent profit now that the land prices were skyrocketing with the arrival of statehood. Francisco, who had just turned fifteen, and Martín, thirteen, wrote to thank their uncle and to say they were content to leave the land in their uncle's hands for the time being. Seven-year-old Francisco Santiago, however, with that tenacity of childhood which always amuses adults, had not forgotten his uncle's promise. He insisted he wanted to come to Texas, and come he did, bundled up by the Mexican family on the Rio Grande into the dusty, spine-jarring stage coach for the long trip to Texas. Fernando welcomed young Francisco into the household in Victoria.

Félix, emboldened by Fernando's successes in court, also challenged those who had taken his land. Although the land transfers which had occurred since the initial purchase increased the problems, the case of the initial land loss was far more clear-cut. It centered on the issue of the payment of taxes for 1839. Edward Linn, who had paid the taxes for Félix, was still available as a witness. A. S. McDonald, the attorney who had originally bought up the Mission Valley League, had died soon after he purchased Félix's ranch. The McDonald estate had failed to pay the 1842–1843 taxes of $44.34 on the property. The attorney had added considerably to his holdings that by this time consisted of 26,366 acres, all of which went back on the block at the sheriff's sale. On March 5, 1845, Thomas Newcomb bought the entire estate, including the Mission League, for $44.34.

To protect the Mission League from trespassers, who evidently included Félix de León, Newcomb leased the land to Peter W. Hays, who had been living on the property for the previous four years. As caretaker, Hays was required to pay an annual rent of only $1 and was allowed to cut timber and clear land "except the motts and groves around the Mission Hill . . . which is hereby reserved and the timber growing on the river within 500 yards above and below the said Mission Hill."[16]

In August 1845 Félix, like his brother, hired attorney A. H. Phillips and, as payment to fight the case, deeded him "one *sitio* with eight *labors* of temporal land and the rest pasture on the west bank of the Guadalupe River . . . originally granted to José María Escalera."[17] Félix had learned from his brother, and he retained titles to land belonging to his neighbors. Thomas Newcomb, obviously foreseeing problems with the newly returned de León family and their attorneys, sold the Mission League two months later to James Dennison of Matagorda for $400. With Edward Linn's testimony, Félix proved that the 1839 taxes had indeed been paid. Félix regained the property and along with Salomé and the six children moved back to the Mission Valley Ranch. Thomas Newcomb skipped town, Peter Hays was ejected from the property, and Dennison lost his $400 investment. The de León family had reason to celebrate.[18]

Meanwhile, down on the San Antonio River, Fernando and his brothers were not the only ones fighting for their land. Carlos de la Garza was also threatened by New Orleans land speculators. After the Texas Revolution, Carlos and Tomasita and their children had remained on his ranch, protected by his *vaqueros* from Indians and by his Irish neighbors from rapacious Anglos. Carlos de la Garza did not enter the world of Anglo politics, just as he had remained out of Tejano politics prior to the war. But he extended his protection over anyone who asked. He fortified his ranch, built additional defensive buildings, and added a small mercantile store run by two Scotsmen. With the blessing and assistance of Bishop Odin, he ran the small Catholic boys school for the education of his own sons and those of his Catholic Irish neighbors. The government of Refugio County conducted its affairs from the safety of his ranch, and his neighbors found protection from Karankawa and Comanche attacks within its walls. He mounted a unit of men to patrol the countryside, much like the men who would later be called the Texas Rangers. He sought no payment. Protecting others was simply expected of a community patriarch. He obeyed the laws and paid his taxes promptly and in full throughout the years of the republic.[19]

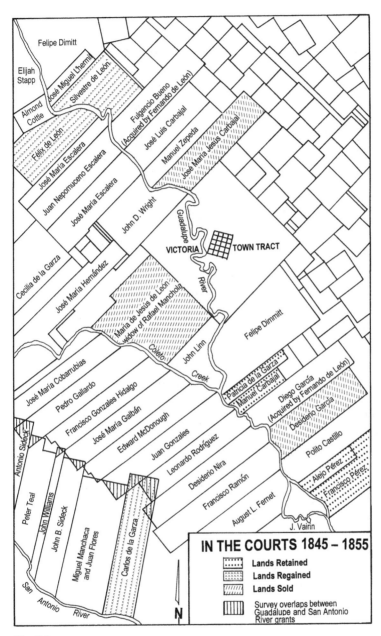

Felipe Dimitt

Elijah
Stapp

José Miguel L'hermit

Silvestre de León

Almond
Cottle

Félix de León

José María Escalera

Juan Nepomuceno Escalera

José María Escalera

Fulgencio Bueno
(Acquired by Fernando de León)

José Luis Carbajal

Manuel Zepeda

José María Jesús Carbajal

John D. Wright

Guadalupe

VICTORIA

TOWN TRACT

Cecilia de la Garza

José María Hernández

María de Jesús de León,
widow of Rafael Manchola

River

Felipe Dimitt

José María Cobarrubias

Pedro Gallardo

Francisco Gonzales Hidalgo

José María Galbán

Coleto

John Linn

Creek

Edward McDonough

Juan Gonzales

Leonardo Rodríguez

Patricia de la Garza
Manuel Carbajal

Diego García
(Acquired by Fernando de León)

Desiderio García

Antonio Sideck

Peter Teal

John Williams

John B. Sideck

Miguel Manchaca
and Juan Flores

Carlos de la Garza

Desiderio Nira

Francisco Ramón

August L. Fernet

Polito Castillo

Alejo Pérez

Francisco Pérez

J. Vairin

San

Antonio

River

IN THE COURTS 1845 – 1855

- Lands Retained
- Lands Regained
- Lands Sold
- Survey overlaps between Guadalupe and San Antonio River grants

N

Map 7.1

In August 1845 Carlos de la Garza and his ranch became the target of General Thomas Taylor Williamson of Shreveport, Louisiana. Williamson had acquired the right to fifty-one sections of land (32,640 acres) from land scrip originally granted to Thomas Green of Richmond, Virginia. Evidently driven by some personal animosity toward Carlos de la Garza, Williamson located his land certificates to include the land on the east shores of the Nueces River, the town of San Patricio, both sides of the Aransas Creek beginning at its junction with the bay, the peninsula of Live Oak Point (part of the Power grant), and the eastern shore of the San Antonio River "so as to cover the claim of Carlos de la Garza."[20] Williamson's wife, who controlled in her own right an additional eighty certificates for 640 acres each, or a total of 51,200 acres, extended the Williamson family claim far up the San Antonio River. Williamson appeared in New Orleans with a title to the lands and sold the fifty-one sections covering the de la Garza ranch to Thomas Brown Lee, a land agent in New Orleans, for $10,000 or approximately thirty cents per acre.[21]

Two years later a confident Thomas Lee arrived in Refugio and began inspecting his lands. Like many of the New Orleans speculators, he planned to divide the thousands of acres and sell them in profitable small quantities of ten or twenty acres. At the county courthouse, which by this time had been moved off of Carlos Rancho and back to Refugio, he attempted to take possession of the lands and register his ownership. Without even a court hearing, the county judge inspected the certificates and declared them invalid, since all of the certificates covered previously titled lands. He did not need to call in Carlos de la Garza. In a fury, Thomas Brown Lee accused the judge of thievery and threatened lawsuits which he swore would tie up the land sales forever. The judge had the sheriff escort Lee from the courthouse and suggested that a return to New Orleans might be conducive to his good health. Lee hired a lawyer to fight for the lands, but unlike the Victoria cases, Carlos de la Garza had strong local support, and Lee was unable to get anywhere with his cases. Thomas Brown Lee lost his entire investment, and the Williamsons made off with their considerable profit. Carlos de la Garza, however, supported by his Irish neighbors, kept Carlos Rancho.[22]

Back in Victoria, Doña Patricia also helped others regain their lands. Rosalía Cisneros came to her for advice. Fernando had granted her husband, Juan Nepomuceno Agatón Cisneros, a league of land where they had lived for over ten years. Like Don Martín, Rosalía's husband had died of cholera, leaving her alone on the ranch with her children. With only the help of her eldest son, Estevan, who was twelve when his father died, she had continued to farm and raise oxen, horses, hogs, and cattle until 1836. When the Mexican troops were defeated, she stayed, and when General Urrea passed through Victoria on his way back to Mexico, she had sent Estevan and the children to Matamoros under the protection of the retreating Mexican forces. She remained behind to care for the ranch until 1837 or 1838, she couldn't remember exactly, she told Doña Patricia, until Estevan came after her to remove her from the danger of Indian raids, which were increasing at the time. She had left the ranch, but she had never sold it.[23]

Rosalía had waited to return until the United States government had taken control, but when she returned in 1846, she had found squatters and settlers who claimed to have bought the land from Eleazar Killpatrick (or Kirkpatrick). Doña Patricia discussed the case with Phillips, who recommended that Rosalía Cisneros hire a lawyer and sue Killpatrick. Rosalía began the case in 1851, frightened to be in the courts but certain that she was in the right. The case dragged on for four years, but the courts, at long last, ruled in her favor. Doña Rosalía Cisneros and her family regained title to her league of land. The court, however, had ruled that she had to pay the $175 court costs. This she refused to do. The sheriff executed a claim against the family homestead which she had just gotten back. The sheriff put the entire 4,428 acres up for sale at auction. The "best and highest bidder" was none other than her son Estevan Cisneros, who paid $27 for the acreage. Doña Rosalía saved herself $148. At another sheriff's auction, Estevan also bought up the Galván league for only $10. The Cisneros family intended to stay on their hard-won land, and after Doña Rosalía's death, the land remained in the hands of her eldest son, Estevan Cisneros.[24]

There were other ways for Tejanos to recover their land than the expense of lengthy court battles. Claim jumpers and squatters fighting to retain their lands were usually impoverished farmers who could be bought off. In 1853 Nicolás Benavides regained a tract of 807 acres by paying Fielding Jones and Stephen Dinkins $215 to leave. Estevan Cisneros had also found a squatter named McGrew on his land, but rather than dispossessing the interloper completely, he offered McGrew 500 acres on the adjacent Galván league to move off the Cisneros property. McGrew accepted without a fight and moved his family to the adjacent ranch.[25] The Tejanos were back to stay.

In 1846 Panchita came home from New Orleans. León de León, her cousin, accompanied her, having just returned from school in Paris. She had almost not recognized the polished and elegant young gentleman who stepped off the boat to greet her. After the first stiffness had passed, however, the two twenty-year-old cousins were soon laughing and talking as they always had. He showed her pictures of the ruling heads of Europe, of the newly crowned Queen Victoria of England, and of Napoleon III, the new emperor of France, and his wife, the Empress Eugenie, whom he had actually seen during a parade. He described the beautiful coaches and carriages in which they rode down the elegant avenues of Paris, the great, gray bastions of the Sorbonne, and the magnificent lifestyle, attending French operas and lingering at outdoor cafés with beautiful French women. Panchita introduced him to her new friend, Cristobal Morales, who had been most attentive during all the balls and masques of the New Orleans winter season, including the grand parties of Mardi Gras. Cristobal, a potential husband for Panchita, had been invited to Victoria to meet the family. The three young people started for home on one of the many ships which sailed almost daily from New Orleans to Matagorda.[26]

The family gathered joyously at Doña Patricia's. Chucha Manchola had every reason to be proud of Panchita, who had become an accomplished young lady with a bright future and a sizable dowry. The convent and the finishing school had refined her. Félix, Salomé, and the family rode down from Mission Valley. Rafael and Trinidad, along with the rest of the Aldretes, drove up in their carriage from Goliad. Trinidad proudly introduced the family to his wife, Andrea Ramírez, and their new baby. After dinner, Cristobal, in proper form, asked the assembled family for permission to marry Panchita. They agreed, and León opened bottles of champagne which he had brought from France. During the next six months, Chucha, Lupita, Francisca, and Doña Patricia helped Panchita prepare the trousseau. They sent to New Orleans and even Paris to buy the silks and laces, the ribbons and kerchiefs, the parasols and fans, and the matching shoes and bonnets. Painstakingly the women sewed the lovely clothes. It was a labor of love from one generation to the next. In 1846, with all the family in attendance, Father Estany performed the marriage at the church in Victoria.[27]

The following year, good news came from Mission Valley. Salomé had just given birth to a third daughter, their seventh child. Félix brought the news to Victoria. He stopped first to let his mother know so that she could begin planning the details of the baby's baptism. Doña Patricia immediately sent for Father Estany so that he could find an appropriate week-

Ostensorium
Church, Victoria
...
Muelle De León

Monstrance said to have been given to the Catholic Church at Victoria by Doña Patricia de la Garza de León. The monstrance is still preserved in St. Mary's Catholic Church in Victoria. Courtesy of Local History Collection, Victory College.

end for the ceremony. Proud and pleased of her growing family and her twenty-second grandchild, Doña Patricia, by now elderly and slow, joined her daughters gathered in the *sala* to begin sewing the white baptismal dress while they planned the festivities. The baby would be named Candelaria after her aunt Candelaria Aldrete, who would act as godmother, along with her husband, José Miguel Aldrete, as the child's godfather.[28]

Choosing a godparent had become an even more critical part of a baby's birth in the new Anglo world. In the past, Tejano parents often chose the godparent from among their relatives. Their preference might be the husband or wife of one parent's brother or sister or a second or third cousin. Gradually, however, with the advent of Texan statehood, the old Tejano families had realized the need to expand their network of protection. Rather than turning to the Irish Catholics in the community, the Tejano families had begun to look to new arrivals for godparenthood connections.

Under the new Anglo regime, Tejano godparents provided protection and help to newly arrived Mexicans who were not relatives, creating new relations with the child and its parents, the *compadres*. In a world in which the Tejano families no longer controlled governmental power and were often denied access to financial resources, the godparenthood network meant safety and support. The Tejano families might have friends and business partners among the Anglo community, such as the Linns, but they did not look to them for financial help. A *compadre* could ask his child's godparent to secure a loan or borrow money to bail him out of jail. Since each child might have a different set of godparents, parents with large families developed an extensive network of religious kin, extending far beyond their own immediate relatives. By 1848 godparenthood had become more than a religious and family obligation. It was a way of creating unity and strength in a community which had lost its political power.[29]

Choosing to be a godparent to more than one child, or for a child from other than one's own family, meant accepting a position of responsibility which not many within the community sought. Because of the potentially heavy financial burden, these godparents of multiple children were often the heads of wealthy, influential families such as the de León clan. By choosing to accept godparenthood status for a half-dozen or more families, the *padrino* and *madrina* received the veneration and respect of the Mexican American community. As more families arrived from Mexico after the war, godparenthood provided a ready means of alliance for the old Tejano families. Thus the landowning elite, in turn, created a loyal group of supporters and established themselves as the patriarchs and matriarchs of the community.[30]

The church encouraged, through godparenthood, the care and concern of the patriarchs and matriarchs for those whom they took under their protective wings. Patriarchs were important, but much of the community's power was wielded by the women. The matriarchs, usually the oldest females in their households, played a critical role in godparenthood relationships. They served more often than the men, frequently standing alone as godmothers for children and their families. By becoming a community godmother, a woman advanced in prestige to a position in which her every wish was a command. No godchild would dare disobey or ignore the request of an elderly godmother. It was these women who demanded proper morals and upright behavior from their godchildren. These *comadres* also understood the intricate relationships which developed between the Tejano families as marriages and godparenthood interconnected one to another to create a Gordian knot which only they could trace. The black-gowned *comadres* also passed on the community history. Godparenthood, like intermarriage, provided one more way for the Tejano community to develop and grow.[31]

Throughout 1846 and 1847, while the de León families fought their court cases and shared in the blessings of new births and marriages, Victoria had been inundated by American troops on their way to invade Mexico. This time, to Doña Patricia's relief, the soldiers, bivouacked outside of town in long rows of tents, were strictly controlled by the American General Zachary Taylor. Punishments of whippings were meted out for drunkenness and disorderly conduct, and, to Doña Patricia's surprise, they were actually carried out. Only the Texas contingent who called themselves Texas Rangers continued to threaten Mexicans and Tejanos wherever they found them. Even they, however, were considerably subdued in comparison to the wild days of the republic. Still, just to be safe, Doña Patricia kept herself and her daughters and granddaughters inside.[32]

Once the troops had moved on, Doña Patricia worried for her daughters and their husbands, the Carbajals, down on the Rio Grande, as well as for the de la Garzas in Soto la Marina. Refugia reported that battles had taken place around Matamoros and that she had kept the family safe and out of the way on their ranch at Camargo. The most they saw of the American soldiers was when their commissary officers were searching up and down the Rio Grande for cattle and mules, for which, she admitted, they usually gave receipts. For two years the war dragged on. In the end, however, by the Treaty of Guadalupe Hidalgo in 1848, the United States had taken all of northwestern Mexico as well as the land from the Nueces River to the Rio Grande. The Mexicans, Refugia reported, were appalled and stunned that almost half their land had been stolen. Many on the north side of the Rio Grande who had suddenly become U.S. citizens could not decide what to do. The peace treaty made little difference to Refugia, but José María Jesús now had more allies among the Anglos who were establishing the little town of Brownsville near the American fort across from Matamoros. He planned to gain their help for his revolution in northern Mexico.[33]

Doña Patricia had other problems to worry about. She was concerned about her three orphaned granddaughters. Pilar was thirteen, Librada twelve, and Matiana was nine. Pilar was approaching marriageable age, and the three girls needed more income than she could offer. Their uncle Ysidro Benavides had died in 1845, just months after the girls had returned to Texas. Over the previous ten years Ysidro had been careful and frugal in his care of Plácido's estate. He had paid the taxes on two town lots, which he rented to Vincent and Gradman, and the Round Top house, which was rented first to C. Vincent and later to attorney James A. Moody. He also paid taxes on Plácido's original league of 4,428 acres, which he rented to Richard West and Cornelius Lane of Linnville. Part of that income he used to pay taxes on 6,021 acres from the Valentín García tract in Calhoun County and an additional 1,107 acres from the Pedro Gonzales land on La Vaca Bay. The girls received more than $300 every year from the estate. After Ysidro's death the courts had appointed Fernando as guardian for the girls. The money had stopped.[34]

In May 1847 Doña Patricia petitioned the court of Victoria County through W. H. Delano, her attorney:

> She has been placed in charge and care of Pilar, Libriata [sic], and Matiana for the last four years and six months. Support of said children has come from her own purse. During the whole period of her said charge she has received nothing from the estate except $100 and a small amount of clothing and necessaries . . . She is pained to say that poverty renders her incapable of doing this any longer. She is informed that the Guardian [her son, Fernando de León] has no funds in his possession. She prays that the court make an order for sale of a portion of the real estate. She prays also that a house in the Town of Victoria known as the Round Top House, a part of the property of said estate may be appropriated for the use of the heirs.[35]

Grimly Patricia questioned her eldest son. He had paid her nothing from the girls' income for two years, and she learned that the estate was still providing him, as guardian, with $381.20 in rents and income every year. Had Fernando taken to gambling with his newfound wealth? Was he using the girls' income to show off for the new Anglos in town? She knew full well he had money. That same year he had just leased four leagues of his land to William Dally and sold 640 acres to Alva Fitzpatrick for $640. He had also sold several lots in town.

Doña Patricia herself was not destitute, either. She still received income from the mortgages on the property in Louisiana and $700 a year on the mortgage on the family home in downtown Victoria. But she needed the money, and besides, José María Jesús Carbajal had just borrowed much of her nest egg, some $6,000, to fund his revolution in northern Mexico.

She turned to Edward Linn to act as the girls' guardian. Edward willingly complied, although he did his best to stay out of the row that was brewing between Fernando and his mother.[36]

What had happened? Fernando should have been the patriarch of the family, supported by his mother. Something had gone terribly wrong. Nineteenth-century Latin American families consisted of dominant males who were prominent public figures and protectors of their relatives. Families also included centralizing women who gathered and disseminated family information. In the case of Victoria, Tejanos like Fernando had lost any power they may have derived from their positions after the arrival of the Anglo Americans. The de León family, as well as others who had been the ruling elite under the Spanish and then the Mexican governments during the years prior to 1836, suddenly found themselves stripped of their positions by the change to the new Texian and later United States governments. Although there were a few who tried to retain public power, most Tejanos, whether grudgingly or willingly, gave up their government occupations. Loss of political power, however, did not affect their positions as prominent public figures.[37]

Tejano men who had been dominant in government prior to the revolution retained economic power and authority in the family. Indeed, economic prowess and social power provided a psychological strength which enabled them to maintain their sense of pride and honor. Their stability within the family and the Mexican-American community gave them the courage to overlook or fight back against racist attacks from Anglos. In the communities they also continued to receive titular tokens of respect, the title of *don*. The family made them prominent, and they continued to protect their relatives.[38]

The centralizing women, or matriarchs, such as Doña Patricia and her daughters, were the glue which held the families together. Even the patriarchal Catholic Church agreed that "the woman was the primary key to the preservation of the family and society."[39] Although the women were expected to respect and obey their husbands, they were never subordinate to their children or their extended kin's children. Fernando, as the eldest son, might become the next patriarch, but he was always expected to obey and respect his mother. Age and position, not gender, were the basis for hierarchical obligations. Women such as Doña Patricia retained control of their own land and wealth, made up their own minds, and played an important role in family decisions. Mexican culture gave its older women the right to demand respect and obedience from the family. They wielded tremendous power within the confines of their own families and their business relationships. Doña Patricia might have been willing to have Fernando maintain the place of hierarchical leader, but when he failed to carry out his patriarchal obligations toward his nieces, she would not abide his presence.[40]

Fernando moved out. Twelve-year-old Francisco Santiago, ever his loyal defender, moved with him. For the first time in his life, Fernando did not have women around him to care for his household, and he needed to find someone. He was fifty years old, but his property certainly made him the most eligible bachelor in Victoria. In San Antonio, María de la Luz Escalera, an opinionated and outspoken forty-four-year-old spinster, could not have agreed more.

Fernando had known the Escalera family since 1833, when they arrived in his father's colony. José María Escalera, Luz' father, had brought the whole family from San Antonio to Victoria just after the outbreak of a smallpox epidemic. During his years in the de León colony, José María's wife had passed away, but he continued to ranch on his league and labor with his daughter Luz to care for him. In 1836 José María sold half of his league to Margaret Wright in order to generate the money to pay taxes on the remainder of the ranch. Four years later, during the worst of the Indian raids, he sold the other half to Philip Dimitt and returned with Luz to San Antonio.[41]

In San Antonio on business in 1848, Fernando met Luz again. Her father had just died, leaving her free to marry, and she and Fernando were reintroduced by mutual friends. Although she had no land wealth, her father had left her a small sum, enough at least for her to live comfortably if she were careful or perhaps for a modest dowry. Fernando found the articulate spinster much to his liking. She had a good head for business, and she certainly had no objection to caring for him in his old age. He saw no need for an extensive courtship. He brought her back to Victoria to reacquaint her with his family and to meet young Francisco Santiago. She liked the family and they liked her, especially Francisco Santiago. Without further ado, Fernando proposed and Luz accepted. It was a good business deal all the way around. The couple was married in the Victoria church before a delighted Tejano community. At Luz' insistence, they adopted an ecstatic Francisco Santiago, and the new family moved out to Fernando's Escondido Ranch. Whether Doña Patricia attended the nuptials is unknown, but Luz became a popular addition to the family.[42]

By 1849 Doña Patricia felt it was important to put her affairs in order. She was in her seventies and not feeling well. In April 1849 she called her daughters together. Cesario de la Garza, one of her relatives from the Power and Hewetson colony at Refugio, had come up to Victoria to help her. He had taken over the guardianship of the three Benavides girls and was proving to be a highly trustworthy and supportive protector. As calmly as arranging a dinner table, Doña Patricia considered the best marriage prospects for Cesario from among her daughters. Of the three, Lupita attracted Cesario, and Doña Patricia was pleased to see the potential for a match. Chucha Manchola assured her mother that she was content and did not need to marry again. Chucha had Panchita and her new husband to live with and all the future grandchildren to look after. Doña Patricia had only to settle the problem of Francisca, who had cared for her so faithfully for so many years. Francisca needed to find a husband. If Luz Escalera could marry at forty-four, certainly thirty-two-year-old Francisca could do so as well. Unlike her brothers and her married sisters, Francisca had never received any land. She counted on her inheritance from her mother to keep her solvent, but she knew she would probably have to move in with either Félix or Fernando someday, since spinster aunts were not expected to live alone.[43]

In 1849 Vicente Dosal, a thirty-four-year-old tailor, arrived from Zacatecas, Mexico. He was not the match whom Doña Patricia would have preferred for her daughter, but he was pleasant and seemed hardworking, and Francisca liked him. Doña Patricia suspected that his avid interest might be due to Francisca's inheritance, but was that not, after all, the point—to buy her last daughter a husband? The arrangements were made, certainly without the fanfare and folderol of Panchita's wedding, but Doña Patricia congratulated herself when Father Estany united Francisca and Vicente Dosal in matrimony at the small Victoria chapel that same year. Ten months later, Francisca gave birth to her first child, a little boy, Jesús.[44]

Doña Patricia, the elderly matriarch, did not like going to court, but in 1849 it was essential. Robert Carlisle and Bridget Quinn had stopped paying their $700 note on the house on the square. At seventy-two, Doña Patricia braved the Anglo court, sailing in imperiously with her cane and her daughters in tow. She needed the mortgage as income for her daughters, so she sued Carlisle and Quinn in the Anglo court. She did not want the house back, and she did not want to sell the property. She wanted to have a dependable inheritance to leave for her two widowed daughters. The case was still in litigation by 1850 when Patricia became ill. The servants were hurriedly sent to summon the family.[45]

Word of Doña Patricia's illness arrived at Mission Valley just as Salomé

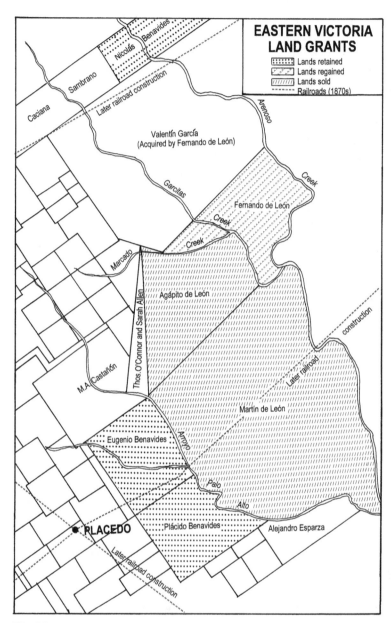

EASTERN VICTORIA
LAND GRANTS

Lands retained
Lands regained
Lands sold
Railroads (1870s)

Benavides

Nicolás

Sambrano

Caciana

Later railroad construction

Arenoso

Valentín García
(Acquired by Fernando de León)

Garcitas

Creek

Fernando de León

Creek

Creek

Creek

Marcado

Agápito de León

Thos. O'Connor and Sarah Allen

Later railroad construction

M.A. Castañón

Martín de León

Arroyo

Eugenio Benavides

Palo

Alto

PLACEDO

Plácido Benavides

Alejandro Esparza

Later railroad construction

Map 7.2

learned from the *vaqueros* that her husband, Félix, had died while working cattle. It was too late for last rites, but Father Estany would say a prayer for Félix' soul when they buried him in the de León family plot in Victoria. Heartbroken, Salomé collected her six sons and daughters. Olivia, eleven, was caring for her two younger sisters, nine-year-old María de Jesús, called Chuchita, and two-year-old Candelaria. At least the boys were old enough to run the ranch and take care of them all. She could count on sensible, level-headed twenty-one-year-old Santiago and twenty-year-old Patricio. Even Samuel could do a man's work at eighteen. Silvestre, however, was something else. He never stayed out of trouble, and almost everyone on the ranch had reprimanded him at one time or another for his constant string of hair-brained pranks. Now, without Félix and his calming influence, Salomé was truly concerned about Silvestre's future. Salomé and her family, dressed in somber black, rode behind the wagon and the coffin on the bumpy road into Victoria.[46]

By October 1850 Patricia de la Garza de León could no longer get around. She had been confined to her bed, and she had called Edward Linn to prepare her will. As the family matriarch, she wanted to make sure that her family was cared for, but she also wanted everyone to know where they stood. She had Edward begin by listing the advances made to her children over the years. He was amazed at how clearly she remembered every advance, every note, every loan she had made in the previous fifty years. She listed all of the money which her children had received from her:

> Fernando de León received $1,611 in cash and stock
> Silvestre de León [deceased] received $777
> Jesusa Manchola received $955
> Guadalupe de la Garza received $417
> Félix de León [deceased] received $910
> Agustina Benavides [deceased] received $519
> Agápito de León [deceased] received $350
> Candelaria Aldrete received $580
> Refugia Carbajal received [illegible] money and stock
> Francisca Dosal received $850.[47]

She then forgave the debts to her daughters and her in-laws, telling Linn to leave "to José María Carbajal the $6,000 he owes me and to Miguel Aldrete the $1,000 he owes me." Edward winced as she came to Fernando. To her eldest son, Fernando, she said, she left nothing and bequeathed "to each of my children [except Fernando] equal portions of the $1,000 that

Fernando borrowed from me to pay debts."[48] Even with Félix gone and no sons left but Fernando, she refused to forgive him.

The rest of the property she divided among the widowed daughters. The Castilian laws of partible inheritance under which Doña Patricia had been raised normally required the equal division of an estate among the heirs. Not all of the estate, however, had to be equally divided, and the law allowed a parent to reward or punish the descendants by granting unequal divisions of the estate. In Spain and in seventeenth- and eighteenth-century Latin America, one-fifth of the estate (a *quinto*) was used for paying funeral expenses and was contributed to pious works. Any money which remained could be given to one or more of the heirs. Of the remaining 80 percent of the estate, one-third (a *tercio*) could also be specifically bequeathed to one of the heirs. Doña Patricia followed the strictures of the old Spanish laws and divided her estate among her daughters.[49]

Women were often favored in wills in both Latin America and in the United States because of their financial vulnerability and the difficulties they faced in making a living through their own work and diligence. Doña Patricia had lived as a widow for fifteen years, and although she had significant support from her extended family, she knew the struggles and hardships which women faced. Patricia's second daughter, forty-year-old María de Jesús Manchola, or Chucha, widow of Rafael Manchola, would have no income and could only look forward to a lifetime of living off her daughter Panchita. Francisca, newly married to Vicente Dosal, also needed funds to ensure the success of her family, especially with the new baby. Only María Guadalupe (Lupita) of the widowed daughters had bright prospects. Cesario de la Garza, in exchange for being named executor of the will, had proposed to Lupita, and she would need no additional income.[50]

Doña Patricia left the mortgages she owned in Louisiana "after deducting the lawyers fees" to Chucha Manchola and to Francisca Dosal. She also left three of the mortgages to Silvestre's sons, Martín, Francisco, and Francisco Santiago. Martín and Francisco had arrived from Soto la Marina two months earlier, both with new wives and families of their own, and Martin had taken the opportunity to sell his land while he was there. To Chucha Manchola and Francisca Dosal she granted each a title to one of the two building lots in Victoria on which she held income-producing mortgages. She divided her cattle between the two women, one-third to Chucha and one-third to Francisca, and left the remainder of the cattle and one yoke of oxen to her fifteen-year-old grandson Francisco Santiago de León, who had just been adopted by Fernando. Evidently, Doña Patricia did not trust Fernando to provide sufficiently for his welfare and wanted to make sure the young boy had some funds of his own in addition to the lands which Fernando had regained for him as part of the suit against Milton H. Hardy.[51]

Unlike the primogeniture laws prevalent in the United States, which kept land together under the eldest son, the partible inheritance laws encouraged the equal division of land, so that each child received an *herencia,* or inheritance. Patricia, however, had no land to give. During the republic, speculators had stolen what land she had left. She asked her daughter Candelaria Aldrete, wife of the very successful José Miguel Aldrete of Goliad, to institute a court case against the Franklin heirs to regain the de León family ranches. Certainly Candelaria could afford to prosecute the case. She did not need the land or the money. The Aldretes owned more than twenty thousand acres of land and hundreds of head of cattle and were the wealthiest of Patricia's sons and daughters. The rest of the family, however, could benefit from the land.[52]

As to the rest of her children, Patricia was less concerned, and she made no provisions for them in her will beyond pardoning their debts to her. With Félix gone, Doña Patricia hoped that Santiago, Patricio, and Samuel would be good guardians for their younger brother and sisters. She expected them to divide the big Mission Valley ranch among the children after Salomé received her part. Refugia Carbajal, like Candelaria Aldrete, enjoyed a comfortable lifestyle, and she stood to inherit all of the extensive Carbajal land holdings in Mexico in the event something happened to José María Jesús, which seemed likely considering his constant revolutionary intrigue. Patricia's grandson León de León lived very well in Mexico, thanks to his excellent education and his sensible investments. Of the three Benavides granddaughters, Pilar had settled in Rio Grande City, while Librada and Matiana divided their time between visiting de León kin in Texas and a small home in Reynosa, Tamaulipas. Their inheritance from their father sustained them very well.[53]

At last Doña Patricia, well aware of the strength of the Linn family in the new Anglo world of Victoria, asked Edward Linn to serve as her executor jointly with her soon-to-be son-in-law Cesario de la Garza. Linn was an Irish Catholic, and she knew he would carry out her wishes in remembering her religious duties. She also hoped that as a powerful political figure Senator John Linn would regain what was owed her by the state of Texas. Edward Linn was to "pay to the Catholic Church all the dues that my parents owed" from the debts that were owed her by the state of Texas for her losses during the Texas Revolution. There was, by late 1850, some realistic hope that Texas would be able to repay the debts incurred in 1836, since the United States government had promised to pay Texas $10 million for its debts as part of the Compromise of 1850. On her deathbed Doña Patricia had done what she could to protect her children. Their success within the Anglo-American economy was up to them. Doña Patricia de la Garza de León passed away in October 1850.[54]

Candelaria Aldrete carried out her mother's wishes and brought suit against the Franklin family. The grant of 22,140 acres on the Garcitas and Arenosa Creeks had been appropriated by Isaac Franklin during the years of the republic. In February 1854 Candelaria sued Franklin for the return of the original grant plus an additional 2,214 acres which belonged to León de León. María Antonia and her husband, Manuel Carbajal, along with all of Félix' children, Luz Escalera, and her adopted son, Francisco Santiago, joined Candelaria in the suit. After the death of Isaac Franklin, Candelaria continued the suit against his heirs. After several more years of litigation the courts at last ruled in her favor, and the de León family regained the entire amount, including León de León's land. Each of the ten de León family members involved in the case received 2,214 acres, and León received the remaining 3,321 acres.[55]

With the death of his mother, Fernando, or, more properly, Don Fernando, could at last aspire wholeheartedly to the title of Tejano patriarch for the Victoria community. Now that he was married to Luz Escalera, the members of the community addressed him as "Don Fernando" and his wife as "Doña Luz." The use of the term *Don* is similar to that of "colonel" or "judge" granted by Southerners to wealthy landholders to whom people in the community could turn for protection or help in times of need. It is interesting to note that there is no equivalent term for Anglo-American women. The notaries and clerks of Victoria may or may not have been aware of what they were writing, but all of the legal and church records included the titles of *Don* and *Doña*, almost as if it were part of the names, for the patriarchs and matriarchs of the community.[56]

Don Fernando, however, was trying to become more acceptable to the Anglo society. In his frequent visits to town from the Escondido Ranch to attend district court, he visited with A. H. Phillips, his lawyer, and spent time with the Anglo elite of the town. He read the New Orleans *Picayune* and discussed the weighty affairs of state with the other affluent gentlemen at the courthouse. When the elite of the town discussed plans to bring a railroad to Victoria, Don Fernando joined his Anglo neighbors in granting land to the railroad. They applauded him in 1852 when he deeded two town lots on Market Square to the Catholic Church "for the use and benefit of the Roman Catholics of the town of Victoria."[57] Not all of them knew that he was merely fulfilling his mother's request. Fernando had continued Doña Patricia's case against Quinn and Carlisle over the mortgage on the property, and when he — or rather her estate — won, Fernando, rather than remortgage the home for his sisters, gave the land to the church.[58]

Anglo landowners, prejudiced though they might be, had to accept Don Fernando as their equal, and he had the wealth to prove that he was. In 1852 Fernando de León's possessions were valued at more than $7,300 for land and goods in Victoria County and an additional $4,000 for land in Calhoun County. The tax assessor missed most of Don Fernando's property, perhaps because much of the land was in other counties. The assessor failed to list 4,428 acres of land on Matagorda Bay originally belonging to Narciso Cabazos, an additional 2,200 acres originally belonging to Pedro Gallardo, 4,428 acres on the Guadalupe acquired from Fernando Bueno, and 7,000 acres from Valentín Garcia. From 1850 to 1852 Fernando sold 2,174 acres for $2,500, enough to keep him and Luz quite comfortably.[59]

Fernando de León made no distinction between sales to Mexicans and sales to Anglo Americans. All who bought land from de León paid the going price of $1 per acre. Of the sixteen sales, only five were to other Mexican Americans. Fernando did not sell land needlessly. He had fought too hard to regain it to squander it recklessly. He sold only when he needed cash. From his return to Victoria in 1845 until 1853 he had sold only 8,503 acres, and he received an income of $4,310. From his land he also paid off his lawyers — Félix B. Webb with two town lots and the faithful A. H. Phillips with a league of 4,428 acres. His lawyers had been well worth the price.[60]

Don Fernando, although raised in the ranching tradition, did not care for the inconvenience of actually herding cattle. He profited handsomely from the sale of land without the difficulty of getting dirty herding, branding, driving, and selling his cattle. The tax rolls in 1852 listed thirty head of horses, fifty head of cattle, and a Negro slave. In 1853 Don Fernando again reported fifty head of cattle. The tax officials questioned the small number of cattle and asked if perhaps Don Fernando was not reporting a full count of his cattle. Don Fernando neither knew nor cared how many cattle he owned, and he replied that there was no way of determining how many cattle ranged free on his property. The tax collectors had to be satisfied with his response and did not press him for more taxes.[61]

Busy in the Anglo world of courts and land sales, Don Fernando had no interest in offering that mark of a patriarch, the willingness to stand as godparent to the Tejano people of his community. It was not until after he married Luz Escalera that his name appeared with hers on the baptismal records, and then only once. In 1851 he served as godfather to an unnamed person, perhaps a ranch hand, who had a daughter at Spring Creek.[62]

Fernando and Luz had moved back to town after 1850, since he needed to be close to his lawyers and the court. While Fernando was busy in court and carousing with his lawyers, Luz visited with her in-laws. Lupita, who had not yet married Cesario, had maintained Doña Patricia's home and continued to welcome Librada and Matiana on their periodic visits, since Pilar was already established in South Texas. Francisca Dosal and her new husband were still in town, and the women spent many amicable days together sewing clothes for Francisca's new baby. Luz brought along fourteen-year-old Francisco Santiago, although he often preferred to attend court with his uncle. Francisco Santiago and Matiana soon found they had much in common. The two fourteen-year-old orphans felt a strong kinship. Luz enjoyed the two youngsters and spent a great deal of time in their company. She took them seriously and often discussed with them the land cases and the problems which their uncle Fernando was facing. The three created a bond which would last for the next thirty years.[63]

In 1852 Francisca Dosal, after a lifetime of service and after less than two years of marriage and a new baby, fell deathly ill. Lupita and Luz felt that it would be best to move her out of Vicente's small home and back into her old room at Doña Patricia's house. Lupita and the girls could look after her and the baby better there. Vicente Dosal could do little but worry, and the women convinced him it would be best if he returned to his shoe shop, where his work would take his mind off Francisca. Dr. Webb, who had helped Fernando when they first arrived in town and to whom Fernando had sold the lot on which the doctor's home and office now stood, did his best to help Francisca. There was little he could do, and sorrowfully, Lupita called Father Estany to administer last rites. Francisca's sisters placed her baby in her arms, and with her tearful husband kneeling by her bed, Francisca quietly passed away. Luz sent the servants for Fernando. One more family member to bury in the de León plot.[64]

Vicente Dosal, to the distress of Lupita and Luz, decided to return to Mexico. His mother and sisters would help him care for Jesús. And since he had also been appointed guardian for Librada and Matiana, he offered to take them back to their sister Pilar and the Benavides relatives on the border. Matiana, in particular, was crushed. She had been so happy with her aunt Luz and with her cousin Francisco Santiago. Luz consoled her and promised that she could come back to visit often. With that small comfort, the girls packed their things. This time, they would not have to ride or camp out along the way. There was actually a coach that stopped at way stations and would take them to the border in only three weeks.

Six months later, at Rancho Escondido seven miles out of Victoria in early 1853, Don Fernando de León, like his brother Félix, died with no warning. Luz, just five years married, made the funeral preparations with the help of Francisco Santiago. Only Fernando's sisters Lupita Garcia de la Garza and Candelaria Aldrete at Goliad and Félix' family from Mission Valley would attend. The Linns would come and probably A. H. Phillips, but those sycophantic friends at the courthouse would never think of him again, except to wonder if they could get their hands on his land. Luz would see that they did not. He was the last of Don Martin's sons, but few remembered the empresario or the establishment of the colony. Those times were gone now. Civilization had arrived, and it was time to move on. Head held high, Luz took young Francisco Santiago's arm, and the two followed the undertaker's hearse to the church.

CHAPTER 8

TEJANOS IN TEXAS, 1853–1880

Genealogical Chart

MARTÍN DE LEÓN (D. 1834)
+ PATRICIA DE LA GARZA (D. 1850)

1. Fernando (d. 1853) + María de la Luz Escalera (d. 1880)
   1-1. Francisco Santiago "Frank" (adopted) + Matilde Ureste (m. 1856, d. 1870; six children) + Justita Wilson (no children)

2. María Candelaria + José Miguel Aldrete
   2-1. José María (b. 1820)
   2-2. José de Jesús (b. 1823) + Salomé Lozano
   2-3. José Trinidad (m. 1844) + Andrea Ramirez
       Five children
   2-4. Rafael (b. 1826)

3. Silvestre (d. 1842) + Rosalía (d. 1838)
   3-1. Francisco (b. 1830)
   3-2. Martin (b. 1832)
   3-3. "Frank" (b. 1836, adopted 1848)

4. "Lupita" (m. 1849) + Cesario de la Garza
   No children

5. Félix (d. 1850) + Salomé Leal (d. 1852)
   5-1. Santiago + Lupita Lozano Moreno (d. 1855) + Guadalupe Berlanga (m. 1875)
       5-1-1. Salomé (b. 1853, d. 1855)
   5-2. Patricio (m. 1858) + Librada de León Benavides (daughter of Agustina and Plácido, 9-2 below)
       Six children
   5-3. Silvestre (d. 1869)

5-4. Olivia (m. 1863) + Crisóforo Lozano

5-5. María de Jesús "Chuchita" (b. 1840)

5-6. Samuel (m. 1874) + Patricia de la Garza

5-7. Candelaria (b. 1847, d. 1855)

6. María Antonia C. de la Garza + Manuel Carbajal (m. 1837)

    6-1. León de León (b. 1824)

7. Chucha Manchola

    7-1. Francisca "Panchita" (m. 1847) + Cristobal Morales

8. Refugia (m. 1832) + José María Jesús Carbajal

    8-1. Antonio (b. 1833)

    8-2. José María (b. 1834)

9. Agustina + Plácido Benavides

    9-1. Pilar (m. 1857) + Cristobal de la Garza

        Five children

    9-2. Librada (m. 1858) + Patricio Leal de León (son of Félix and Salomé, 5-2 above)

        Six children

    9-3. Matiana (b. 1836)

10. Francisca (d. 1852) + Vicente Dosal

    10-1. Jesús (b. 1850)

On one of those lovely spring days when the sky is brilliant blue and the breezes soft, the wildflowers all in glorious bloom, in early May 1856, Doña Luz Escalera de León, widow of the late landowner Fernando de León, and her twenty-year-old adopted son and business partner, Francisco Santiago, stepped into their trim, high-wheeled, new black surrey for the three-hour trip to Victoria. The slave whom Francisco had inherited from Fernando finished loading Francisco's trunks onto the ranch wagon, and Francisco's *caporal*, his foreman, ceremoniously climbed up and took the reins of the powerful draft horses to follow the carriage into town. Francisco turned and waved at the assembled crowd on the wide porch of the Rancho Escondido. He loosened the reins on the restive horses and the small caravan of carriage and wagon set off. Francisco Santiago was getting married.

It had been only two years since Don Fernando's death. The probate court had completed their review of Fernando's estate the year before, and Doña Luz had been pleased but not particularly surprised to find that she was the wealthiest widow in the county. She had inherited 19,253.5 acres of land plus seventeen town lots. Francisco Santiago, in his own right, owned 14,628 acres made up of the 8,000 acres which Fernando had left him plus the Cabasos league on Lavaca Bay and Guajardo's half-league, also on the bay. The eligible young bachelor was, by the estimate of the tax assessor, worth more than $7,600. Francisco, who had become "Frank" to his friends among the American community, had been accepted in both cultures. He had proved his devotion to the Tejano community, serving as godfather on six different occasions and as wedding sponsor for his cousin Santiago. Many of the mothers, both Anglo and Tejano, with marriageable daughters had hoped for an alliance with the powerful de León clan. Francisco had finally chosen Matilde Ureste, the daughter of Don Guadalupe Ureste.[1]

The Ureste family was a large and hardworking clan that had arrived from Mexico soon after Texas statehood. In 1835 Don Guadalupe Ureste and his wife, Francisca García from Matamoros, Mexico, had come to Victoria, where the couple had acquired almost five hundred acres from Francisco de León out of the Silvestre de León league as well as several town lots. Don Guadalupe had increased his holdings over the years. In December 1854 Francisco Santiago had served as godfather for Don Guadalupe's son Inocencio. It may have been at the Christmas festivities of that year when he met Matilde. During December the Tejanos of Victoria, just like Catholics throughout the Spanish-speaking world, exchanged food and

Fandango by Theodore Gentilz shows a party like many held during the Christmas festivities throughout Texas and Mexico. Gift of the Yanaguana Society, Courtesy of Daughters of the Republic of Texas, San Antonio.

drinks as they celebrated the Nativity with a *posada*. Singing pilgrims lighting their way with candles reenacted the holy family's search for lodging in Bethlehem. They carried the images of Joseph and the Virgin Mary on a donkey as they paraded through the streets, knocking at the doors of homes asking for shelter for the soon-to-be-born Christ child. The groups inside sang the refrains refusing them entrance, and the procession moved on to the next house. At the last house, the pilgrims were admitted for a glorious festival and celebration with food, dancing, and the breaking of the *piñata*.[2] Francisco Santiago, with the approval of both Doña Luz and Don Guadalupe, courted and at last asked for permission to marry Matilde. It was a beneficial connection for both parties, and the two families agreed to the wedding.

Amidst the happiness of the wedding plans, Doña Luz remained concerned over the situation of Félix' family at Mission Valley Ranch. Salomé had died in 1852, two years after her husband, leaving the surviving family members to fend for themselves. The three older boys—Santiago, twenty-seven, Patricio, twenty-six, and Silvestre, a very rowdy twenty-one—had been left to take care of their younger sisters—Olivia, María Jesús, and

Candelaria—and their youngest brother, Samuel. Certainly Santiago had tried to take care of the home, but most of the burden for running the household fell on twenty-year-old Olivia and her seventeen-year-old sister Chuchita. Both girls needed husbands, and with Francisco moving to his own ranch, Doña Luz wanted to be with family. It was time to sell Fernando's Rancho Escondido.[3]

Doña Luz knew she would have no trouble selling the Escondido. After the death of Fernando many Anglos had hoped to profit from the widow de León. They had found that she was a particularly tough-minded business-woman. She was sensible and careful with the land she had inherited from Fernando. When she sold land she made a good profit, but she saw no need to hoard large quantities of money or to buy up more property. She needed money to live comfortably, to travel if she chose, and to help her family and her people. Her land sales supplied her with more than enough for that. Since she had no children of her own and all of her de León nieces and nephews owned their own property, she was free to sell the land or to give it away as gifts to whomever she chose. No one took advantage of the sensible widow. Nor did she abandon Fernando's efforts to win land back in court.

Doña Luz became a frequent, if reluctant, visitor to the district court. During the turbulent years of the Texas Revolution, Fernando had gained title to the Pérez league. By 1845 Antonio Pérez had returned to reclaim the four thousand acres near the small town of Bloomington, just south of Victoria. He filed against Doña Luz in the case of *Antonio Pérez et al. v. María de Jesús Escalera or de León* [sic] for partition of the land. Doña Luz and Phillips discussed their options. Phillips felt certain they could win the whole league, and Doña Luz, unwilling to back down, told him to carry on the case. For two years she accompanied Phillips into the court-room, at times sweltering and other times freezing, as they brought in affidavits, swore witnesses, and referred to Fernando's notes. Doña Luz did not, however, attend the inebriated gatherings in the evenings after court. At last, in 1855 the judge ruled in her favor. She had not felt guilty, for the Pérez family still retained two other leagues of land upon which they lived.[4]

No sooner had Doña Luz dispensed with the Pérez case than Phillips called her into his office again. With all her land wealth, everyone felt free to take her to court. Jacoba Bueno had returned from Mexico to sue over the Fulgencio Bueno league, which had also been left in Fernando's hands after the revolution. She had filed *Jacoba Bueno et al. v. M. De Jesús Escalera or de León*, another action for partition. Again Phillips called in the usual witnesses. Senator Linn, who was in from Austin, testified for Fernando, as did Ed Linn, his brother, and Carlos Lasso, Antonio Cabassos, and José Castillo, all of whom had known Fernando in the years before the revolution. Even Lupita de la Garza, Fernando's sister, and Doña Luz herself were called on to testify. After weeks of testimony, Jacoba Bueno lost the case. She paid more than $100 in court costs for the witnesses and the lengthy trial and returned to Mexico. Doña Luz's victories had convinced others not to challenge her in court.[5]

Doña Luz sold land once or twice a year. She had learned to speak enough English to deal with the land purchasers herself, when they came to call on her, but she preferred to have the assistance of Francisco Santiago, who acted as her lawyer and partner and co-signed the documents with her. During her first year as a widow Doña Luz sold two hundred acres to Charles Johnson for $1 an acre. She soon learned that sometimes land prices were up and sometimes they were down, and she had to take what she could get. In 1856 she had sold one league of land (4,428 acres) to Fielding Jones for forty-five cents an acre, earning only $2,000 on the sale. The following year, early in 1857, Matiana Benavides had written from the Rio Grande and asked about selling some land. Her uncles had been unable to find a buyer for her, and Doña Luz had encouraged her to wait until the prices went back up. After 1857 both Matiana and Doña Luz sold their land at $1 per acre and often $2 and $3 per acre.[6]

Doña Luz and her sister-in-law Lupita, recently married to Cesario de la Garza, had remained active in church affairs. A women's group had been formed to support the church which would later take the name Las Guadalupanas from Our Lady of Guadalupe. The matriarchs, many of them descendants of the original colonists, made a sociable group, cooking food and decorating the church during festivals, sewing drapes for the sanctuary and clothes for the figures of the saints, and embroidering vestments for the priest.

Over their sewing they discussed the disgraceful activities of the Anglo women. There was a new movement against the consumption of alcohol, and the Temperance Marchers had paraded right down the center of town with placards and drums, some of them dressed most inappropriately, showing their underclothes. Those strange Anglo women had ranted against liquor, then some few had even begun to attack the institution of slavery. The many slave owners in Victoria had been furious, but even the Anglo women's irate husbands had not been able to stop the women marchers. The Catholic church ladies, as they plied their needles, acknowledged that both liquor and slavery were issues which needed to be addressed, but there were far less shameful ways to do it. These Anglo women were even demanding the right to vote, and that, the matriarchs agreed, was an incredibly foolish idea. Doña Luz and her compatriots, with raised eyebrows, shook their heads at the dreadful behavior and bent their energies toward working for the church and their Tejano community.

On Sunday, May 14, 1856, friends and well-wishers, Anglo and Tejano, Catholic and Protestant, crowded into the brightly decorated church to hear Francisco and Matilde exchange their wedding vows. After the service, the entire town turned out for the feast. Long trundle tables had been laden with giant *cazuelas*, or casseroles, of rice and beans and squash and tomatoes. Rich sauces were poured over the massive piles of tender barbecued beef, goat, and pork. Freshly made tortillas steamed in enormous baskets. Mounds of cakes and sweets and candies covered other tables, and whiskey and tequila flowed from giant kegs under the trees. It was a party which few would soon forget.

With Francisco and Matilde gone, Doña Luz closed up the big Escondido Ranch. As the *patrona* she was responsible for her employees, their families, and their welfare. She could not take all of them to Mission Valley, which already had its own compliment of *vaqueros* and servants. Many would move over to Francisco's new ranch and work as faithfully for him as they had for her. She was certain that he would care for them as a good *patrón* should, protecting their families, providing them with homes and food, standing as godfather for their children, and helping them when they were in need. Others chose to work for other Tejano ranchers, while a few went to work on the Anglo ranches. The Anglos, however, held a different attitude toward their workers. Some of the Anglos were so concerned with their profits that they fired their cowboys at the end of the trail drives, leaving them with little but their horses and saddles to make it through the long, cold winters. Little wonder that many turned to thieving and rustling cattle in their poverty, for who knew better than they where cattle hid during the winters?

Doña Luz had found a buyer for the beautiful Escondido Ranch in Joseph Weisiger. He was impressed with the comfortable, roomy ranch house, the bunk houses, the small homes for the ranch hands, the extensive corrals and pens, the solid barns and spacious horse stalls. Weisiger willingly paid $13,284, or better than $3 per acre. That much money would keep Doña Luz comfortable for many years, with more than enough to lend to family and friends when they needed it. While she was settling her affairs, she also helped Felix' sons and daughters to divide the Mission Valley Ranch among them as well as the town lots which Félix still owned. Santiago, Patricio, Silvestre, and Olivia each received 738 acres plus two town lots. The land for the youngest, María de Jesús and ten-year-old Samuel, was held in trust by Patricio. All except the wild Silvestre chose to stay on the ranch and to keep the land together.[7]

Twenty-seven-year-old Santiago, the eldest of the family, had done his best. He had married Guadalupe "Lupita" Lozano Moreno the year his mother died, and he had tried to take care of both families, knowing he was responsible for his sisters and his wild brother Silvestre. His young wife and his sisters had worked together to keep the ranch going and caring for eleven-year-old Samuel, and the women made a good team. In August 1854 the de León family had gathered in Victoria to celebrate the baptism of Santiago and Lupita's first child. The baby was named Salomé after Santiago's mother. Olivia, who had become a close confidante and friend of the happy Lupita, was overjoyed when Santiago asked her to act as godmother to little Salomé. For her godfather, Santiago called on Raphael Aldrete, his cousin from Goliad. Within two years, however, in November 1855, both Lupita and little Salomé died at the Mission Valley Ranch. Candelaria, the youngest of the family, also passed away. It had been a terrible blow. Santiago gave up the care of the family, and Olivia, Chuchita, and Samuel moved in with their brother Patricio.

Patricio, two years younger than Samuel, always sober, serious, and scholarly, became the family patriarch. He had married his cousin, Librada de León Benavides, one of Aunt Agustina and Uncle Plácido's daughters. After the death of Lupita and Candelaria, it was Patricio who took over the main ranching duties and the care of the family. Although Santiago remained on the ranch, the burden of keeping the big ranch going fell to Patricio. He continued his guardianship of Chuchita and Samuel from 1856 until 1871. Meanwhile, Patricio and Librada were planning their own family, and he was grateful for the help from Doña Luz, Olivia, and María Jesús.

Rebellious and defiant at twenty-one, Silvestre had gone out on his own. He turned his back on his Tejano family and joined the hard-drinking, fast-living sons of the old Anglo families. "Sil," as he was known among his Anglo drinking buddies, needed money. Much to Doña Luz's disapproval, he had promptly sold two of his town lots, one for $450 and the other for $600. Refusing to live on his portion of the family ranch, he went into the cattle business with Andrew Oliver, with whom he bought 200 acres on Garcitas Creek. Doña Luz liked Andrew Oliver and hoped that he would help mend Silvestre's bad habits.[8]

Of the remaining three children, Olivia had begun at fifteen to run the household for her brothers and sister. At a time when she should have been finding a husband, she faced the problems of commanding a dozen or more servants. She supervised the purchase of food supplies, sent *vaqueros* to town when they were running low, decided on meals and managed their preparation, oversaw the housecleaning, organized the washing and ironing, and delegated whatever jobs needed to be done. For two years she had gotten help from Santiago's wife until her tragic death and then from Patricio's wife, Librada. It had not been easy, but Olivia had learned quickly. Her sister Chuchita had helped as well. It had been a difficult time for the two girls, but they had become mature women, resilient and resourceful. Little Samuel, not quite ten, had also become adept at helping around the ranch.[9]

During the 1850s those who had the money to invest in carts and oxen had profited from the increasing trade coming in from Indianola, Matagorda, and Corpus Christi. Carting was a very risky business because the Anglo merchants objected to the Tejano competition, which was usually less expensive. While the de León family opted for the safer return from cattle and horses, Carlos de la Garza, on the road to the coastal communities, had made a profit from carting. He owned four carts and teams, which he had used to carry goods to and from the coast. Although Don Carlos always sent outriders and guards with each wagon, several of his teamsters had been attacked by the envious Anglos. Gangs of marauders burned cargo, killed oxen, and threatened carters riding alone or unarmed. With the railroads gradually making their way in from the coast, Don Carlos cut his losses, sold off his carts, and turned to other avenues of profit.[10]

De León family gatherings were no longer held in the increasingly Anglo town but on the ranches, in particular at the Mission Valley Ranch. Births and baptisms, with all the festivities, now took place upriver at Mission Valley, where a small chapel accommodated the extended family. Patricio's wife, Librada, gave birth to their first child, Agustina, in 1857. The couple had agreed on Patricio's first cousin Matiana as godmother to the baby, if she would be willing to make the long trip from the Rio Grande.

Matiana, now twenty-two, had come into her inheritance and wanted to return to Texas to inspect her lands. She had received one-third of her father's estate and the income from the town lots, ranches, and buildings. With the money she could travel comfortably and live well. If necessary she could sell land for additional income. Above all, however, she was dedicated to her Texas family, among whom she had spent all her early years. The baptism of Librada and Patricio's daughter Agustina, planned for Christmas Eve 1857, proved to be an excellent opportunity to return to the family ranch at Mission Valley. Matiana's sister Pilar had also married in Texas, and she and her husband, Cristobal de la Garza, asked Matiana to serve as godmother to their first son, Patricio, born in 1858. Matiana felt pleased to offer her protection as godmother to any of her friends and relations in Victoria who might ask.[11]

During the 1850s the Spanish-speaking community of Victoria had grown rapidly. A combination of political problems in Mexico and the chance for a good life in Texas had attracted many Mexicans across the border. A number of them, with friends or relatives in Victoria, had migrated to town. Some, as Doña Luz knew, had tried carting since it had proved profitable, if only for a few years. Others, with connections to local families, had either bought or received land from the old settlers and started ranches of their own. If they had the right social connections, they married into the old Tejano ranching families, as Matilde Ureste had done. Still others, with smaller dreams and less capital to invest, bought or rented farms or town lots and became farmers or small merchants. Some Mexicans, skilled in both business and handling cattle, and who had a little money to invest, provided a much-needed group of cattle brokers to buy cattle in Victoria or Goliad or along the San Antonio and Guadalupe River valleys and move the herds to the coast for sale. Those with no funds but with family in Texas could still expect a job or a place to stay on the Tejano ranches or the small farms springing up around Victoria.

Francisco Santiago, as a leader of the Tejano community, had encouraged many of the young men arriving from Mexico whom he found in town or on the ranches of his friends and relatives. With their excellent knowledge of cattle and horses as well as a powerful desire to improve themselves and their families, one of the quickest ways for the newly arrived Mexicans to profit was to become cattle agents and sell herds not only for Don Francisco but for others as well. They needed not only good business sense but also the confidence of the ranchers for whom they acted as agents. That was not difficult among the Tejanos. The new arrivals, many of whom were related to those already living in Victoria, became automatically part of the large extended families, whether through marriage or through godparenthood. They could be counted on to support their relatives.

Don Francisco and Matilde led the way in providing godparenthood to more than twenty-three of the growing number of Mexican-Tejano families, regardless of whether they were wealthy or poor, relatives or merely friends. A score of the other ranchers did so as well. The network of *compadres* and *comadres* grew, even as intermarriages created additional bonds, extending family connections. Gradually, the Mexican-Tejano community was becoming one solid, integrated whole.

The family ties also united the Tejano community economically. During the 1850s, with the support and protection of the United States, Texas was developing an infrastructure and a growing economy. Almost all of the Tejanos engaged in some form of cattle raising. With Indianola expanding, ranch owners like Santiago and Patricio at Mission Valley and their cousin Francisco Santiago, or Frank, on Garcitas Creek, found Mexican stockmen, trustworthy *compadres* or blood relatives, who bought cattle in Victoria and surrounding counties and trailed the cattle to Indianola, Corpus Christi, or Brownsville twice a year. The herds varied in size from a few dozen to as many as several hundred head of cattle. In the port cities, local agents bought the cattle from the stockmen and shipped the cattle to New Orleans or New York. The stockmen returned to Victoria with saddlebags loaded with silver and gold coins with which they could buy more cattle.[12]

Among the newcomers were Manuel Flores and his cousin Regalón. Manuel had moved to Victoria and married Felipa Carbajal, setting himself up as an entrepreneurial stockman. With Felipa's dowry, land she received from her Carbajal uncles, he invested in herds which his cousin Regalón drove to the coast. As a new member of the extended de León family, Manuel Flores and his cousin could be trusted to handle the de León cattle trade. In 1852 Regalón Flores took forty head of horses and two hundred head of cattle to the coast for Patricio, Silvestre, Francisco, and other Victoria cattlemen. With cattle selling for as much as $10 a head, the trip was particularly lucrative both for Regalón and for the ranchers.[13]

Francisco Santiago, out on Garcitas Creek, had taken a particular interest in Pedro Answaldo (or Ansualdo), one of the newly arrived Mexican immigrants. Francisco had learned of him in 1853 when he bought 182.5 acres on Arenosa Creek from Don Fernando de León. Pedro was educated and signed for his property with a bold, elegant script. Francisco had attended the wedding feast in early spring of 1855 when twenty-two-year-old Pedro married fourteen-year-old Altagracia Cruz, also from Mexico. Francisco had also served as godfather when their second child, María Paulita, was born in 1858. Pedro had invested in two ox carts and teams with which he hauled goods to and from the coast, often for Francisco or the de León family. Pedro added two more yoke of oxen and two more wagons to his small business during the late 1850s as trade increased between Victoria and the coast. As his business expanded, he brought the Lara family from Mexico to help on the small farm and with the carting business. Pedro even registered a cattle brand in Altagracia's name when she turned twenty-seven and helped her purchase a small herd of cattle. Pedro had become a solid, successful member of the community, worth $875, and willing to serve as godfather for others in Victoria.[14]

Francisco Santiago, along with his adoptive mother, Doña Luz, had also reached out to help Prudencio Espetia and his wife, María de los Santos Rodríguez. Prudencio, at forty years of age, had arrived from Mexico in 1852 and may have become acquainted with Francisco through work as a carpenter on the construction of the new ranch house. In 1858 Prudencio had saved enough money to buy a small farm from Doña Luz three miles south of town on the Guadalupe River. She charged him only fifty-eight cents per acre, or $140 for the 242-acre tract on which he kept a small herd. Francisco had stood as godfather for Prudencio's sons and had gone with him to the courthouse to register brands for the two boys, Rómulo and Manuel, when each of them turned nine. As their godparents, Francisco and Doña Luz helped the boys by giving each of them a few cows to start their own herds.[15]

Like many of the Tejano ranchers, Don Guadalupe Ureste, Matilde's father, had created a successful village on his ranch. The paternalism which he practiced was protective for those who lived on his lands. He not only extended godparenthood protection to the children of his ranch hands, but he also extended the hospitality of the ranch to the relatives and families of his workers as well.[16]

Don Guadalupe had hired Manuel Cano and his brother Felipe as ranch hands when the two arrived as young men from Mexico during the 1850s with their spinster sister Matilde, for whom Don Guadalupe also found work. Two years later, Don Guadalupe had welcomed their brother Miguel to the ranch, hired him as a *vaquero*, and had helped pay for the wedding feast when Miguel married a local girl, María Elena Cano, in 1854. He also paid for the feasts for the baptisms of their first two children, which were held in the ranch chapel. As the other ranch hands married and had children, they had called on each other to become godparents and on Don Guadalupe himself.[17]

Matilde Cano, the cheerful little spinster from the Ureste Ranch, offered her help as godmother to more than thirty children in Victoria from 1856 to 1896. At first her name appeared with Don Guadalupe's *vaqueros*. Then, because of her popularity, she began moving up in the hierarchy of the Tejano society. No longer was she just at the baptisms of the *vaqueros'* children, but she was asked to be godmother to the children of the "old Spanish families" as well. She was chosen not so much for what she could give but for who she was, a kind, caring, compassionate leader of the community. At age thirty-five she finally married Moses Johnson, a neighbor who may not have been Catholic since his name appears only once as godfather. She remained active in community affairs until 1896.[18]

Just as Soto la Marina had been the center for family gatherings fifty years earlier, by the 1860s the Tejano families who had moved to Mexico now returned to their roots in Victoria for weddings and births. Doña Luz had established her own household where, at fifty-two years of age, she had given a home to Manuel Flores and Felipa Carbajal and their three children, along with a *mozo* from Mexico, Antonio de la Garza, and a maid, Josefa Navarro. Matiana Benavides, meanwhile, had taken up residence with Patricio and Librada at Mission Valley. It was Matiana's cousin's sister who was coming to Victoria to have her wedding to Juan de Hoyos. She wanted to marry in the presence of her de León and Benavides kin as well as her entire extended family. It was important to the Tejano and Mexican extended families to come together to provide support for each other. Never was the success of the individual jeopardized or compromised by a lack of help. These habits of familial responsibility were not necessarily better adapted to the frontier environment than the Anglo traits of individualism, but the Tejano extended family, which consisted of dozens of relations, provided economic and social protection in time of need. The Anglo-American concept of individualism and drive to get ahead had come at the expense of the extended family. The Anglo-American women and their tiny families who were left alone in the wilderness while their husbands went in search of new homes or to sell goods in town had suffered when they had no family nearby.[19]

As more and more Anglos arrived in Victoria in the 1850s, the de León family had learned to adjust to their ways. There had been racist sneers and snide comments from the newly arrived Anglo Americans who coveted the vast acreage of the Tejano families. In some areas, such as Refugio, Goliad, and down on the Nueces, the racism escalated to violence and attacks on the Mexican ranchers. Anglos interested in cutting in on the carting trade between San Antonio and the coast carried out particularly vicious attacks against the Mexican carters, who were often killed and their goods stolen. Without the support of the authorities, there was little the Mexican families could do to fight back. Many turned to each other for protection. Francisco, Doña Luz, Patricio, and his brothers had learned to ignore the jibes during the court cases which forced the squatters off their lands. Fernando himself had struggled to be accepted by both cultures, even, perhaps, joining the Anglo churches. For Francisco Santiago, or Frank, the transfer was easier. There were still supporters and defenders of the Tejano families among the early settlers such as the Linns who labeled them "old Spanish" families. The incoming Mexicans, in turn, could look to these old Spanish families for their protection and defense.

Economically, the Tejanos had no need to go to Anglo banks for funds. They depended on each other and their godparenthood relationships to support them with loans and financial help, as Doña Patricia and Doña Luz had proved time and again. With the arrival of every new worker, the old Tejano families continued to receive the infusion of Spanish cultures and customs which helped them maintain their own Tejano frontier mentality and habits.[20]

For many of the Tejanos, there was danger both socially and economically in having a daughter marry an Anglo. From the Tejano view, there would be no joining of extended families, no strengthening of the clan, no betterment for all. From the Anglo perspective, on the other hand, the conservative Tejano families were the main obstacle to advancing in the business world. The Tejanos, thought the Anglos, prevented the "development and recognition of individual abilities that would help elevate the Latin community."[21] Doña Luz and the Tejanos disagreed. For them amassing fortunes at the expense of others and then not sharing it with the family was selfish. Only when individual abilities were used for the good of the whole did the families and the community prosper, the Tejanos argued. The success of one was the insurance which protected all of the members. The family cared for its own, good and bad, rich and poor. For the Tejanos of Victoria, the family was the basis for existence.[22]

While clouds of a civil war loomed on the distant horizon in late 1860, the family celebrated the marriage of Matiana's sister Librada to Juan de Hoyos. The threat of war was discussed, but it was not something which disturbed the wedding feast. Librada and Juan remained in Texas with their cousin Patricio and his wife, Librada, for another year along with Matiana and the de León families at the Mission Valley Ranch. By coincidence, both Libradas, known in the Spanish culture as *tocayas*, a form of relation in which kin have the same name, gave birth to children the same year. Patricio and Librada had a girl named Francisca Estanislada, born in May, while Librada and Juan de Hoyos had a little girl named Francisca in October. The de Hoyos family asked their cousin José María Benavides and his wife, Josefina, to serve as godparents. Thus they had carried on the name of Francisca, and the babies became the third and fourth in the line of Panchitas. After the de Hoyos couple returned to the border, they did not lose contact with their Texas kin. In 1862, when Librada had her second child, Julianita, two of their Texas relatives traveled to Reynosa, Tamaulipas, to serve as godparents. In grateful recognition of their support ten years later, in 1871, Librada granted to her two cousins and *comadres* title to 717 acres out of the original Benavides league of land which Librada had inherited. Librada saved 990 acres of the Texas land for her own children, Panchita and Julianita.[23]

National politics broke into the affairs of the de León and Benavides families during November and December 1860. Although Santiago, Patricio, and their cousin Francisco had discussed the growing debate over slavery, they had taken little interest when Abraham Lincoln, the Republican candidate, had been elected. By January 1861, however, when South Carolina and five other states seceded from the Union, the Tejano men found themselves facing the dilemma of choosing sides. Like the difficult decisions their fathers had to make twenty-four years earlier, now Santiago, Patricio, and their cousin Francisco, as well as the Benavides boys across the county and Carlos de la Garza's sons down on the San Antonio had to choose sides. Texas teetered on the edge of secession as Victoria citizens split over the issue of slavery and secession.

The Tejano ranchers since the early days under Mexico had never approved of slavery. Of them all, Don Fernando had been the only one to own a slave, and when Doña Luz and Francisco had inherited him, they had done their best to manumit him. Only the laws of Texas prevented them from freeing their slave. But it was obvious to Santiago at Mission Valley and Francisco on the Garcitas that if they did not support the Southern sympathizers, who seemed to hold a slender majority in Victoria, the de León families might be in danger from vengeful Southern Anglos. The newly arrived Germans had staunchly opposed slavery and had voted strongly against separating from the Union. The pro-Southerners had

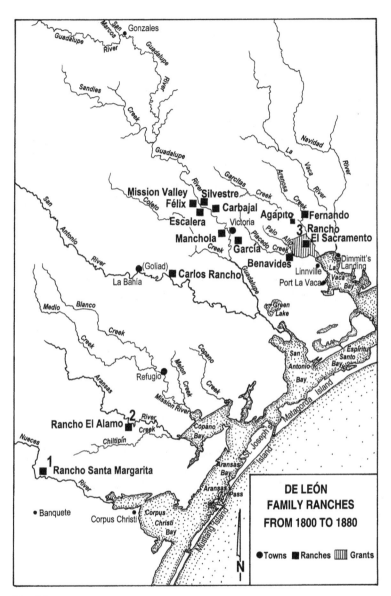

Map 8.1

sent two delegates to the Secessionist Convention called by the Legislature in Austin. By the middle of February 1861 word reached Victoria that the convention had passed an Ordinance of Secession and that the people of the state had been asked to ratify the separation from the Union. The Victoria *Advocate* and the New Orleans *Picayune* reported that statewide, the secessionists carried the vote, and in Victoria 313 voted for separation and 88 against. The de León family along with many of the Tejano and Mexican families, after considerable discussion over family tables, remained aloof from the increasingly bitter dispute.[24]

In early 1861 the Union commander of the United States Army in Texas in San Antonio had surrendered his supplies and equipment to a group of newly deputized Confederate mounted volunteers and had moved his 2,700 troops downriver to Green Lake, just outside of Victoria, to await transports out of Matagorda. Most Southerners, including the de León family in Victoria, expected the Union to quietly accept the separation of half the country, although Sam Houston, who had refused to condone secession, warned that the country would choke in blood. Sam Houston proved to be more prescient than most. Lincoln and the North refused to accept the loss of the Southern states. In April 1861 the local newspaper reported that gun batteries of the city of Charleston fired on U.S. troops in Fort Sumter, and the country stumbled headlong into the bloodbath which Houston had predicted.[25]

Many of the Southern supporters, seeking to form cavalry units, placed ads in the Victoria *Advocate* calling young men to arms. They were encouraged to come "whip the Yankees" and for the joy of doing of noble deeds for the glory of the South. As the Tejano families discussed the options, the women united in opposition to the men leaving Texas at all. Already Union ships were threatening the coastline, and if there was to be an invasion, the Tejanos needed to protect their homes and families. Unlike Doña Patricia, who had been forced from her home in 1836, Doña Luz, Doña Matilde, and the others were not about to leave. The men could glory in their martial ardor, wear their uniforms, and fire off their guns, but they would not do it on some battlefield in Tennessee.

Francisco Santiago acceded to Doña Luz's dictates. With his cousins at Mission Valley he joined the Victoria Cavalry Company, a local independent company for coastal defense which "employed a drill sergeant and armed themselves." In Refugio County their cousins Trinidad Aldrete and his brother Rafael were respectively appointed first lieutenant and captain of the Jeff Davis Home Guard. Another cousin, Santos Benavides from Laredo, created the Benavides Company, a cavalry unit much like the unit his uncle Plácido Benavides had led during the Texas Revolution. At Carlos Rancho the sons of Carlos de la Garza were enrolled in the Davis Guard Reserve Company of mounted infantry.[26]

Of all of the brothers, only Silvestre de León chose combat outside Texas. Silvestre, now twenty-six, joined Company A of Waller's 13th Cavalry Battalion. Led by Captain James P. B. January, a veteran of the Texas Revolution and the Mexican War, the unit formed at Garcitas Creek and marched for Louisiana in April 1862. They were assigned to Brigadier General Arthur Pendleton Bagby's Brigade in the cavalry division of Major General Thomas Green. Silvestre and his unit soon had all the glory they cared for. They fought Union forces throughout western Louisiana in a series of short, bitter, bloody battles. On September 8, 1862, after less than a year in the service, Silvestre and several members of Waller's unit were captured by Union forces at Bonnet Carré, Louisiana. While the rest of his unit gained laurels by defeating Union General Nathaniel Banks at Mansfield and at Pleasant Hill, Silvestre suffered through the remainder of the war in a Union prisoner of war camp without sufficient food, clothing, or shelter, conditions common to all of the Civil War prisons.[27]

Doña Luz and the de León family in Victoria continued their daily routines. Olivia provided a bright spot in their lives when she married Crisóforo Lozano, a widower with three children and a recent arrival from Mexico. As Olivia's dowry, Crisóforo received part of the Mission Valley Ranch and joined his new brothers-in-law in cattle ranching. Like Santiago and Patricio and their cousin Frank, he also offered godparenthood protection to the old Tejano families who were now his relatives, as well as to other newly arrived Mexicans.[28]

The Union ships closed their stranglehold on the ports of the coast, gradually cutting off the supplies on which the South depended. The women learned to live with the reports of attacks on Matagorda, Indianola, and Port Lavaca, always fearing that the next attack might be on Victoria. Santiago and Francisco engaged in cavalry skirmishes against Union advances and fought off Yankee attempts to gain anything more than a toehold on the coast.

During November 1862 their cavalry company was called to battle. Three Union gunboats entered Pass Caballo and attacked the town of Indianola. The Southern defensive cavalry units fought off the Union attack. Santiago and Francisco, to the relief of the family, were not injured, but the Northerners captured the town, drove the Southern forces from the coast, and closed the small port. The cavalry unit could do nothing to remove the Union troops who controlled the coast until May 1864, when they once again left the town only to return for good the following year.[29]

During the war the Tejanos profited by supplying the Confederate forces with food and horses. In 1863 David Benavides, one of the de León family cousins, in addition to selling horses and cattle to the Confederacy made a handsome profit by using his three wagons and eighteen yoke of oxen to carry cotton from East Texas to the Mexican port of Matamoros. David unloaded cotton at the port of Brazos de Santiago, where incoming British ships traded weapons, powder, medicines, and supplies for the cotton and paid in bullion. Once in Mexico, David could shop for the whole family in Mexican markets at Matamoros or pick up supplies at the Carbajal or Benavides ranches at Camargo and Mier. The carting and cotton trade continued until 1864, when the Union ships captured Brownsville and effectively blocked the supply lines into the South. David and other Mexican entrepreneurs, however, still used the markets along the Rio Grande and inland at Saltillo to supply their families.[30]

In Victoria there was little for Santiago, Patricio, and the Victoria Cavalry Company to do but make an occasional foray against the Yankee forces on the coast. The soldiers spent the evenings drinking and playing cards, mostly a form of gambling known as *monte*. *Monte*, or mountebank, was a game played with forty cards in which the players bet that two cards, drawn from either the top or bottom of the deck and placed face up, would match, in suit, the next card drawn. Santiago had taken to gambling with the sons of the oldest families in Victoria. In addition to Santiago de León, the Victoria sheriff caught Ed and Charles Linn, Ches King, William Van Norman, Edward Allen, and Peter Farrell. The group was jailed several times in 1863 and 1864 and again in 1868 and 1870 for "betting at a Monte Bank."[31]

After their arrest the young men were bailed out by their fathers. Santiago was bailed out by his mortified brother Patricio. The various family lawyers, perhaps because of the influential position of the young men in the community, convinced the judge to carry the cases over for three years and finally got the charges dismissed in 1864. C. L. Thurmond and C. O. Weller, who had kept the gaming table, did not have their cases dismissed until the February term of 1866.[32]

When the Civil War ended in 1865 Silvestre returned from the Union prison in Louisiana, bitter and demoralized. His business partner and agent, Andrew Oliver, had taken good care of his business while he was gone, and Sil was worth more than $5,700. In addition to his part of the

Mission Valley Ranch, he owned 1,050 acres, more than three hundred cattle, and sixty-seven horses. Oliver would have made a handsome profit for the partnership by selling both horses and cattle to the Southern Army, except that the bankrupt Confederate government paid in scrip and devalued currency which by the end of the war was worthless. The land, cattle, and horses which the two men owned still held their value. In 1866 Andrew Oliver moved to San Antonio. He remained in contact with the de León family, extending a kind invitation to Sil to come up for Christmas and sending kind regards to Doña Luz.[33]

Without the stabilizing influence of his partner, Sil took up his old habits of drinking, playing pool, and gambling, along with the worst of Victoria's young rowdies. C. L. Thurmond and C. O. Weller, the owners of the gaming table, along with Sil, James W. Allen, A. Acheson, R. Hanna, and N. D. J. Hatfield, were caught by the sheriff and again brought up on charges of gambling at pool. The judge continued the cases, but this time Silvestre, Charles Linn, and their drinking friends stood trial. There was no reprieve. The judge ruled them all guilty and fined each one $25. Silvestre and Charles Linn appealed their cases. Of the two young men, Silvestre's case was dismissed, while Charles was required to pay his fine.[34]

Sil had begun to drink heavily. He ran up large bills for half-gallon jugs of bourbon with William G. Neely and Company. He sold his land, and the money vanished as he gambled and drank his way through town. In 1867 he came to Doña Luz and Doña Matiana to borrow money. He offered his acreage in Mission Valley as collateral. The women agreed to hold the mortgage on his land. The loan failed to keep him afloat. In 1868 he sold his cattle and horses to his cousin Frank for $1,500, and that money, too, soon disappeared. As a member of the family, Silvestre had to be cared for, but the women also realized the importance of teaching him a lesson. Reluctantly, Doña Luz and Doña Matiana foreclosed on Silvestre. Unlike Anglo bankers who would have taken everything he had, the women left him a twenty-acre tract where his ranch house stood. In June 1869 Silvestre de León was discovered drowned in the Guadalupe River; some suggested it had been a suicide. He had little to show for his life but the land his family had protected for him. From what was left of Silvestre's property, his cousin Frank satisfied some of the claims of Matiana Benavides and Luz Escalera.[35]

With the end of the war and the defeat of the South, the de León family, like the Anglo Victorians, had to accept Union rule. Northern forces arrived and demanded the rebuilding of the South. It made little difference to the Tejano families. Resentful Anglo Southerners reelected the same officeholders who had controlled the state before the war, refused to offer equal rights to the newly freed blacks, and returned unregenerate secessionist ex-Confederates to Washington as their representatives. Northerners were shocked and dismayed by the lack of contrition in the South. In late 1865 the Republican-dominated Congress in Washington refused to seat the incoming delegates, and within two years the Congress, now controlled by what Southerners depicted as vengeful, radical Republicans, overturned the Southern constitutions and governments. The South was divided into five military districts, with Texas and Louisiana lumped into the 5th Military District under General Philip Sheridan at New Orleans.[36]

The Yankees were in charge and made sure everyone knew it. Even Santiago and Francisco and the other Tejano families, insulated and relatively safe on their ranches, felt the impact of the government officials who felt it was their duty to pacify the South. Major General David S. Stanley, commanding general of the 4th Corps of the U.S. Army, arrived in Victoria with his troops and took over the home of the banker Abraham Levi. The troops moved into other homes, removed the government officials whom they deemed disloyal, and replaced them with Unionists and Republicans. The new officeholders tried to control the rising tide of violence and the increasing use of guns and knives among the local populace. They did not, however, count on Tejano pride.[37]

Twenty-six-year-old Samuel, the youngest of Félix' sons, perhaps because of his brother's bad reputation around town, had become particularly sensitive to slights to his honor. He frequented the German Schutzen Hall, or meeting place, on Coleto Creek. In January 1871 Samuel got into a fight with a German named Alcide Willemen, who assaulted Sam with a six-shooter. The sheriff, a Republican officeholder, arrested Willemen, and the judge found the German guilty of simple assault and let him off with a fine of $5. Sam apparently did not feel that his honor had been satisfied. In September of that year he returned to the Schutzen Meeting Hall carrying a gun. The witnesses, three Germans — Alcide Willemen, William Albright, and Albert Schubert — testified that Sam had come into the hall on Coleto Creek while a meeting was in progress. Sam was arrested by the sheriff, and rather than call on his brothers, he asked his friends Tobe Reeves and Allan Thinner to bail him out. Eight months later, on April 27, 1872, the case was dismissed.[38]

It was probably not surprising, considering Sam de León's recent problems with the Germans, that on June 6, 1872, a month and a half after the dismissal of his case, Sheriff John D. Sneigr and Victoria Mayor William Billings, both outsiders unfamiliar with the de León family, stopped him on the streets of Victoria and attempted to frisk him for a gun. After a ten-minute altercation in which no gun was found, the sheriff let de León go. In a fury, Sam de León immediately went to the courthouse and charged that both men

> unlawfully and without authority of law and without a legal warrant of arrest did arrest and falsely imprison and detain contrary to the wishes and without the consent of this affiant . . . for the space of ten minutes or less and did there and then unlawfully and without authority of law search the person of this affiant contrary to the form of the statute in such cases.[39]

The case was brought to trial the next day, June 7. The jury, under the rules of the Reconstruction government, was required to swear the test oath of 1862, affirming that they "had never voluntarily supported the Confederacy."[40] The oath effectively removed all ex-Confederates. The jury of six Anglos, much to the surprise of Samuel and his de León supporters, found the sheriff and the mayor guilty and fined them $35 each. Sheriff Sneigr demanded a new trial, which the judge granted and ordered to take place June 8. For this second trial the jury found it impossible to agree, and the defendants were discharged. Court again convened on June 10. This time the Charge to the Jury required that

> [I]f from the evidence in this case you believe William Billings as Mayor of the City of Victoria had good reason to believe that Saml [sic] de León was violating the law by carrying deadly weapons, then it was his duty to arrest de León even though de León really was not carrying such weapons. Had the Mayor in such case failed to make the arrest he would have been liable to punishment for failure to do his duty.[41]

A new jury again found the mayor and sheriff of Victoria guilty, only this time the fine was reduced to $5 each. The mayor and sheriff filed for a new trial, but the judge refused their request, and they were forced to pay their fine. Samuel, with his honor avenged, returned to the safety of the Mission Valley Ranch.[42]

Unlike his brothers, Patricio de León remained on the right side of the law. A staunch member of the Catholic Church, he and his wife, Doña Librada, offered their protection as godparents to more than a dozen families in Victoria. He served on juries, got along well with his Anglo neigh-

Librada Benavides de León was the granddaughter of Martín and Patricia de León. Librada, the daughter of Agustina de León and Plácido Benavides, was orphaned at age seven. Courtesy of the de León family, Victoria, Texas.

Patricio de León, also grandson of Martín de León, married his cousin Librada. He was the son of Salomé Leal and Félix de León, Agustina's brother. Courtesy of the de León family, Victoria, Texas.

bors, and supported the standards of the community. With considerable humiliation, he also bailed out his younger brothers frequently. He learned much from his brothers' brushes with the law, eventually apprenticed with the de León family lawyers, and went on to read for the bar. He became a respected lawyer in his own right. In 1874, with the end of Reconstruction, he was appointed a deputy sheriff for Victoria County. Within ten years Patricio had been commissioned a deputy county clerk, and in addition to his regular duties he spent years translating all of the Spanish language records into English.[43]

Francisco Santiago, still in close contact with the family at Mission Valley Ranch and his adoptive mother, Doña Luz, had done his best to maintain the family honor. Like Patricio, Frank worked hard to preserve his upstanding and stellar reputation. He and Matilde, his wife, and Doña Luz were often at the church, standing up for one godchild after another, attending baptisms for almost all the new babies, and celebrating at the marriage feasts of the many members of the Tejano community. By either godparenthood or marriage, they were soon related to most of the Tejanos and newly arrived Mexicans. Frank also served on juries and upheld the law.[44]

Other Tejanos also supported law and order. Don Guadalupe Ureste, like his son-in-law Frank, had worked hard on his ranch but did not hesitate to fight for his rights in the Anglo courts. In 1860 he and Francisco Garza sued James C. Scott for debt on a note of $620.80. In a trial before twelve Anglo jurors, the court found in Don Guadalupe's favor. Like the de León family, however, Don Guadalupe also had trouble with the younger generation.[45]

Don Guadalupe's four sons, Florencio, Inocencio, Julián, and Romualdo, became the bane of their father's existence. In April 1873, during the height of Reconstruction, Florencio was accused of stealing a bay horse colt belonging to W. J. Lewis. Don Guadalupe and the family attorney, D. Alexander, secured bond for his son. Don Guadalupe paid for the attorney, and Florencio was found not guilty. Five months later Florencio was back in court, this time for stealing an unbranded colt from José María Gonzales. Bond was again posted by Guadalupe Ureste, this time with a very weak and wobbly signature, and D. Alexander, the lawyer. Once again Florencio Ureste was found not guilty. In January 1874 Florencio was arrested for aggravated assault with a loaded quirt on John Chambers, who drew a knife on him. Florencio was found not guilty by reason of self-defense. In 1874 Florencio Ureste was involved in a fight and sued Jackson

Chambers for assault. The case was dismissed when Jackson Chambers died of unknown causes.[46]

Frustrated over his son's indiscretions, the elderly and ailing Don Guadalupe in 1876 moved back to his family home in San Antonio, leaving the boys in Victoria. He died not long afterward. Florencio, upon his father's death, cleaned up his act, but Inocencio, the second son, began to get into trouble. In late 1876 Juan Mora and Inocencio Ureste were caught stealing a hog worth $5 from Roberto Gonzales. Crisóforo Lozano, Olivia's new husband, who may have been Mora's employer, signed for him as security, and the judge released Mora on his own recognizance. Inocencio had two of his brothers, Florencio and Julián, sign as his security since his father was gone. Perhaps the judge felt that the two younger Urestes were not as trustworthy as their father, and the judge required a $250 bond for Inocencio. The bond was rescinded when both Mora and Ureste were found not guilty. In July 1883 the state accused Inocencio Ureste of murdering Alex Semand with a pistol. Inocencio's brothers and his mother came to his defense, and he was bailed out and found not guilty.[47]

Frank de León and the other members of the Tejano community were relieved when the Ureste boys finally gave up their wild ways. Perhaps maturity had cured their transgressions. In 1878 Florencio Ureste took over the family affairs and began to pay the taxes for his mother, Francisca Garcia Ureste. By the 1880s he was his mother's agent and paid taxes on her 431 acres, one wagon, sixty cattle, two yoke of oxen, six hogs, and $25 worth of corn. He also acted as her agent and sold some of her cattle to A. G. Hugo of De Witt County for $1,500. Florencio had at last become a respectable and accepted member of the Tejano and Anglo communities. So proper had he become that, like his many Tejano relatives, he was called to serve on juries in the Victoria County courts that he had known so well as a teenager.[48]

The Tejano families, scattered across Victoria and the surrounding counties, were as relieved as the Anglos to learn of the end of Northern control in the South in 1876. The Radical Republicans and the Northern troops left Texas. Two factors spurred the economy of the area, which would one day become known as the "Cradle of the Cattle Industry." The first was the rapid increase of industrialization in the Northeast. Northern businessmen and a growing number of British and Scottish investors had capital to finance new industries and the money to buy up large cattle ranches. The Northern factories, with their rapidly expanding labor force, all needed Texas beef. The second factor was transportation. For cattle ranching to reach its full profit potential, cattle had to be moved quickly and with the least loss of weight to the urban centers of the Northeast and Midwest, where hungry laborers waited. Railroads were expanding across the country to fill that need.[49]

Few railroad owners, however, had made the cattle connection prior to the Civil War. Edward Piper, in 1846, took six months to drive cattle from Kansas to Ohio. In 1853 an Illinois merchant drove a herd from Texas to New York in only a year and a half. In 1867 Joseph McCoy of Illinois, after several disheartening rejections by communities and railroads, finally convinced Abilene, Kansas, to provide stock pens to hold Texas cattle, and he induced the officials of the Hannibal and St. Joseph Railroad to provide the cattle cars necessary to move the cattle from Texas to the Northeast. Within three years, by 1870, more than 300,000 cattle were being shipped each year out of Abilene, Kansas. Cattle trails connected Texas and Kansas, and the boom was on.

For ten years, from 1876 to 1886, Anglos, Englishmen, Scotsmen, and Eastern entrepreneurs invaded the cattle kingdoms which had once belonged almost exclusively to the Tejanos. Doña Luz, Doña Matiana, Francisco Santiago, and many other Tejanos sold portions of their lands to the rapidly expanding population of Anglo ranchers, who had to learn the cattle-herding techniques from their Tejano neighbors. The newcomers expanded their holdings at the expense of the old families, whether Tejano, Irish, or Anglo. With the potential for incredible profit and with the advent of barbed wire with which they could fence out the Tejanos and control the water sources, the new cattle barons bought up not just hundreds but thousands and even millions of acres. The saying around the ranches soon became, "If the owner won't sell, his widow will." Some of the Tejano families fought back, but midnight raids, shots in the night, and dead bodies at dawn forced many to flee for the border. Others moved in with relatives and friends, counting on the kinship network which still supported them.[50]

Not all Tejanos lost their lands. Many, such as the de León family at Mission Valley, the Benavides clan on the east end of the county, and the Carlos de la Garza family on the San Antonio River, joined the cattle boom and made a profit by taking cattle to Corpus Christi and Galveston and shipping them to New Orleans and New York. In Corpus and Galveston the Tejano stockmen continued to deal with agents they knew and trusted, although many also went "up the trail" to take herds to the railheads in Kansas. During the cattle boom years from 1870 until the disastrous droughts and blizzard of 1885–1886, some Tejanos lost land, but dozens of Mexicans arrived in Texas to profit from the cattle industry.[51]

The old Tejano families, by the third and fourth generations, had divided their lands among their children and their children's children. Each time, the parcels became smaller and smaller, but all received their *herencia*. Félix had divided his land among his six children. Although Silvestre had died, his aunt and cousin returned his portion of the ranch to his brothers and sisters. Santiago had remarried, this time to Guadalupe Berlanga, and Samuel, just two years after all his problems with the sheriff, had married Patricia de la Garza, a distant cousin. Patricio and Librada along with Olivia and Crisóforo Lozano, and Chucha and her husband all had growing families among whom they would, in turn, divide their land. Doña Luz and Doña Matiana continued to sell pieces of their once-vast holdings. They lent money to friends and family in need and gave hundreds of acres to their relatives as dowries and as gifts. Doña Librada, Matiana's sister, gave property to her cousins, nephews, and nieces who had stood as godparents for her children. Godparenthood and the land tied the families together. The Tejano and Mexican families continued to stand as godparents for each other's children, forming closer and more complex ties among the small community.

There were opportunities even for the less wealthy who also used the support of the Tejano society to better themselves. The Cano family had remained on Don Guadalupe's ranch until it was divided among his four sons. Miguel continued to work for the Ureste sons, while his brother became a landowner and rancher in his own right. After the war Manuel bought 4.6 acres from Alcide Willemen, the same German who had the altercation with Samuel de León, and the following year registered his own brand. By 1877 Manuel Cano, by then forty years old, had a city lot valued at $200, two horses, thirty head of stock horses at $8 each, and one jack. The following year he had sold ten of his horses and bought a $50 wagon, and his property had increased in value to $250. He sold horses and cattle, but much of his income came from selling mules, which were still commonly used for carrying goods. He had his ranch and his own property in town, and he could still visit his brother out on the Ureste ranch.[52]

Prudencio Espetia, like the Canos, had invested in his own land and achieved a modest prominence in Victoria society. His children were connected by godparenthood to Francisco and Doña Luz, but he wanted more. He purchased an additional 200 acres from J. M. Brownson, a very good deal at seventy-five cents per acre, although he had to take a mortgage to do it. By 1877 Prudencio was worth almost $1,000 and held his original 242 acres of land free and clear plus the second 200 acres under a mortgage. He and his wife, Maria de los Santos, had married off their three older daughters—Maria Florentina in 1868, and six years later, Maria Isabela and Teresa María Francisca had a double wedding in November. Meanwhile, seventeen-year-old Juana and thirteen-year-old Anselma helped their mother around the house. The two sons, sixteen-year-old Rómulo and fourteen-year-old Manuel, helped their aging father with the farm. The few head which Francisco and Doña Luz had given the boys when each of them turned nine years old had grown into a profitable and sizable herd. Prudencio paid off the mortgage in 1878 and passed on to his children their *herencia* of land.[53]

The society was changing. A new, more modern generation was taking over, and out at Mission Valley, Doña Luz, the elderly matriarch, passed away in 1892, a respected and much-loved member of the Victoria community. Hundreds of the old Tejano families, her own de León and Escalera and Benavides and Carbajal and Aldrete relations, as well as the many Mexicans to whom she had extended her support and friendship attended her funeral. Her black-gowned *comadritas* lit candles for her and prayed for her soul. Her land was gone, but it had gone for the good of her people. She had given away or sold it all, giving the money to the poor of the community, helping the needy, and supporting the building of the new Catholic church where she was laid to rest. Doña Luz had indeed been the godmother of the Victoria Tejanos.

Francisco Santiago de León, her beloved adopted son, with hard work and a knowledge of the cattle and horse business, had become an accepted member of the Anglo community and one of the wealthiest of the "old Spanish families," but he had not turned his back on his Tejano people. After the war he was worth more than $7,700, with six thousand acres of the Fernando de León league, seventy-nine horses, one hundred cattle, four yoke of oxen, one cart, and six hogs. Francisco, like his adoptive father, Fernando, tended to underreport the number of cattle he owned. In 1876, while reporting only one hundred head of cattle to the tax man, Frank sold one-third interest in a thousand head of his own branded cattle "ranging in Victoria, Jackson, Calhoun and adjoining counties" for $490 in silver.[54] His assessments for the following year included sixty horses, ten of which were good riding stock, and the same one hundred cattle, in addition to the family ranch of 9,242 acres from the Valentín Garcia grant, 120 bushels of corn, two yoke of oxen, and several wagons. He also listed $500 cash in hand, the silver from the previous year's cattle sale, a gun, and a dog. After his first wife, Lupita Ureste, passed away, he married Justita Wilson, and she cared for the younger of his six children. By 1878 Frank had used his cash to invest in three hundred head of good $25 horses, but he had also seen a possibility to diversify. He went into the ambulance business, converting one of his wagons into a town ambulance. He profited handsomely during the next ten years from his investments. By the time he turned fifty-two, Frank's position within the Mexican community as well as the Anglo society was assured. He continued to profit from horse sales and protect members of the Tejano community. In 1889 Frank was elected deputy sheriff for Victoria County, a position he held until his death.[55]

The Tejano and Mexican-American families of Victoria kept their shared beliefs in paternalism, love of family, open-handed hospitality, and strong religious faith. They struggled for survival, fought for their beliefs, and supported and protected their own. Regardless of their successes or failures, they were linked to each other in unbreakable kinship bonds. The powerful kinship and godparenthood networks, with the blessings of the Catholic Church, created a society in which, as they can still say today, "We are all cousins here."

EPILOGUE

If Martín de León were to return to his town so many years after his death, what would he have said of the contributions of his family to the settlement of Texas? Was their struggle characteristic of life on the frontier of northern New Spain? What lessons about the Hispanic past can the de León family offer their descendants and other Mexican Americans throughout the Southwest today?

Martín de León was by no means unique among those who faced the frontier experience of the Spanish in Texas. On the contrary, he and his extended family were typical of the settlers found in northern New Spain during the late eighteenth and early nineteenth centuries. The history of the de León family reveals much about the *norteño* settlers on the *despoblado*, the unsettled lands of the north. As the de León case shows, these early settlers survived as family units, supporting and defending each other. Their lives were not luxurious, but they did eke out a passable living. They maintained resilience in the face of adversity and retained strength of character that kept their families and their community united and strong.

First, the case of the de León family demonstrates that many Spanish trailblazers settled the northern frontier, and not all of them came from wealthier backgrounds. Bernardo de León was one among thousands who moved north to find better lives. Tejano scholars are beginning to explore the stories of other early settlers, such as the Benavides brothers, the Carbajal family, the thousands of de la Garza kin. Their stories likewise will reveal struggles and successes. Presently, there is no evidence that the de León family was among the wealthy elite of northern New Spain. The de León name does not appear among those granted the giant estates along the Rio Bravo del Norte by the king. Had Martín's family been among the *ricos*, he would have been entitled to a commission as colonel with the militia, a position that he never attained. Nor was the family part of the peasant poor, for Martín was well educated, although he never received a university education. Whether his mule train was his own or whether someone else hired him is unknown. Muleteering was an avocation that required intelligence, skill, courage, and honesty, but not necessarily social position or wealth. The frontier, therefore, provided opportunities for many among the rising middle classes of New Spain.

A second point in the story of Martín de León provides evidence that frontier settlers learned to adapt to new political and economic concepts as three sovereignties changed around them. They began their lives on the Spanish frontier as a product of the expansion and growth triggered by the Bourbon reforms of Charles III and the great land rush started by José de Escandón. When Mexico City merchants imposed taxes, restricting hope among the northern settlers for profit from legal trade, the frontier families countered by developing a successful contraband trade with New Orleans. Little wonder that many of the embittered settlers were among the first revolutionaries and supporters of independence from the Spanish crown.

A third lesson from the de León story shows Mexican frontier settlers to have been people of vision. Once the new federalist Mexican government had been instituted in 1824, de León, influenced by his upbringing during the heady years of the Escandón settlements, saw the possibilities for growth for his family in the lands of Texas. He took advantage of the empresario system and the changing land laws to lay claim to ranches in the river valleys of Texas for his family. He also opened land to other immigrants from Mexico. As with frontier settlements the world over, Tejanos encouraged their relatives and friends in Mexico to come across the Rio Grande to settle in the new colony. Difficulties did not deter the new Mexican immigrants, and they came in trickles and then floods to take advantage of the land and the possibilities for a new and better life. That siphon effect still continues today.

The fourth concept evident from the story of the de León family is a more complex view of the interactions that took place during the 1820s and 1830s between the Mexican and the incoming Anglo-American and European settlers. Not all Tejanos hated all Anglo Americans or vice versa. De León's colony, multinational from the start, encouraged people of all nationalities to interact and to know each other as individuals. What hatreds and conflicts existed occurred at a personal level. Friendships also developed with little regard to race or nationality. The support and companionship between the de León family and the Linns, as well as the antagonisms between Fernando and his enemies, were typical of the kinds of relationships that took place between Tejanos and Anglos.

A fifth deduction from the de León family experience is that no simplistic view will suffice to explain the attitudes of the Tejanos toward Texas independence. The years of the Texas Revolution were a period of indecision and conflict for the de León sons and daughters, much as were the decisions forced on the northern ranchers during the years of Mexican independence. Tejano families, unsure of where their best interests lay, made difficult political choices to keep their families alive. The de León family provides a particularly clear view of the differences of opinion. Some of the men chose to fight with the Texians, others supported the legally constituted government, while others still chose to simply remove themselves from the fray. Whichever side one chose, there were repercussions, as there always are in times of civil war.

The stories of the de León women also provide an instructive new view of Hispanic women on the frontier. The Tejana women were not silent witnesses to history, obedient to their families' wishes. Patricia de la Garza was a partner in marriage and in her husband's business. It was her dowry that made the settlement at Nuestra Señora de Guadalupe Victoria possible, and it was her support that made the colony a success. She and her daughters and daughters-in-law proved their strength and stamina in the face of the same frontier hardships faced by the men. The women, however, also accepted the dangers and traumas of childbirth. By her example, Doña Patricia taught her daughters to make decisions for themselves, to demand respect, to sell land, to persist in lawsuits, and to protect their community, their religion, their culture, and their people. By their example, they also influenced the new Texas laws relating to women that provided the rights of community property, a concept unknown to the newly arrived Anglos. These Tejanas became the nucleus of the community that still exists today, in large part thanks to their tenacity.

A last lesson to be learned from the de León saga is that accommodation to the new Anglo culture was an option for the Texas Mexicans. Just because they became part of the new Anglo world, however, did not mean that Tejanos also accepted land loss. The de León family, along with dozens of other Tejano residents of the new Texas, confronted those who threatened their land inheritance. Many were determined to regain their lands and succeeded in using Anglo courts to fight for their rights. The courts upheld their demands. On their lands and among their Tejano people, accommodation acted as a shield to prevent them from becoming pawns in the Anglo economy. They bought and sold cattle, traded corn and produce, and developed their own protected economy based on godparenthood relationships. When they did sell their land to Anglo buyers during the 1870s, they moved to town and bought or built up businesses that served the Tejano community. Some made successful lives for themselves and their families, while others struggled and failed, even with family support. Through kinship ties, all of the Tejano families continued to acknowledge the old traditions and customs and to celebrate the richness and strength of the Spanish and Mexican civilizations.

Mexican Texans, then, have historically been tough, resilient, and hardworking. The communal unity, the family love, and the fighting spirit of the de León family are typical of the Tejanos in the communities of old established Mexican families. These characteristics are equally typical of those who arrived during the revolutions in Mexico from 1910 to 1930 and among the new immigrant families whose drive and ambition has brought them across the border in the recent past. The Tejano cultural traits of family, religion, community, and *compadrazgo* still found today among many of the de León descendants and the Tejano communities today are rich reminders of a proud past. To know the history of the de León family is to appreciate the strength, the courage, and the convictions the Spanish Mexican settlers of Texas.

Notes

1. Although no detailed records exist of Martín de León and his family during this period, the family did live in Cruillas, northern New Spain, at a time when the Spanish Empire was calling for soldiers. In a quote at the beginning of a history of Alonso de León, a father asks his best friend, as the friend sets out to explore the far north, to take his fourteen-year-old son "that he should know adventure." Throughout the rest of his life, young de León always opted for adventure. At fourteen, his age at the time our story begins, he might have wanted to join the exciting world of Bernardo de Gálvez, but somebody, perhaps his father, prevented him from going. David J. Weber, *The Spanish Frontier in North America* (New Haven: Yale University Press, 1992), 267–268; E. A. Montemayor, Eric Beerman, and Winston De Ville, *Yo Solo: The Battle Journal of Bernardo de Gálvez during the American Revolution* (New Orleans: Polyanthos, 1978).

2. Weber, *Spanish Frontier*, 267–268.

3. Ibid.

4. Michael C. Meyer and William L. Sherman, *The Course of Mexican History* (New York: Oxford University Press, 1983), 241–243.

5. Benedict Leutenegger, *The Zacatecan Missionaries in Texas, 1716–1834: Excerpts from the Libros de los Decretos of the Missionary College of Zacatecas, 1707–1828* (Austin: Texas Historical Survey Committee, 1973), 7–9.

6. Juan Rodríquez-Castellano and Caridad Rodríquez-Castellano, *Historia de España: breve resumen* (New York: Oxford University Press, 1939), 88–91; Patricia Osante, *Orígenes del Nuevo Santander (1748–1772)* (Mexico City: Universidad Nacional Autónoma de México Instituto de Investigaciones Históricas; Ciudad Victoria: Universidad Nacional Autónoma de Tamaulipas, 1997), 100–102; Armando Alonso, *Tejano Legacy: Rancheros and Settlers in South Texas, 1734–1900* (Albuquerque: University of New Mexico Press, 1998), 27–29.

7. The people who came with Escandón were not those whom Timothy E. Anna calls the *léperos*, the beggar poor. Bishop-elect Manuel Abad y Queipo of Michoacan had divided Mexican society into the rich and the poor, but Escandón's settlers did not fit this arbitrary division. On this northern frontier, these settlers were the *petite bourgeoisie*, defined by Mexican scholar Luis Villoro as middle-class, and they were

looking for a chance to better themselves; Luis Villoro, *El proceso ideológico de la revolución de independencia* (Mexico City: Universidad Autónoma de México, 1967), 17–20; see also Timothy E. Anna, *The Fall of the Royal Government in Mexico City* (Lincoln: University of Nebraska Press, 1978), 11, 18–19. Among those from Nuevo Santander who went on to become leaders in the revolutionary movement of 1810 were two of the key players in the Texas revolts, Juan Bautista de las Casas, a retired militia captain from Nuevo Santander, and José Bernardo Gutiérrez de Lara, a settler from Revilla in Nuevo Santander; Donald E. Chipman, *Spanish Texas, 1519–1821* (Austin: University of Texas Press, 1992), 232–233, 234–236.

8. Osante, *Orígenes*, 220; Manuel Barrera, *Then the Gringos Came: The Story of Martín de León and the Texas Revolution* (Laredo, Tex.: Barrera Publications, 1992), 11.

9. Osante, *Orígenes*, 222–224; Anna, *Fall of the Royal Government*, 11, 18–19.

10. Osante, *Orígenes*, 222–224; Villoro, *El proceso ideológico*, 17–20.

11. Osante lists those who received both haciendas and *ranchos*, and although there is a Cristóbal de León listed who received a rancho at two leagues from Santander, there is no mention of Bernardo de León. For the de la Garzas, two names are listed, José and Xavier, who received haciendas near the Hacienda de Dolores, but there is no mention of any de la Garzas receiving land in or near Soto la Marina; see index in Osante, *Orígenes*, for names of hacienda owners.

12. Osante, *Orígenes*, 183.

13. Anna, *Fall of the Royal Government*, 19; Charles A. Hale, *Mexican Liberalism in the Age of Mora, 1821–1853* (New Haven and London: Yale University Press, 1968), 38–39, 46–56.

14. Osante, *Orígenes*, 183–184; A. B. J. Hammett, *The Empresario: Don Martin de León* (Kerrville, TX: Braswell Printing, 1971) 10; Barrera, *Then the Gringos Came*, 11–12.

15. Osante, *Orígenes*, 220.

16. José Miguel Ramos Arizpe, quoted in Alonso, *Tejano Legacy,* 46; Chipman, *Spanish Texas*, 168; Osante, *Orígenes*, 219; Hammett, *Empresario*, 10–24; Barrera, *Then the Gringos Came*, 2–6. Both Hammett and Barrera claim Spanish ancestry and great wealth for Bernardo de León, but there are no records of his having received any grants of a large hacienda. The lack of land would have placed Bernardo among the landless poor, which makes his son's later success all the more interesting since it indicates that Bernardo's ambition and desire to get ahead enabled him, and later his son, to overcome considerable obstacles.

17. Kathryn Stoner O'Connor, *The Presidio La Bahía del Espíritu Santo de Zuñiga, 1721 to 1846* (Austin: Von Boeckmann-Jones, 1966), 9–17.

18. Captain Domingo Ramón, under the orders of the Marquis of San Miguel de Aguayo, had founded the presidio of Nuestra Señora de Loreto de la Bahía del Espíritu Santo on April 4, 1721, at or near the site of La Salle's French settlement on Matagorda Bay. A year later the mission of Nuestra Señora del Espíritu Santo de Zuñiga was founded three-quarters of a league from the fort on Garcitas Creek. Due to problems between Captain Ramón and the Indians, the Garcitas site was aban-

doned, and the presidio and mission were moved in April 1726. According to recent archeological investigations, the next site was in present-day Victoria, Texas. Several months later the complex was again moved up the Guadalupe to what is now called Mission Valley. For the next twenty-six years, while the mission and presidio were at Mission Valley, the Indian neophytes grew corn and vegetable crops and began to develop the huge herds for which the mission became justly famous; Manuel Ramírez de la Piscina, Mission Records, Box 122, Folder 13, Spanish Archives, Archives and Records Division, Texas General Land Office, Austin, Texas (hereinafter GLO); Julia Coopwood, "History of the La Bahía Settlements during the Administration of Captain Manuel Ramírez de la Piscina, 1750–1767," (master's thesis, University of Texas, 1938), 30–34, 78–79; Herbert Eugene Bolton, *Texas in the Middle Eighteenth Century* (Berkeley: University of California Press, 1915; reprint Austin: University of Texas Press, 1970), 255–256; O'Connor, *Presidio La Bahía*, 20–21; Edward Werner Heusinger, *Early Explorations and Mission Establishments in Texas* (San Antonio, Tex.: Naylor, 1936), 150.

19. Coopwood, "History of the La Bahía Settlements," 78–92.

20. The inspection by Lieutenant Colonel Don Angel Martos y Navarrete provided much of the information available on Captain de la Piscina; Coopwood, "History of the La Bahía Settlements," 69–82; Bolton, *Texas in the Middle Eighteenth Century,* 240–259; Fray Juan Agustín Morfi, *History of Texas, 1673–1779,* trans. Carlos E. Castañeda (Albuquerque: Quivira Society, 1935), 99–102; Max L. Moorehead, *The Presidio: Bastion of the Spanish Borderlands* (Norman: University of Oklahoma Press, 1975), 65–66, 91–92, 239–242; Sandra L. Myres, *The Ranch in Spanish Texas, 1691–1800* (El Paso: Texas Western Press, 1969), 12.

21. Osante, *Orígenes,* 161–163, 185–187.

22. Escandón received the remaining 25,095 pesos from the original grant of 115,700 pesos which the viceroy had promised. He also begged an additional 12,000 pesos to purchase 3,500 *fanegas* (1 *fanega* = 1.5 bushel) of corn which he needed to distribute among the residents of his villas. In addition, Escandón asked for 10,000 pesos to purchase tobacco, notions, dry goods, and machetes to keep the Indians peaceful; Osante, *Orígenes,* 209–211. According to Osante, Escandón also put pressure on his *hacendados* to supply funds to keep the colony viable; Osante, *Orígenes,* 185–189, 207–208.

23. Osante, *Orígenes,* 184–186, 188–189. Osante argues that Escandón had no real altruism and had from the beginning counted on using the king's funds to keep his colony alive.

24. Osante, *Orígenes,* 171–176, 191–192.

25. Osante, *Orígenes,* 252.

26. Ibid., 123–124, 184–186, 215–216, 218.

27. Ibid., 253. Mexican scholar Dr. Israel Cabazos Garza suggested at a conference in Mexico that the northerners, irritated over the high taxes, "nacieron encabronados" (were born angry).

28. Weber, *Spanish Frontier*, 237–238; François Chevalier, *Land and Society in Colonial Mexico: The Great Hacienda*, trans. Alvin Eustis, ed. Lesley Bird Simpson (Berkeley: University of California Press, 1963), 220–221; William B. Taylor, "Landed Society in New Spain: A View from the South," *Hispanic American Historical Review* 54, no. 3 (August 1974): 399, 409; Osante, *Orígenes*, 123–124, 184–186, 215–216, 218; Jesús F. de la Teja, "St. James at the Fair," *The Americas* 57, no. 3 (January 2001): 408–409.

29. Rodríquez-Castillano, *Historia de España*, 91–92; David A. Brading, *Miners and Merchants in Bourbon Mexico, 1763–1810* (Cambridge: Cambridge University Press, 1971), 24–26.

30. Chevalier, in *Land and Society*, suggests that the name *reales de minas* "probably came from the name of the flag, or *pendón real* flown above these camps," 39.

31. Chevalier, *Land and Society*, 39–42; Osante, *Orígenes*, 190, 213; Clara Elena Suárez Argüello, *Camino real y carrera larga: La arriería en la Nueva España durante el siglo XVIII* (Mexico City: Centro de Investigaciones y Estudios Superiores en Antropología Social, 1996), 44–48; Brading, *Miners and Merchants*, 263–291.

32. Lawrence F. Hill, *José de Escandón and the Founding of the Nuevo Santander* (Columbus: Ohio State University Press, 1926), 142–145; Roberto Villaseñor E., *El Coronel Don José Escandón y la conquista del Nuevo Santander* (Mexico City: Boletín del Archivo General de la Nación, 1979), 37–39.

33. A *sitio* is given as approximately 4,428 acres, and a *caballería* in Mexico is defined as approximately 106 acres; GLO.

34. Brian Robertson, *Wild Horse Desert: The Heritage of South Texas* (Edinburgh, Tex.: Hidalgo County Historical Museum, 1967), 23; Osante, *Orígenes*, 255–256.

35. Osante, *Orígenes*, 126, 190, 213; Meyer and Sherman, *Course of Mexican History*, 254; Hammett, *Empresario*, 8–10; Barrera, *Then the Gringos Came*, 8–9. Both Hammett and Barrera claim for Martín de León an excellent education at a university in Monterrey. Several factors suggest that such was not the case. Although there were Jesuit seminaries in Monterrey prior to 1767, by the time Martín was old enough to attend a seminary in Monterrey in 1770, the Jesuits had been removed and any seminaries in Monterrey would have closed down. In 1824, when Martín de León applied for his empresarial contract from the Provincial Delegation at San Antonio, he stated that he was a native of the town of Cruillas. Max Berger, "Education in Texas during the Spanish and Mexican Periods," *Southwestern Historical Quarterly* 51 (July 1947), 45; Frederick Eby, *The Development of Education in Texas* (New York: Macmillan, 1925), 60–61; Brading, *Miners and Merchants*, 346.

36. Hammett, *Empresario*, 8; Barrera, *Then the Gringos Came*, 3–4.

37. Suárez Argüello, 23–24.

38. Suárez Argüello, *Camino real*, 44.

39. Suárez Argüello argues that the muleteers were instrumental in carrying the ideas and news of the independence movement throughout the central parts of Mexico some forty years later, in 1810; Suárez Argüello, *Camino real*, 24, 44.

40. David Ringrose, "Transportation and Economic Stagnation in Eighteenth-

Century Castile," *Journal of Economic History* 28 (March 1968), 58-60; Suárez Argüello, *Camino real*, 47; Osante, *Orígenes*, 179.

41. Suárez Argüello, *Camino real*, 44-47; Osante, *Orígenes*, 189.

42. Suárez Argüello, *Camino real*, 44.

43. Ibid., 44-45.

44. Ibid., 43-45.

45. Suárez Argüello, *Camino real*, 202-203, translation by the author.

46. Hammett, *Empresario*, 8-9; Barrera, *Then the Gringos Came*, 10-11.

47. "Strength Report and Daily Record of the Occurrences at San Antonio de Béxar for February, 1780, February 28, 1780," quoted in Robert H. Thonhoff, *El Fuerte del Cíbolo: Sentinel of the Béxar-La Bahía Ranches* (Austin: Eakin Press, 1992), 57.

48. Odie B. Faulk, "The Presidio: Fortress or Farce?" in *New Spain's Far Northern Frontier: Essays on Spain in the American West, 1540-1821*, ed. David J. Weber (Dallas: Southern Methodist University Press, 1979), 73.

49. Ibid., 409.

50. Ibid.

51. "Historia de Nuevo León con noticias sobre Coahuila, Tejas y Nuevo México por el Capitán Alonso de León," anonymous, in *Documentos inéditos o muy raros para la historia de México*, ed. Genaro García (Mexico City: Editorial Porrúa, 1975), 107; Osante, *Orígenes*, 24-36; Elizabeth A. H. John, *Storms Brewed in Other Men's Worlds: The Confrontation of Indians, Spain, and France in the Southwest 1540-1795* (College Station: Texas A&M University Press, 1975), 660.

52. Osante, *Orígenes*, 34-36; David A. Brading, "Government and Elite in Late Colonial Mexico," *Hispanic American Historical Review* 53 (August 1973): 409-414.

53. Coopwood, "History of the La Bahía Settlements," 59-61; "Historia de Nuevo León," 110; Alonzo, *Tejano Legacy*, 50.

54. "Historia de Nuevo León," 110; see Osante, *Orígenes*, 28-35.

55. John, *Storms Brewed*, 634-635.

56. Ibid., 750-757; Osante, *Orígenes*, 234, 261; Coopwood, "History of the La Bahía Settlements," 60-65.

57. John, *Storms Brewed*, 750-757; Osante, *Orígenes*, 234, 261.

58. Although de León's biographers argue that de León was of the "grandee" or elite class, there is no evidence which indicates that de León was a wealthy Spanish officer. Had his family had either wealth or connections, he would have been appointed a colonel or lieutenant colonel. That he was only a captain indicates his lower status as a *criollo*.

59. Asunción Lavrin and Edith Couturier, "Dowries and Wills: A View of Women's Socioeconomic Role in Colonial Guadalajara and Puebla, 1640-1790," *Hispanic American Historical Review* 59, no. 2 (May 1979): 293.

60. Inventory of Goods of Patricia de la Garza signed at Presas del Rey, January 1, 1801, vol. 1, p. 34, Index to Deed Records, Victoria County Clerk's Office, Victoria County Courthouse, Victoria, Texas (hereinafter VCCO).

61. Hammett, *Empresario*, 8–9, 20–25; Barrera, *Then the Gringos Came*, 10–11; Victor M. Rose, *Some Historical Facts in Regard to the Settlement of Victoria, Texas: Its Progress and Present Status* (Laredo, Tex.: Daily Times Print, 1883), 104–105; William H. Oberste, *Texas Irish Empresarios and Their Colonies*, 2d ed. (Austin: Von Boeckmann-Jones, 1973), 68; Inventory of Goods of Patricia de la Garza, Patricia de la Garza to P. B. Cocke, deed, January 24, 1837, Index to Deed Records, VCCO; Lavrin and Couturier, "Dowries and Wills," 288–295.

62. "Libro formado por el Capitán de Milicias y primer Alcalde Constitucional de La Bahía del Espíritu Santo," Archivo General de la Nación, Mexico City (hereinafter AGN); Census of Santa Margarita Ranch, Sergeant José de Jesús Aldrete, November 10, 1811, Bexar Archives (BA) at the Center for American History, Austin (CAH); Martín de León to Salcedo, Petition to Ferdinand VII, 1800, Martín de León Papers (hereinafter MLP), O'Connor Room, Victoria County Public Library, Victoria, Texas (hereinafter O'CVL); Alonso de León, "Relación del descubrimiento, población y pacificación de este Nuevo Reino de León: temperamento y calidad de la tierra," in *Documentos inéditos*, ed. Genaro García, 15; Israel Cavazos Garza, *El General Alonso de León, descubridor de Texas* (Monterrey, Mexico: Real Ayuntamiento de Monterrey, 1993), 14–15; Osante, *Orígenes*; Villaseñor E., *El Coronel*, 232.

CHAPTER 2

1. Inventory of Goods of Patricia de la Garza, Index to Deed Records, VCCO.

2. Nava to Muñoz, very secret, July 30, 1795, Chihuahua, quoted in Odie B. Faulk, *The Last Years of Spanish Texas, 1778–1821* (The Hague: Mouton, 1964), 115.

3. Faulk, *Last Years*, 118–119; Paul Horgan, *Great River: The Rio Grande in North American History* (New York: Rinehart, 1954; reprint, Austin: Texas Monthly Press, 1984), 397–400; Gerald Ashford, *Spanish Texas: Yesterday and Today* (Austin: Jenkins Publishing, 177–188.

4. Census of 1811, CAH-BA.

5. Hammett, *Empresario*, 8–10; Barrera, *Then the Gringos Came*, 4, 16–17.

6. Martín de León to Salcedo, Petition to Ferdinand VII, 1800, O'CVL-MLP.

7. Francisco Solano, *Cedulario de tierras: compilación de legislación agraria colonial (1497–1820)* (Mexico City: Universidad Nacional Autónoma de México, 1984), 537–539; Brading, "Government and Elite," 392; Hammett, *Empresario*, 11–12; Barrera, *Then the Gringos Came*, 20–22.

8. Chevalier, *Land and Society*, 176.

9. Solano, *Cedulario de tierras*, 537–539.

10. Willard B. Robinson, "Colonial Ranch Architecture in the Spanish-Mexican Tradition," *Southwestern Historical Quarterly* 83 (October 1979), 126.

11. Martín de León to Salcedo, Petition to Ferdinand VII, 1800, O'CVL-MLP; Nettie Lee Benson, "Bishop Marín de Porras and Texas," *Southwestern Historical Quarterly* 51 (July 1947): 26–29.

12. Jesús F. de la Teja, *San Antonio de Béxar: A Community on New Spain's Northern

Frontier (Albuquerque: University of New Mexico Press, 1995), 117. The archives at GLO do not show a recorded title for the Rancho de Santa Margarita, although de León's request for the land is on file. That the de León family did take up residence on the ranch is indicated by the census records for 1811, which list family names and those of their ranch hands and a teacher.

13. Robinson, "Colonial Ranch Architecture," 129–130; Willard B. Robinson, *Gone from Texas: Our Lost Architectural Heritage* (College Station: Texas A&M University Press, 1981), 7–12; Mary Crownover Rabb, untitled article, in *Texas Tears and Texas Sunshine*, ed. Jo Ella Powell Exley (College Station: Texas A&M University Press, 1985), 5–18.

14. Robinson, "Colonial Ranch Architecture," 130; Eugene George, *Historic Architecture of Texas: The Falcón Reservoir* (Austin: Texas Historical Commission and Texas Historical Foundation, 1975), 28, 48.

15. Adobe bricks were mud and straw blocks four inches thick by twelve inches wide by eighteen inches long. They are still regularly used for house construction in the countryside throughout Mexico. Environmental architects in New Mexico have adopted adobe as a building material and have found that these *trombé* walls absorb the heat during the day, keeping the interiors cool and comfortable, and then slowly release the warmth into the room during the cool nights.

16. Robinson, "Colonial Ranch Architecture," 130–139; George, *Historic Architecture*, 48–49. Any archeological evidence there might be to indicate whether Martín de León ever constructed a *casa grande* like the Casa Blanca south of the Nueces River has been destroyed by the construction of the town of San Patricio in the early 1830s. The kind of houses which were built are typical of all of the ranch houses in the area, and the style is still found to the present day in such places as Coyoacan, a suburb of Mexico City, where an adobe ranch home existed within the past thirty years almost identical to those described for Texas. The single difference was the addition of windows to the homes of the twentieth century.

17. Robinson, "Colonial Ranch Architecture," 130–139; George, *Historic Architecture*, 48–49.

18. Ibid.

19. Robinson, "Colonial Ranch Architecture," 126; Horgan, *Great River*, 356–358. Horgan suggests that the severity of the furniture may have stemmed from the Spanish attitude that "in penance resided virtue." Even the king himself did not indulge in extravagant physical comforts since "wealth brought its discomforts to be suffered in patience" (355).

20. Patricia Osante in *Orígenes de Nuevo Santander* (219) suggests a "virtual absence" of artisans by 1750, when out of sixty-five men dedicated to artisan trades, there were three bricklayers, seven blacksmiths, and nine carpenters. George, *Historic Architecture*, 48; Horgan, *Great River*, 355; Robinson, "Colonial Ranch Architecture," 131–132.

21. Robinson, "Colonial Ranch Architecture," 131–132; Osante, *Orígenes*, 219.

22. Henry F. Brown, *Baptism through the Centuries*, (Mountain View, Calif.: Pacific

Press Publishing Association, 1965), 16-24; Emil Brunner, *The Christian Doctrine of God*, trans. Olive Wyon (Philadelphia: Westminster Press, 1979), 57-59.

23. Lavrin and Couturier, "Dowries and Wills," 285-287; Horgan, *Great River*, 353-354; Brown, *Baptism*, 16-24, 29-30; Bruner, *Christian Doctrine*, 57-59.

24. Ashford, *Spanish Texas*, 191.

25. Petition, Martín de León to the King, No. 42, copy in O'CVL-MLP; Moorehead, *Presidio*, 72-73, 92-93, 172, 224; Kathryn Garrett, *Green Flag over Texas: A Story of the Last Years of Spain in Texas* (Austin: Jenkins Publishing; New York: Pemberton Press, 1969), 11.

26. Ashford, *Spanish Texas*, 191.

27. Ibid.

28. Request by Pobladores at Trinidad de Salcedo, Box 129, Folder 46, GLO; Ashford, *Spanish Texas*, 191-192.

29. Jack Jackson, *Los Mesteños: Spanish Ranching in Texas, 1721-1821* (College Station: Texas A&M University Press, 1986), 489; Mattie Austin Hatcher, "The Opening of Texas to Foreign Settlement, 1801-1821, Austin, Texas," *University of Texas Bulletin* no. 2714 (April 8, 1927): 92; Bando of October 18, 1805, published by Don Ignacio Pérez at San Antonio de Béxar, GLO; list of habitations at Trinidad de Salcedo by Pedro Lopez Prieto, March 25, 1810, GLO; land sales for Trinidad de Salcedo, GLO.

30. Faulk, *Last Years*, 120-123; Oakah L. Jones Jr., *Los Paisanos: Spanish Settlers on the Northern Frontier of New Spain* (Norman: University of Oklahoma Press, 1979), 55; Garrett, *Green Flag*, 11-14; Ashford, *Spanish Texas*, 191-193.

31. Carlos Castañeda, *Our Catholic Heritage in Texas*, vol. 5, *The Mission Era: The End of the Spanish Regime 1780-1810* (Austin: Von Boeckmann-Jones, 1942), 211-215.

32. El Obispo del Nuevo Reyno de León, Monterrey, August 21, 1809, to the Viceroy, Archbishop Lizana, original manuscript in the W. B. Stephens Collection, CAH, quoted in Benson, "Bishop Marín," 32.

33. Ashford, *Spanish Texas*, 194.

34. Faulk, *Last Years*, 125-126; Ashford, *Spanish Texas*, 193-194; Garrett, *Green Flag*, 14.

35. Faulk, *Last Years*, 97-98; Abraham P. Nasatir, *Borderland in Retreat: From Spanish Louisiana to the Far Southwest* (Albuquerque: University of New Mexico Press, 1976), 121-122, 124; Jackson, *Los Mesteños*, 469-470, 516.

36. Jackson, *Los Mesteños*, 471, 504.

37. Regarding horses see William E. Doolittle, "Las Marismas to Pánuco to Texas: The Transfer of Open Range Cattle Ranching from Iberia through Northeastern Mexico," *Yearbook, Conference of Latin Americanist Geographers* 13 (1987), 4-7; Richard W. Slatta, *Cowboys of the Americas* (New Haven: Yale University Press, 1990), 93-96, 107, 225; John E. Rouse, *The Criollo: Spanish Cattle in the Americas* (Norman: University of Oklahoma Press, 1977), 191-192; Myres, *Ranch in Spanish Texas*, 11-20; C. J. Bishko, "The Peninsular Background of Latin American Cattle Ranching," *Hispanic American Historical Review* 32 (November 1952), 491-515; Ray August, "Cowboys

v. Rancheros: The Origins of Western American Livestock Law," *Southwestern Historical Quarterly* 96 (April 1993), 457–459; Report of the Mustang Fund, La Bahía del Espíritu Santo, December 1807, CAH-BA; S-49-1, St. Landry Parish, La., Clerk of Court Conveyances, 1805–1971, Index, Louisiana Division, New Orleans Public Library, New Orleans, La. (hereinafter NO).

38. Zebulon M. Pike, quoted in Ashford, *Spanish Texas*, 180; Jesús F. de la Teja, "Discovering the Tejano Community in 'Early' Texas," *Journal of the Early Republic* 18, no. 1 (spring 1998), 82; Kathleen Mullen Sands, *Charrería Mexicana: An Equestrian Folk Tradition* (Tucson: The University of Arizona Press, 1993), 27–28, 88, 98–99, 105, 176; Don Worcester, *The Spanish Mustang: From the Plains of Andalusia to the Prairies of Texas* (El Paso: University of Texas Press, 1986), 12–13; Francis Haines, *Horses in America* (New York: Thomas Y. Crowell, 1971), 41; Thomas A. Dwyer, "From Mustangs to Mules," in *Mustangs and Cow Horses*, eds. J. Frank Dobie, Mody Boatright, and Harry Ransom (Dallas: Southern Methodist University; Austin: Publications of the Texas Folk Lore Society, 1940), 48–49.

39. Noah Smithwick, *The Evolution of a State, or, Recollections of Old Texas Days*, comp. Nanna Smithwick Donaldson (Austin: University of Texas Press, 1983), 11.

40. De la Teja, *San Antonio de Béxar*, 112–113; Sands, *Charrería Mexicana*, 93.

41. Slatta, *Cowboys*, 43.

42. José Cisneros, *Riders across the Centuries: Horsemen of the Spanish Borderlands* (El Paso: Texas Western Press, 1984), 59, quoted in Sands, *Charrería Mexicana*, 37.

43. Robinson, "Colonial Ranch Architecture," 126; Sands, *Charrería Mexicana*, 37.

44. The destruction of the cattle herds by San Antonio ranchers is covered by Jesús F. de la Teja in *San Antonio de Béxar*, 105–114, and in his "Sobrevivencia económica en la frontera de Texas; los ranchos ganaderos del siglo XVIII en San Antonio de Béxar," *Historia Mexicana* 42, no. 4 (April–June 1993), 837–865.

45. Martín de León to the Chief of the Department at Béxar, August 4, 1807, BCC-SP. *Relación que manifiesta los CCs de esta Villa*, Goliad, July 27, 1832, GLO; Hobart Huson, *Refugio, A Comprehensive history of Refugio County: From Aboriginal Times to 1953*, vol. 1 (Woodsboro, Tex.: Rooke Foundation, 1953–1955), n. 82; Roy Grimes, *300 Years in Victoria County* (Austin: Nortex Press, 1985), 385; Testimony given in *Rosalía Cisneros v. Edwards*, 1846 Court Case, Victoria County Court records, Victoria College/University of Houston Library Archives (hereinafter VC/UH).

46. De la Teja, "Sobrevivencia económica," 840–841; de la Teja, "Discovering the Tejano Community," 80–89.

47. Interview with Arturo Castillo, December 1999, Key West, Florida.

48. Horgan, *Great River*, 362–363.

49. Ibid., 363–364.

50. Sands, *Charrería Mexicana*, 32, 46–47; Slatta, *Cowboys*, 39; Jane Clements Monday and Betty Bailey Colley, *Voices from the Wild Horse Desert: The Vaquero Families of the King and Kenedy Ranches* (Austin: University of Texas Press, 1997), xxiv.

51. Sands, *Charrería Mexicana*, 46–47; Slatta, *Cowboys*, 39–40; Horgan, *Great River*,

361–371; Madeline Gallego Thorpe and Mary Tate Engels, *Corazón Contento* (Lubbock: Texas Tech University Press, 1999), 35–36.

52. James S. Griffith and Celestino Fernández, "Mexican Horse Races and Cultural Values: The Case of Los Corridos del Merino," *Western Folklore*, 47, no. 2 (April 1988), 134; Nora E. Ramírez, "The Vaquero and Ranching in the Southwestern United States, 1600–1970" (Ph.D. diss., University of Indiana, 1978), 211; Sands, *Charrería Mexicana*, 46, 274.

53. De la Teja, *San Antonio de Béxar*, 147–148; Horgan, *Great River*, 366–370.

54. Anna, *Fall of the Royal Government*, 35–63.

55. Ibid.

56. Ibid., 70–73; Faulk, *Last Years*, 132; Garrett, *Green Flag*, 36–37; Ashford, *Spanish Texas*, 200–201.

57. Félix Almaráz, *Tragic Cavalier: Manuel Salcedo of Texas, 1808–1813* (Austin: University of Texas Press, 1971), 9–10, 110–112; de la Teja, *San Antonio de Béxar*, 147–150; Thorpe and Engels, *Corazón Contento*, 107–128; Ashford, *Spanish Texas*, 196–198.

58. Anna, *Fall of the Royal Government*, 67–69.

59. Jesús F. de la Teja, "Rebellion on the Frontier," in *Tejano Journey, 1770–1850*, ed. Gerald E. Poyo (Austin: University of Texas Press, 1996), 17–19; Anna, *Fall of the Royal Government*, 3, 7, 19.

60. Almaráz, *Tragic Cavalier*, 118; de la Teja, "Rebellion on the Frontier," 18–19; Garrett, *Green Flag*, 38–40.

61. Both of Martín de León's biographers claim that de León was a republican, although they provide no evidence to support the claim, and his allegiance to either side can be argued. Hammett, *Empresario*, 12; Barrera, *Then the Gringos Came*, 30–32; Almaráz, *Tragic Cavalier*, 118–119, 156–158; Garrett, *Green Flag*, 40–43; Ashford, *Spanish Texas*, 202–203.

62. Garrett, *Green Flag*, 54–57; Ashford, *Spanish Texas*, 203–206; de la Teja, "Rebellion on the Frontier," 19–21.

63. Garrett, *Green Flag*, 143–145; Almaráz, *Tragic Cavalier*, 144–146, 157–158.

64. Almaráz, *Tragic Cavalier*, 160–164; Faulk, *Last Years*, 134; Garrett, *Green Flag*, 141–143; de la Teja, "Rebellion on the Frontier," 20–21.

65. Garrett, *Green Flag*, 151.

66. Ibid., 163–165, 168; Almaráz, *Tragic Cavalier*, 163–164.

67. Garrett, *Green Flag*, 173–176.

68. Hammett, *Empresario*, 13; Barrera, *Then the Gringos Came*, 31.

CHAPTER 3

1. Almaráz, *Tragic Cavalier*, 174–176; Garrett, *Green Flag*, 208–210; de la Teja, "Rebellion on the Frontier," 21–22; Rie Jarratt, "Gutiérrez de Lara, Mexican Texan: The Story of a Creole Hero," in *The Mexican Experience in Texas* ed. Carlos E. Cortés (New York: Arno Press, 1976), 42–44; Chipman, *Spanish Texas*, 234–236.

2. Almaráz, *Tragic Cavalier*, 168-172; Garrett, *Green Flag*, 175-179; Jarratt, "Gutiér-rez de Lara," 5-16, 20-29; Kathryn Garrett, "The First Constitution of Texas, April 17, 1813," *Southwestern Historical Quarterly* 40 (April 1937), 301.

3. Jarratt, "Gutiérrez de Lara," 20-29.

4. Almaráz, *Tragic Cavalier*, 175-176; Garrett, *Green Flag*, 223-229; de la Teja, "Rebellion on the Frontier," 24-25.

5. Grimes, *300 Years*, 60; Nettie Lee Benson, "The Provincial Deputation," in *Mexico: Harbinger of Provincial Autonomy, Independence, and Federalism* (Austin: University of Texas Press, 1992), xi, 19; Jesus F. de la Teja, "Land and Society in 18th-Century San Antonio de Bexar, A Community on New Spain's Northern Frontier" (Ph.D. diss., University of Texas, 1988), 69-70; Wilbert H. Timmons, *Tadeo Ortiz: Mexican Colonizer and Reformer*, Southwestern Studies, Monograph 43 (El Paso: Texas Western Press, 1974), 5, 13; Benson, "Provincial Deputation," 23, 24-25; Janicek, "The Development of Early Mexican Land Policy: Coahuila and Texas, 1810-1825" (Ph.D. diss., Tulane University, 1985), 58, 63.

6. Gloria Candelaria Genealogical Records (hereinafter Candelaria), María Candelaria de Aldrete de León, Austin, Texas.

7. A. H. Verrill, *The Real Story of the Pirate* (New York: D. Appleton and Co., 1923), 346-355; Cyrus H. Karraker, *Piracy Was A Business* (Rindge, N.H.: Richard R. Smith, Publisher, 1953), 226-227; Robert Carse, *The Age of Piracy* (N.Y.: Rinehart and Co., 1957), 244-247.

8. Verrill, *Real Story*, 350.

9. Karraker, *Piracy Was A Business*, 227; Carse, *Age of Piracy*, 245; Verrill, *Real Story*, 350-352.

10. The piracy in Galveston, the Gulf of Mexico, and the Caribbean was not halted until 1823 when American Commodore Porter, stationed at Key West, joined the British in exterminating the last few pirate colonies. Although some suggest Jean Lafitte was killed in 1823 with sixty of his men in a battle against a British sloop of war, later sources maintain that the Lafittes had moved to Isla Mujeres off the Yucatan peninsula in 1823 and that Lafitte died of natural causes in Yucatan in 1825. Hammett, *Empresario*, 13; Barrera, *Then the Gringos Came*, 42-43; Verrill, *Real Story*, 355, 369; Carse, *Age of Piracy*, 246-247; Harris Gaylord Warren, *The Sword Was Their Passport: A History of American Filibustering in the Mexican Revolution* (Baton Rouge: Louisiana State University Press, 1943).

11. Candelaria, María Candelaria de Aldrete de León; de la Teja, *San Antonio de Béxar*, 149-150.

12. Jones, *Los Paisanos*, 21; Nettie Lee Benson, "Texas as Viewed from Mexico," *Southwestern Historical Quarterly* 90 (January 1987): 219; Chipman, *Spanish Texas*, 236-239.

13. Josefina Zoraida Vázquez, "Los Primeros Tropiezos," in *Historia General de México*, vol. 3 (Mexico City: El Colegio de México, 1976), 5; William Edward Syers,

Texas, The Beginning, 1519-1839 (Waco, Tex.: Texian Press, 1978), 136, 137; Jones, *Los Paisanos*, 21; Benson, "Texas as Viewed from Mexico," 219; Chipman, *Spanish Texas*, 236–239.

14. Dora Elizondo Guerra, "Whose Water Is This Anyway, and Keep Your Plow Out of My Cornfield: Men, Women, and Culture in Spanish Colonial Texas," *South Texas Studies* (2000), Victoria Community College, 173–174.

15. Mrs. T. C. Allan, comp., and Mrs. Thomas O'Connor, contributor, "Reminiscences of Mrs. Annie Fagan Teal," *Southwestern Historical Quarterly* (April 1931), 321.

16. Ibid.

17. Benson, "Texas as Viewed from Mexico," 219; Chipman, *Spanish Texas*, 238–239. Patricia de la Garza, having given birth to seven of her ten children in Texas, would have laughed had she known that Jane Long would be named "The Mother of Texas" by later Anglo arrivals.

18. Benson, "Provincial Deputation," xi, 19, 23, 24–25; Jaime E. Rodríguez O., *The Emergence of Spanish America: Vicente Rocafuerte and Spanish Americanism, 1808-1832* (Berkeley: University of California Press, 1975), 1–2, 40–48.

19. Benson, "Texas as Viewed from Mexico," 220.

20. Ibid.

21. Ibid.

22. Rodríguez O., *Emergence of Spanish America*, 51–53; Benson, "Texas as Viewed from Mexico," 220–221; Ashford, *Spanish Texas*, 230–231.

23. Rodríguez, *Emergence of Spanish America*, 44–46; Chipman, *Spanish Texas*, 240–241; Timmons, *Tadeo Ortiz*, 5, 13; Janicek, "Development," 58, 63.

24. Some authors, including Jane Long, his wife, suggest that Long was killed at the instigation of Texas Governor José Félix Trespalacios. Jones, *Los Paisanos*, 21; Benson, "Texas as Viewed from Mexico," 219; Chipman, *Spanish Texas*, 238–239.

25. Benson, "Texas as Viewed from Mexico," 220.

26. Quoted from *Archivo histórico diplomático mexicano*, in Timmons, *Tadeo Ortiz*, 15.

27. Timmons, *Tadeo Ortiz*, 15; Eugene C. Barker, *The Life of Stephen F. Austin, Founder of Texas, 1793-1836: A Chapter in the Westward Movement of the Anglo-American People* (Austin: University of Texas Press, 1985), 25–27.

28. Oberste, *Texas Irish Empresarios*, 32.

29. Estella Martínez Zermeño, "Mi Familia," in *Papers of the 250th Anniversary of the Founding of La Bahía, South Texas Studies* (Spring 2000), Victoria, Texas.

30. Lucas Alamán, *Historia de Méjico*, vol. 5 (Mexico City: Editorial Jus, 1942), 434, 807; Benson, "Texas as Viewed from Mexico," 230, 231; Timmons, *Tadeo Ortiz*, 16.

31. Ibid.

32. Janicek, "Development," 10–12; Austin Papers, CAH. Empresario contracts in Martín de León Papers (hereinafter DLC), April 15, 1824, GLO; Green De Witt contract, April 15, 1825, GLO; Power and Hewetson contract June 11, 1828, GLO; Benson, "Texas as Viewed from Mexico," 249; Thomas Lloyd Miller, *The Public Lands of Texas, 1519-1970* (Norman: University of Oklahoma Press, 1972), 21; Barker, *Life of*

Stephen F. Austin, 123; *Colección de las leyes y decretos expedidos por el congreso general de los Estados-Unidos Mejicanos en los años de 1829 y 1830* (Mexico City: Imprenta de Galván, 1831), 64–65; Gilberto M. Hinojosa, *A Borderlands Town in Transition: Laredo, 1755–1870* (College Station: Texas A&M University Press, 1983), 66.

33. Hammett, *Empresario*, 13–15; Barrera, *Then the Gringos Came*, 60–61.

34. Petition of Martín de León to Baron de Bastrop, Provincial Deputation, April 8, 1824, at San Fernando de Béxar, GLO-DLC; Gregg Cantrell, *Stephen F. Austin: Empresario of Texas* (New Haven: Yale University Press, 1999), 176–177; Mary Virginia Henderson, "Minor Empresario Contracts for the Colonization of Texas, 1825–1834," *Southwestern Historical Quarterly* 31 (April 1928): 295–299, and 32: 4–10; Grimes, *300 Years*, 60; Hammett, *Empresario*, 24–25; Rodríguez, *Emergence of Spanish America*, 55.

35. Hammett, *Empresario*, 20–21; de León Colony Papers, GLO-DLC.

36. Michael P. Costeloe, *La primera república federal de México, 1824–1835: un estudio de los partidos políticos en el México Independiente*, trans. Manuel Fernández Gasalla (Mexico City: Fondo de Cultura Económica, 1975), 24. Roy Grimes in *300 Years in Victoria County* suggests that the name Victoria was left out "perhaps by oversight" (60). Martín de León's original petition in the General Land Office does not mention Victoria, and there was little reason to suppose that de León had anything more than religion in mind when he suggested the name. Guadalupe Victoria, at the time, was not yet president of the republic and only one of a triumvirate. Victor M. Rose in *Some Historical Facts* claims that Guadalupe Victoria was de León's "warm personal friend" (10–11). This supposition, which is unsubstantiated, is highly unlikely since Guadalupe Victoria was never in Texas, nor is there any evidence of Martín de León ever going to Mexico City. The more logical conclusion is that the Provincial Deputation, trying to ingratiate itself with the ruling triumvirate, added Victoria after discussion with de León.

37. Resolution of the Provincial Deputation, San Fernando de Béxar, April 13, 1824, BCC-SP. There has been considerable controversy over whether de León's colony ever had specific boundaries, since his original petition did not list them. The decree of the Provincial Deputation does specify the boundaries when his empresario contract was granted.

38. Alamán, *Historia de Méjico*, 736–737.

39. Benson, "Texas as Viewed from Mexico," 244; H. P. N. Gammel, *The Laws of Texas, 1822–1897* (Austin: Gammel Book Co., 1898), 1:99; Gifford White, *1830 Citizens of Texas* (Austin, Tex.: Eakin Press, 1983), 3; Janicek, "Development," 11–14; Miller, *Public Lands*, 21.

40. Gammel, *Laws of Texas, 1822–1897*, 99; Janicek, "Development," 11–14; Miller, *Public Lands*, 21; Barker, *Life of Stephen F. Austin*, 124–127; *Colección de las Leyes y Decretos*, 64–66.

41. Court cases involving surveyor Edward Linn as witness to boundary disputes, Corporation Journal, City Hall Minutes, 1845–1855, City of Victoria, City Secretary's Office, Victoria, Texas.

42. Hammett, *Empresario*, 10; Barrera, *Then the Gringos Came*, 60-61; L. Randall Rogers, *Two Particular Friends of Stephen F. Austin* (Waco: Texian Press, 1990), 61; Candelaria, Family Group Records prepared from Victoria County census records by Gloria Candelaria, Victoria Hispanic Genealogical and Historical Society of Texas, Victoria, Texas (hereinafter FGR).

43. Interview with Joe Janak, Victoria County Extension Agent, Victoria, Texas, January 2000.

44. Ibid.; Hammett, *Empresario*, 58-59.

45. Town Plat, VCCO.

46. Charles R. Cutter, *The Legal Culture of Northern New Spain, 1700-1810* (Albuquerque: University of New Mexico Press, 1995), 19; Petition for *licencia de capilla* and priest for Guadalupe Victoria, reel 85, frames 230-231, 986, and reel 88, frames 713-714, CAH-BA; Janelle Scott, "Patricia de la Garza de León," manuscript, January 8, 1982, Special Collections, Texas Women's University Library, Denton, Tex.; Hammett, *Empresario*, 18-19, 21-23; Barrera, *Then the Gringos Came*, 55-58.

47. Scott, "Patricia de la Garza de León," 10.

48. Hammett, *Empresario*, 10-11; Barrera, *Then the Gringos Came*, 70-71; Family Group Records prepared from La Bahía and Victoria census data, Gloria Candelaria, Victoria County Genealogical Society, Victoria, Texas.

49. Plat of Victoria County, August 1921, GLO; land grant deeds, GLO-DLC. A note from Kate O'Connor indicates that Ware was a "squatter on land awarded to Empresario de León and was included among the colonists," in Rose, *Some Historical Facts*, 189. Although de León has been accused of being antagonistic toward Anglo Americans, his willingness to admit these settlers does not reflect any racial antipathy. Henderson, "Minor Empresario Contracts," 6-7; Index to Deed Records, VCCO; Rose, *Some Historical Facts*, list of settlers, 189; Jean Louis Berlandier, *Journey to Mexico during the Years 1826 to 1834*, trans. Sheila M. Ohlendorf, Josette M. Bigelow, Mary M. Standifer (Austin: Texas State Historical Association and Center for Studies in Texas History, 1980), 328-383.

50. Alcalde of Goliad Juan José Hernandez to the Governor of the State, March 26, 1825, GLO-DLC; Record of Translations, No. 55, GLO; original letter in Saltillo Municipal Archives, Saltillo, Coahuila, Mexico (hereinafter SM).

51. José Antonio Saucedo to Excelentísimo Señor Governador del Estado de Coahuila y Texas, D. Rafael González, July 14, 1825, SM; Saucedo to Gonzales, June 10, 1825, GLO-DLC; Record of Translations, p. 56, GLO; González to José Antonio Saucedo, May 17, 1825, Catálogo del Fondo Presidencia Municipal, SM; José Antonio Saucedo to Juan Martín de Veramendi, April 11, 1825, CAH-BA; De León to Saucedo, n.d., photocopy, O'CVL-MLP; Padilla to Jefe, October 6, 1825, GLO-DLC; original in CAH-BA, same date.

52. Martín de León to Political Chief, March 24, 1826, CAH-BA.

53. J. Thomas to Stephen F. Austin, April 15, 1824, in Cantrell, *Stephen F. Austin*, 177.

54. Vázquez, "Primeros Tropiezos," 70.

55. Ibid.; Miller, *Public Lands*, 21; Cantrell, *Stephen F. Austin*, 176-177.

56. Barker, *Life of Stephen F. Austin*, 123; Andreas V. Reichstein, *Rise of the Lone Star: The Making of Texas*, trans. Jeanne R. Willson (College Station: Texas A&M University Press, 1989), 38.

57. Edward A. Lukes, *De Witt Colony of Texas* (Austin: Jenkins Publishing Co.; New York: Pemberton Press, 1976), 59–63.

58. Ethel Ziveley Rather, "De Witt's Colony," *Quarterly of the Texas State Historical Association* 8, no. 2 (October 1904); Ethel Ziveley Rather, *De Witt's Colony* (Austin: University of Texas Press, 1905), 113.

59. Padilla to Jefe Político, October 6, 1825, GLO-DLC. Grimes, *300 Years*, 66; Rather, "De Witt's Colony," 103, 106. Using 2.63 miles as the length of a league, Port Lavaca, or Old Station, is approximately 20 miles, or close to 8 leagues, from the nearest coastal islands.

60. Lukes, *De Witt*, 67.

61. Martín de León to Governor González, n.d., photocopies in O'CVL-MLP.

62. Martín de León to Saucedo, November 12, 1826, CAH-BA.

63. David J. Langum, *Law and Community on the Mexican California Frontier: Anglo-American Expatriates and the Clash of Legal Tradition, 1821–1846* (Norman: University of Oklahoma Press, 1987), 5.

64. Jerold S. Auerbach, *Justice Without Law?* (New York: Oxford University Press, 1983), supra note 13 at 8, quoted in Langum, *Law and Community*, 142.

65. Joseph F. McKnight, "Stephen Austin's Legalistic Concerns," *Southwestern Historical Quarterly* 89 (January 1986), 254, 250, 254.

66. Langum, *Law and Community*, 8.

67. Ibid., 5–7, 142.

68. W. Bishop and W. Attree, *Report of the Debates and Proceedings of the Convention for the Revision of the Constitution of the State of New York, 1846*, quoted in Langum, *Law and Community*, 144.

69. Cutter, *Legal Culture*, 85; Langum, *Law and Community*, 142–143.

70. Cutter, *Legal Culture*, 92–93.

71. Ibid., 87; Cantrell, *Stephen F. Austin,*

72. John J. Linn, *Reminiscences of Fifty Years in Texas* (New York: D. and J. Sadler and Co., 1883; reprint, Austin: State House Press, 1986), 201.

73. José Miguel Ramos Arizpe, *Memoria que el Doctor D. Miguel Ramos de Arizpe, cura de borbón y diputado en las presentes cortes generales y extraordinarias de España por la provincia de Coahuila, una de las cuatro internas del oriente en el reino de México presenta a el Augusto Congreso* (Guadalajara: Oficina de Don José Fruto Romero, 1813; reprint, trans. Nettie Lee Benson, Austin: University of Texas Press, 1950), 10–13; José Castro (Secretaría de Guerra y Marina, to Commandants of Coahuila y Texas, Organización del Ramo de Tabaco, June 3, 1825, CAH-BA; Plegatoria del Ramo de Papel Sellado y Tabaco del Presidio de la Bahía del Espíritu Santo, January 1, 1826–December 12, 1826, State Records of Coahuila and Texas, SM; Suárez Argüello, *Camino real*, 115–120.

74. Cuaderno Borrador de José Antonio Saucedo of April 15, 1825, letter dated July 12, 1825, CAH-BA.

75. Rather, "De Witt's Colony," 110; Saucedo to Martín de León, October 9, 1826, in José Antonio Saucedo's Cuaderno Borrador of January 4, 1826, CAH-BA.

76. Saucedo to Gren deWit[sic], October 25, 1826, Cuaderno Borrador de José Antonio Saucedo of January 4, 1826, CAH-BA; Saucedo to La Bahía, October 29, 1826, CAH-BA; Green De Witt to Saucedo, November 8, 1826, CAH-BA; La Vaca Station, Thomas Powell to José Antonio Saucedo, "Report on arrival in Texas after having been expelled by force of arms and declaring that he will make a demand for goods seized by de León and Manchola," August 20, 1827, CAH-BA; Rather, "De Witt's Colony," 111.

77. Francis Smith to Sor. Jefe de este Departamento, November 29, 1826, CAH-BA; Kerr to Austin, November 11, 1826, Austin Papers, CAH; Rather, "De Witt's Colony," 111.

78. Receipt for all embargoed tobacco from the Arroyo de la Baca to el Muelle del Jacinto, Bahía, December 24, 1826, SM; Report on Tobacco, La Bahía Presidio, May 20, 1827, SM; Saucedo to Martín de León, November 30, 1826, in Cuaderno Borrador de José Antonio Saucedo, January 4, 1826, CAH-BA; Francis Smith to José Antonio Saucedo, November 29, 1826, CAH-BA, Martín de León to Saucedo, n.d., CAH-BA.

79. Rafael Manchola to Mateo Ahumada, October 29, 1826, CAH-BA, quoted in Andrés Tijerina, *Tejanos and Texas under the Mexican Flag, 1821–1836* (College Station: Texas A&M University Press, 1994), 124; see also Jesús F. de la Teja, "The Colonization and Independence of Texas: A Tejano Perspective," in *Myths, Misdeeds, and Misunderstandings: The Roots of Conflict in U.S.–Mexican Relations,* ed. Jaime E. Rodríquez O. and Kathryn Vincent (Wilmington, Del.: Scholarly Resources, 1997), 89.

80. Tijerina, *Tejanos and Texas,* 123–124.

81. Martín de León to Saucedo, August 15, 1825, CAH-BA.

82. Martín de León to Saucedo, May 16, 1825; Martín de León to Saucedo, April 12, 1825, CAH-BA.

83. Henderson, "Minor Empresario Contracts," 31: 299; Barker, *Life of Stephen F. Austin,* 167–168, 170–171, 175–177; Rather, *De Witt's Colony,* 112–113.

84. Saucedo to Alcalde Constitutional del Puerto de Nacogdoches, June 14, 1825, in the Cuaderno Borrador of José Antonio Saucedo, CAH-BA; Barker, *Life of Stephen F. Austin,* 112.

85. Anastacio Bustamante to Political Chief, August 18, 1827, CAH-BA.

86. Rather, *De Witt's Colony,* 114.

87. McKnight, "Stephen Austin's Legalistic Concerns," 254–255; Barker, *Life of Stephen F. Austin,* 241.

88. Saucedo to Martín de León, September 5, 1826, in Cuaderno Borrador de José Antonio Saucedo, January 4, 1826, CAH-BA; Martín de León to Alcalde of La Bahía, March 28, 1825, CAH-BA; Martín de León to José Antonio Saucedo, September 1, 1826, CAH-BA; Cantrell, *Stephen F. Austin,* 177.

CHAPTER 4

1. Huson, *Refugio,* 160–161; O'Connor, *Presidio La Bahía,* 126–127.

2. Letter from Martín de León, Goliad (GOL), June 18, 1829, 123:0542–60, CAH-BA; Meyer and Sherman, *Course of Mexican History,* 319–320.

3. José María Sánchez, *Viaje a Texas en 1828-1829* (Mexico City: Colección de Papeles y Documentos Históricos Mexicanos, 1939), 30. Descriptions of La Bahía both by Jean Louis Berlandier and the Boundary Commission in 1829 and by Almonte in 1834 describe the town with considerable scorn; Berlandier, *Journey to Mexico,* 1:123.

4. Ibid., 30–32, 44–46.

5. Ibid., 30.

6. Sánchez, *Viaje a Texas,* 30; Henderson, "Minor Empresario Contracts," 31: 299; O'Connor, *Presidio La Bahía,* 74–75; T. R. Fehrenbach, *Lone Star: A History of Texas and the Texans* (New York: Collier Books, 1968), 159–161; Oberste, *Texas Irish Empresarios,* 34–37, 42, 132.

7. Edith Louise Kelly and Mattie Austin Hatcher, eds., "Tadeo Ortiz de Ayala and the Colonization of Texas, 1822-1833," *Southwestern Historical Quarterly* 32 (July 1928): 74, 315.

8. Barker, *Life of Stephen F. Austin,* 149–152; Oberste, *Texas Irish Empresarios,* 64.

9. Oberste, *Texas Irish Empresarios,* 141, 143.

10. Allan and O'Connor, "Reminiscences," 321. The term "Spanish" as used by Annie Fagan Teal refers to the Mexicans but may have been commonly used because the Irish viewed these early families as Spanish due to the recent transition from Spain to Mexico.

11. Sánchez, *Viaje a Texas,* 30; Juan Nepomuceno Almonte, "Statistical Report on Texas," trans. Carlos E. Castañeda, *Southwestern Historical Quarterly* 28 (January 1925), 177–222. This statistical report is a shorter version of his complete report, which was filed in secret with the Mexican government upon his return. The report, "Informe secreto sobre la present situación de Texas," has been printed in the appendix of Juan Nepomuceno Almonte, *Como México perdió Texas* (Mexico City: Talleres de Impresión Instituto Nacional de Antropología e Historia, 1987), page 31 of the original text, 14 of the appendix. Marriage records for La Bahía and the Goliad area were lost during the years of the Texas Revolution. The only reference to Carlos de la Garza's wedding is in Huson, *Refugio,* 84, 160–161, 173; Grimes, *300 Years,* 85, 105, 125; Assessment of Taxes, 1852, Box II 16B, VC/UH. Carlos de la Garza's name appears on the enlistment records of the presidio but not among the members of the town council of La Bahía, "Libro formado por el Capitan de Milicias," La Bahía, vol. 320, foja 60, Sección Historia, AGN.

12. Henderson, "Minor Empresario Contracts," 32:11; Oberste, *Texas Irish Empresarios,* 80.

13. Henderson, "Minor Empresario Contracts," 32:11–12; Oberste in *Texas Irish Empresarios* (80-81) claims that Power and Hewetson encouraged the locals to apply

for titles since Power could thereby more easily acquire title to his five league and five labor grant as soon as the first hundred families were settled. In spite of the problems, many of the La Bahía residents, as evidenced by the appendix in Oberste, after page 310, did receive title to their lands; List of Titles issued by José Jesús Vidaurri in Powers and Hewetson Colony, in Oberste, *Texas Irish Empresarios*, 310 et passim.

14. Chipman, *Spanish Texas*, 253; Joseph W. McKnight, *The Spanish Elements in Modern Texas Law* (Dallas: J. W. McKnight, 1979), 8.

15. William Madsen inaccurately suggests that the "Latin wife . . . did not resent her subordinate role nor envy the independence of Anglo women"; William Madsen, *Mexican-Americans of South Texas* (New York: Holt, Rinehart and Winston, 1964), 19. He fails to see the tremendous power that these women wielded within the confines of their own families and their business relationships. Susan E. Keefe, "Ethnic Identity: The Domain of Perceptions of and Attachment to Ethnic Groups and Cultures," *Human Organization* 51 (spring 1992): 38; Micaela Di Leonardo, *The Varieties of Ethnic Experience: Kinship, Class, and Gender among California Italian-Americans* (Ithaca: Cornell University Press, 1984), 215–218; Suzanne Forrest, *The Preservation of the Village: New Mexico's Hispanics and the New Deal* (Albuquerque: University of New Mexico Press, 1989), 180.

16. Judith E. Brown, *The Science of Human Nutrition* (New York: Harcourt Brace Jovanovich, 1990), 177–178.

17. Brett Williams, "Why Migrant Women Feed Their Husbands Tamales: Foodways as a Basis for a Revisionist View of Tejano Life," in Linda Keller Brown and Kay Mussell, co-editors, *Ethnic and Regional Foodways in the U.S.: The Performance of Group Identity* (Knoxville: University of Tennessee Press, 1984), 113; Elizondo Guerra, "Whose Water Is This Anyway?"; Richard A. García, *Rise of the Mexican American Middle Class: San Antonio, 1929–1941* (College Station: Texas A&M University Press, 1991), 122; Joe S. Graham, "El Rancho in South Texas," in *Bulletin* (Denton: University of North Texas, 1994), 27–28.

18. Brown and Mussell, *Ethnic and Regional Foodways*, 113–115.

19. E. Perdiguero Gil, *El mal de ojo: de la literatura antisuperticiosa a la antropología médica*, cited in Elizondo Guerra, "Whose Water is This Anyway?"

20. Graham, "El Rancho," p. 27.

21. Carlos E. Castañeda, *Our Catholic Heritage in Texas*, vol. 7, *The Church in Texas since Independence, 1836–1950* (Austin: Von Boeckmann-Jones, 1958), 25.

22. Hammett, *Empresario*, 69–70.

23. Castañeda, *Our Catholic Heritage*, 7:73.

24. Oberste, *Texas Irish Empresarios*, 80–83.

25. Ibid., 149; Henderson, "Minor Empresario Contracts," 31:299.

26. Berlandier, *Journey to Mexico*, 384.

27. Almonte, *Como México perdió Texas*, 44–45; Almonte, "Statistical Report on Texas," 177–222.

28. Fernando's command of English is evident from a subscription to the New Orleans *Daily Picayune*; subscription in VC/UH.

29. Hammett, *Empresario*, 10–11; Barrera, *Then the Gringos Came*, 62–70; Candelaria, FGR.

30. Linn, *Reminiscences*, 37–38; Grimes, *300 Years*, 61; Rose, *Some Historical Facts*, 12.

31. Meyer and Sherman, *Course of Mexican History*, 321–322; Cantrell, *Stephen F. Austin*, 219–221; Margaret Swett Henson, *Juan Davis Bradburn: A Reappraisal of the Mexican Commander of Anáhuac* (College Station: Texas A&M University, 1982), 42–45; Oberste, *Texas Irish Empresarios*, 129, 131, 138–139.

32. Malcolm McLean, "Tenoxtitlán, Dream Capital of Texas," *Southwestern Historical Quarterly* 70 (July 1966) 25–27; Barker, *Life of Stephen F. Austin*, 282; Fehrenbach, *Lone Star*, 54.

33. Henson, *James Davis Bradburn*, 58–60.

34. Nodé Quintellen McMillen, "Surveyor General: The Life and Times of José María Jesús Carbajal," manuscript, Rosanky, Tex., 1990, 16–20; Henson, *James Davis Bradburn*, 58–59.

35. McMillen, "Surveyor General," 16–20.

36. Henson, *James Davis Bradburn*, 65–67.

37. Vito Alessio Robles, *Coahuila y Texas desde la consumación de la Independencia hasta el tratado de paz de Guadalupe Hidalgo* (Mexico City, 1945), 1:145–146.

38. Hewetson to R. Muzquiz, [1832], Deed Records, Vol. 1, p. 97, VCCO; Almonte, "Statistical Report on Texas," 177–222; full report in "Informe secreto sobre la presente situación en Texas, 1834," in Almonte, *Como México perdió Texas*, 44–45; Martín de León contract, Record of Translations, GLO; Henderson, "Minor Empresario Contracts," 31:299–302; Oberste, *Texas Irish Empresarios*, 42–45; Rather, "De Witt's Colony," 113; Cantrell, *Stephen F. Austin*, 217.

39. Rather, "De Witt's Colony," 142; Henderson, "Minor Empresario Contracts," 32:7; Angel Navarro to the Governor of the State, January 10, 1835, Eberstadt Collection, CAH; Ramón Músquiz to Fernando de León, request for Deed, included in Document 4, "Resolution of the General Government of the State in favor of the Mexicans established on the Coast," Deed Records, VCCO; Plat Map, Victoria County, August 1921, GLO.

40. Candelaria, Plácido Benavides and José María Jesús Carbajal.

41. Grimes, *300 Years*, 60–61; Rose, *Some Historical Facts*, 12; Robinson, "Colonial Ranch Architecture," 140; Linn, *Reminiscences*, 28–29, 36–37.

42. McMillen, "Surveyor General," 20; Candelaria FGR, José María Jesús Carbajal.

43. Hammett, *Empresario*, 10–12; McMillen, "Surveyor General," 20–21; Candelaria FGR, José María Jesús Carbajal.

44. Hammett, *Empresario*, 10–12; Candelaria FGR, Plácido Benavides; Linn, *Reminiscences*, 28–29, 37–38; Grimes, *300 Years*, 60–61; Rose, *Some Historical Facts*, 12.

45. Barker, *Life of Stephen F. Austin*, 326.

46. McMillen, "Surveyor General," 21-25; Cantrell, *Stephen F. Austin*, 247-250.

47. Manuel de Mier y Terán to Lucas Alamán, July 2, 1832, in Cantrell, *Stephen F. Austin*, 255.

48. Ohland Morton, *Terán and Texas: A Chapter in Texas-Mexican Relations* (Austin: Texas State Historical Association, 1948), 178; Cantrell, *Stephen F. Austin*, 255.

49. Meyer and Sherman, *Course of Mexican History*, 325-326; Cantrell, *Stephen F. Austin*, 262-263.

50. Rather, "De Witt's Colony," 145; David J. Weber, ed., *Troubles in Texas, 1832: A Tejano Viewpoint from San Antonio*, trans. Conchita Hassell Winn and David J. Weber (Austin: Wind River Press, 1983), 2-3.

51. Cantrell, *Stephen F. Austin*, 262.

52. Although there is little written proof of the views of the de León family during this period other than Manchola's resolution, the actions of the men throughout the next several years indicated their adherence to the different camps. Neither Félix nor José Miguel Aldrete fought with the Anglos during the revolution, but Fernando, Silvestre, Benavides, and Carbajal all did. Cantrell, *Stephen F. Austin*, 262-263.

53. Ibid., 263-264.

54. Western to Austin, January 19, 1832, Nacogdoches Archives, Texas State Library, quoted in Barker, *Life of Stephen F. Austin*, 356; Minutes of the Ayuntamiento, October 14, 1832, "Libro formado por el Capitan de Milicias," AGN; Weber, *Troubles in Texas*, 3.

55. Rather, "De Witt's Colony," 145; *Gaceta del Gobierno Supremo del Estado de Coahuila y Texas, 1833*, Eberstadt Collection, Box 3N177, no. 2, CAH; Weber, *Troubles in Texas*, 1-3.

56. Cantrell, *Stephen F. Austin*, 262-263.

57. Meyer and Sherman, *Course of Mexican History*, 326-327; Jones, *Santa Anna*, 40-44; Mena L. Flores, *El General Don Antonio López de Santa Anna* (Mexico City: n.p., 1950); Wilfrid H. Callcott, *Santa Anna: The Story of an Enigma Who Once Was Mexico* (Hamden, Conn.: Archon Books, 1964), 56-67; Antonio López de Santa Anna, *The Eagle: The Autobiography of Santa Anna*, ed. Ann Fears Crawford (Austin: Pemberton Press, 1967).

58. Cantrell, *Stephen F. Austin*, 264-265.

59. Stephen F. Austin to Ayuntamiento of Béxar, October 2, 1833, in Cantrell, *Stephen F. Austin*, 271.

60. Cantrell, *Stephen F. Austin*, 271-274.

61. Candelaria FGR, de León family.

62. Barker, *Life of Stephen F. Austin*, 369; William Ransom Hogan, *The Texas Republic: A Social and Economic History* (Austin: University of Texas Press, 1986), 229, 234; Henderson, "Minor Empresario Contracts," 32:11; Patrick Ireland Nixon, *The Medical Story of Early Texas, 1528-1853* (Lancaster, Pa.: Mollie Bennett Lupe Memorial Fund, 1946), 138; Hogan, *Texas Republic*, 228.

63. Hammett, *Empresario*, 10–12; Candelaria, de León family.

64. Charles E. Rosenberg, *The Cholera Years, The United States in 1832, 1849, 1866* (Chicago: University of Chicago Press, 1963), 3; Rob Pollitzer, "Cholera Studies: History of the Disease," *Bulletin of the World Health Organization* 10 (1954), 458; F. B. Smith, *The People's Health, 1830–1910* (London: Croom Helm, 1979), 232. Office of the Chief, July 1, 1834, Department of Bexar, to Ayuntamientos, Papers of the Medical History of Texas, vol. 3, 270–273, CAH; H. Villasana Haggard, "Epidemic Cholera in Texas, 1833–1834," *Southwestern Historical Quarterly* 40 (July 1936–April 1937), 225, 228.

65. R. E. McGrew, "The First Cholera Epidemic and Social History," *Bulletin of the History of Medicine* 34 (January–February 1960), 62–64; W. E. Van Heynigen and John R. Seal, *Cholera: The American Scientific Experience, 1847–1980* (Boulder, Colo.: Westview Press, 1983) 1–2; Rosenberg, *Cholera Years*, 2–4; Smith, *People's Health*, 230; Barker, *Life of Stephen F. Austin*, 373, 382–385; Haggard, "Epidemic Cholera," 229; Ramón Muzquiz to Ayuntamiento at Goliad, July 2, 1834, Papers of the Medical History, vol. 3, CAH; Plácido Benavides to Ramón Múzquiz, July 9, 1834, in Haggard, "Epidemic Cholera," 229.

CHAPTER 5

1. Candelaria FGR Austin, Martín de León family.

2. Ibid.

3. "Tortillas," Box 26B, VC/UH.

4. Box 26B, VC/UH.

5. Ibid.

6. Arnoldo de León, *The Tejano Community, 1836–1900* (Albuquerque: University of New Mexico Press, 1982), 6–7.

7. Roll 162: 0922–23, August 19, 1834, CAH-BA.

8. Will of Patricia de la Garza de León, Index to Deed Records, vol. 1, VCCO; McMillen, "Surveyor General," 59.

9. Fernando de León to Martín de León, January 1834, Index to Deed Records, VCCO.

10. Decree of April 19, 1834, in Malcolm McLean, *Papers Concerning Robertson's Colony in Texas* (Arlington: University of Texas at Arlington: 1983), 10:54–55; Cantrell, *Stephen F. Austin*, 306–307.

11. Leonardo Manso purchases, Index to Deed Records, VCCO.

12. McMillen, "Surveyor General," 63.

13. Paul D. Lack, *The Texas Revolutionary Experience: A Political and Social History, 1835–1836* (College Station: Texas A&M University Press, 1992), 14–15; Reichstein, *Rise of the Lone Star*, 96–97, 101–108; Cantrell, *Stephen F. Austin*, 298–299.

14. Kerr to Gail Borden, Jr., Lavaca, June 3, 1835, in McLean, *Papers Concerning Robertson's Colony*, 20:373.

15. Sue Watkins, ed., Texas Surveyors Association, Historical Committee, comp., *One League to Each Wind: Accounts of Early Surveying in Texas* (Austin: Von Boeckmann-

Jones, 1980), 6-8; State Colonization Law of Coahuila y Texas, March 24, 1825, in McLean, *Papers Concerning Robertson's Colony,* 10:27.

16. State Colonization Law of Coahuila y Texas, March 24, 1825, in McLean, *Papers Concerning Robertson's Colony,* 20:27; Watkins, ed., *One League,* 7-8.

17. Blake Collection, 39: 15-16, April 26, 1832, CAH; José María Jesús Carbajal, GLO.

18. Watkins, *One League,* 7-8; McLean, *Papers Concerning Robertson's Colony,* 10:41-43.

19. Box 26A, VC/UH.

20. McLean, *Papers Concerning Robertson's Colony,* 10:41-43.

21. McLean suggests that Samuel May Williams "used the Upper Colony as a training ground for surveyors like Francis W. Johnson to learn how to survey 11-league grants, which could be located for a fee of $2,000 each," although a later surveyor, John J. Dix, set the price for a 1,903-acre tract for José Vaellos at $28. McLean, *Robertson's Colony,* 10:30; Marilyn J. Good, ed., Texas Surveyors Association, Historical Committee, comp., *Three Dollars per Mile: Accounts of Early Surveying in Texas* (Burnet, Tex.: Eakin Press, 1981), 54.

22. Robles, *Coahuila y Texas,* 2:407; Cantrell, *Stephen F. Austin,* 271-273.

23. Juan Nepumoceno Almonte, *Informe secreto sobre la presente situación de Texas, 1834* (Mexico City: INAH, 1987), 18-19; Cantrell, *Stephen F. Austin,* 293-294; Reichstein, *Rise of the Lone Star,* 112; Lupita Barrera, "Footprints on the Land: Early Hispanics of Texas," display at Lyndon Baines Johnson Library, 1998-1999, containing a twenty-*vara* Gunter chain, circa 1840, from the collection of Darrell D. Shine, land surveyor, Silsbee, Texas.

24. James McPherson, *The Battle Cry of Freedom,* quoted in Lack, *Texas Revolutionary Experience,* 15.

25. Cantrell, *Stephen F. Austin,* 298-299.

26. Almonte, *Informe Secreto,* 31-32; Cantrell, *Stephen F. Austin,* 294-295; Reichstein, *Rise of the Lone Star,* 75-76.

27. Correspondencia al H. Congreso de Matamoros, Marzo 1835, Expediente 18, Caja 3 de Presidenciales/Independencia, 1835-1836, Archivo de Casamata, Matamoros, Tamaulipas, Mexico.

28. McLean, *Papers Concerning the Robertson Colony,* 10:40-41; Fernando de León grants, 1835, Index to Deed Records, VCCO. The majority of land grant titles in the Victoria County records are for 1835, although many of the titles indicate that the owners had arrived between 1828 and 1832.

29. McLean, *Papers Concerning the Robertson Colony,* 10:50-51; Grimes, *300 Years,* 76-77; Cecil Alan Hutchinson, "Valentín Gómez Farías, A Biographical Study" (Ph.D. diss., University of Texas, 1948), 353; Meyer and Sherman, *Course of Mexican History,* 324-336.

30. Cantrell, *Stephen F. Austin,* 300-301; McLean, *Papers Concerning the Robertson Colony,* 10:40-41, 50-51.

31. McLean, *Papers Concerning the Robertson Colony,* 10:40–41, 50–51.

32. Margaret Swett Henson, *Samuel May Williams, Early Texas Entrepreneur* (College Station: Texas A&M University Press, 1976), 67–68; Cantrell, *Stephen F. Austin,* 300–302.

33. McMillen, "Surveyor General," 69.

34. Linn, *Reminiscences,* 37–38.

35. Huson, *Refugio,* 137–142; Grimes, *300 Years,* 135.

36. Lack, *Texas Revolutionary Experience,* 24–25.

37. Ibid., 27–29.

38. Cantrell, *Stephen F. Austin,* 310–314.

39. Scott, "Patricia de la Garza de León," 2–3. Although there is no written documentation of the decisions of the de León men, their actions during 1835 and 1836 clearly indicated their positions in regard to the Texas Revolution.

40. Cantrell, *Stephen F. Austin,* 310–311; Lack, *Texas Revolutionary Experience,* 32–33.

41. Huson, *Refugio,* 212.

42. O'Connor, *Presidio La Bahía,* 250–254; Huson, *Refugio,* 212.

43. Linn, *Reminiscences,* 105, 107.

44. Stephen L. Hardin, *Texian Iliad: A Military History of the Texas Revolution, 1835–1836* (Austin: University of Texas Press, 1994), 15; Huson, *Refugio,* 212–213.

45. Hardin, *Texian Iliad,* 15–16; Grimes, *300 Years,* 129, 135; Hobart Huson, *Captain Phillip Dimitt's Commandancy of Goliad, 1835–1836* (Austin: Von Boeckmann-Jones, 1974), 32–33; Huson, *Refugio,* 213; Carlos E. Castañeda, *Our Catholic Heritage in Texas, 1519–1936,* vol. 6, *The Transition Period: The Fight for Freedom, 1810–1836* (Austin: Von Boeckmann-Jones, 1950), 277, 284.

46. Hardin, *Texian Iliad,* 28.

47. Ibid., 28–29; Cantrell, *Stephen F. Austin,* 316–322.

48. Stephen L. Hardin, "Efficient in the Cause," in *Tejano Journey, 1770–1850,* ed. Gerald E. Poyo (Austin: University of Texas Press, 1996), 50–54, 68.

49. Hardin, *Texian Iliad,* 44.

50. Linn, *Reminiscences,* 119–120; Hardin, *Texian Iliad,* 44.

51. Huson, *Captain Phillip Dimitt's Commandancy,* 101; Hardin, *Texian Iliad,* 42.

52. Cantrell, *Stephen F. Austin,* 324–327.

53. Ibid., 327–238.

54. Hardin, *Texian Iliad,* 67–68.

55. Castañeda, *Our Catholic Heritage,* 6:277; Grimes, *300 Years,* 81.

CHAPTER 6

1. L. H. W. Johnson to the Honorable Provisional Government of Texas, Matagorda, in John H. Jenkins, ed., *The Papers of the Texas Revolution, 1835–1836* (Austin: Presidial Press, 1973), 4:214.

2. Linn, *Reminiscences,* 259; Grimes, *300 Years,* 88, 135; Rose, *Some Historical Facts,* 190–191.

3. James S. Fannin to the Honorable Provisional Government of Texas, in Jenkins, ed., *Papers of the Texas Revolution*, 4:220–221.

4. K. W. Donovan, *History of Pirates and Pirating* (Key West, Fla.: Conch Republic Printing Press, 1972), 2–5.

5. Johnson to the Government, in Jenkins, ed., *Papers of the Texas Revolution*, 4:211–215.

6. Ibid., 4:214.

7. Ibid., 4:213.

8. Linn, *Reminiscences*, 259; McLean, *Papers Concerning the Robertson Colony*, 11:240–242.

9. Barrera, *Then the Gringos Came*, 131.

10. Hardin, *Texian Iliad*, 109–111.

11. Ibid., 158–160; Grimes, *300 Years*, 84; Castañeda, *Our Catholic Heritage*, 6:284.

12. Hardin, *Texian Iliad*, 160; Grimes, *300 Years*, 129, 135; Huson, *Refugio*, 213; Castañeda, *Our Catholic Heritage*, 6:284.

13. Grimes, *300 Years*, 84; Castañeda, *Our Catholic Heritage*, 6:284; Carlos E. Castañeda, *The Mexican Side of the Texan Revolution [1836] by the Chief Mexican Participants* (Washington, D.C.: Documentary Publications, 1971), 16–18; José Urrea, "Diary of the Military Operations of the Division Which under His Command Campaigned in Texas," in Castañeda, ed. *Mexican Side of the Texan Revolution*, 228–235; Lack, *Texas Revolutionary Experience*, 164–165; Huson, *Refugio*, 330.

14. Hardin, *Texian Iliad*, 170–174; Urrea, "Diary of the Military Operations," 228–235.

15. Huson, *Refugio*, 385; Allan and O'Connor, "Reminiscences," 322–323; Hardin, *Texian Iliad*, 17; Lack, *Texas Revolutionary Experience*, 194; Urrea, "Diary of the Military Operations," in Castañeda, ed. *Mexican Side of the Texas Revolution*, 228–235; Huson, *Refugio*, 330.

16. Linn, *Reminiscences*, 247–249.

17. Grimes, *300 Years*, 129, 135; Huson, *Refugio*, 213; Castañeda, *Our Catholic Heritage*, 6:284.

18. José Urrea, *Diario de las operaciones militares de la division que al mando del General José Urrea hizo en la campaña de Tejas* (Victoria de Durango, Mexico: n.p., 1838), 25–26; *Morning Courier and New York Enquirer*, July 28, 1836, quoted in Hardin, *Texian Iliad*, 65.

19. There are no details of Doña Patricia's actions during this time. Her actions both before and after this incident indicate that she would have come to her son's aid. That a general would have accepted her commands is supposition based on the ingrained obedience to matriarchs which Mexican men have always maintained. On Fernando's capture by General Urrea see Grimes, *300 Years*, 88.

20. Hardin, *Texian Iliad*, 66.

21. Isaac D. Hamilton vertical file, CAH; Craig H. Roell, "Plácido Benavides," in *The Handbook of Victoria County* (Austin: Texas State Historical Association, 1996), 4–6; Hardin, *Texian Iliad*, 66.

22. Pedro Delgado, *Mexican Account of the Battle of San Jacinto* (Deepwater, Tex.: W. C. Day, 1919), 7–8.

23. Antonio López de Santa Anna, "Manifesto que de sus operaciones en la campaña de Tejas y su captura," in Carlos E. Castañeda, ed., *Mexican Side of the Texan Revolution [1836] by the Chief Mexican Participants*, ed. Carlos E. Castañeda (Washington, D.C.: Documentary Publications, 1971), 16.

24. Hardin, *Texian Iliad*, 200–201.

25. Ibid., 202–213.

26. Ibid., 215–216.

27. "Sumaria aberiguacion sobre la retirada del Exto. de operaciones sobre Tejas verificada por el Sr. General de División don Vicente Filisola," Tomo 200, Acervo 113, Archivo de Guerra y Marina, AGN.

28. Linn, *Reminiscences*, 248; Grimes, *300 Years*, 86; Lack, *Texas Revolutionary Experience*, 152–154.

29. Again, there is no proof of Doña Patricia's activities during this time. Given what is known of her personality, however, there is little doubt that she would have come to her son's aid again and that she would have expected her orders to be obeyed by General Rusk, just as she had from General Urrea. In Rusk's case, however, it would not have been upbringing and obedience to a matriarch, but proper Southern manners. Barrera, *Then the Gringos Came*, 140.

30. Smithwick, *Evolution of a State*, 102.

31. Ibid.

32. Whether she ever received payment from the poverty-stricken Texian government is unknown. Lack, *Texas Revolutionary Experience*, 205.

33. Grimes, *300 Years*, 87.

34. Huson, *Refugio*, 398; Philip Dimitt to Thomas Rusk, from Corpus Christi, June, 1836, Thomas Jefferson Rusk Papers, CAH.

35. In testimony given by Fernando de León in *Rosalía Cisneros v. Kirkpatrick* in 1852, Fernando had located the trunk among his mother's possessions after her death. In it were all the titles to lands in the Victoria colony, including those to which Fernando had laid claim.

36. Fairvax Catelet to Editor, Velasco, July 20, 1836, in Jenkins, ed., *Papers of the Texas Revolution*, 495–496.

37. Passenger lists of Vessels Arriving in New Orleans, July 18, 1836, M259-14, microfilm, NO; Thomas J. Rusk to P. Dimitt, June 22, 1836, in Thomas Jefferson Rusk Papers, Correspondence, CAH.

38. Fernando de León, Petition to the Legislature, December 1849, Records of the Legislature, Archives Division, Texas State Library, Austin.

39. Henry Teal and H. Carnes to Gen. Rusk, June 2, 1830, and Tho. J. Rusk to Col. James Smith, June 17, 1836; and Thos J. Rusk to Citizens, Broadside; and Thomas J. Rusk to Alexander Somerville, June 19, 1836, in Jenkins, ed., *Papers of the Texas Revolution*, 7:203.

40. P. Dimmitt to T. Rusk, July, 1836, Rusk Papers, Texas State Archives, Austin (hereinafter TSA); Lack, *Texas Revolutionary Experience*, 206; Passenger lists of Vessels Arriving in New Orleans, July 18, 1836, M259-14, microfilm, NO. Grimes in *300 Years* (135) maintains that the family "assembled at Linnville and took ship for New Orleans."

41. *History of New Orleans.*

42. The genealogical records indicate that Matiana Benavides was born in Opelousas in 1837, and Plácido died there in 1837, thus placing the family in that town during this period.

43. Tax Rolls, 1839, 1840, 1841, Victoria County, VCCO. This document is a small, coverless, lined notebook of about one hundred pages which was found in a metal cabinet in the Victoria County Clerk's Office.

44. Hammett, *Empresario*, 59–60.

45. Linn, *Reminiscences*, 260.

46. *Menifee v. De León*, November, 1839, Victoria District Court, District Clerk's Office, Victoria County (hereinafter VDC); Sheriff to James Robinson, January 28, 1840, Deed Records, vol. 2, p. 140, VCCO; *McGuffin v. De León*, Case 11, November 1839, VDC; *De León v. Sutherland*, September 4, 1850, 3:207, VDC; October 15, 1845, 2:228, VDC; *Sutherland et al. v. De León*, Case 14, March 20, 1839, VDC; court cases for 1841, 1842, 1844, VC/UH; Sheriff's Sales, 1839 and 1840, Deed Records, VCCO.

47. Sheriff's sale, Fernando de León to George Sutherland and John S. Menifee, April 9, 1839, vol. 1, p. 108; Sheriff's sale, Fernando de León to Andrew Neill, January 8, 1840, vol. 1, p. 133; Sheriff's Sale, Property of Fernando de León, 6¾ leagues of land sold to G. Sutherland on Garcito [sic] and La Bacca [sic] Bay remained, 1839 Property Inventory, VCCO; Sheriff's sale, One lot on northeast corner of the square, sold to satisfy judgement in favor of James Kerr, May 6, 1839, Deed Records, VCCO; Sheriff's sale to J. Schenks, Execution against Fernando de León for taxes for 1840 in the sum of $1340.60.

48. *State v. Félix de León*, Court Case No. 212, VC/UH.

49. Thomas Newcomb to Peter W. Hays, Indenture of Lease, vol. 2, p. 163, March 6, 1845, VCCO.

50. Silvestre de León was not listed among those in Opelousas, Louisiana, during the court session for the tutorship of León de León, and since all of the family was present, save for the Aldretes and the Garcías, it is evident that Silvestre, too, had returned to Texas.

51. The sales by Sheriff Pridham included names such as Richardson, Mahaney, Coughlin, Cyrus, Vance, O'Donovan, Ternit, Barrow, Rogers, Eaton, Sawyer, McCoy, Hayes, Turner, Cottel, Neill, Cheney, Milby, Halber, Graban, and Smalley; P. W. Pridham, Assessor to J. O. Wheeler, vol. 4, 1848, 1849, 1850, Index to Deed Records, VCCO.

52. Andrew Forest Muir, ed., *Texas in 1837: An Anonymous Contemporary Narrative*

(Austin: University of Texas Press, 1958), 148–160; Smithwick, *Evolution of a State*, 194–200.

53. Smithwick, *Evolution of a State*, 200–202.

54. "Republic and State Land Grants," pamphlet, Archives and Records Division, GLO.

55. "Republic and State Land Grants," Key to Index, GLO.

56. "History of the General Land Office," pamphlet, GLO.

57. Hogan, *Texas Republic*, 81–82.

58. Leonardo Manso purchases, Index to Deed Records, VCCO; Leonardo Manso to Pedro W. Grayson, Deed, vol. 1, p. 196, April 6, 1836; Gail Borden Jr. and John P. Borden executors of P. W. Grayson to Levi Jones and A. T. Burnley of Galveston, Deed, vol. 2, p. 228, May 22, 1845, Deed Records, VCCO.

59. Patricia de la Garza to Martín de León, 1801, Presas del Rey, in Patricia de la Garza to P. B. Cocke, Deed, vol. 1, p. 34, January 24, 1837, Deed Records, VCCO.

60. Patricia de la Garza to P. B. Cocke, Deed, vol. 1, p. 34, January 24, 1837, Deed Records, VCCO.

61. María Antonia de la Garza, Tutorship of León de León, son, vol. 1, p. 94, January 3, 1837, Index to Deed Records, VCCO.

62. María Antonia de la Garza, Executrix for Minor, León de León to P. B. Cocke, Deed, vol. 1, p. 94, January 23, 1837, Deed Records, VCCO.

63. Ibid.

64. María de Jesús de León Manchola to P. B. Cocke, January 23, 1837, Deed Records, VCCO.

65. Smithwick, *Evolution of a State*, 194–195, 200.

66. Muir, *Texas in 1837*, 155.

67. Ibid.; Lack, *Texas Revolutionary Experience*, 43.

68. Muir, *Texas in 1837*, 52, 155.

69. Smithwick, *Evolution of a State*, 199–200.

70. *Morning Star*, Houston, May 2, 1844, CAH.

71. VOCC, Victoria County.

72. Candelaria FGR, Carbajal family, Benavides family, Austin.

73. Meyer and Sherman, *Course of Mexican History*, 232–240.

74. Estate of Plácido Benavides, June 8, 1838, Vol. 2, p. 43–46, Probate Records, VCCO.

75. Candelaria FGR, Desiderio family, Austin.

76. Barrera, *Then the Gringos Came*, 138–139, 143–144. Family stories upon which Barrera bases his book indicate that it was Agápito who was shot by "Mustang" Gray in 1836. Agápito, however, had died in 1834, as evidenced by the fact that his widow, María Antonia, married Manuel Carbajal in 1835. Since Silvestre was in Texas during 1842 and was killed during that time, it appears that the story relates to Silvestre rather than to Agápito.

77. Linn, *Reminiscences*, 322.

78. Barrera, *Then the Gringos Came*, 138-139, 143-144; Linn, *Reminiscences*, 322-324.

79. Estate of Sylvester [sic] De León, M. H. Hardy, Adm[inistrato]r, April 1843, vol. 1, p. 67; May 1843, vol. 1, p. 69; August 1843, vol. 1, p. 75; December 1843, vol. 1, p. 79; February 1844, vol. 1, p. 82; May 1844, vol. 1, p. 87; and vol. 1, p. 237 for records of Bond, inventory, and appraisement, Application of Creditor for order of Sale, Report of Appraisers, Records of Sale of Land; M. H. Hardy, administrator of the Estate of Sylvester de León (deceased) to T. Newcomb, vol. 2, p. 54, September 25, 1843; M. H. Hardy to W. S. Van Norman, February 27, 1843, Deed Vol. 2, p. 80; Milton H. Hardy to James Ingram, Indenture, Vol. 2, p. 73, September 25, 1843, VCCO.

CHAPTER 7

1. Miguel Aldrete of Goliad to Charles Cuvelier of New Orleans, Deed Records, VCCO.

2. Smithwick, *Evolution of a State*, 78.

3. Candelaria FGR, de León family, Austin.

4. Matiana Benavides to Luz Escalera de León, n.d., O'CVL-MLP.

5. Victoria City Council Minutes, 1845-1848, city secretary's office.

6. Father Vincent had been a simple parish priest in Lyons, France. With the help of the Gondi family, he established the Vincentian missionary order and a seminary at Saint-Lazare, the motherhouse of the order, in Paris. Providing their own money and missionaries, by 1847 the Vincentian friars in Texas, led by Bishop Odin, had established dozens of churches, including Our Lady of Guadalupe of Victoria, and the chapel of Santa Gertrudis on Don Carlos' Ranch on the San Antonio River; Castañeda, *Our Catholic Heritage*, 7:106. Father Estany's name appears as priest for marriages and baptisms which covered the area from Corpus Christi to Goliad, Refugio, and Victoria, although he had been assigned to Victoria by Bishop Odin.

7. *Patricia de la Garza v. Robert Carlisle and Bridget Quinn*, Case No. 24, Fall Term 1849, settled Fall Term 1851, 25-A District Clerk's Miscellaneous Records, Civil Court Docket, VC/UH.

8. What Fernando had to face during his attempts to regain his land is supposition based on the fact that he did appear as a witness in the court cases, that he did hire and pay for Phillips' services, and that he did win the cases. It is interesting to note that he never gave up wanting to be accepted in the new Anglo world. He later joined his Anglo neighbors in granting land for the railroad, and he subscribed to the New Orleans *Picayune*. He also might have joined one of the Protestant churches, to his mother's dismay.

9. Hogan, *Texas Republic*, 254.

10. Fernando de León to Dr. Felix B. Webb, 1945, Deed Records, VCCO; *Fernando de León v. A. Neill*, Ejectment, Case No. 30, Spring Term 1847; *Fernando de León v. S. A. White*, Ejectment, Case No. 59, Spring Term 1847; *Murphree and Van Bibber v. Fernando*

de León, Ejectment, Case No. 82, Spring Term 1847; *Fernando de León v. M. I. Hardy*, Ejectment, Case No. 18, Spring Term 1847; all in Civil Court Docket, 1847–1859, District Court, VC/UH.

11. *Fernando de León v. James Robinson*, Spring Term 1847, Case No. 29, Ejectment; and *Fernando de León v. T. W. Robinson, Adm. of James Robinson, dec'd*, Ejectment, Bar Docket, Spring Term 1851, Civil Court Docket, 1847–1859, District Court, VC/UH.

12. David C. Humphrey, *Austin: An Illustrated History* (Northridge, Calif.: Windsor Publishing, 1985), 5–22; David C. Humphrey, "Austin, Texas," in *The New Handbook of Texas* (Austin: Texas State Historical Association, 1996), 299.

13. Ibid.

14. Ibid.

15. Hogan, *Texas Republic*, 253; Milton Hardy sales for 1843, Deed Records, VCCO. *De León v. Hardy*, 7 Tex. 466, Texas Supreme Court Records (RG201), TSL-A; Estate of Silvestre de León, PM 1:238, VOCC; Fernando de León, Weisiger Collection, Folder 77, Box 4, VC/UH; Martín de León to A. H. Phillips and Vincent McRae, Deed Records, vol. 4, p. 346, VCCO.

16. 1839 Property Inventory, VCCO. Félix de León, June 8, 1838, Mark and Brands Book, VCCO; Daniel McDonald, Sheriff, to A. S. McDonald, Indenture, vol. 2, p. 40, September 8, 1841, VCCO; Thomas Costello, Sheriff, from Thomas Newcomb, receipt, vol. 2, p. 81, March 4, 1844, VCCO; Thomas Costello, Sheriff, to Thomas Newcomb, Indenture, vol. 2, p. 161, March 5, 1845, VCCO; Thomas Newcomb to Peter W. Hays, Indenture of Lease, vol. 2, p. 163, March 5, 1845, VCCO; Thomas Newcomb to James Dennison of Matagorda, Deed, vol. 2, p. 263, October 19, 1945, VCCO.

17. Félix de León to A. H. Phillips, Deed, vol. 2, p. 214, August 16, 1845, VCCO.

18. Thomas Newcomb to James Dennison, of Matagorda, deed, vol. 2, p. 263, October 19, 1945, VCCO; Félix de León to A. H. Phillips, Deed, vol. 2, p. 214, August 16, 1845, VCCO; Probate Records for Félix de León, December 1856, vol. 2, p. 29, VCCO.

19. Huson, *Refugio*, 517; Inventory for 1863 (Census) by Thurmond A & C, Box I7A, VC/UH; Letter, 1842, Bishop Odin, Correspondence, Catholic Archives of Texas, Austin (hereinafter CAT).

20. General Thomas Taylor Williamson with his wife Tersah [sic] Ann to Thomas Brown Lee of New Orleans, Deed, vol. 3, p. 658, August 7, 1845, VCCO.

21. Ibid.

22. Williamson to Thomas Brown Lee, August 7, 1845, Deed Records, Victoria County, VCCO; tax rolls for 1863 and 1876 indicate that Carlos de la Garza was still in full possession of his lands by his death; Inventory for 1863 (Census) by Thurmond A & C, Box I7A, VC/UH.

23. *Rosalía Cisneros v. E. Killpatrick*, 36-A Depositions of T. J. Rusk and Fernando de León, Fall Term 1851, VC/UH.

24. *R. Cisneros v. Eleazar Killpatrick* [variously Sizeneros, Sisnaros, Sesnaros; also Kirkpatrick], Court Case No. 1325, VC/UH; Sheriff's Sales, November 14, 1855, Deed Records, Victoria County, VCCO.

25. N. Benabides [sic] to Fielding Jones and Stephen Dinkins, Deed Records, Victoria County, VCCO; Stephen [Estévan] Sisneras [Cisneros] to John McGrew, Deed Records, VCCO.

26. There is no record of these incidents other than the fact that Panchita and León had been brought up together and were in school at the same time—León in Paris and Panchita in New Orleans. Barrera, *Then the Gringos Came,* 85, 165; Receipts from the Convent of the Immaculate Conception, New Orleans, O'CVL-MLP.

27. Candelaria FGR, Manchola family, Austin.

28. Candelaria FGR, de León family, Austin.

29. Hugo J. Nutini, *San Bernardo Contla: Marriage and Family Structure in a Tlaxcalan Municipio* (Pittsburgh: University of Pittsburgh Press, 1968), 20; Forrest, *Preservation of a Village,* 31; Brown, *Baptism,* 26–29; Richard Griswold del Castillo, *The Los Angeles Barrio, 1850–1890: A Social History* (Berkeley: University of California Press, 1979), 97–99; Ramon A. Gutierrez, *When Jesus Came, the Corn Mothers Went Away: Marriage, Sexuality, and Power in New Mexico, 1500–1846* (Stanford: Stanford University Press, 1991), 182; de la Teja, *San Antonio de Bexar,* 150–152.

30. Most families served only once as godparents. Of the 211 individuals reviewed, 148, or approximately 70 percent, were godparent to only one child. In these cases of single godparenthood, the child was usually the son or daughter of a brother or sister. The remaining 30 percent, or 63 individuals, were willing to accept godparenthood status for two or more children. Of those 63, only 16 families sponsored more than three children. St. Mary's Church, baptismal records, CAT.

31. Madsen, *Mexican Americans,* 19.

32. "Daily Reports, 1845, 1846," Reports of Gen. Zachary Taylor, Records of the Mexican American War, National Archives, Washington, D.C.

33. War Department, Reports of the Commissary Office, 1846, 1847, 1848, Department of the Army, National Archives, Washington, D. C.; Letters, Colonel Williamson to City of Matamoros, Caja 1847–1848, Seccion Presidencial/Independencia, Archivo de Matamoros, Casamata, Matamoros, Mexico.

34. Estate of Plácido Benavides, June 8, 1838, vol. 2, p. 43–46, Probate Records, VCCO.

35. Petition of Patricia de la Garza, May term, 1847, filed for record December 29, 1848, vol. 1, p. 527, VCCO.

36. Patricia de la Garza from R. Carlisle and Bridget Quinn, Mortgage, vol. 1, p. 32, September 23, 1838, Deed Records, VCCO; Fernando de León to William Dally, Lease, vol. 3, p. 131, February 16, 1847, and Fernando de León to Alva Fitzpatrick, January 13, 1847, vol. 3, p. 105, Deed Records, VCCO; Will of Patricia de la Garza, Probate Records, VCCO; Final Record of Guardian, vol. 1, p. 527, May 1847, Probate Records, VCCO.

37. Elizabeth A. Kuznesof, "History of the Family in Latin America: A Critique of Recent Work," *Latin American Research Review* 24, no. 2 (1989), 175–176; Douglas Monroy, " 'Our Children Get So Different Here': Film, Fashion, Popular Culture, and the

Process of Cultural Syncretization in Mexican Los Angeles, 1900–1935," *Aztlán* 19 (spring 1988–1990), 80; Carey McWilliams, *North from Mexico: The Spanish-Speaking People of the United States* (New York: Greenwood Press, 1970), 50; Ernest L. Schusky, *Variation in Kinship* (New York: Holt, Rinehart and Winston, 1974), 3; Madsen, *Mexican Americans*, 46.

38. Kuznesof, "History of the Family," 175–176; Madsen, *Mexican Americans*, 46.

39. R. A. García, *Rise of the Mexican American Middle Class*, 127.

40. Madsen, *Mexican Americans*, 19; Kuznesof, "History of the Family," 176–180.

41. Index to Deed Records, José María Escalera, Juan Nepomuceno Escalera, VCCO.

42. Fernando de León to Luz Escalera, 1848, Marriage records, St. Mary's Catholic Church, CAT; Index to Deed Records, Luz Escalera de León, Francisco Santiago de León, VCCO.

43. Candelaria FGR, de León family, Austin.

44. Candelaria FGR, Dosal family, Austin.

45. *Patricia de la Garza v. Robert Carlisle and Bridget Quinn*, Case No. 24, Fall Term 1849, settled Fall Term 1851, 25-A District Clerk's Miscellaneous Records, Civil Court Docket, VC/UH.

46. Candelaria FGR, Félix de León family, Austin.

47. Ibid.

48. Probate Records, Will of Patricio [sic] Garza de León, October 17, 1850, vol. 2, p. 591, VCCO.

49. Marti Lamar, "Choosing Partible Inheritance: Chilean Merchant Families, 1795–1825," *Journal of Social History* 28 (fall 1994): 125–126.

50. Candelaria FGR, Manchola, Dosal, and García families, Austin.

51. Will of Patricia de la Garza de León, VCCO.

52. An 1870 Map of Refugio County indicating Aldrete land holdings, GLO; Guadalupe de León to Cesario de la Garza, Marriage records, VCCO; letters in O'CVL-MLP.

53. Letters in O'CVL-MLP; Martín de León and Francisco de León to Francisco Santiago de León, Power of Attorney and Deed Records, October 1850, VCCO.

54. Gilbert G. González and Raúl Fernández, "Chicano History: Transcending Cultural Models," *Pacific Historical Review* 63, no. 4 (November 1994), 480–481. The Aldretes of Refugio had retained large quantities of land since José Miguel Aldrete, as a Mexican government official, had acquired far more than his original league and labor. The Aldretes remained powerful landowners in Refugio until the 1880s; see Huson, *Refugio*, 212–215.

55. *Aldrette [sic] et al. v. Franklin's Heirs*, Partition, Spring Term 1854, Case No. 77-209, Fee Book, 1858, Box II 24A, VC/UH; *Western v. De León* Case 16 (1838), VDC. León de León to Andrew Oliver, Deed, vol. 6, p. 395, May 24, 1856, Deed Records, VCCO; *Aldrete et al. v. Franklin Heirs*, Case 209, District Court of Victoria, August 17, 1859, Civil Minutes of the District Clerk, 4:579, VDC.

56. Antonio Domínguez Ortiz, *Ciclos y temas de la historia de España: clases privilegiadas en el Antiguo Régimen* (Madrid: Ediciones ISTMO, 1979), 133.

57. A. H. Phillips, as agent of F. de León, Assessment of Taxes, 1852, Box II 16B, VC/UH; Fernando de León to the Right Reverend John M. Odin, Lot 4, Block 111, Range 8, in vol. 5, p. 232, Deed Records, VCCO; A. H. Phillips as agent of Fernando de León, Victoria County Property Assessments, for 1853, Box II 16B, VC/UH; Patricio de León as agent of Ferdinand [sic] de León's Estate, Assessment of Taxes, 1855, Box II 16B, VC/UH.

58. Subscription receipt in O'CVL-MLP; history of St. Mary's Catholic Church, Linn, *Reminiscences*, 200-201.

59. Fernando de León, Index to Deed Records, 1845-1855, VCCO.

60. Fernando de León, Grantee, Index to Deed Records, 1845-1855, VCCO.

61. Patricio de León as agent of Ferdinand [sic] de León's Estate, Assessment of Taxes, 1852, 1853, 1855, Box II 16B, VC/UH. A handwritten note in the tax assessments book for 1853 lists a number of ranchers who had not reported a full count of their cattle. Among those on the list is Fernando de León, and all of the rest are Anglo names. On the back of the list is Fernando de León's explanation.

62. Linn, *Reminiscences*, 200-201; unnamed person, birth of a daughter, December 28, 1851, at Spring Creek, Baptismal Records, St. Mary's Catholic Church, CAT.

63. Candelaria FGR, Benavides, Escalera, Dosal, and de León families, Austin.

64. Ibid., Dosal family.

CHAPTER 8

1. Luz Escalera, and Francisco S'tgo de León, Index to Deed Records, VCCO; Luz Escalera de León, and Frank S. de León, Assessment of Taxes, Victoria County Property Assessments for 1853, 1855, Box II 16B, VC/UH.

2. Jeffrey M. Pilcher, *Que Vivan los Tamales!* (Albuquerque: University of New Mexico Press, 1998), 52.

3. Luz Escalera de León and Frank S. de León, Assessment of Taxes, Victoria County Property Assessments for 1853, 1855, Box II 16B, VC/UH.

4. *Antonio Pérez et al. v. Fernando de León and wife*, August 27, 1853, Case 194, Civil Clerk's Docket, Box 25A, District Clerk Miscellaneous Records, VC/UH; *Antonio Pérez et al. v. F. de Leon and Wife*, Case No. 194, in Fee Book, p. 255, August 1853, Box II 24A, VC/UH; *Antonio Pérez et al. v. Maria de Jesus Escalera or de León*, September 7, 1854, 25-A District Clerk Miscellaneous Records, Civil Court Docket, Case 239, VC/UH; *Antonio Pérez et al. v. Luz Escalera de León*, August 27, 1855, Box 25A District Clerk Miscellaneous Records, Civil Court Docket, 1850s, VC/UH, and same in Fee Book, p. 257, Case No. 304, August 27, 1855, Box II 24A, VC/UH.

5. Cases No. 194, No. 239, No. 343, and No. 348, *Jacoba Bueno et al. v. María de Jesús de León or Escalara [sic]*, November 10, 1855, October 20, 1856, 25-A, District Clerk Miscellaneous Records, Civil Court Docket, 1850s, VC/UH; *Jacoba Bueno et al. v. M. De Jesus Escalera or De Leon*, Fee Book, p. 389, Case 348, n.d., VC/UH. Although

no resolution is given on these two cases, the deed records for the sale of property by Luz Escalera de León indicate that she did keep the Bueno league, and no Bueno family is found in any of the other records in Victoria County.

6. Luz Escalera de León, Index to Deed Records, 1854, 1855, 1857, VCCO.

7. Index to Deed Records for Luz Escalera de León and relevant deeds in Deed Records, VCCO; Letter, Luz E. de León to Matiana Benavides, October 6, 1857, Mission Valley, O'CVL-MLP.

8. Silvestre de Leon, Assessments of Taxes for 1857, Box II 16B, VC/UH.

9. Candelaria FGR, José Félix de Leon, Austin.

10. Manuel García, Assessment of Taxes, 1852, Box II 16B, VC/UH; Carlos de la Garzer [sic], Victoria County Property Assessments, 1853, Box II 16B, VC/UH; Assessment of Taxes 1855, Box II 16B, VC/UH; Assessments of Taxes for 1857, Box II 16B, VC/UH; Assessments for 1877, Ledgers, VC/UH.

11. Estanisla Francisca, Baptismal Record, July 20, 1861, St. Mary's Catholic Church, CAT; Venabides [sic] heirs, Probate records, November 1850, Volume 1A, p. 268, VCCO.

12. Victoria County Property Assessments, 1853, 1855, 1857, 1877, Box II 16B, VC/UH.

13. Regalón Flores, Assessment of Taxes, 1852, Box II 16B, VC/UH.

14. Fernando de León to Pedro Answalda [sic], Deed, October 4, 1953, vol. 5, p. 472, Deed Records, VCCO; Pedro Ansualdo [sic] to Alta Gracia Cruiz [sic], February 22, 1855, Marriage Records, VCCO; Pedro Answalder [sic] Assessment of Taxes, 1855, Box II 16B, VC/UH; Baptism Records for Maria Paulita, 1856, Maruicio, 1859, Maria Theresa, 1861, Cecilia, 1866, Ana Maria, 1868, St. Mary's Catholic Church, 1840–1881, microfiche, CAT; Pedro Answalder [sic], Assessments of Victoria County for 1857, Box II 16B, VC/UH; Altagracia de Ansalda [sic], September 12, 1868, Mark and Brands Book, VCCO; Baptism records for Anna Maria Cabassos, July 13, 1869, St. Mary's Catholic Church, Victoria, Texas, microfiche, CAT; Pedro Answaldua [sic], County Tax Assessments Ledgers 1877, VC/UH.

15. "Beef Shipping at Indianola," *(Victoria) Texian Advocate,* Thursday, September 26, 1850, microfilm, CAH; Baptismal Records for María Isabel (1853), Maria Genoveva (1855), Juana María (1857), Rómulo (1859), Manuel Pedro (1861), and Anselma (1863), St. Mary's Catholic Church, Victoria, 1840–1881, CAT; George Miller to Prudencio Espetia, vol. 7, p. 308, July 13, 1858, Deed Records, VCCO; Inventory for 1863 (Census) by A & C Thurmond, Box 17A, VC/UH; Brand Records for Rómulo Espetia (1867) and Manuel Espetia (1870), Mark and Brands Book, VCCO; J. U. Brownson to Prudencio Aspetia [sic], vol. 15, p. 588, December 5, 1877, Deed Records, VCCO; County Tax Assessments, 1877, Ledgers, VC/UH.

16. Patricia Seed, *To Love, Honor, and Obey* (Austin: University of Texas Press, 1987), 7; Kenneth M. Stampp, *The Peculiar Institution: Slavery in the Ante-Bellum South* (New York: Holt, Rinehart and Winston, 1956).

17. Marriage records, Miguel Cano and Maria Elena Biereal [Villareal], Decem-

ber 2, 1854, VCCO; Plácido Cano, Baptism Records, December 15, 1856, St. Mary's Catholic Church, microfiche, CAT; Amado John, born January 19, 1858, baptized March 20, 1858, on the rancho of Guadalupe Ureste, Baptism Records, St. Mary's Catholic Church, microfiche, CAT; Fulgencio Licón, Baptism Records, 1860, St. Mary's Catholic Church, CAT; Isidora Licón, Baptism Records, 1863, St. Mary's Catholic Church, CAT; Peter Rodríguez, Baptism Records, 1862, St. Mary's Catholic Church, CAT.

18. Baptism Records, St. Mary's Catholic Church, CAT.

19. Kuznesof, "History of the Family," 175-176; Monroy, "Our Children," 80; McWilliams, *North from Mexico*, 50; Schusky, *Variation in Kinship*, 3; Madsen, *Mexican Americans*, 46.

20. Patricia de la Garza de León, Will, Index to Deed Records, VCCO; Mortgages in Index to Deed Records, Luz Escalera de León, VCCO.

21. Richard Griswold del Castillo, "Only for My Family," *Aztlán* 16, no. 1-2 (1985), 147; Kuznesof, "History of the Family," 168.

22. Family letters, Matiana Benavides to Patricio de León, in de León archives, VCL; Gerald E. Poyo and Gilberto M. Hinojosa, "Spanish Texas and Borderlands Historiography in Transition" *Journal of American History* (September 1988) 38-40; Nutini, *San Bernardino Contla*, 19; William A. Vega, Thomas Patterson, James Sallis, Philip Nader, Catherine Atkins, and Ian Abramson, "Cohesion and Adaptability in Mexican-American and Anglo Families," *Journal of Marriage and the Family* 48 (November 1986), 857, 865; Kuznesof, "History of the Family," 168, 175; Schusky, *Variation in Kinship*, 3.

23. Juan de Hoyos to Librada Benavides, 1860 Marriage Records, St. Mary's Catholic Church, CAT; Francisca Benavides, Baptismal Record, 1861, St. Mary's Catholic Church, CAT; Librada B. de Hoyos of Reynosa to J. M. Benavides and Ynes Villareal, November 4, 1871, vol. 13, p. 435, Deed Records, VCCO.

24. Grimes, *300 Years*, 252.

25. Ibid., 252-258.

26. Confederate Records, Santiago, Patricio and Silvestre de León, Trinidad and Rafael Aldrete, Santos Benavides, and de la Garzas, in Adjutant General's Record Group, TSA.

27. Charles D. Spurlin, ed., *West of the Mississippi with Waller's 13th Texas Cavalry Battalion* (Hillsboro: Hill Junior College Press, 1971), 69; Grimes, *300 Years*, 260.

28. Marriage and baptismal records for Crisóforo Lozano and Olivia de León Lozano, St. Mary's Catholic Church, CAT; Candelaria, "Spanish-surnamed Citizens of Victoria, 1860 Census," May 2000.

29. Grimes, *300 Years*, 264.

30. Ibid., 269.

31. VDC, August Term 1862, Box II 24A, Criminal Docket, VC/UH.

32. VDC, August Term 1862, August Term 1863, August Term 1864, Box II 24A, Criminal Docket, 1860s, VC/UH.

33. Letter from Andrew Oliver to Sil de Leon, 1867, in O'CVL-MLP.

34. *State v. Silvestre de León, James W. Allen, A. Acheson, R. Hanna, N. D. J. Hatfield, C. L. Thurmond, C. O. Weller,* for playing pool, Box II 30B, Victoria County District Clerk Case Papers, VC/UH.

35. Assessments of Victoria County for 1857 by W. L. Harrison, Box II 16B, VC/UH; Silvestre de León to Louis Jecker, vol. 7, p. 398, December 1, 1858, Deed Records, VCCO; Sil de León and A. Oliver, July 2, 1859, Mark and Brands Book, VCCO; Joseph and Andreas Nonnemacher to A. Oliver and Silvt [sic] de León, vol. 8, p. 43, December 2, 1859, Deed Records, VCCO; Francisco de León, by attorney Rafael Aldrete to Silvestre de León, Deed, October 15, 1860, vol. 8, p. 322, Deed Records, VCCO; Confederate Records, Adjutant General's Record Group, Lorenzo de Zavala State Library, Archives Division, Austin; Inventory for 1863 (Census) by A. and C. Thurmond, Box 17A, VC/UH; William J. Neely and Co., Account Book, Box 17A, VC/UH; Silvestre de León to Luz Escalera de León and Miss Matiana Benavides, Mortgage, April 26, 1867, vol. 10, p. 89, Deed Records, VCCO; Probate Records for Silvestre de Leon, May 3, 1872, vol. 3, p. 342, VCCO; Letter from Sil de León to Cousin Señora Doña Matianita Benavides, October 23, 1867, in O'CVL-MLP; Bill of Sale, Silvestre de León to Frank S. de León, March 11, 1868, vol. 10, p. 128, VCCO; Probate Records, April 2, 1872, Ledger for 1870–1873, VC/UH.

36. Randolph B. Campbell, *Grassroots Reconstruction in Texas, 1865–1880* (Baton Rouge: Louisiana State University Press, 1997), 11–14.

37. Grimes, *300 Years,* 270–278.

38. *State v. Alcide Willemen,* January 3, 1871, Box II 30B, VC/UH; *State v. Samuel de León,* September 17, 1871, Box II 30B, Victoria County District Clerk Case Papers, VC/UH.

39. *State of Texas v. John D. Sneigh [sic, Sneigr] and William Billings,* June 6, 1872, VC/UH.

40. Campbell, *Grassroots Reconstruction,* 18.

41. *State v. John D. Sneigr and William Billings,* Case No. 1119, June 10, 1872, VC/UH.

42. Ibid.

43. *State v. Henry Davidson and Ben Hawkins,* January 2, 1874, VC/UH; Deputation of Patricio de León, November 13, 1886, Bonds Ledger 1880, VC/UH.

44. Francisco Santiago ("Frank") de León, St. Mary's Church Records, 1860–1880, CAT; Jury Lists, 1872, 1874, 1878, VC/UH.

45. *Garza and Ureste, Plaintiffs, v. Jas. C. Scott, Defendant,* Judgment, September 2, 1860, Rendered February 27, 1866, vol. 10, p. 32, VC/UH; *State v. W. A. Welch, Wm. Wall, Jesse Davidson, and John Keefe,* Case No. 1627, July 1876, VC/UH; *State v. Jackson Chambers,* January 9, 1874, VC/UH.

46. *State v. Florencio Ureste,* April 1, 1873, VC/UH; *State v. Florencio Urista [sic],* Case No. 1262, 1273, Theft of a colt, Fee book 1858, Box II 24A, VC/UH; *State v. Florencio Urista [sic],* January 9, 1874, Aggravated assault, VC/UH; *State v. Florencia Urista [sic],* July 1874, Case No. 1359, Fee Box 1858, Box II 24A, VC/UH.

47. *State v. Florencio Ureste*, April 1, 1873; *State v. Florencio Ureste*, September 1873, Court cases, VC/UH; Case No. 1722, *State v. Juan Moya and Ynocencio [sic] Ureste*, November 11, 1876, VC/UH; Guadaloupe Uriste [sic] to S. Goldman and L. Goldman, Deed, March 15, 1855, vol. 6, p. 167 VC/UH; Guadalupe Uresta [sic] to Francisca García Uresta, Deed, November 22, 1870 (grants to his wife 442 8/10 acres in consideration of the love and affection which I have for my wife), vol. 11, p. 563; *State v. Inocencio Ureste*, July 26, 1883, 25A, District Clerk Miscellaneous Records, VC/UH.

48. Corporation of Victoria to Gaudalupe Ureste [sic], Deed, August 23, 1850, Farm Lot 5, vol. 4, p. 225, Deed Records, VCCO; Assessment of Victoria County 1857 by W. L. Harrison, Box II 16B, VC/UH; Baptism records for Inocencio Ureste, February 27, 1854, and Romualdo Ureste, May 3, 1858, St. Mary's Catholic Church, microfiche, CAT; Inventory of Property assessed for taxes for 1878 by F. R. Pridham, Victoria County assessor, Box II 6, VC/UH; F. Uresti [sic], agent of Francisca G. Ureste to A. G. Hugo of De Witt County, Bill of sale, August 9, 1879, for cattle, $1500, vol. 14, p. 364, VC/UH; Clerk Miscellaneous Records, Juror's Time Book, May Term 1883, Box 25A, VC/UH.

49. Marshall W. Fishwick, "The Cowboy: America's Contribution to the World's Mythology," *Western Folklore* 11 (April 1952): 78; Carlos A. Mayo, "Landed but Not Powerful: The Colonial Estancieros of Buenos Aires (1750–1810)," *Historical American History Review* 71, no. 4 (November 1991): 779; Slatta, *Cowboys*, p. 25; Jerome O. Steffen, *Comparative Frontiers: A Proposal for Studying the American West* (Norman: University of Oklahoma Press, 1980), 55.

50. Huson, *Refugio*, 212–218, 238.

51. Steffen, *Comparative Frontiers*, 57, 69; Edward Everett Dale, *The Range Cattle Industry: Ranching on the Great Plains from 1865 to 1925* (Norman: University of Oklahoma Press, 1930, reprint 1960), 5–6; Sandra L. Myres, "The Ranching Frontier: Spanish Institutional Backgrounds of the Plains Cattle Industry," in *Essays on the American West*, ed. Sandra L. Myres, Blaine T. Williams, Robert Williamson, and Roy A. Billington (Austin: University of Texas at Arlington, 1969), 22; Mody C. Boatright, "The American Myth Rides the Range: Owen Wister's Man on Horseback." *Southwestern Review* 36 (summer 1951): 163.

52. Baptismal records, Plácido son of Miguel and Elena Oriol [sic], Manuel Cano and Matilda Cano as godparents again, December 15, 1856, St. Mary's Catholic Church, CAT; Porphiria de Jesús daughter of Miguel Cano and Ellena [sic] Biareal [sic], December 12, 1865, godparents Francisco S. de León and Mathilda de León, Victoria, CAT; Deed Records, F. M. Moody and Mary J. to Phillip [sic] and Matilda Cano, one town lot 4, Bl. 62, R. 5 for $40 in Assessments of Victoria County, 1857, Box II 16B, VC/UH; Alcide Willemen, to Manuel Cano, August 14, 1866, vol. 1, p. 201, Deed Records, VCCO; Mark and Brands Book, Manuel Carno[sic] April 12, 1867, and May 20, 1874, VCCO; County Tax Assessments, Manuel Cano, 1877, Ledgers, VC/UH, and Inventory of Property Assessed for Taxes for 1878, Manuel Cano, VC/UH.

53. Baptismal Records for María Isabel (1853), Maria Genoveva (1855), Juana María (1857), Rómulo (1859), Manuel Pedro (1861), and Anselma (1863), St. Mary's Catholic Church, 1840–1881, microfiche, CAT; George Miller to Prudencio Espetia, July 13, 1858, vol. 7, p. 308, Deed Records, VCCO; Inventory for 1863 (Census) by A. and C. Thurmond, Box 17A, VC/UH; Brand Records for Rómulo Espetia (1867) and Manuel Espetia (1870), Mark and Brands Book, VCCO; J. U. Brownson to Prudencio Aspetia [sic], December 5, 1877, vol. 15, p. 588, Deed Records, VCCO; County Tax Assessments, 1877, Ledgers, VC/UH.

54. Frank S. de León to M. A. Oliver, Bill of Sale, March 21, 1876, vol. 14, p. 14, Deed Records, VCCO.

55. A. H. Phillips as agent of Francisco S. de León, Victoria County Property Assessments, 1853, Box II 16B, VC/UH; A. Oliver as agent for Frank S. de León, Assessments of Victoria County, 1857, by W. L. Harrison, Box II 16B, VC/UH; Inventory for 1863 (Census) by A. and C. Thurmond, Box 17A, VC/UH; County Tax Assessment Ledgers 1877, VC/UH; Inventory of Property Assessed for Taxes for 1878 by F. R. Pridham, Box II 6, VC/UH; Court Case of *Frank S. de León v. Leonidas Salas*, Box 36A, District Clerk Depositions, July 24, 1889, Miscellaneous Papers, Affidavit Information, Case No. 1214, VC/UH.

Bibliography

ARCHIVAL SOURCES

Archivo de Matamoros, Casamata, Matamoros, Mexico
Archivo General de la Nación (AGN), Mexico City
    Minutes of the La Bahía Ayuntamiento, 1821–1834, Sección História, vol. 320
    Trial Records for General José Urrea, Sección Guerra y Marina
Bexar County Courthouse (BCC), San Antonio, Texas
    Spanish Archives (SP) for San Antonio de Béxar
Candelaria, Gloria, Genealogical Records (Candelaria), Austin, Family Group Records (FGR) prepared from Victoria County census records by Gloria Candelaria, Victoria Hispanic Genealogical and Historical Society of Texas, Victoria
Catholic Archives of Texas (CAT), Austin
    Bishop Odin, Correspondence
Center for American History (CAH), University of Texas at Austin
    Austin Papers
    Bexar Archives (BA)
    Blake Collection
    Eberstadt Collection
    Papers of the Medical History of Texas
    Thomas Jefferson Rusk Papers
J. P. Bryan Collection, Houston, Texas
    Spanish Collection Materials
Lorenzo de Zavala State Library, Archives Division, Austin
    A. J. Houston Collection
    Confederate Records in Adjutant General's Record Groups
    Records of the Legislature
    T. J. Rusk Collection
National Archives, Washington, D.C.
    Records, Mexican American War, Reports of the Commissary Office
New Orleans Public Library, New Orleans, La. (NO), Archives Division
    St. Landry Parish Clerk of Court Conveyances
    Southwest Louisiana Church and Civil Records, 1831–1840.

Saltillo Municipal Archives (SM), Saltillo, Coahuila, Mexico
    Catalogo del Fondo Presidencial
Texas General Land Office (GLO), Archives and Records Division, Austin
    De León Colony Papers (DLC)
    Empresario Contracts
    Maps of South Texas Counties
    Record of Translations
    Republic and State Land Grants
    Surveying Division
Texas State Archives (TSA), Austin
    Rusk Papers
Victoria, City Secretary's Office
Victoria College/University of Houston (VC/UH) at Victoria College, Library Archives, Victoria
    Assessment of Taxes
    Court Records
    General Files
Victoria County Clerk's Office, Victoria (VCCO)
    Brand Records
    Deed Records
    Index to Deed Records
    Marriage and Death Records
    Probate Records
Victoria District Court (VDC), District Clerk's Office, Victoria County
Victoria County Public Library, O'Connor Room, Victoria (O'CVL) Martín de León Papers (MLP)
Victoria Hispanic Genealogical and Historical Society of Texas Archives

SECONDARY SOURCES

Alamán, Lucas. *Historia de Méjico*. Vol. 5. Mexico City: Editorial Jus, 1942.

Allan, Mrs. T. C., comp., and Mrs. Thomas O'Connor, contributor. "Reminiscences of Mrs. Annie Fagan Teal," *Southwestern Historical Quarterly* (April 1931).

Almaráz, Félix. *Tragic Cavalier: Manuel Salcedo of Texas, 1808–1813.* Austin: University of Texas Press, 1971.

Almonte, Juan Nepomuceno. *Como Mexico perdió Texas.* Mexico City: Talleres de Impresión Instituto Nacional de Antropología e Historia, 1987.

———. *Informe secreto sobre la presente situación de Texas, 1834,* Mexico City: Instituto Nacional de Antropología e Historia, 1987.

———. "Statistical Report on Texas." Trans. Carlos E. Castañeda. *Southwestern Historical Quarterly* 28 (January 1925): 177–222.

Alonso, Armando C. *Tejano Legacy: Rancheros and Settlers in South Texas, 1734–1900.* Albuquerque: University of New Mexico Press, 1998.

Anna, Timothy E. *The Fall of the Royal Government in Mexico City.* Lincoln: University of Nebraska Press, 1978.

Ashford, Gerald. *Spanish Texas: Yesterday and Today.* Austin: Jenkins Publishing, 1971.

Auerbach, Jerold S. *Justice Without Law?* New York: Oxford University Press, 1983.

August, Ray. "Cowboys v. Rancheros: The Origins of Western American Livestock Law." *Southwestern Historical Quarterly* 96 (April 1993): 457–490.

Barker, Eugene C. *The Life of Stephen F. Austin, Founder of Texas 1793–1836: A Chapter in the Westward Movement of the Anglo-American People.* Austin: University of Texas Press, 1985.

Barrera, Manuel. *Then the Gringos Came: The Story of Martín de León and the Texas Revolution.* Laredo, Tex.: Barrera Publications, 1992.

Benson, Nettie Lee. "Bishop Marín de Porras and Texas." *Southwestern Historical Quarterly* 51 (July 1947): 16–40.

———. "The Provincial Deputation." In *Mexico: Harbinger of Provincial Autonomy, Independence, and Federalism.* Austin: University of Texas Press, 1992.

———. "Texas as Viewed from Mexico." *Southwestern Historical Quarterly* 90 (January 1987): 219–291.

Berger, Max. "Education in Texas During the Spanish and Mexican Periods." *Southwestern Historical Quarterly* 51 (July 1947): 41–53.

Berlandier, Jean Louis. *Journey to Mexico during the Years 1826–1834.* Trans. Sheila M. Ohlendorf, Josette M. Bigelow, and Mary M. Standifer. Austin: Texas State Historical Association and Center for Studies in Texas History, 1980.

Bishko, C. J. "The Peninsular Background of Latin American Cattle Ranching." *Hispanic American Historical Review* 32 (November 1952): 491–575.

Boatright, Mody C. "The American Myth Rides the Range: Owen Wister's Man on Horseback." *Southwestern Review* 36 (summer 1951): 157–163.

Bolton, Herbert Eugene. *Texas in the Middle Eighteenth Century: Studies in Spanish Colonial History and Administration.* Berkeley: University of California, 1915. Reprint, Austin: University of Texas Press, 1970.

Brading, David A. "Government and Elite in Late Colonial Mexico." *Hispanic American Historical Review* 53 (August 1973): 389–414.

———. *Miners and Merchants in Bourbon Mexico, 1763–1810.* Cambridge: Cambridge University Press, 1971.

Brown, Henry F. *Baptism Through the Centuries.* Mountain View, Calif.: Pacific Press Publishing Association, 1965.

Brown, Judith E. *The Science of Human Nutrition.* New York: Harcourt Brace Jovanovich, 1990.

Brown, Linda Keller, and Kay Mussell, eds. *Ethnic and Regional Foodways in the U.S.: The Performance of Group Identity.* Knoxville: University of Tennessee Press, 1984.

Brunner, Emil. *The Christian Doctrine of God.* Trans. Olive Wyon. Philadelphia: Westminster Press, 1950–1979.

Callcott, Wilfrid H. *Santa Anna: The Story of an Enigma Who Once Was Mexico.* Hamden, Conn.: Archon Book, 1964.

Calvert, Robert A., and Arnoldo de León. *The History of Texas,* Wheeling, Ill.: Harlan Davidson, 1996.

Campbell, Randolph B. *Grassroots Reconstruction in Texas, 1865-1880.* Baton Rouge: Louisiana State University Press, 1997.

Cantrell, Greg. *Stephen F. Austin: Empresario of Texas,* New Haven: Yale University Press, 1999.

Carse, Robert. *The Age of Piracy.* New York: Rinehart and Co., 1957.

Castañeda, Carlos E., ed. *The Mexican Side of the Texan Revolution [1836] by the Chief Mexican Participants.* Washington, D.C.: Documentary Publications, 1971.

———. *Our Catholic Heritage in Texas, 1519-1936.* Vol. 3, *The Mission Era: The Missions at Work, 1731-1761.* Austin: Von Boeckmann-Jones, 1938.

———. *Our Catholic Heritage in Texas, 1519-1936.* Vol. 5, *The Mission Era: The End of the Spanish Regime 1780-1810.* Austin: Von Boeckmann-Jones, 1942.

———. *Our Catholic Heritage in Texas, 1519-1936.* Vol. 6, *The Transition Period: The Fight for Freedom, 1810-1836* (Austin: Von Boeckmann-Jones, 1950).

———. *Our Catholic Heritage in Texas, 1519-1936.* Vol. 7, *The Church in Texas since Independence, 1836-1950.* Austin: Von Boeckmann-Jones, 1958.

Chevalier, Francois. *Land and Society in Colonial Mexico: The Great Hacienda.* Trans. Alvin Eustis and ed. Lesley Bird Simpson. Berkeley: University of California Press, 1963.

Chipman, Donald E. *Spanish Texas, 1519-1821.* Austin: University of Texas Press, 1992.

Cisneros, José. *Riders across the Centuries: Horsemen of the Spanish Borderlands.* El Paso: Texas Western Press, 1984.

Colección de las leyes y decretos expedidos por el Congreso General de los Estados-Unidos Mejicanos en los años de 1829 y 1830. Mexico City: Imprenta de Galván, 1831.

Coopwood, Julia. "History of the La Bahia Settlements during the Administration of Captain Manuel Ramírez de la Piscina, 1750-1767." Master's thesis, University of Texas at Austin, 1938.

Costeloe, Michael P. *La Primera República Federal de México (1824-1835): un estudio de los partidos políticos en el México independiente.* Trans. Manuel Fernández Gasalla. Mexico City: Fondo de Cultura Económica, 1975.

Cutter, Charles R. *The Legal Culture of Northern New Spain, 1700-1810.* Albuquerque: University of New Mexico Press, 1995.

Dale, Edward Everett. *The Range Cattle Industry: Ranching on the Great Plains from 1865 to 1925.* Norman: University of Oklahoma Press, 1930, and reprint, 1960.

de la Teja, Jesús. "The Colonization of Texas: A Tejano Perspective." In *Myths, Misdeeds, and Misunderstandings: The Roots of Conflict in U.S.-Mexican Relations.* Ed. Jaime E. Rodríquez O. and Kathryn Vincent. Wilmington, Del.: Scholarly Resources, 1997.

————. "Discovering the Tejano Community in Early Texas." *Journal of the Early Republic* 18, no. 1 (spring 1998): 73–98.

————. "Land and Society in 18th Century San Antonio de Béxar, A Community of New Spain's Northern Frontier." Ph.D. diss. University of Texas at Austin, 1988.

————. "Rebellion on the Frontier." In *Tejano Journey, 1770–1850.* Ed. Gerald E. Poyo. Austin: University of Texas Press, 1996.

————. *San Antonio de Béxar: A Community on New Spain's Northern Frontier.* Albuquerque: University of New Mexico, 1995.

————. "Sobrevivencia económica en la frontera de Texas: los ranchos ganaderos del siglo XVIII en San Antonio de Béxar." *Historia Mexicana* 42 (April–June 1993): 837–865.

————. "St. James at the Fair." *The Americas* 57 (January 2001): 408–409.

de León, Arnoldo. *The Tejano Community, 1836–1900.* Albuquerque: University of New Mexico Press, 1982.

————. *They Called Them Greasers: Anglo Attitudes toward Mexicans in Texas, 1821–1900.* Austin: University of Texas Press, 1983.

Delgado, Pedro. *Mexican Account of the Battle of San Jacinto.* Deepwater, Tex.: W. C. Day, 1919.

DiLeonardo, Micaela. *The Varieties of Ethnic Experience: Kinship, Class, and Gender among California Italian Americans.* Ithica: Cornell University Press, 1984.

Domínguez Ortiz, Antonio. *Ciclos y temas de la historia de España: clases privilegiadas en el Antiguo Régimen.* Madrid: Ediciones ISTMO, 1979.

Donovan, K. W. *History of Pirates and Pirating.* Key West, Fla.: Conch Republic Printing Press, 1972.

Doolittle, William E. "Las Marismas to Pánuco to Texas: The Transfer of Open Range Cattle Ranching from Iberia through Northeastern Mexico." *Yearbook of the Conference of Latin Americanist Geographers* 13 (1987): 3–11.

Dwyer, Thomas A. "From Mustangs to Mules." In *Mustangs and Cowhorses.* Ed. J. Frank Dobie, Mody Boatright, and Harry Ransom, 48–49. Dallas: Southern Methodist University; Austin: Publications of the Texas Folklore Society, 1940.

Ebright, Malcolm. "Introduction: Spanish and Mexican Land Grants and the Law." *Journal of the West* 27 (July 1988): 3–11.

Eby, Frederick. *The Development of Education in Texas.* New York: Macmillan, 1925.

Elizondo Guerra, Dora. "Whose Water Is This Anyway, and Keep Your Plow Out of My Cornfield: Men, Women, and Culture in Spanish Colonial Texas," 173–174. *South Texas Studies* (2000). Victoria Community College, Victoria, Tex.

Exley, Jo Ella Powell, ed. *Texas Tears and Texas Sunshine.* College Station: Texas A&M University Press, 1985.

Faulk, Odie B. *The Last Years of Spanish Texas, 1778–1821.* The Hague: Mouton and Co., 1964.

————. "The Presidio: Fortress or Farce?" *New Spain's Far Northern Frontier: Essays on Spain in the American West, 1540–1821.* Ed. David J. Weber. Dallas: Southern Methodist University Press, 1979.

Fehrenbach, T. R. *Lone Star: A History of Texas and the Texans.* New York: Collier Books, 1968.

Fishwick, Marshall W. "The Cowboy: America's Contribution to the World's Mythology." *Western Folklore* 11 (April 1952): 77–92.

Flores, Mena L. *El General Don Antonio Lopez de Santa Anna.* Mexico City: n.p., 1950.

Forrest, Suzanne. *The Preservation of the Village: New Mexico's Hispanics and the New Deal.* Albuquerque: University of New Mexico Press, 1989.

Gammel, H. P. N. "Proceedings of the Convention." *Laws of Texas, 1822–1897.* Vol. 1. Austin: Gammel Book Co., 1898.

García, Genaro, ed. *Documentos inéditos o muy raros para la historia de México.* Mexico City: Editorial Porrúa, 1975.

Garcia, Richard A. *Rise of the Mexican American Middle Class: San Antonio, 1929–1941.* College Station: Texas A&M University Press, 1991.

Garrett, Kathryn. "The First Constitution of Texas, April 17, 1813." *Southwestern Historical Quarterly* 40 (April 1937): 290–308.

———. *Green Flag over Texas: A Story of the Last Years of Spain in Texas.* Austin: Jenkins Publishing; New York: Pemberton Press, 1969.

Garza, Israel Cavazos. *El General Alonso de León, Descubridor de Texas.* Monterrey, Mexico: Real Ayuntamiento de Monterrey, 1993.

George, Eugene. *Historic Architecture of Texas: The Falcón Reservoir.* Austin: Historical Commission and Texas Historical Foundation, 1975.

González, Gilbert G., and Raúl Fernández. "Chicano History: Transcending Cultural Models." *Pacific Historical Review* 63, no. 4 (November 1994): 469–497.

Good, Marilyn J., ed., and Texas Surveyors Association, Historical Committee, comp. *Three Dollars per Mile: Accounts of Early Surveying in Texas.* Burnet, Tex.: Eakin Press, 1981.

Graham, Joe S. "El Rancho in South Texas." *Bulletin.* Denton: University of North Texas, 1994.

Griffith, James S., and Celestino Fernández. "Mexican Horse Races and Cultural Values: The Case of Los Corridos del Merino." *Western Folklore* 47, no. 2 (April 1988): 134.

Grimes, Roy, ed. *300 Years in Victoria County.* Victoria, Tex.: Victoria Advocate Publishing Co., 1968. Reprint, Austin: Nortex Press, 1985.

Griswold del Castillo, Richard. *The Los Angeles Barrio, 1850–1890: A Social History.* Berkeley: University of California Press, 1979.

———. "Only for My Family." *Aztlán* 16, no. 1–2 (1985): 145–176.

Gutiérrez, Ramón A. *When Jesus Came the Corn Mother Went Away: Marriage, Sexuality, and Power in New Mexico, 1500–1846.* Stanford: Stanford University Press, 1991.

Haggard, H. Villasana. "Epidemic Cholera in Texas, 1833–1834." *Southwestern Historical Quarterly* 40 (July 1936–April 1937): 216–231.

Haines, Francis. *Horses in America.* New York: Thomas Y. Crowell, 1971.

Hale, Charles A. *Mexican Liberalism in the Age of Mora, 1821–1853.* New Haven and London: Yale University Press, 1968.

Hammett, Arthur B. J. *The Empresario: Don Martín de León (The Richest Man in Texas).* Kerrville, Tex.: Braswell Printing, 1971.

Hardin, Stephen L. "Efficient in the Cause." In *Tejano Journey 1770–1850.* Ed. Gerald E. Poyo. Austin: University of Texas Press, 1996.

———. *Texian Iliad: A Military History of the Texas Revolution, 1835–1836.* Austin: University of Texas Press, 1994.

Hatcher, Mattie Austin. "The Opening of Texas to Foreign Settlement, 1801–1821, Austin, Texas." *University of Texas Bulletin* no. 2714 (April 8, 1927).

Henderson, Mary Virginia. "Minor Empresario Contracts for the Colonization of Texas, 1825–1834." *Southwestern Historical Quarterly* 31 (April 1928): 295–324, and 32 (July 1928): 1–28.

Heusinger, Edward Werner. *Early Explorations and Mission Establishments in Texas.* San Antonio, Tex.: Naylor, 1936.

Henson, Margaret Swett. *Juan Davis Bradburn: A Reappraisal of the Mexican Commander of Anáhuac.* College Station: Texas A&M University Press, 1982.

———. *Samuel May Williams, Early Texas Entrepreneur.* College Station: Texas A&M University Press, 1976.

Hill, Lawrence F. *José de Escandón and the Founding of the Nuevo Santander.* Columbus: Ohio State University Press, 1926.

Hinojosa, Gilberto M. *A Borderlands Town in Transition: Laredo, 1755–1870.* College Station: Texas A&M University Press, 1983.

Hogan, William Ransom. *The Texas Republic: A Social and Economic History.* Austin: University of Texas Press, 1986.

Horgan, Paul. *Great River: The Rio Grande in North American History.* New York: Rinehart, 1954. Reprint, Austin: Texas Monthly Press, 1984.

Humphrey, David C. *Austin: An Illustrated History.* Northridge, Calif.: Windsor Public, 1985.

———. "Austin, Texas." In *The New Handbook of Texas.* Austin: Texas State Historical Association, 1996.

Huson, Hobart. *Captain Phillip Dimitt's Commandancy of Goliad, 1835–1836.* Austin: Von Boeckman-Jones, 1974.

———. *Refugio, A Comprehensive History of Refugio County: From Aboriginal Times to 1953.* 2 vols. Woodsboro, Tex.: Rooke Foundation, 1953–1955.

Hutchinson, Cecil Alan. "Valentín Gomez Farías, a Biographical Study." Ph.D. diss., University of Texas at Austin, 1948.

Jackson, Jack. *Los Mesteños: Spanish Ranching in Texas, 1721–1821.* College Station: Texas A&M University Press, 1986.

Janicek, Ricki S. "The Development of Early Mexican Land Policy: Coahuila and Texas, 1810–1825." Ph.D. diss., Tulane University, 1985.

Jarratt, Rie. "Gutiérrez de Lara, Mexican Texan: The Story of a Creole Hero." In *The Mexican Experience in Texas*. Ed. Carlos E. Cortés. New York: Arno Press, 1976.

Jenkins, John H., ed. *The Papers of the Texas Revolution, 1835-1836*. Austin: Presidial Press, 1973.

John, Elizabeth A. H. *Storms Brewed in Other Men's Worlds: The Confrontation of Indians, Spain, and France in the Southwest 1540-1795*. College Station: Texas A&M University Press, 1975.

Jones, Oakah L. Jr. *Los Paisanos: Spanish Settlers on the Northern Frontier of New Spain*. Norman: University of Oklahoma Press, 1979.

———. *Santa Anna*. New York: Twayne Publishers, 1968.

Karraker, Cyrus H. *Piracy Was a Business*. Rindge, N.H.: Richard R. Smith, Publisher, 1953.

Keefe, Susan E. "Ethnic Identity: The Domain of Perceptions of and Attachment to Ethnic Groups and Cultures." *Human Organization* 51 (spring 1992): 35-43.

Kelly, Edith Louise, and Mattie Austin Hatcher, eds. "Tadeo Ortiz de Ayala and the Colonization of Texas, 1822-1833." *Southwestern Historical Quarterly* 32 (July 1928): 74-86, and (April 1929): 311-343.

Kuznesof, Elizabeth Anne. "The History of the Family in Latin America: A Critique of Recent Work." *Latin American Research Review* 24, no. 2 (1989): 168-186.

Lack, Paul D. *The Texas Revolutionary Experience: A Political and Social History, 1835-1836*. College Station: Texas A&M University Press, 1992.

Lamar, Marti. "Choosing Partible Inheritance: Chilean Merchant Families, 1795-1825." *Journal of Social History* 28 (fall 1994): 125-145.

Langum, David J. *Law and Community on the Mexican California Frontier: Anglo-American Expatriates and the Clash of Legal Tradition, 1821-1846*. Norman: University of Oklahoma Press, 1987.

Lavrin, Asunción, and Edith Couturier. "Dowries and Wills: A View of Women's Socioeconomic Role in Colonial Guadalajara and Puebla, 1640-1790." *Hispanic American Historical Review* 59, no. 2 (May 1979): 280-304.

Leutenegger, Benedict. *The Zacatecan Missionaries in Texas, 1716-1834: Excerpts from the Libros de los Decretos of the Missionary College of Zacatecas, 1707-1828*. Austin: Texas Historical Survey Committee, 1973.

Levine, Lawrence W. *Black Culture and Black Consciousness*. New York: Oxford University Press, 1977.

Linn, John J. *Reminiscences of Fifty Years in Texas*. New York: D. and J. Sadlier and Co., 1883. Reprint, Austin: State House Press, 1986.

Lukes, Edward A. *De Witt Colony of Texas*. Austin: Jenkins Publishing, 1976.

McGrew, R. E. "The First Cholera Epidemic and Social History," *Bulletin of the History of Medicine* 34 (January-February 1960): 61-73.

McKnight, Joseph W. *The Spanish Elements in Modern Texas Law*. Dallas: J. W. McKnight, 1979.

———. "Stephen Austin's Legalistic Concerns." *Southwestern Historical Quarterly* 89 (January 1986): 239-268.

McLean, Malcolm D. "Nashville-on-the-Brazos." Vol. 11 of *Papers Concerning Robert-son's Colony in Texas (December 6, 1831–October 1833)*. Arlington: University of Texas at Arlington Press, 1980.

———. "Ranger Rendezvous." Vol. 10 of *Papers Concerning Robertson's Colony in Texas (December 6, 1831–October 1833)*. Arlington: University of Texas at Arlington Press, 1980.

———. "Tenoxtitlán, Dream Capital of Texas." *Southwestern Historical Quarterly* 70 (July 1966): 23–43.

———. "Those Eleven-League Grants." Vol. 7 of *Papers Concerning Robertson's Colony in Texas (December 6, 1831–October 1833)*. Arlington: University of Texas at Arlington Press, 1980.

McMillen, Nodé Quintellen. "Surveyor General: The Life and Times of José Maria Jesús Carbajal." Manuscript. Rosanky, Tex., 1990.

McWilliams, Carey. *North from Mexico: The Spanish-Speaking People of the United States*. New York: Greenwood Press, 1970.

Madsen, William. *Mexican-Americans of South Texas*. New York: Holt, Rinehart and Winston, 1964.

Mayo, Carlos A. "Landed but Not Powerful: The Colonial Estancieros of Buenos Aires (1750–1810)." *Historical American History Review* 71 (November 1991): 761–779.

Meyer, Michael C., and William L. Sherman. *The Course of Mexican History.* New York: Oxford University Press, 1983.

Miller, Thomas Lloyd. *The Public Lands of Texas 1579–1970*. Norman: University of Oklahoma Press, 1972.

Monday, Jane Clements, and Betty Bailey Colley. *Voices from the Wild Horse Desert: The Vaquero Families of the King and Kenedy Ranches*. Austin: University of Texas Press, 1997.

Monroy, Douglas. " 'Our Children Get So Different Here': Film, Fashion, Popular Culture, and the Process of Cultural Syncretization in Mexican Los Angeles, 1900–1935." *Aztlán* 19 (spring 1988–1990): 79–108.

Montemayor, E. A., Eric Beerman, and Winston De Ville. *Yo Sólo: The Battle Journal of Bernardo de Gálvez during the American Revolution*. New Orleans: Polyanthos, 1978.

Moorehead, Max L. *The Presidio: Bastion of the Spanish Borderlands*. Norman: University of Oklahoma Press, 1975.

Morfí, Fray Juan Agustín. *History of Texas, 1673–1779*. Trans. Carlos E. Castañeda. Albuquerque: Quivira Society, 1935.

Morton, Ohland. *Terán and Texas: A Chapter in Texas-Mexican Relations*. Austin: Texas State Historical Association, 1948.

Muir, Andrew Forest, ed. *Texas in 1837: An Anonymous Contemporary Narrative*. Austin: University of Texas Press, 1958.

Myres, Sandra L. *The Ranch in Spanish Texas, 1691–1800*. El Paso: Texas Western Press, 1969.

———. "The Ranching Frontier: Spanish Institutional Backgrounds of the Plains

Cattle Industry." In *Essays on the American West*. Ed. Sandra L. Myres, Blaine T. Williams, Robert Williamson, and Roy A. Billington. Austin: University of Texas at Arlington, 1969.

Nasatir, Abraham P. *Borderland in Retreat: From Spanish Louisiana to the Far Southwest*. Albuquerque: University of New Mexico Press, 1976.

Nixon, Patrick Ireland. *The Medical Story of Early Texas, 1528–1853*. Lancaster, Pa.: Mollie Bennett Lupe Memorial Fund, 1946.

Nutini, Hugo G. *San Bernardino Contla: Marriage and Family Structure in a Tlaxcalan Municipio*. Pittsburgh, Pa.: University of Pittsburgh Press, 1968.

Oberste, William H. *Texas Irish Empresarios and Their Colonies*, 2d ed. Austin: Von Boeckmann-Jones, 1973.

O'Connor, Kathryn Stoner. *The Presidio La Bahía del Espiritu Santo de Zuñiga, 1721 to 1846*. Austin: Von Boeckmann-Jones, 1966.

——— (Mrs. Thomas), contributor. "Reminiscences of Mrs. Annie Fagan Teal." Comp. Mrs. T. C. Allan. *Southern Historical Quarterly* 34 (April 1931): 321.

Osante, Patricia. *Orígenes del Nuevo Santander (1748–1772)*. Mexico City: Universidad Nacional Autónoma de México Instituto de Investigaciones Históricas; Ciudad Victoria: Universidad Nacional Autónoma de Tamaulipas, 1997.

Pilcher, Jeffrey M. *Que Vivan los Tamales!* Albuquerque: University of New Mexico Press, 1998.

Pollitzer, Rob. "Cholera Studies: History of the Disease." *Bulletin of the World Health Organization* 10 (1954): 421–461.

Poyo, Gerald E., and Gilberto M. Hinojosa. "Spanish Texas and Borderland Historiography in Transition." *Journal of American History* 75 (September 1988): 38–40.

Rabb, Mary Crownover. Untitled article. In *Texas Tears and Texas Sunshine*. Ed. Jo Ella Powell Exley. College Station: Texas A&M University Press, 1985.

Ramírez, Nora E. "The Vaquero and Ranching in the Southwestern United States, 1600–1970." Ph.D. diss., University of Indiana, 1978.

Ramos Arizpe, José Miguel. *Memoria que el Doctor D. Miguel Ramos de Arizpe, cura de Borbón y diputado en las presentes cortes generales y extraordinarias de España por la provincia de Coahuila, una de las cuatro internas del oriente en el Reino de México presenta a el augusto Congreso*. Guadalajara: Oficina de Don José Fruto Romero, 1813; reprint, trans. Nettie Lee Benson, Austin: University of Texas Press, 1950.

Rather, Ethel Ziveley. *De Witt's Colony*. Austin: University of Texas Press, 1905.

———. "De Witt's Colony." *Quarterly of the Texas State Historical Association* 8 (October 1904): 95–191.

Reichstein, Andreas V. *Rise of the Lone Star: The Making of Texas*. Trans. Jeanne R. Willson. College Station: Texas A&M University Press, 1989.

Ringrose, David. "Transportation and Economic Stagnation in Eighteenth-Century Castile." *Journal of Economic History* 28 (March 1968): 58–60.

Robertson, Brian. *Wild Horse Desert: The Heritage of South Texas*. Edinburg, Tex.: Hidalgo County Historical Museum, 1967.

Robinson, Willard B. "Colonial Ranch Architecture in the Spanish-Mexican Tradition." *Southwestern Historical Quarterly* 83 (October 1979): 123–150.

———. *Gone From Texas: Our Lost Architectural Heritage*. College Station, Tex.: Texas A&M University Press, 1981.

Robles, Vito Alessio. *Coahuila y Texas desde la consumación de la Independencia hasta el tratado de paz de Guadalupe Hidalgo*. 2 vols. Mexico City: Talleres Gráficos de la Nación, 1945–1946.

Rodríguez O., Jaime E. *The Emergence of Spanish America: Vicente Rocafuerte and Spanish Americanism 1808–1832*. Berkeley: University of California Press, 1975.

Rodríguez-Castellano, Juan, and Caridad Rodríguez-Castellano. *Historia de España: breve resumen*. New York: Oxford University Press, 1939.

Roell, Craig H. "Plácido Benavides." *The Handbook of Victoria County*. Austin: Texas State Historical Association, 1996.

Rogers, L. Randall. *Two Particular Friends of Stephen F. Austin*. Waco: Texian Press, 1990.

Rose, Victor M. *Some Historical Facts in Regard to the Settlement of Victoria, Texas: Its Progress and Present Status*. Laredo, Tex.: Daily Times Print, 1883. Reprinted as *Victor Rose's History of Victoria*. Ed. J. W. Petty Jr., Victoria, Tex.: Book Mart, 1961.

Rosenberg, Charles E. *The Cholera Years, the United States in 1832, 1849, 1866*. Chicago: University of Chicago Press, 1963.

Rouse, John E. *The Criollo: Spanish Cattle in the Americas*. Norman: University of Oklahoma Press, 1977.

Sánchez, José María. *Viaje a Texas en 1828–1829*. Mexico City: Colección de Papeles y Documentos Históricos Mexicanos, 1939.

Sands, Kathleen Mullen. *Charrería Mexicana: An Equestrian Folk Tradition*. Tucson: University of Arizona Press, 1993.

Santa Anna, Antonio López de. *The Eagle: The Autobiography of Santa Anna*. Ed. Ann Fears Crawford. Austin: Pemberton Press, 1967.

———. "Manifesto que de sus operaciones en la campaña de Tejas y su captura." In *The Mexican Side of the Texan Revolution [1836] by the Chief Mexican Participants*. Ed. Carlos E. Castañeda. Washington, D.C.: Documentary Publications, 1971.

Schusky, Ernest L. *Variation in Kinship*. New York: Holt, Rinehart and Winston, 1974.

Scott, Janelle. "Patricia de la Garza de León." Manuscript. 1982. Special Collections, Texas Women's University Library, Denton, Tex.

Seed, Patricia, *To Love, Honor and Obey*. Austin: University of Texas Press, 1987.

Slatta, Richard W., *Cowboys of the Americas*. New Haven: Yale University Press, 1990.

Smith, F. B., *The People's Health, 1830–1910*. London: Croom Helm, 1979.

Smithwick, Noah. *The Evolution of a State or Recollections of Old Texas Days*, comp. Nanna Smithwick Donaldson. Austin: University of Texas Press, 1983.

Solano, Francisco de. *Cedulario de tierras: compilación de legislación agraria colonial (1497–1820)*. Mexico City: Universidad Nacional Autónoma de México, 1984.

Spurlin, Charles D., ed. *West of the Mississippi with Waller's 13th Texas Cavalry Battalion*. Hillsboro: Hill Junior College Press, 1971.

Stampp, Kenneth M. *The Peculiar Institution: Slavery in the Ante-Bellum South.* New York: Holt, Rinehart and Winston, 1956.

Steffen, Jerome O. *Comparative Frontiers: A Proposal for Studying the American West.* Norman: University of Oklahoma Press, 1980.

Suárez Argüello, Clara Elena. *Camino real y carrera larga: la arriería en la Nueva España durante el siglo XVIII.* Mexico City: Centro de Investigaciones y Estudios Superiores en Antropología Social, 1996.

Syers, William Edward. *Texas: The Beginning, 1519-1834.* Waco, Tex.: Texian Press, 1978.

Taylor, William B. "Landed Society in New Spain: A View from the South." *Historical American History Review* 54 (August 1974): 387–413.

Thonhoff, Robert H. *El Fuerte del Cíbolo: Sentinel of the Béxar–La Bahía Ranches.* Austin: Eakin Press, 1992.

Thorpe, Madeline Gallego, and Mary Tate Engels. *Corazón Contento.* Lubbock: Texas Tech University Press, 1999.

Tijerina, Andrés. *Tejanos and Texas Under the Mexican Flag, 1821-1836.* College Station: Texas A&M University Press, 1994.

Timmons, Wilbert H. *Tadeo Ortiz: Mexican Colonizer and Reformer.* Southern Studies, monograph 43. El Paso: Texas Western Press, 1974.

Urrea, José. *Diario de las operaciones militares de la división que al mando del General José Urrea hizo en la campaña de Tejas.* Victoria de Durango, Mexico: n.p., 1834.

———. "Diary of the Military Operations of the Division Which under His Command Campaigned in Texas." In *The Mexican Side of the Texan Revolution* by the *Chief Mexican Participants.* Ed. Carlos E. Castañeda. Washington, D. C.: Documentary Publications, 1971.

Van Heynigen, W. E., and John R. Seal. *Cholera: The American Scientific Experience, 1847-1980.* Boulder, Colo.: Westview Press, 1983.

Vázquez, Josefina Zoraida. "Los Primeros Tropiezos." In *Historia General de México.* Vol. 3. Mexico City: El Colegio de México, 1976.

Vega, William A., Thomas Patterson, James Sallis, Philip Nader, Catherine Atkins, and Ian Abramson. "Cohesion and Adaptability in Mexican-American and Anglo Families." *Journal of Marriage and the Family* 48 (November 1986): 857–865.

Verrill, A. H. *The Real Story of the Pirate.* New York: D. Appleton and Co., 1923.

Villaseñor E., Roberto. *El Coronel Don José Escandón y la conquista del Nuevo Santander.* Mexico City: Boletín del Archivo General de la Nación, 1979.

Villoro, Luis. *El proceso ideológico de la revolución de independencia.* Mexico City: Universidad Nacional Autónoma de México, 1967.

Warren, Harris Gaylord. *The Sword Was Their Passport: A History of American Filibustering in the Mexican Revolution.* Baton Rouge: Louisiana State University Press, 1943.

Watkins, Sue, ed., and Texas Surveyors Association, Historical Committee, comp. *One League to Each Wind: Accounts of Early Surveying in Texas.* Austin: Von Boeckmann-Jones, 1964.

Weber, David J. *The Spanish Frontier in North America.* New Haven: Yale University Press, 1992.

———, ed. *Trouble in Texas, 1832: A Tejano Viewpoint from San Antonio.* Trans. Conchita Hassell Winn and David J. Weber. Austin: Wind River Press, 1983.

White, Gifford. *1830 Citizens of Texas.* Austin, Tex.: Eakin Press, 1983.

Williams, Brett. "Why Migrant Women Feed Their Husbands Tamales: Foodways as a Basis for a Revisionist View of Tejano Life." In *Ethnic and Regional Foodways in the U. S.: The Performance of Group Identity.* Ed. Linda Keller Brown and Kay Mussell. Knoxville: University of Tennessee Press, 1984.

Worcester, Don. *The Spanish Mustang: From the Plains of Andalusia to the Prairies of Texas.* El Paso: University of Texas Press, 1986.

Zermeño, Estella Martínez. "Mi Familia." In Papers of the 250th Anniversary of the Founding of La Bahía, *South Texas Studies* (spring 2000), Victoria, Tex.

Zorrilla, Juan Fidel. *Historia de Tamaulipas.* Ciudad Victoria, Tamaulipas: Dirección General de Educación y Cultura, 1987.

Index

The numbers in brackets following names refer to the genealogical charts at the beginning of each chapter.

Gray, Mabry (Mustang), 182–183
Grayson, Peter W., 176
Green, Thomas, 196, 231
Grey, Thomas, 93
Grymes, John R., 66
Guadalupe Victoria (Manuel Félix
  Fernandez), 78–79, 80
Guadalupe Victoria. *See* Victoria
Guajardo, Juan, 101; half league, 216
Guardia Victoriana, 158–159, 164, 182
Guerrero, Vicente, 99, 109
Gutierrez de Lara, José Antonio, 73
Gutiérrez de Lara, José Bernardo,
  58–59, 63–64

Hamilton, Isaac D., 163
Hannah Elizabeth, 154–155, 191
Hannibal and St. Joseph Railroad, 240
Hardy, Milton, 183, 191, 209
Hardy, Thomas, 193
Hatfield, N. D. J., 233
Hawkins, Littleberry, 111
Hays, Peter W., 194
Headrights, 175–176
Hemphill, John, 192
Henry, Patrick, 4
Hernández, José María, 84
Hernández, Juan José, 84
Hernández family, 168
Herrera, Simón, 44, 45, 46, 58, 60, 64
Hewetson, James, 98, 100, 101, 113
Hidalgo y Costilla, Miguel, 54–55, 58, 63
Horses, 47, 48–49, 53, 65, 92, 147, 149,
  154, 158, 191, 232
Houston, Sam, 137, 149, 154, 156, 158–
  159, 161, 163–164, 171, 173–174, 187,
  230
Houston *Morning Star* (newspaper), 180
Hugo, A. G., 239
Humboldt, Alexander von, 134
Hurd, W. A., 155
Hyne, Peter, 100

Indianola, 188, 222, 224, 231
Indians, 26, 50, 58, 87, 181–182, 187–189

Ingram, Thomas, 183
Irish, 73, 99, 100–101, 103, 106, 125, 148,
  158–159, 166, 192, 194, 200, 209
Iturbide, Agustín, 71, 73–74, 79–80, 117

Jackson, Andrew, 66, 137, 176
Jackson, Thomas, 176
*Jacoba Bueno et al. v. M. De Jesús Escalera
  or de León*, 218–219
January, James P. B., 231
Jeff Davis Home Guard, 230
Jefferson, Thomas, 41, 44, 45
Johnson, Charles, 219
Johnson, Frank, 156
Johnson, Moses, 226
Jones, Fielding, 197
Jones, Levi, 176

Karankawa (tribe), 13, 114, 135, 145, 171,
  194
Kerr, James, 87, 88–91, 94, 113, 115,
  133–135, 146–147
Kerr, Peter, 154–156
Killpatrick (or Kirkpatrick), Eleazar, 197
King, Amon, 158–159, 161
King, Ches, 232
King, George, 178
Kirkpatrick. *See* Killpatrick (or Kirk-
  patrick), Eleazar

La Bahía, 12, 23, 29, 32, 33, 44, 47, 49,
  60, 66–68, 71–72, 81–82, 84, 91, 93,
  95, 98–99, 101, 106–107, 109, 113, 145,
  173. *See also* Goliad; Nuestra Señora
  de la Bahía del Espíritu Santo de
  Zúñiga
Lafitte, Jean, 66–67, 70
Lafitte, Pierre, 66
Lamar, Mirabeau B., 171, 173–174, 187
Land, 35, 36, 73, 76, 80, 98–101, 111–
  112, 130–133, 141, 166, 173–175, 241;
  certificates, 175; Commission, 176;
  Commissioner, 80, 84, 86, 101, 129;
  scrip, 176; speculators, 86, 113, 130;
  theft, 179–180

CPSIA information can be obtained
at www.ICGtesting.com
Printed in the USA
FSHW010613061219
64681FS